D0330974

even the
terrible
things seem
beautiful
to me now

SECOND EDITION

even the terrible things seem beautiful to me now

*on hope, loss,
and wearing sunscreen*

mary schmich

Chicago Tribune

MIDWAY

AN AGATE IMPRINT

CHICAGO

Chicago Tribune: R. Bruce Dold, Publisher & Editor-in-Chief; Peter Kendall, Managing Editor; Christine W. Taylor, Managing Editor; Amy Carr, Director of Content/Life + Culture; Angela Rozas O'Toole, Deputy Metro Editor; Jennifer Day, Books Editor

First edition published 2013. Second edition 2019.

Printed in the United States

10 9 8 7 6 5 4 3 2 1   19 20 21 22 23

ISBN-13: 978-1-57284-280-9
ISBN-10: 1-57284-280-6
eISBN-13: 978-1-57284-836-8
eISBN-10: 1-57284-836-7

The Library of Congress has cataloged an earlier edition of this book as follows:

Schmich, Mary.
 Even the terrible things seem beautiful to me now : the best of Mary Schmich / Mary Schmich.
      pages cm
  Summary: ""A collection of columns from Chicago Tribune columnist, Mary Schmich"--Provided by publisher"-- Provided by publisher.
  ISBN 978-1-57284-145-1 (pbk.) -- ISBN 1-57284-145-1 (pbk.)
 1. Chicago (Ill.)--Social life and customs. 2. Families--Illinois--Chicago. I. Title.
 F548.52.S278 2013
 977.3'11--dc23
                               2013019130

Cover design by Morgan Krehbiel
Cover artwork by iStock/Ekely
Interior illustration of Mary Schmich by Tom Bachtell

Midway Books is an imprint of Agate Publishing. Agate books are available in bulk at discount prices. For more information, visit agatepublishing.com.

To my mother, who inspired so many columns, including the one that gave me the title for this book.

And to Bill.

contents

CHAPTER 13: The Journey of Joan Lefkow 337

CHAPTER 14: 2012 Pulitzer Prize Winners 365

introduction

One night in the winter of 1992, I was sitting at my kitchen table in Atlanta when the phone rang. An editor from Chicago was on the line.

For nearly five years, I'd been living in Georgia, where I spent most of my childhood, covering the South for the Tribune. I loved the work and the territory. But now the editor had a question:

Did I want to come back to Chicago and write a column?

There had been a time when I wouldn't have hesitated. In fact, when I arrived at the Tribune in 1985, Koky Dishon, who was the first woman on the paper's masthead, sat me down in her office and asked how I imagined my journalistic future.

"I'd like to write a column," I said cheerily.

She rolled her eyes. "Yeah, you and everybody else."

And so I shoved that notion aside and went about the lifelong business of learning to be a reporter. The years I spent writing about the South — rushing to hot news in Florida and South Carolina, searching for stories along the back roads of Alabama and Tennessee, trying to comprehend how Chicago connected to Mississippi — was the best education I've ever had. It taught me how complicated the world is, and the more I saw the world's complexities, the less I trusted the kind of opinions formulated on newspaper columnist deadlines.

Column-writing, I came to suspect, required a higher level of certitude than I could muster honestly and a higher degree of bluffing.

Queasy with that truth, I told the editor to give me a couple of days to think. I hung up. I thought for a while — just long enough to hear an inner voice say, "Are you crazy? You're going to turn down a column in the great city of Chicago?"

That was thousands of columns ago.

Choosing which of those columns would make sense in this book was hard when I sifted through them for the first edition in 2013. It was harder as we prepared this second edition.

A lot has changed in the intervening years. The country has a new president. Chicago has a new mayor. Gay marriage was made the law of the land. The Black Lives Matter and #MeToo movements have shifted our ways of seeing, talking, being. The Cubs won a World Series. One of my best friends died.

I've removed a few columns from the first edition to make space for newer ones that reflect some of those changes.

What hasn't changed through all these years is the relationship I've developed with Tribune readers. Thousands of you have shared your opinions and your stories in response to mine. We've traveled through our place and time together, arguing over politics, loving our friends and family, remarking on the weather.

I hope the columns in this book reflect that wide range of our shared life.

I'm infinitely grateful to Ann Marie Lipinski, who offered me the column job, and to all of you who have done me the honor of reading what I've written. You've made my life infinitely richer.

FROM THE DESK OF

Mary Schmich

There's a famous building at 435 North Michigan Avenue in Chicago. It's called Tribune Tower.

For most of the 20th century and on into the 21st, it was the home of the newspaper for which it was built. For more than three decades, I was one of the lucky Chicago Tribune employees who wheeled in and out of its revolving doors, sometimes remembering to pause and admire the flying buttresses, the arched windows, the inspiring quotations carved into the lobby's marble walls.

But the newspaper industry changed. New technology drove the old print paper into decline. The journalistic mission stayed the same, but the financial model didn't. One consequence? The Tower, as we called it, was sold to developers who are turning it into condos.

In the late spring of 2018, the Tribune left its old home. As we packed to go, I documented the move on Facebook, routinely posting photos of objects in my cubicle, and with each object a brief story.

I've included a few of those posts in this book.

chapter 1

....

my mother

Still Getting to Know Her

My mother turns 70 today, Mother's Day, and though I've known her more than half her life, I can't claim to know her.

I could present reams of data about her life: Born and raised in Macon, Ga. Married at the age of 29 and by the age of 39 had given birth to eight children. Fine pianist until arthritis slowed her hands. Lived for a while with her husband and children in a string of single, seedy Phoenix motel rooms and never lost her sense of humor. Very weird sense of humor.

I could even provide some plausible interpretation of these facts, but I wouldn't get it right. The older I get, the more my mother seems to me as opaque as stone.

I have friends who feel the same way. We marvel that we know stunningly intimate details about each other without knowing half as much about our mothers. It's not that we don't get along with our mothers, but getting along is not the same as knowing. It is, in fact, sometimes a convenient substitute.

When did your mother go through menopause? Did she ever love a man besides your father? Did she, does she, love your father? Was her heart ever broken? How does she feel about sex? What does she really think about her life? About your life?

Do you know these things? Are you sure?

Growing up, you don't think about whether you know your mother. She's just there, as functional as furniture. Later, it is hard to start asking questions, even if, as I do, you consider her a friend.

My own mother's life comes to me in glimpses and glimmers. She has taken to making surprising remarks at odd moments, as if after years of hoarding her inner life, she now wants to share some of what she kept hidden. Or maybe she has simply decided that only in revealing her life will she herself come to see it clearly.

A few weeks ago, while we sat at TV tables in her apartment, eating dinner in front of "Designing Women," I described a big, sumptuous wedding I had recently attended. She looked pensive.

"If I had it to do over again," she said, "I would have a very small, intimate wedding. It never occurred to me that I could do that. Mother wanted something grand. And I didn't question it."

She was talking softly, without resentment, analyzing her own life with the dispassionate curiosity of a historian.

"But then, women didn't question much of anything in those days," she said. "When we got married, we were supposed to give up everything that came before, without question, and do things we weren't trained to do."

She laughed. "Like bake." She paused. "I gave up music. And to do what? To iron sheets?"

Until that moment, I hadn't known that in the early years of her marriage, my mother had actually ironed sheets. More important, I hadn't known she had ever noticed, or cared, how much she gave up.

So now I knew, and we went back to watching TV. I had learned a little more about my mother, accompanied by a sitcom laugh track.

My brothers and sisters and I occasionally talk about the facts and feelings we should extract from our mother before it's too late. Each of us knows a detail or two that the others don't, and if we pool our puzzle pieces, we can put together a picture of her greater than what any of us could alone. Still, there remain huge gaps.

We'll get Mom to tell us about her life on video, we sometimes say. We never quite get around to it, in part, I think, because as much as we want to know her better, we are afraid of knowing her. Afraid most, I think, of knowing her disappointments.

I suspect she would see that as the naivete of children and tell us that what we perceive as loss and failure she sees simply as life.

It's inevitable that mothers remain a mystery to their children, and maybe it's best that way. But here's an idea for Mother's Day. If you're lucky enough that your mother is still alive, ask her a question, just one, that might help you know her a little better. A lot of mothers would probably like to be asked.

SUNDAY, MAY 11, 1997

Nothing Like Our Mothers

The women I know spend a fair amount of time discussing how different we are from our mothers. We are so different that we sometimes wonder if we crawled into our cribs straight from some alien's womb.

How are we different from our mothers? We count the ways.

We put up with less from men, we ask for more from work. We are franker about sex and finickier about our coffee. We curse more and iron less, and we're not as apt to believe that everything from war to rush-hour gridlock can be solved by prayer.

We are not certain we are happier, but we figure we must be because one thing is for sure: We wouldn't want to live the way our mothers have.

We wouldn't want their difficult marriages, disappointments and weird habits. We wouldn't want the wounds and warts that fate and men and they themselves have inflicted on their lives.

No indeed, we infinitely prefer our own difficult relationships and disappointments, our vastly superior wounds and warts and weird habits, to our mothers' discount brands.

Like most of my women friends, I've spent most of my life convinced that the differences between me and my mother were as wide as Texas and as permanent as taxes. We've always liked and respected each other, but what could be more different from an employed woman with no children than a woman who had eight kids in nine years in her 30s and stayed home to raise them?

And yet, recently something strange has happened. My sense of our differences is diminishing. I become more like my mother. She becomes more like me. Or maybe we weren't so different all along.

I am not talking about physical similarities, the knobbiness of our hands, the oddities of our toes, the feathery cough before we speak. I am talking about something more profound.

From my mother I inherited a love for books and music and a curiosity about the world, and these have traveled with me into the work I do, the habits I keep, the dreams I dream.

My mother, on the other hand, dreamed of being a writer or an actress or a pianist, but she raised her kids instead, ignoring the piano for those 30 years, locking herself in the bathroom to find the time and privacy to read.

Our circumstances have been different, but we share aptitudes and attitudes, and it is these shared qualities that enabled me to build a different life.

My mother's differences and mine, I've come to see, are steeped in our similarities.

A friend of mine once said that she felt her mother's life and hers were matching puzzle parts. Alone, their lives seemed fractured, but together, they add up to the girl who got it all.

It's true for many mothers and daughters. What we perceive as differences are, in many ways, just complementary parts.

I've opened up the world to my mother: Look, Mom! Life in the Big City! Fun at work! Travel! She gave me a different gift, a large and generous family, and that family was the base from which I could go exploring.

My own mother's mother was a south Georgia sharecropper's daughter who married the boss at the textile mill. I asked my mother the other day if she had felt different from my grandmother.

"Of course!" she said, and laughed. "I thought my mother was a nice lady, but she was not as bright as I was, and she was hopelessly strait-laced. I have since learned my mother was reading books much more interesting than what I was reading at the time."

She was silent for a moment. "I'm really rather ashamed of my attitude."

I told her how different my women friends and I imagine we are from our mothers and asked how that made her feel.

"I hope most mothers just roll their eyes and let it go," she said. "Or, I hope they think with joy, 'This world is getting better. The next generation is smarter than mine.'"

Is that what you think, Mom?

"Oh," she said, and laughed again, "once in a while."

My mother's remarks are a clue that this conviction of difference gets passed through the generations. When the daughters of the women my age are our age, they will probably swear that they're nothing like their moms. Which will make them just the same.

On this Mother's Day, ponder this puzzle: No woman is ever like her mother. Except in her delusion that she's not.

Forever Five Years Old

Sometimes lately I snap awake in the middle of the night and say out loud, "I miss my mother." In that moment, I feel both middle-age and 5 years old, and my mother appears in front of me as a woman both young and ancient.

Lying there in the dark, I often feel her fingers graze my neck the way they did one Thanksgiving afternoon when she was 35 and I lazed in her lap while she fiddled with my hair.

And always on those wakeful nights, I feel what my fingers feel all these years later whenever I lean down to hug her hello or goodbye. I feel her papery, soft skin and the shrinking bones that seem hardly sturdier than eggshells.

Finally, I sink back to sleep, away from the black questions of 3 a.m., away from wondering: How will I bear it when my mother's gone? Why don't I see her more while she's still here?

There are perfectly good reasons I don't see my mother more. They're the same reasons millions of other people don't see their mothers more. We live in a world that makes it easy and acceptable for children and their parents to live like citizens of independent countries.

I have a life and people I care about in the city where I live. My mother has a life and people she cares about in the city where she lives. To see each other, we have to jump the hurdles of money, time and distance. The busier I am and the frailer she gets, the higher these hurdles seem.

Like so many people I know, I tell myself that the geographical gap between me and my mother — to whom I am otherwise very close — is natural, even right. Parents send their children into the world like kites, and the generous ones, the brave ones, the ones like my mother, eventually relax their grip on the string and take both pride and courage from watching their children fly.

Or so I tell myself. The adult in me believes it; the 5-year-old just wants her mama.

And that's the problem. Inside most every busy, competent adult is a 5-year-old who still needs her mother. The older my mother gets, the more often that 5-year-old in me emerges in the middle of the night, grieving prematurely for a loss that, with some luck, will not come for a long time.

"You feel that way even though she probably made you crazy the last time you talked to her, right?" says a friend who is made routinely crazy by a mother she adores.

Of course my mother makes me crazy. Doesn't yours? And she makes me crazier now than she ever did when I was younger. Now she makes me crazy just by getting old. The 5-year-old in me wants her to cut it out. Get over it. Shape up, Mother.

My impatience is irrational, unfair, immature, and I would never admit it if so many other perfectly reasonable adults hadn't admitted the same unreasonable, childish thoughts to me.

The craziness I feel over my mother getting old — the impatience and anger bred of fear — is compounded by the distance. From 2,000 miles away, all I can do is listen, advise, harangue and hope across the telephone wires.

"I decided I was going to die," my mother, who never complains, said on the phone not long ago. She slipped this fact into our chit-chat as idly as if she were announcing her plans for breakfast.

She laughed. I didn't. She explained the symptoms that for several days had led her to this conclusion.

"So," she said, "I started getting my affairs organized. You know, that old thing of not wanting to be wearing dirty underwear when you go to the hospital."

She said she was better now, however, and had decided to live another 20 years. She was still laughing. I still wasn't. I hung up and bought a plane ticket.

And on this Mother's Day, my inner 5-year-old would like to make a suggestion to all the adult 5-year-olds out there: Go see your mother. Let her make you crazy while she still can.

Miss Lil

My mother was 14 the first time she made her way up the red dirt road to Laurel Falls Camp, where a woman named Miss Lil slyly taught Southern white girls the history of the Negro. This was in the racially segregated South of 1937, long before much of anyone could have dreamed that February would one day be designated our national Black History Month.

My mother's British uncle had decided that year that it was time for his starstruck niece to spend her mind on something besides movie heartthrob Nelson Eddy. Her parents were happy to have him subsidize Mary Ellen's summer at Laurel Falls where, it was said, a girl could learn not only to ride and hike but to write and think.

What my grandparents and the parents of many Laurel Falls girls didn't seem to realize, though, was that up there amid the forests and waterfalls of the Georgia hills, Lillian Smith was teaching her campers to defy their Southern way of life.

"To wake up the little sleeping beauties that our Anglo-American culture has anesthetized, or rather put in a deep freeze," Smith once wrote of her camp-marm subversions.

At first, my mother didn't like Miss Lil, this gray-haired, big-nosed woman with a remote smile who answered questions by asking questions.

But she loved the series of skits, labored over for a full summer, that attempted to synopsize the history of black people from Africa to Atlanta. And she loved Haile Selassie, a horse that shared a name, she learned, with the emperor of Ethiopia.

She couldn't know then that Miss Lil would become a renowned civil rights champion whose writing appeared in publications as diverse as Redbook and the Chicago Defender. In the five summers she spent there, my mother knew only that she loved this camp and the way it allowed her to believe something her heart had always felt — that black people were as fully human as she was.

"Miss Lil was trying to raise a different generation of white girls," she says. "She never said that. She didn't say a whole lot unless we questioned her. She just let it occur to us that blacks were equal. Or I don't know if at that point we thought about equality per se. But we just became upset, upset about the way black people were treated."

The last summer my mother spent at Laurel Falls, a half-dozen or so older "leadership" girls would gather at night around the fireplace in the old stone library to hear Miss Lil read from her book in progress. They'd never heard things like this, the story of love between a black girl and a white boy in a small Southern town.

Soon afterward, Lillian Smith published her book, "Strange Fruit," named after Billie Holiday's famous song about lynching. It sold 3 million copies, rode to No. 1 on the best seller list, and the parents of Laurel Falls girls finally realized the kind of racial education Miss Lil was up to. My grandfather was particularly incensed that she'd named a character Prentiss, spelled just like he spelled his name.

After that, when Miss Lil invited my mother to be the camp's music director for a summer, she said no.

"In a different generation, I would have gone," she says. "But in this generation, I knew that it would just kill my parents."

Later, though, under Miss Lil's influence, my mother went to work as a counselor in a Boston Girl Scout camp that, shockingly, invited black girls for the first time that summer.

"In defense of the parents of our generation — well, I don't need to defend them — but for generations they had been told that blacks did not have basic intelligence," my mother says. "They learned blacks were not equal. Miss Lil taught us that they were. Without saying it. We just did the history."

My mother still wonders if she could and should have done more to make the South change faster, but her small rebellions mattered. One of those was simply to raise her children with stories of Miss Lil and Miss Lil's lessons.

Here's one of the Miss Lil lessons I inherited: We're all products not only of the past, but of what we learn about the past. Do the history. And remember that black history is white history, too.

How to Be a Good Mother

When my mother was in her 20s a doctor told her that because she'd lost an ovary after an appendix attack she would have trouble getting pregnant. Her eight children can't help but wonder how big the family zoo would have been if both ovaries had been firing at full throttle.

Bringing up eight kids was unlikely work for my mother on other grounds too. She never yearned the way some women do to be a mother, and she was never maternal in the cliche sense of the word. She was an imagining girl who loved books and who would rather play the piano than play with dolls. In college, she read plays late at night and smoked cigarettes and fantasized a life on the stage more than a life in the kitchen.

"I didn't even think I liked children until I had my own," she once told me with a laugh, and she brought a casual, though friendly, air to her parenting.

Not long ago, I asked her what she dreamed for her kids when they were young. Her reply was simply, "I wanted you to have your own dreams."

I've always thought that allowing her kids to choose their own dreams, their own lives, was the secret to the fact that my mother raised decent kids who still turn to her for inspiration and good company. She has rarely criticized how we dress, eat, think or live and has only rarely supplied direct advice, seeming to understand that when it comes to kids, formulas work only in a bottle.

But if you can't give advice at the age of 79, when can you? On the occasion of this Mother's Day, I asked the woman who was never supposed to have children for some tips on child rearing. She balked. She dawdled. And finally e-mailed this:

Subjects to Be Taught in Motherhood School

1. **Optimism 101.** (Warning: If you make less than a B+ you have flunked.) This class stresses — excellent word — that there will always be difficult times, especially when your children are in their late teens and are not only always right, right, right, but find Mother incredibly stupid, stupid, stupid. This too shall pass. Not that you, Mother, will ever become a fount of wisdom, but you will be considered sufficiently improved to get you introduced to your children's friends.

2. **Courage.** A course requiring many field trips, such as visits to the school principal's office, and putting up with folks who want to know what your REAL job is.
3. **Generosity.** This has nothing to do with learning what "things" to buy your kids. It deals with getting the balance right: allowing them a certain freedom of choice. Making bombs in the basement is not open to discussion.
4. **Q&A.** (Do not skip this class!) Be prepared for your children to ask questions that you can't answer. Regardless of what you may think, you do not know everything. Be prepared to admit it. One important discussion question: Am I an interesting person to anyone besides other mothers? Become interesting.
5. **Learning to Laugh, Learning to Listen.** Very difficult. Do not attempt motherhood without these two Ls. And remember that no two children are ever exactly alike. Cherish and encourage the differences. Of course, this means you can no longer shout, in a moment of anger, "You're just like your father!"
6. **Love.** No teacher found yet, so just do the best you can. Follow your heart. Pray. And take the other classes!

She added this postscript:

"After my own mother died, when I was 36, a part of me died, too, the part of me that felt I had approached perfection. I thought it would return someday, but so far it never has."

When I was younger I sometimes wished for a mother who gave me more practical advice on how to live, who taught me how to find the right bra or how to make money or how to properly roast a chicken.

But each of us gets what our particular mother has to give, and what my mother had available were the ethereal gifts of optimism, generosity, humor, dreams.

She also gave us what her mother gave her and it's one of the greatest comforts any mother can bestow: a sense that there's one person in the world who knows all your flaws and still thinks you're close to perfect.

My Mother's Refrigerator

Millions of words have been written about the difference between the so-called greatest generation and us wimps who have followed, but after a recent visit from my mother I realize that one aspect of the gap has not been fully addressed:

Leftovers.

To my mother, a refrigerator packed with leftovers is a Goodwill of edibles, a place where second-hand meals unwanted by the persnickety are thrilling to those with more generous attitudes toward food.

To put it another way, reaching into my refrigerator when my mother's in town — or into hers when I'm visiting — is like diving for hidden treasure, only the treasure is apt to be borderline moldy and the only sparkle comes from the tinfoil wrapping.

During any visit from my mother, and for a while after she leaves, I'm apt to reach into the fridge and wonder: What's this? Ah, a foil-covered coffee cup containing five spoonfuls of leftover canned vegetable soup. It wasn't good to begin with. It has not improved with age. But my mother couldn't stand to see it go to waste.

And this? Oh, that's right. It's half a cup of rice Mama scraped off her dinner plate, with a few specks of other food collected in the harvest.

Lifting a piece of foil from a bowl, I recall the conversation that led to the preservation of its contents.

"Honey," my mother had said as I headed toward the disposal with the salad. "Don't throw that away."

"Mother, it's three leaves of greasy, soggy lettuce and one really sorry-looking cherry tomato."

"I'll eat it for breakfast."

"Breakfast? Breakfast is for cereal. Eggs. Scones. Fresh food for a new day."

She had beamed a maternal smile, the kind suggesting that one day when I grew up, I'd understand. "Breakfast is whatever you make it."

That's a beautiful philosophy as applied to life, but some things are hard to stomach at 7 a.m.

Obviously, lovers of leftovers are of all ages, races and creeds, and saving leftovers is the proper thing to do. But I'm talking about the radicals, people who not only save every uneaten molecule of every meal but later eat every last one. And even though we live in an age of sophisticated, disposable, zipping, locking products designed to conserve leftovers, those radicals are likelier to belong to my mother's generation.

Like many people I know, I often forget leftovers I've saved. Until my mother visits.

"Mother, what are you eating?" I'll say when I discover her at some lunch she has rustled up on her own.

"I found this in your refrigerator."

"Oh my God. That's been there for weeks. Doesn't that look a little blue-green to you?"

"It doesn't smell bad. Would you like some?"

My mother also goes to restaurants primarily to hijack leftovers. To her, a restaurant is not a place to eat a meal; it's a place to stock up on future meals. No sooner has the waiter set the plate on the table than she exclaims, "Oh, I am going to have some good leftovers!"

She often leaves with a box containing the leftovers of everyone at the table, as well as the remains of the bread basket. She also likes to stuff her pockets with packets of Sweet'n Low and butter.

"But it's free," she'll say when I note that her jacket is bulging with contraband as we leave.

In truth, I admire that she doesn't take food for granted, and I once asked her to speculate on her passion for saving and consuming food others would deem past its prime. Was it having lived through the Great Depression? World War II?

Maybe, she said, but it was also the result of raising eight kids. She wouldn't eat until we were done, and then she would settle for whatever was on our plates.

She's left town now, and my refrigerator is looking a little less mysterious. But when I tossed out a moldy bread end the other day, I couldn't help a flush of shame as I heard her voice, kind and reasonable: "Honey, that would still be good if you just trimmed the edges."

A State of Chronic Emergency

When your parents reach a certain age, they and you enter a state of chronic emergency.

You try not to dwell on the dangers: a fall or a heart attack, a stroke or a disease, a mind that closes its shutters to the world. But if your parents have had the good fortune to live until they're old, there comes a point when there's no escaping the shadow of the loss to come. You live poised for the alarm.

A few days ago, while in Oregon visiting my mother and out for a walk with my cell phone, I was talking to a friend who was in just this state of parental red alert.

Her father was in the hospital, again. Maybe he had a week left, she said, or a year, who knew. It wasn't the first time he'd been on the brink.

That's part of living in the state of parental emergency. Your mother or father teeters at the brink and then, miraculously, retreats. You relax, but not entirely, knowing there will be at least one more trip to the edge.

As my friend talked, my cell phone beeped. I glanced at the screen. It read "Mama." I kept on talking to my friend about her father. After I hung up, I walked for a while in silence. Then I checked my mother's voice mail.

Twenty minutes later, I was in an urgent-care waiting room. With my brother at her side, my tiny, white-haired mother sat curled in a wheelchair, her chin on her knees in a vain attempt to blunt the pain.

For several weeks, even as she'd lain in bed with pneumonia, she'd been having pain attacks. The pain always went away, eventually, so she pretended not to worry. This attack had been too crippling to ignore.

In the examination cubicle, nurses and a doctor came and went, scraping the curtain back and forth, exuding efficient cheer. Blood was drawn, urine sampled, X-rays taken.

That evening a doctor suggested emergency surgery. After more deliberation, it was determined surgery could wait at least until morning. Ultimately, after a whirlwind week of medical appointments, an operation was scheduled for this coming Tuesday.

"I don't really understand everything they're telling me," my mother said at one point. "I think what they're saying is that I'm old."

One challenge to all of us with elderly parents is to accept that fact: They're old.

My mother, at 84, is stooped by osteoporosis and gnarled by arthritis. She has had a heart attack. Her lively mind has slowed.

Now she has discovered that she has an unusual, dangerous hernia in her lower abdomen, as well as one that has allowed her stomach to migrate into her chest, right behind her heart. Meanwhile, the night after the day in urgent care, she woke up at 3:30 a.m., choking and unable to speak. The paramedics came.

This story isn't novel. Millions of adult children and millions of our parents know this uniquely lonely but widely shared grief and fear. The loss is inevitable.

The most we can hope for is to give our parents a little courage in the process and to find some for ourselves.

"All of my weakness seems to have come upon me at once," my mother said the other night. She was lying in the dark. I knelt down next to her. We cried.

The next morning I found her sitting next to a sunny window. She pointed to the yard.

"A blue jay," she said. "Isn't that exciting?"

We sipped coffee and watched the birds, and as much to herself as to me, she said, "You have to be old to appreciate the beauty of your life. Even the terrible things seem beautiful to me now."

This is the courage my mother gives to me, this will to find beauty, even during an emergency.

The Time That's Left

My mother put down her fork, picked up her glass of wine and took a sip. I had taken her out to dinner, and we were talking about nothing much.

"I keep wondering," she said, without preamble, "what I'm going to do with the time I have left."

In the length of a swallow, she had segued from nothing much to something huge.

"I could have a year," she went on. "Or 10. However long it is, I can't spend it all just sitting in the chair and staring at the yard."

A few months ago, it looked as if my mother, who is 85, might not last a few more weeks. But she got an extension on the deadline, which was great, except that the question now pesters her like a bill collector:

What are you going to do with the time you have left?

When my mother asked that question, I heard an echo of Mary Oliver's poem "The Summer Day." I quoted it here once before, and readers still write to ask about it. It's worth revisiting, especially this time of year.

Here are the last few lines:

> I don't know exactly what a prayer is.
> I do know how to pay attention, how to fall down
> into the grass, how to kneel down in the grass,
> how to be idle and blessed, how to stroll through the fields,
> which is what I have been doing all day.
> Tell me, what else should I have done?
> Doesn't everything die at last, and too soon?
> Tell me, what is it you plan to do
> with your one wild and precious life?

However you phrase it — as poetically as Mary Oliver, or as bluntly as my mother — it's a question that doesn't pose itself only at 85. In old age, it may knock at the heart like a firefighter at the door, but at any age it's one of life's basic quandaries.

Every now and then, most of us imagine we have answered the question. Start a job, make a move, get married, have a kid, plant a garden, renovate the kitchen. Problem solved.

We construct our days to avoid having to answer the question again, jamming the hours with routines and obligations — which, if we are lucky, add up to a sense of purpose — that squeeze out space for the existential squirm.

But the question never goes away. It shifts, it hides. When those routines and obligations are disrupted, it pounces again.

You may lose a job, your health, your house, a pet, someone you love, which is to say you may lose your habits and a piece of who you think you are. Now what are you going to do with the time you have left?

The question gets tougher to answer even as it grows more pressing. When my mother considers what she will do with her remaining time, she works within the shrinking boundaries of her body.

Her fingers are so gnarled that she unpries them one by one, lifting the thumb off the index finger, the middle finger off the ring finger, opening her joints by pressing her palm on the arm of a chair.

So much for the hands that once flew through Chopin, easily gripped a pen to write. Those pastimes, gone. And even though she still goes out, to lunch, to church, to a book club, walking is a chore.

So she sits a lot.

"I'm counting the roses," she said when I found her in her chair a couple of days after our dinner conversation. She looked pleased. "I keep getting different answers."

And maybe that's the truth at any age: The answer keeps changing. You learn to find pleasure in pondering the question.

FRIDAY, SEPT. 4, 2009

September Light

September light.

The days get shorter, the shadows longer.

"How late does it stay light in Chicago now?" my mother says. I've just flown west to visit her.

Seven? I say. Seven thirty? The light fades so fast these days I'm not sure.

Out the window of the chain restaurant where we're having dinner, the sun is setting on a parking lot and a supermarket. In the September twilight, even the concrete seems to soften.

Then for no clear reason, my mother, who is 86, says, "I'm sure I've told you this story . . ."

I say, probably, but carry on. I used to get impatient when she repeated her life stories, impatient with her memory gaps, impatient that she'd boxed herself up as anecdotes. But lately I listen more carefully, knowing my chances to listen are numbered.

"Then you know the story of how my mother was so desperate for me to get married that she called the priest at St. Joseph's and told him to find me a husband."

I do know that story, how after a studious spiritual search, my mother chose to become a Catholic in a time and place — Macon, Ga., the 1950s — when being Catholic verged on social suicide.

My mother's mother, a strict Baptist, phoned the priest at the white Catholic church in town. My grandmother told the priest that her daughter was 28, unmarried and had, tragically, become Catholic; she would never find a husband without his help.

"The Baptists," my grandmother told the priest, "don't want her anymore."

So the priest introduced my mother to every traveling salesman who made it through his sanctuary. One of them was an itinerant insurance man who worked out of Chicago. My father.

"But you know," my mother says now, the sun vanishing behind her in the parking lot, "it was that priest I loved."

What?

"If he had asked me to run off with him," she says, and I don't think she's kidding, "I would have followed him anywhere."

My mother loved my father, but in the past couple of years, she has made several revelations — just a few sentences here and there, always over half a glass of wine — that have made me think, "Who is this woman?"

So, I say, the priest — I remember how much she talked about him when I was little — what made him so special?

"He was just, I don't know," she says, "different. I could talk to him. Someone once told me she saw him standing on a sidewalk at dawn watching the sun rise, with his arms flung wide and he was saying, 'Isn't it wonderful? Isn't it wonderful?'"

That's just the kind of thing my mother would do and that my father never would have dared.

I ask her if she knows where the priest is now.

She gazes out the window. The sky is that uniquely September shade of dusky yellow that seems to lead to some far horizon.

"Oh, dead," she says, "I'm sure. A few years ago, someone told me he was in a nursing home, happy as a clam and mad as a loon."

She turns back to me and smiles. I'm thinking about September — how there's something about September light that makes remembering more urgent and more tender than at any other time of year — when she says: "How late does it stay light in Chicago now? Have I asked you that already?"

Mama Writes a Poem

My mother announces she has written a poem she wants to put on her gravestone.

"It was just here," she says, shuffling through mounds of papers, magazines and wadded Kleenex on the coffee table next to the sofa where she spends most of her days now, sleeping. "It's not really for my grave since I want to be, oh . . ."

She adjusts her new oxygen tube and sighs.

"Oh, what's the word?" she says. Lately the right words flutter away like startled birds.

I say, "Cremated."

"Anyway, it was just here," she says. "I want you to see it."

For a while now, she has been scribbling notes on every kind of paper. Big sheets, little sheets, lined, unlined, white, yellow, blue. I find the scraps in nests of dust bunnies while I'm cleaning.

There are unfinished grocery lists, usually involving coffee; lists of things to tell her children (Tell Joe I found earring); lists of people to call, though she rarely phones anyone anymore.

There are lists of lyrics to find, from old songs no one she knows has heard of: "Alone." "Me and the Moon." "In My Solitude."

There are single-sentence commentaries on things she's seen on TV: Michael Feinstein probably the most talented and obnoxious pianist I have ever heard.

Several scraps involve stories she intends to write about her 1920s Southern childhood. I recently came across a yellow legal pad with the heading "Topics to Write About." The two-page list included:

Climbing the magnolia tree, "peeling" magnolia buds.

Living on the right side of the railroad track. Black settlement across our side road.

Mother making dresses for me to wear to school, making me think we were rich, when we were in depression financial trouble.

Delma & me: our shared bed, ukuleles, trips, heartbreaks.

I stack my mother's paper scraps in tidy piles, trying not to read them, especially not her reflections on God and my father. Too naked. Which may be what she wants.

Maybe, in the same way she now lets her children bathe her, she hopes we'll stumble on her inner truths before she dies. Maybe she wants to be sure we remember her life at least partly in the way she remembers it. Maybe these scraps are her trail of clues.

How she writes at all is a mystery. One hand — a hand that once whizzed over the piano playing Beethoven, Big Band, gospel — is permanently closed into a claw.

The other hand opens just enough to let a pen slip between her fingers so she can scrawl things like these lines from a Leonard Cohen song:

> Ring the bells that still can ring
> Forget your perfect offering
> There is a crack in everything
> That's how the light gets in.

The day after she tells me about the poem she's written for her funeral, whenever that may be, she says, "I found it."

With a smile, she hands me a pink, lined sheet, on which she's written in shaky block letters:

> Roses for remembrance
> Daffodils to sing
> Let us do a sundance
> To honor everything!
> (No, I can't dance, honey —
> My legs just barely wiggle
> But I am gonna try it, kid.
> And you are free to giggle.)
> So what if I should slip and fall
> And break stuff while I sing?
> I'm using all that I've got left
> To honor everything!

....

I Read to My Mother

Every night at bedtime for the past couple of weeks, I've read a poem to my mother.

I sit next to the old sofa she prefers to her new, metal hospital-style bed and I leaf through her copy of "Good Poems," edited by Garrison Keillor. It's a fat hardback with a blue jacket, and I muse over the titles she has starred, the stanzas she has bracketed, the pages she has bookmarked with toilet paper.

Here, I said a few nights ago, talking over the wheeze of the oxygen machine, here's a passage you marked in "What I Learned From My Mother," by Julia Kasdorf.

> *I learned that whatever we say means nothing,*
> *what anyone will remember is that we came.*

"Oh, that's nice," she said, and pretty soon she was asleep, coaxed by the drug that eases the anxiety that's caused by the drug that helps her breathe.

My mother and I started this bedtime routine after she went into the hospital with pneumonia two weeks ago, then came home on hospice care, permanently unable to walk.

After several years of decline and rebound and decline again — if you have an elderly parent, you know the cycle — she has been given a loose official deadline. Three to six months. Two weeks if she gets another respiratory infection.

Whatever the count, the goal now is not recovery, but comfort until the end.

And so the ritual of the poems.

One night, noting that she'd written "COPY" next to the title, I read "Perfection Wasted," by John Updike.

> *And another regrettable thing about death*
> *is the ceasing of your own brand of magic,*
> *which took a whole life to develop and market —*

She smiled, and drifted off.

She sleeps for a couple of hours each night, then wakes up and rings a little bell to say she needs to be lifted to the portable commode or wants a sip of juice or has to have a light turned on.

She needs a lamp, she says, with a flutter of panic, because she wants to see the clock. It's as if she senses she can hold on to life as long as she has light and the time.

"Here's one by Mary Oliver," I said one evening, holding up the page where she'd written a big "Yes!"

> Whoever you are, no matter how lonely,
> the world offers itself to your imagination,
> calls to you like the wild geese, harsh and exciting —

When the poem was done, I asked what she was thinking.

"What a wonderful world I have lived in."

I have friends whose mothers died young and others whose mothers died suddenly but many more whose mothers leave this way, fading and flaring through old age, like the last shred of wick.

This process, difficult and bountiful, may be the greatest common bond of my generation.

One day last week, the hospice nurse, who drops by routinely, reached for her ringing cell phone.

"I have to take this," she said. It was her mother's nurse, calling from Florida.

I think about all those other fading mothers while I read poems to mine at night. I think about what little rituals their children seek to make the last days feel kind, the conclusion close to right, the relationship close to complete.

And yet all that really matters is that, given the chance, you came.

SUNDAY, AUG. 8, 2010

Who Stole My Mother?

For a couple of days after my mother died, I wandered past the living room sofa where she took her final breath and repeatedly blurted, "Where did my mother go?"

It was an involuntary utterance, like speaking in tongues, an expression more of baffled curiosity than of grief.

"Where did my mother go? Who stole my mother?"

I'd known she was dying. The doctors said so. It was never clear that she believed them, but she had shrunk to 75 pounds. Exertions as simple as sitting up or lying down felt to her like wind sprints. Every day she filled in fewer words in the newspaper crossword puzzle.

So, yes, the signs were there.

But no matter how prepared you think you are, death startles.

Where did that warmth go, that breath, that laugh, that voice?

You can spend hours Googling a disease — in my mother's case, pulmonary fibrosis — and still not be able to compute how a life, especially one you love, vanishes in a single exhale.

On the morning my mother died, the first Friday in July, I was out for breakfast in Chicago. I was ordering two eggs, scrambled, when I saw a voice mail from my brother.

My heart bounced. This was the call, the call that anyone with an elderly parent braces for for weeks, months, years.

But it couldn't be that call. Just five days before, I'd been laughing with my mother — her name was Mary Ellen — and rolling her wheelchair along the river while she exclaimed over the ducks and roses.

"It's Mom," my brother said when I called back. "She's passing."

"Passing? What? When?"

"Right now."

"OK," I said, too startled to think clearly, "I'm on my way."

I was racing home on my bicycle when it hit me. On my way where in such a hurry? She was in Oregon. I was in Chicago.

I called back.

"Put me on speaker phone."

"She's gone."

Over the years in this column, I've written a lot about my mother.

Her Southern childhood. Her difficult marriage. Her eight children. Her love of books, music, people, squirrels. Her habit of eating cold dinner leftovers for breakfast. The bright spirit that in her old age shone through her broken body.

Many of you have sent me stories in return, of caring for your own parents, or of what it is to be an elderly parent. Thank you for sharing your stories with me, and for letting me share my mother with you.

In the weeks since my mother has been gone, I've ceased to be startled.

For a while a strange thought popped to mind — "I've got to call my mother to tell her my mother died" — but that's subsided too.

Her death has come to feel natural, right.

Where did she go? Mystery keeps the living alert. And it helps every now and then to read this bit of poem by Mary Oliver:

> *To live in this world*
> *you must be able*
> *to do three things:*
> *to love what is mortal;*
> *to hold it*
> *against your bones knowing*
> *your own life depends on it;*
> *and, when the time comes to let it go,*
> *to let it go.*

FRIDAY, SEPT. 17, 2010

Canceling My Mother's Paper

With a traitor's leaden heart, I recently canceled my mother's subscription to her local newspaper.

I'd anticipated harder tasks when I went to Oregon a couple of weeks ago to start dismantling her home. Friends who had already gone through this kind of ritual had warned me: Pace yourself. Saying goodbye to the tangible evidence of a parent's life can be exhausting. You might stumble on things you didn't want to know. You'll find things you can't bear to discard but can't stand to keep. And the dust!

I walked into the house girded for battle, then was surprised when the days passed in what felt like meditation.

I spent peaceful hours sitting on a box in the garage or on some closet floor, sifting, usually in silence.

I discovered that all those times I'd phoned my mother and she'd said, "I'm getting organized for my death," she was telling the truth.

She had gathered precious documents in a little green metal box: her birth certificate and marriage certificate, my father's death certificate, the bill for his coffin.

In a yellow plastic file, she had assembled a lifetime of psychological evaluations of my youngest sister, who had always lived with her.

She had created cardboard folders for each of her children, eight in total, and in each one inserted school photos, report cards, letters. I was perversely delighted to see my eighth-grade C in conduct.

And every morning while I sorted and pondered, the newspaper landed outside the house.

For the first couple of days when I opened the front door, the paper startled me. It lay there like a ghost, an intruder from a vanished time. I could still see my mother bending over, picking it up.

The newspaper — The Eugene Register-Guard — had been my mother's morning sun, and fetching it was the first act in her day. She always spent at least an hour with it, musing on the news, agreeing or disagreeing with the columnists, clipping her favorite stories.

The climax was the daily crossword puzzle; she asked for it even on the morning she died.

Now she was gone and the paper kept coming, and it unnerved me in a way nothing else in the house had.

I had to cancel it. But how could I?

My mother belonged to a generation that loved printed newspapers in a way no one will again. What we now call newspapers will live and prosper, but they'll do it in a different way, maybe one day without paper, and they're unlikely to command the single-minded dedication of my mother's generation.

Canceling her paper would feel to me like canceling her history, newspaper history and my own past as a newspaper writer.

So at first I tossed the paper on the sofa, unread. I had other things to do. Finally, though, I started reading it. And liking it.

It was a mix of national stories from good news services and local stories from a smart staff that was clearly working very hard. I liked the fact that it's one of the few papers still run by a family.

All of that made it even harder to cancel, so I waited until I got back to Chicago.

"If you ever want to resubscribe," said the nice man who answered when I called, "just let us know."

I hung up hoping that some young person would subscribe instead and see what she'd been missing.

A Visit From Beyond

My mother came to visit me the other night for the first time since she died.

She has appeared briefly in my dreams several times since her last morning nearly two years ago, but always as if in a video, a memory to be watched, not a person to be touched. This dream was different.

In the dream, my mandolin case — I started playing mandolin shortly after my mother's death — was sitting on my dining table. Hearing a noise come from it, I walked over, perplexed. I flipped the latches, lifted the lid.

The mandolin was gone. In its place lay my mother.

She was dressed the way her body had been laid out for its final viewing, in the same flowered skirt and little brown vest, her hands stacked on her waist.

Her eyes popped open.

I don't know which was greater, the relief that my mother was alive or the horror of it. Either way, I had to get her out of this crazy coffin.

"Mama," I said, grasping one of her hands. "Get up. Get up."

She shook her head and smiled, as if to say, no, she was too tired. I persisted. I'd always been her self-appointed personal trainer, coaxing her into activity even when she was disinclined, and in the dream, I resumed that role.

"Come on, little lady. Up. Up. Let's walk."

She relented, and then we walked around for a long time, the way we used to, shuffling while she leaned on my arm. I felt her familiar small bones, her papery skin, the pulse of her blood and breath, a wisp of her white hair against my shoulder. She never spoke.

Eventually, wordlessly, she made it clear that she was too tired to go on, so I picked her up, the way I used to pick her up to bathe her or set her in her wheelchair, and placed her back in the mandolin case.

She looked up at me, smiled, and without moving her lips, transmitted these words: "It's OK, honey. I like it here. It's peaceful."

Then I did what every instinct, every desire told me not to do, the thing she so clearly wanted. I closed the lid.

When I woke up, I cried a little, and then I felt something entirely unexpected. Refreshed, released, complete. What a windfall. I had gone walking with my mother one last time, and I hadn't even known how much I needed to.

Memories of dreams are unreliable, I know, but this one shook me so much that I immediately told it to several people. A couple of them, who have lost their own mothers, said the equivalent of "Oh. Sure. I've had those visitations."

If you'd asked me before this if I believed in something as outlandish as visits from the dead, I would have rolled my eyes. I'd still roll my eyes, with less conviction.

Here's a thing about the death of your mother, or anyone else you love: You can't anticipate how you'll feel afterward. People will tell you; a few may be close to right, none exactly right.

I couldn't have foreseen all the good things that have followed my mother's death. The renewed energy, the surprising sweetness of grief. The tenderness I feel for strangers on walkers. The deeper love I have for my siblings and friends. The desire to play the mandolin. The gift of a visitation.

Here's another thing about the death of someone you love: It teaches you respect for the mysteries.

On June 1, 1997, a mock graduation speech I wrote as a column ran in the Tribune. It began: Wear sunscreen.

A few months later, I found a strange voice mail on my phone.

The caller had a strong Australian accent. He identified himself as Baz Luhrmann and went on to explain that he made movies and that he was putting some of the music from his movies on a CD.

His assistant, Anton, had brought him a graduation speech by Kurt Vonnegut and he thought it would be fun to put it to music. When they reached out to Vonnegut for permission, however, they discovered that, although it had rocketed around the newfangled thing called the Internet wearing Vonnegut's name, I'd written it.

"I have an idea for the material," he said. He asked me to call.

I called.

He turned that column into a spoken-word song, which to everyone's surprise turned into a hit widely known as "The Sunscreen Song."

chapter 2

....

advice, etc.

Wear Sunscreen

Inside every adult lurks a graduation speaker dying to get out, some world-weary pundit eager to pontificate on life to young people who'd rather be Rollerblading. Most of us, alas, will never be invited to sow our words of wisdom among an audience of caps and gowns, but there's no reason we can't entertain ourselves by composing a Guide to Life for Graduates.

I encourage anyone over 26 to try this and thank you for indulging my attempt.

Ladies and gentlemen:

Wear sunscreen.

If I could offer you only one tip for the future, sunscreen would be it. The long-term benefits of sunscreen have been proved by scientists, whereas the rest of my advice has no basis more reliable than my own meandering experience. I will dispense this advice now.

Enjoy the power and beauty of your youth. Oh, never mind. You will not understand the power and beauty of your youth until they've faded. But trust me, in 20 years, you'll look back at photos of yourself and recall in a way you can't grasp now how much possibility lay before you and how fabulous you really looked. You are not as fat as you imagine.

Don't worry about the future. Or worry, but know that worrying is as effective as trying to solve an algebra equation by chewing bubble gum. The real troubles in your life are apt to be things that never crossed your worried mind, the kind that blindside you at 4 p.m. on some idle Tuesday.

Do one thing every day that scares you.

Sing.

Don't be reckless with other people's hearts. Don't put up with people who are reckless with yours.

Floss.

Don't waste your time on jealousy. Sometimes you're ahead, sometimes you're behind. The race is long and, in the end, it's only with yourself.

Remember compliments you receive. Forget the insults. If you succeed in doing this, tell me how.

Keep your old love letters. Throw away your old bank statements.

Stretch.

Don't feel guilty if you don't know what you want to do with your life. The most interesting people I know didn't know at 22 what they wanted to do with their lives. Some of the most interesting 40-year-olds I know still don't.

Get plenty of calcium. Be kind to your knees. You'll miss them when they're gone.

Maybe you'll marry, maybe you won't. Maybe you'll have children, maybe you won't. Maybe you'll divorce at 40, maybe you'll dance the funky chicken on your 75th wedding anniversary. Whatever you do, don't congratulate yourself too much, or berate yourself either. Your choices are half chance. So are everybody else's.

Enjoy your body. Use it every way you can. Don't be afraid of it or of what other people think of it. It's the greatest instrument you'll ever own.

Dance, even if you have nowhere to do it but your living room.

Read the directions, even if you don't follow them.

Do not read beauty magazines. They will only make you feel ugly.

Get to know your parents. You never know when they'll be gone for good. Be nice to your siblings. They're your best link to your past and the people most likely to stick with you in the future.

Understand that friends come and go, but with a precious few you should hold on. Work hard to bridge the gaps in geography and lifestyle, because the older you get, the more you need the people who knew you when you were young.

Live in New York City once, but leave before it makes you hard. Live in Northern California once, but leave before it makes you soft. Travel.

Accept certain inalienable truths: Prices will rise. Politicians will philander. You, too, will get old. And when you do, you'll fantasize that when you were young, prices were reasonable, politicians were noble and children respected their elders.

Respect your elders.

Don't expect anyone else to support you. Maybe you have a trust fund. Maybe you'll have a wealthy spouse. But you never know when either one might run out.

Don't mess too much with your hair or by the time you're 40 it will look 85.

Be careful whose advice you buy, but be patient with those who supply it. Advice is a form of nostalgia. Dispensing it is a way of fishing the past from the disposal, wiping it off, painting over the ugly parts and recycling it for more than it's worth.

But trust me on the sunscreen.

SUNDAY, MARCH 25, 2012

My Workplace, Myself?

Out for a walk on Friday morning, I saw a familiar face coming toward me, a face that I've seen day after day for years.

In the middle of the park we stopped to talk as readily as friends would, though we were never exactly friends. Our banter through the years had occurred mostly on opposite ends of my employee ID as I pressed it onto the card reader on my way into the building.

He'd been one of the Tribune's security guards, around as long as I could remember, always quick with a hearty greeting or a wry quip.

"I'm gone now, you know," he promptly said.

I was glad he'd brought it up so I didn't have to decide whether I should. Many of the security guards were recently replaced by guards from another firm, and the old crew's forced departure made many employees sad.

I said I was sorry he was gone, a comment he might have taken as an opening to rant against the company or the country or the economy. In his position, I probably would have picked at least one of the above.

Instead he smiled and said he'd been taking long walks rather than just sitting around. He patted his belly.

"Gotta work this off," he said, and laughed.

I said something about missing the old guards, how it was strange not to see their familiar faces, how much a part of the place so many of them had been, that I hoped everything was OK.

He shrugged.

"Thousands have left before," he said, sweeping his hand through the air, his tone philosophical. "Thousands will leave after."

I've been thinking about that line — thousands have left before, thousands will leave after — since we waved goodbye with a generic "See you around" and walked off in our opposite directions.

Wherever you work, you're likely to think of it as yours.

My office. My job. My desk. My workplace, myself.

You bring to your work all the possessiveness, ownership, entitlement and sense of safety that go with the word "my." All the self-delusion.

On an average day, we allow ourselves the fiction that we own a piece of our workplace. That's part of what it takes to get the job done.

Deeper down, we know it's all on loan. There's nothing like layoffs — when it happens to you or someone you know — to drive that truth home.

In any workplace, people come, people go. The building may stay the same, the brand name, the basic values, the candy machines.

But the people? We're all temps. Even the ones who think they hold the title to the place.

Losing your job involuntarily is the toughest way to leave a workplace you thought of as yours, and in this economy it's far too common.

But layoffs aren't the only way people vanish. They take buyouts, retire, die. The fortunate few move on to something better.

And just like that, workers who seemed as permanent as the sun, maybe as vital, disappear from an office, a school, a store, a team, a community of co-workers. The place goes on.

I still catch glimpses of some of the people who have vanished from my office, some a long time ago, some, like the security guards, just the other day. As long as there are people around to remember them, a part of them will linger.

But, as John, the security guard, so wisely pointed out, thousands have left before, thousands will leave later.

In work, as in the rest of life, we're all just passing through.

The Good Boss

In honor of National Bosses Day, here's a primer on what makes a good boss.

The good boss doesn't strut as if he were your superior in the game of life. He understands that all power is fleeting and borrowed, a fancy suit on loan.

The good boss has a boss too, and he tries to please her, but he doesn't forget that his real power comes not from the realms above him but from the rank-and-file.

The good boss listens. He listens well enough that he sees the problem before it turns into a crisis. But if it turns into a crisis, the good boss doesn't hide.

Even the good boss thinks he's busier than you are, but he understands that your time is important too.

He answers your e-mails, though rarely as fast as you answer his.

The good boss knows what you want above all: respect. Not that a raise would hurt.

The good boss does not work on his BlackBerry while talking to you. He does not badmouth colleagues in your presence, even if you wish he would. He tries to make everyone feel special and included.

The good boss is self-aware. He knows that every memo he sends out is scrutinized like CIA code: What does it really mean when he says "Good job"?

The good boss knows that it is the sad lot of all bosses to be resented by someone, but he genuinely tries to understand how his behavior affects others.

The good boss doesn't say "Don't take it personally" when delivering bad news. He knows that work is personal.

The good boss has the courage to deal with bad employees.

The good boss tells you when you've screwed up and he forgives you — in the same conversation. He does not take credit for your ideas, nor does a good boss demand credit when he gives you an idea.

Still, it never hurts to thank him. So I'll note that I got the previous two tips from my boss.

The good boss is not afraid of people as smart as he is. He lets them help him look good.

The good boss does not tell you everything he knows, but he does not lie. And he doesn't confuse dissent with disloyalty.

The good boss sees what you do best and matches your job to your talents. He gives you room to bloom.

The good boss remembers how he felt about bosses before he was one. He makes an effort to understand what you do and how you feel, so you forgive him if he never quite gets it.

A good boss reveals just enough about his personal life to remind you that bosses are people too. This never involves sex.

The good boss is not sexist, racist or the biggest clown at parties. Having said that, I have to say that the most brilliant boss I ever had had a couple of those failings.

The good boss doesn't take bonuses when the workers can't get a raise. He doesn't cling to a bad idea just because it was his.

A good boss realizes he can't be too friendly with people who call him boss, but he knows when to be generous and kind, and when to accept those offerings.

A good boss knows how to apologize and how to laugh, sometimes at himself.

And a good boss understands how much we all yearn for a good boss.

SUNDAY, NOV. 2, 1997

Big F Friends, little f friends

Even if you don't believe anything else Mayor Richard Daley says about the latest City Hall scandal, you have to admit that one observation he made last week is true.

"You have very few friends in life," he said, "and those who say they're your friends — many of them are not your friends."

As most of us use it, friend is actually two words. There are friends with a little "f" and friends with a big "F." The first is a large group with sloppy admission standards, the other an elite, time-tested crew. What's the difference?

A little f friend identifies herself when she calls.

A big F Friend doesn't have to.

A little f friend opens a conversation with a full news bulletin on her life.

A big F Friend says, "What's new with you?"

A little f friend thinks the problems you whine about are recent.

A big F Friend says, "You've been whining about the same thing for 14 years. Get off your duff and do something about it."

A little f friend has never seen you cry.

A big F Friend has shoulders soggy from your tears.

A little f friend doesn't know your parents' first names.

A big F Friend has your parents' phone numbers in her address book.

A little f friend knows almost nothing about your family.

A big F Friend knows the medical history, dietary habits and marital troubles of everyone on your family tree.

A little f friend brings a bottle of wine to your party.

A big F Friend comes early to help you cook and stays late to help you clean.

A little f friend calls you at 10 p.m. just to chat.

A big F Friend knows you hate to be called after 9.

A little f friend tells you you look good even when you don't.

So does a big F Friend.

A little f friend wonders about your romantic history.

A big F Friend could blackmail you with it.

When you get a disease or a divorce, a little f friend drops out of sight because she doesn't know what to say.

A big F Friend finds something to say.

A little f friend is someone whose middle name you couldn't even guess.

You know your big F friend's middle name, and when you make fun of it, she laughs along.

A little f friend is jealous of your successes.

A big F Friend enjoys your moments in the sun because she knows about your dark nights of the soul.

A little f friend feels that as time passes and your lifestyles diverge you have nothing left to talk about.

A big F Friend believes that as your lives grow different, you help each other see life through a wider lens.

A little f friend has no clue when your birthday is.

No matter where you are on your birthday, a big F Friend finds you to wish you a happy one, then forgives you when you forget hers.

A little f friend tabulates her share of the dinner check right down to the penny.

Neither you nor a big F Friend worries about a couple extra bucks, confident that over the years it will even out.

A little f friend waits for an invitation to visit.

A big F Friend invites herself.

When a little f friend visits, she acts like a guest.

When a big F Friend visits, she opens your refrigerator, puts her feet on the sofa, talks back to your husband and reprimands your children.

A little f friend thinks the friendship is over when you argue.

A big F Friend knows that a friendship's not a Friendship until you've had a fight.

Should College Make You Happy?

What made you happy in college? Here are a few of my paths to bliss:

> *Breakfast in the all-you-can-eat dining hall.*
> *Lunch in the all-you-can-eat dining hall.*
> *Dinner in the all-you-can-eat dining hall.*
> *Pizza at midnight.*
> *Doughnuts at 2 a.m.*
> *Baggy clothes to disguise the consequences of all of the above.*
> *Sleeping late.*
> *Sleeping, period.*
> *Staying up all night.*
> *No exercise.*
> *Love.*
> *Weeping over love.*
> *Waiting until the last minute to study for the test.*
> *Coffee at 4 a.m.*
> *Etc.*

And if those Princeton Review people had come around and asked, "Overall, how happy are you?" what would I have said? I'd have had to report that I was too fat and tired and profoundly fretful right then to have a clue. Could they check back after I'd had something to eat?

Of course, nobody was roaming campuses with a happy-o-meter in those days. But now the Princeton Review annually measures collegiate jolliness, and in its latest guide, released this week, we learn that the happiest students in America are right here in Chicago, at DePaul University.

Maybe you saw the story in the Tribune Tuesday? Accompanied by a photo of grinning students in a dining hall? The photo suggested that DePaul life was a hoot. Could be. But could it also be that those smart students at that fine school were guffawing over the idea of a college happiness survey?

As it turns out, the second-happiest campus in the nation, down from a previous rank of No. 1, is my alma mater, Pomona College in Claremont, Calif. As a proud alum who would recommend Pomona enthusiastically, this high score should make me happy.

Instead, I'm thinking, "What is wrong with kids today? Whatever happened to the ecstasy of agony? In my day, it was being miserable that made you proud! Get it together, people. You can be happy when you're older. Now is the moment to wallow in torment!"

I once heard someone say that happiness is for people who are either stupid or not paying attention. Please, happy readers. Do not write to tell me this person was whacked out. He was. He also believed that anyone who didn't drink too much was either stupid or not paying attention.

But the valid point in his warped perspective is that there's a time and a place to travel deep into the soul of existence, down into the restless dark where the Big Questions squirm, and that place often is college. A good college education will prepare you for patches of happiness later in life — it will introduce you to people and passions that stick for good — but a good college experience is not necessarily one that in the moment you'd call happy.

Dostoyevsky, sad songs, dorm food, your first serious excursion into loneliness. Now that's the grim college stuff of which happiness is built — later. In college, as in the rest of life, it's often misery that shows the way to understanding what lights and lightens the heart.

I have a cheerful friend who attended another of the colleges on this year's top 10 happiest list. Was she happy at her happy college? Only in retrospect, and even so she remembers the agonies.

"College is supposed to be about suffering and struggle, isn't it?" she says. "It's like childbirth. Later, you say, 'It was so beautiful.' But not right then."

She adds, "And isn't being named the happiest college one step shy of being the biggest party school?"

Hey, she said it. I didn't. So I don't want to hear from any readers unhappy with that remark.

More than many other people, Americans are obsessed with the notion of happiness — pursuing it, analyzing it, peddling it, measuring it, comparing their own with everybody else's. But life is not the SAT. You can't score it. You can't check your score against mine and declare who's best.

So those students at the least-happy colleges should not despair. Remember: If you're unhappy at college, it doesn't mean you're going to a bad college. It doesn't even mean you're having a bad time at college. Sometimes unhappiness can be happy. Have another doughnut and think about it.

SUNDAY, SEPT. 6, 2009

What I've Learned From Work

I've been working since I was 16. I've been a waitress and a writer, a college admissions officer and a movie-theater candy-counter clerk. In honor of Labor Day, here are some things that working has taught me about work.

1. Work is hard. That's why it's called work.
2. Calm down. The work that must get done will get done. Or you're fired.
3. Deadlines are the enemy of perfection. They're also your best friend.
4. Your boss has a boss too. That explains half the crazy things she — or he — does.
5. Listen to the assignment. You may think it's stupid. But be sure you understand what you're being told to do before you do the thing you think is smarter.
6. As one of my first bosses told me: Be loyal to individuals, but never be loyal to an institution because it will not be loyal to you.
7. Some bosses are very wise.
8. Your job is harder than other people think, but not as hard as self-pity tells you.

9. Looking busy and working effectively aren't the same. But only the fortunate few get credit for making work look effortless.

10. Your boss doesn't understand what you do. Let her — or him — know occasionally.

11. It's easier to second-guess the boss than to be the boss.

12. As a business-school professor once told me: Power doesn't corrupt; power reveals. That knowledge won't change your workplace, but it might change your perceptions.

13. Keep your psychodrama to yourself and not only because your work chums could wind up as your superiors or subordinates.

14. Sad but true: Work is a bond, but the workplace can be as ferocious as "Survivor." You can rarely be sure your work friend is your true friend until you're off the island.

15. The above is especially true of workers at different levels of power.

16. Flattery won't get you far. If it does, it's called sucking up.

17. Respect. You can't expect it if you won't give it. This applies to the ranks above and below you.

18. Don't quit when you're mad. Or drunk.

19. Alcohol never helps get the job done. Never.

20. Sad but true: Team players don't always come in first.

21. Neither do sick people who won't take sick days. Stay home.

22. Find work you love. If you can't, find things to love about your work. If that fails, remind yourself that there's always, always someone with a worse job.

23. Work pays for the fun.

24. Everyone feels underappreciated.

25. At least once in your working life, you will hear at least two of these phrases: "Don't take it personally." "We've decided to move in a different direction." "I wish I could offer you more, but . . ."

26. The boss is not thinking about you as much as you're thinking about the boss. But she — or he — wants your approval too.

27. Bosses are like the weather and the pop charts — they change. You're likely to outlast more than one.

28. Yes, you are lucky to have a job. But that's not license for your employer to exploit you.

29. Power trumps talent. And effort. And experience. All the way up the ranks.

30. Work gives life purpose. But it's not the only purpose. It's a piece of your identity. But it is not you.

Panic Is My Muse

Sometimes when I get anxious — which, really, never happens, because serious professional people are in control of everything all the time because otherwise they get fired, and, um, where was I?

Oh, right. Sometimes when I get anxious, I look for solace in a couple of little sayings I've invented for myself in my otherwise 99.9 percent cool and collected life.

One of these sayings is: "Panic is my muse."

For example, in moments when I have nothing with which to fill this column — which, really, is not happening right now — I recite that sentence to myself several times.

Panic is my muse.

Panic is my muse.

Panic is my muse.

I've found over the years that repeating those four little words has a mystically soothing and clarifying effect on an agitated brain. They remind me that panic, like distress of all kinds, can be productive. Unfortunately, for panic to be productive, you have to calm down enough to use it.

So, if during my anxiety attacks — not that I'm having one today! — if in those rare occurrences I can't sufficiently sedate myself by chanting, "Panic is my muse," I recite another of my self-invented mantras: "Deadlines crowd out doubt."

In other words, when you're worried about what you should be doing, or fretting that what you're doing isn't good enough, nothing puts you out of your misery faster than having no choice but to get it done.

You may think I'm repeating and elaborating on these phrases simply to fill space, which would be the case if I were in any way panicked about getting this column done, which you better believe I am. But I'm also trying to make a point about how people keep their battered psychic boats afloat on the herky-jerky sea of daily life.

Many of us have little mantras — invented or adopted — that help us survive the anxieties of our ordinary days.

One friend often silently quotes her minister to herself: "Want what you have."

Another friend likes to mutter: "It always gets done." Whatever "it" is — finishing a project, catching a plane, picking up the kids — if it has to happen, it will.

Another likes to chant to herself: "Soon this will be over." A dentist drilling in her head? "Soon this will be over, soon this will be over." An awful dinner party? "Soon this will be over, soon this will be over."

Yet another friend printed his self-help mantra on a plastic label that he keeps taped to his pen-and-pencil desk set. It says: "Stay calm and try to adjust."

Like many of the other mantras mentioned, this is an elaborate way of saying, "Accept." Once when asked by a famous author to state his philosophy of life, my calm, adjusted friend said just that: "Acceptance."

The famous author shrugged. "What else is there?"

So true, and yet so hard to remember in the midst of an anxious moment, which is why we have to remind ourselves of this basic truth in a variety of ways.

Some people rely on standard-issue formulas: One foot in front of the other. Be here now. It'll look different tomorrow. Don't sweat the small stuff.

Others, on the other hand, have truly unique approaches.

"A self-help mantra?" mused one friend I quizzed. "How about 'To hell with 'em all but six — save 'em for pallbearers.'"

This gentleman is still working on the concept of acceptance. But, hey, whatever gets you through.

Sometimes our self-help mantras are specific to our jobs. A newspaper colleague finds deep consolation on a bad day by humming to herself, "Tomorrow they'll be wrapping their garbage in it."

One of my all-purpose favorites is something someone told me when I lived in balmy California and was about to visit New York for the first time. It was January, and I'd never endured a northern winter.

"Relax and let the wind roll over you," he said.

The secret to staying comfortable in the cold, he explained, was to not clench. He meant it as a physical tip, but it works in psychological ways as well. Fight the inevitable and you only suffer more.

Here's one last line I made up to help me through rocky moments. It's a good thing to chant on the days when the thing that you get paid to do doesn't come easy: "This is why they call it work."

Portions

Words sometimes land in your mind like birds on a wire. They flutter in, sit there, flutter off, come back, distract you at inconvenient hours.

That bird of a word for me lately is "portion."

I hear the word sometimes when I'm thinking about my friends and family, other times when I'm confronted by the news.

A cyclone hits Myanmar and the death count rises as inexorably as the sun. Bodies wash onto the riverbanks. Corpses rot in the mud.

What a small portion those human beings got.

Then an earthquake hits China and the death count rises as inexorably as the moon.

"What do I have left in the world?" asked a Chinese man quoted in a story by Evan Osnos, the Tribune's China correspondent. The man had lost his wife, his son, his home. "I have nothing," he said. "I have nothing."

Nothing but life itself. His portion, swiftly and terribly reduced, was still bigger than what was allotted to the dead.

Until I started inexplicably obsessing on the word, hearing it like a mantra, thinking, out of the blue on many days, "So this is my portion," I had never thought specifically about what "portion" meant.

I knew it meant 10 potato chips, seven Triscuits and never quite enough ice cream. I knew it meant a part of a whole, as in a rhubarb pie.

Until I Googled "portion," though, I didn't know it meant a dowry, the money a woman brings to her husband through marriage. I had never heard of Bible portions and Torah portions.

Most significantly, I didn't know "portion" means fortune, fate. I have recently learned that the Greek word "moira" signifies both fate and portion.

The word "portion," as it has been chirping in my brain, is some combination of its definitions: allotment and lot, quantity and destiny.

We learn as children that portions are limited and that people get different amounts of things.

"He got more!" is one of childhood's great laments.

"More" was my first word.

From the beginning of life, we chafe at the boundaries of enough. We grow up trying to correct the inequities of the servings we have been given.

If we fully grow up, we also try to correct the inequities of the servings given to others. We don't have to look as far as China and Myanmar to notice how unevenly life distributes its bounty.

A few days ago I was talking to a man involved in building a mixed-income community on the site of an old Chicago housing project.

"I used to think life should be fair," he said.

Now, after years of working with people who have a lot and those who don't, he has concluded that life simply isn't fair. You can do your best to reapportion the goodies, but there will always be people who get the granite countertops and the ones short on food.

Families are further proof that life portions out luck in random ways.

I think especially of my youngest sister, who is mentally disabled, who on an average day literally trembles with medicine and the fluctuations of a troubled mind. Her portion is so much smaller than mine that I want to rage against her unfair share as if it were my own. Her limited portion reminds me how capriciously big mine is. But the other day when I was musing on this notion to myself, she started talking about other mentally ill people she knows, ones abandoned by their families.

"Compared to them," she said, "I have a lot."

She does. So many of us do. There's always somebody with more, with a bigger slice of brains and beauty, a bigger scoop of fame and money, a heftier helping of love and time. But in this world of cyclones and earthquakes, a lot of us have potato chips to spare.

SUNDAY, SEPT. 3, 2000

Dad's Work Ethic

Most of us learn our notions and habits of work in childhood, usually from our parents. I learned mine from my father, and I've been trying to recover ever since.

My mother taught her children to wonder, to ponder, to dream, but my father taught us to get off our dreamy butts and, as he loved to bark, "use a little elbow grease!"

Weekends in our household were not the rhapsody of leisure enjoyed by so many of our friends. "Today's a workday!" my father would proclaim on the typical Saturday or Sunday. So, while our friends were playing tennis or lounging at the pool or lurking at the mall, we would be busily applying elbow grease — his term for effort — to mowing lawns, scrubbing toilets, making curtains and otherwise engaging in the infinite tasks of home improvement.

To my father, work was as vital to life as breath, and he breathed that spirit into his children. Too bad if some child or other felt sick or tired on a designated workday. "Goldbricker!" he would scold, and though none of us had a clue what a goldbricker was exactly, we knew we had violated our father's primary commandment: Thou shalt not be lazy.

My father didn't just preach non-stop work, he modeled it. For the last 15 of his 60 years, he painted houses. We lived in Phoenix then, and he often started work at 5 a.m. to beat the heat. Several of my younger siblings worked with him — before school, after school, weekends — giving up childhood's normal diversions to paint and sand and wash the brushes.

"You have a family of little worker bees, don't you?" a friend's mother once said. I glowered at her, but proudly.

Work was our family virtue, our collective identity. For years, I brought that to my paying jobs — Work 'til midnight? Sign me up! — and into my home life. Well into my adulthood, you could find me on any given Saturday on an outside ladder scrubbing windows or inside vacuuming the corners of some closet. Once a friend popped in on a summer afternoon to find me digging into the grooves of a stove knob with a toothpick, trying to remove the greasy gunk. She gave me a sad look.

"What kind of childhood did you have?"

Finally, a few years ago, I began to think that maybe a little less effort would yield different but equal rewards. Perhaps the work ethic my father instilled in us was in some ways just a work compulsion. He had no hobbies, no extracurricular pleasures, no means of relaxing except his Camels and Christian Brothers burgundy and TV football games.

In some measure, work and its stresses killed him, along with the co-conspirators of cigarettes and alcohol, all of which finally added up to cancer.

I admired his capacity for work; still do. On the days when I don't feel like working, I recall that he never shirked, "shirker" being another of his favorite insults. Long before "Just do it" was an advertising slogan, he just did it. He did it hungover. He did it sick. He did it outdoors when it was 115 in the shade.

And, unlike my soft generation, so many of whom think we shouldn't have to work unless the work is "meaningful," he believed that meaning was a function of the worker, not the work. You, the worker, could find meaning in any kind of work if you did it to the best of your ability.

He found meaning in a baseboard trimmed without a misplaced speck of paint, in walls that were as smooth as seamless silk. At his funeral, one of his customers told me, "Your father wasn't a house painter. He was an artist." She said she sometimes rubbed her hands on the kitchen cabinets he had sanded and painted, marveling that wood could feel so much like glass.

But if I could have granted my father one wish — my wish — it would have been that he learn to find pleasure and meaning in something beyond work. He probably would have lived longer. That's a lesson for a lot of us.

But even as I say that, I feel his skeptical ghost hovering. I'm writing this — Can writing really be called work? — on the Friday of Labor Day weekend, the annual weekend on which Americans are supposed to honor labor by relaxing. I plan to knock off early. And I hear his voice chiding, "You call that elbow grease?"

WEDNESDAY, DEC. 6, 2000

Gwendolyn Brooks: Show Your Neck

When I heard that Gwendolyn Brooks had died Sunday at age 83, I reflexively touched my throat. For a long time, Gwendolyn Brooks has made me think about my throat.

Fifteen years ago, I went to interview Brooks, a product of Chicago's South Side, about her role as the nation's first female African-American poetry consultant. On a sunny winter's day in Washington, D.C., I found her in the Jefferson building of the Library of Congress, an Italian Renaissance extravaganza of marble columns and sculpted angels, very, very far from the poor, rambunctious Chicago she praised and mourned and re-created in her poems.

She sat with her back straight, ankles crossed, in a plaid pinafore and flat black patent leather shoes, looking, deceptively, as proper as a schoolmarm. For a while, she talked about the practicalities and philosophies of poetry. "Poetry," she said, "is life distilled."

And yet her remarks kept looping back to age. To how it felt to be a woman growing old. To things she wished young women understood about being young.

"My face is beginning to fall," she said wistfully, wryly. "What you do when you get to be my age is you just don't look in the mirror except for natural hygienic reasons. But you don't look in the mirror and love what you see the way you used to. Because, you know, I'm not the most beautiful girl that was ever born." She laughed and slapped the couch. "But I used to like what I saw in the mirror. I would look and primp. So you just quit doing that."

I put that remark in the story I wrote. But there were two related remarks I didn't include, two baubles of wisdom I've repeated often to my friends.

She had been talking about poetry when, out of the blue, she said, "Good for you for showing your neck." Confused, I reached toward my throat, not particularly aware until then that I was wearing a V-neck shirt.

She fingered the scarf around her throat. "I'm sorry I didn't expose mine more when I could." Women, she said, should show their necks while they're young enough to have attractive necks to show.

Then she began to talk about how young women not only didn't show their necks enough, they didn't show their voices. Had I noticed, she asked, how many young women spoke as if they were being strangled? How they spoke not from the gut and the heart but from some traffic jam in their throats? They needed to reach down through that constriction, she said, and pull their voice up from somewhere deep and true.

Until that moment, I'd never thought about it. For the 15 years since, I've noticed it almost every day, particularly in women in their 20s and 30s, sometimes in older women, sometimes in myself. And every time I hear a tiny, tinny voice coming from a woman clearly capable of more, I want to grab the strangled speaker on Gwendolyn Brooks' behalf and bellow: Speak up, girl! Speak out! Speak true! You can!

Gwendolyn Brooks had a voice. When she was young, if recordings are a fair accounting, her voice could sound eerily like the feathery, genteel voice of Jackie O. And yet in later years, though she could still speak shyly and primly, her voice was clear and commanding.

Maybe that physical strength of voice correlated to her transformation in the late 1960s, when she rejected mainstream publishing houses in favor of small black presses, stopped straightening her hair and began writing specifically to her fellow African-Americans, believing her mission was to help them define themselves.

When she read her poetry aloud, as she often did to packed audiences of varied skin shades, her voice rumbled through a room like a freight train. When she laughed, the furniture seemed to shake. Her voice spanned at least an octave, from wind chime to diesel engine.

Brooks used her voice as a ticket to freedom and meaning. That voice, on paper and in person, carried her and her message all over the world. She'll be remembered for her voice, and for the lessons it brought to the thousands of young people whose educations she took as personally as a mother might.

And so on the occasion of the passing of one of Chicago's great poets and teachers, I share these two lessons that otherwise might go overlooked: Show your neck. Free your voice.

FRIDAY, NOV. 21, 1997

Be Like Joe

For the past few weeks, I have walked through the world disfigured. I have felt the looks of friends and strangers land on my face as heavily as bricks. I've watched their eyes lock on the raw landscape of my forehead, then dart away, then sneak back, pulled by the magnet of curiosity.

I've heard the unspoken question even close friends wouldn't ask out loud, "What's wrong with you?" I've heard them silently invent various nutty answers.

My excursion through life as a freak began with a dot near my hairline. It was tiny, but troubling enough that I went to the dermatologist. She peered through a magnifying glass and pronounced, "Actinic keratosis." She prescribed a cream designed to keep the sun-damaged dot from progressing into something dangerous. Then she added, "Why don't you use it on your whole forehead while you're at it?"

So for three weeks, I spread the magic cream on half my forehead, and before long — shazam! — it was a screaming, bright red horror show.

If you can hide a problem — with your body, your job, your relationships — you can kid yourself that in some slight way you've controlled it. But with an overt physical deformity, there is no disguise or control.

With my forehead aflame, I could practically hear the circus barker cawing, "Over here, folks! Take a gander! Be amazed!" while, throbbing with embarrassment, I muttered, "Anybody looks at me, I kill 'em."

I tried a hat, but it looked ridiculous. I tried makeup, but it looked worse. I met my vanity and my cowardice face to face, and that was the least pleasant sight of all.

I could occasionally half-forget my forehead, until a startled look from someone reminded me as vividly as any mirror.

I grew annoyed. Annoyed that everyone looked but almost no one asked. Annoyed that those who asked tended toward something discreet like, "My God!!! What happened?!?"

But I eventually realized there was no right response. I was simply trying to ease my discomfort by blaming others for it. For consolation, I turned to three little words that became my mantra: Be like Joe.

"Look people in the eye," I told myself. "Don't shrink. Don't hide. Be brave. Be like Joe."

Finally, hoping to learn better how to walk boldly through the world when you're wearing an abnormality as conspicuous as a Halloween costume, I called Joe up.

"Do you have any tips, Joe?"

Joe declined to offer tips, but he did tell me, in his usual thoughtful, amused way, what it was like to look abnormal not just for a few weeks, but for a lifetime.

"Even after all these years, you still play psychological games, still talk to yourself about it," Joe said. "People see you and do double takes, and you tell yourself, 'Hey, I would do the same thing.' You tell yourself it's normal to look at anything that's different."

Joe is the fourth of my five brothers and the father of three children. He is also the owner of two abnormally short arms that have no elbows and two unusually small hands that have no thumbs.

He has learned to handle a fork and knife as deftly as a magician. His penmanship is perfect. When he is called upon to shake hands, in social situations or with customers he meets as a traveling salesman, he bravely extends his right hand, the one with thin gnarled fingers that have no joints.

I've never once heard Joe complain about his arms, but I've seen him unable to button his top shirt button or tie his tie or scratch his back. I've seen him when people stared.

Sometimes, he said, he wants to hide, and does, but just as often he confronts the curiosity head on. Once, during a week when his daughter's school was focusing on people with physical differences, he went to talk to her kindergarten class.

"Who knows why I'm here today?" he asked the 5-year-olds. A hand shot up. A little girl's dead-earnest voice: "Because you're bald?"

This is what it means to be like Joe — to openly confront the difficult, to see the humor in the unspeakably hard, to answer your sister's questions willingly and frankly, even though, until she felt abnormal, she never asked.

"Does it get easier?" I said.

"Having a family certainly eased my social issues. But it never totally leaves my conscious state."

Knowing that my trip through the abnormal will end soon, I can afford to say I'm glad I took it. It has made me understand better what Joe and so many others have learned in harder and deeper ways, that normalcy is an unkind standard.

SUNDAY, APRIL 29, 2012

The Perfect College

Every year about this time, when the future is rapping hard on the doors of high school seniors, I get a smattering of letters from students.

They write because they haven't gotten into the college of their dreams, and they're wondering if I have any guidance or consolation.

One of these letters arrived in my email last week, from a suburban Chicago student who had been wait-listed at her preferred college.

"I have been simultaneously encouraged by everyone to stay optimistic," she wrote, "but also choose another school and mentally commit to it. The former advice was easy to follow. The latter, quite challenging. I have become one of those kids caught in a desperate love affair with a place they've only spent a few hours at. It pains me to evoke this cliche, but . . . As long as I still have a hope, I am going to hope with all my heart."

I'm sympathetic. The heart is a single-minded creature, and there's virtue in the tenacity of hope.

But she's on to more than she may know when she calls her desire for this college "a desperate love affair."

Desperate love affairs are often conducted in the haze of romantic myth, fogged up by the notion that there is only one true beloved, without whom life will be just a shadow of its glorious possibilities.

This romantic myth can apply to colleges as surely as it does to human mates, and in both cases it obscures the truth: There is no perfect One, and there's more than one path to a good life.

I never yearned for one special college the way many students do. The reasons are various. By the time college was in my viewfinder, my parents had more urgent preoccupations, and so I felt no parental pressure. My friends were staying close to home for school, so I felt no peer pressure. Nor did my school counselor foster the idea that applying to college was an Olympic-level competition in which she who aims highest is likeliest to die happiest.

I applied to one school, Pomona College in California, figuring that if I got in and they gave me financial aid, I'd go, and if they didn't? Well, I'd hang with my friends at Arizona State.

I did get into Pomona — I might not qualify today — and it changed my life. I found lifetime friends, learned how to learn, grew up. I feel loyal and indebted to the place.

But I also believe that what I gained there I could have gained at a number of other schools. I know people who went to state universities whose college years were equally fruitful.

And I've seen desperate love affairs with colleges turn into bad dates, pricey bad dates.

I know a couple of smart Chicago-area women, now in their 20s, who went away to expensive colleges they'd yearned for, only to wind up unhappy. They came back, closer to home, and prospered, less expensively.

One beauty of being 18 is the intensity of desire. You want, you dream, you reach. And the broad things so many of us want at that age — knowledge, adventure, opportunity, love in its assorted forms — are likely to be things we want all through our lives.

But the specifics — that school, that job, that person — are not as important as they seem in the clutch of desire. Love can change its direction, and in the end, college is like everything else:

It doesn't make you. Your future lies in what you make of it.

Reunion Time

"We don't look as old as they do, do we?" muttered my old college friend. It was reunion weekend and we were walking toward a group of alumni gathered on a lawn.

"Let's hope not," I muttered back, squinting at the class year scribbled on their name tags. "They're 20 years older than we are."

This is the kind of conversation heard all across America in the spring, the nation's official reunion season, a time when former classmates return to the alma mater seeking to answer life's deepest questions: How old do I look? How old do they look? We're not really this old, are we?

At first glance, the answers are not pretty.

Well, that guy's eaten a few too many Oreos since he left the dining hall. And who would have thought that dude would have turned white-haired so soon? At least he still has hair.

And her — she wasn't blond in college, was she? But I swear that dingy-haired woman behind her once had locks as gold as summer. And her — she obviously hasn't had her eyes done.

And check out that freak, the one who hasn't gained a line or an ounce in all these years. Revoke her class credentials.

For every assessment you make or hear, of course, you know an equally dispassionate analysis is being made of you.

It doesn't matter that you just had a manicure or a haircut or an antioxidant-and-avocado-detox-anti-aging facial. Someone is still whispering to someone else that you could use a double shot of Botox or some tooth bleach or at least a long vacation.

You suspect that "You look great!" is code for, "Hey, I thought you'd look worse!"

You thank God for low lights, name tags and the open bar.

But something funny happens after the shock of the initial reunion sightings and assessments. Once you match your youthful classmates with these middle-age relations, once you get used to the fact that time has robbed every single one of you of something — or added it in the wrong places — you stop noticing the thinning hair and padded waists, the doubled chins and rutted foreheads.

What you notice is the voice. The eyes. The hand gestures and the laugh.

They're eerily unchanged. And though it's not visible to the current college kids who drift past thinking, "Geezers," before long, among yourselves, the younger selves are shining through.

You stop thinking about looks, start talking about life.

You trade resumes. Doctor, lawyer, rancher. Teacher, preacher, mom or dad.

Then the talk goes deeper. There's mention of a divorce. A disabled child. A disease conquered or in progress.

Someone says something like, "My male friends warned me about getting involved with a younger woman," and explains that after raising kids with her husband she's raising another with her female partner.

You share stories of the deaths of parents. Of distant travels and surviving dreams. You see someone you were once in love with and you remember why you were, and why it's better for you both that it didn't last. You see someone you might have fallen in love with and wonder if it's better that you didn't.

You eat some more.

And you stop hearing the question that nagged before you came, "Why would I go to a reunion?" You know why now. It's not mostly to revisit memories. It's to share trip notes with your fellow travelers through time. It's to allow your fully alive but often hidden younger self back out on parade. That self can never be fully seen by people who know your past only through your stories.

We often measure our lives in events — the accumulation of things we do and things that happen to us. Reunions remind us that though events may polish us, dent us, turn us upside down or dress us up in different clothes, we are in some basic measure simply who we are. We still are who we were.

So when some reunion shutterbug says, "Smile," you do, with pleasure. And even though later when you see the pictures you'll see that, yeah, you all do look older, you'll also notice something really funny — those smiles have hardly changed at all.

I f I had to name the thing I love most about my job —
there are many — it would be meeting people I'd otherwise never meet and introducing them to the Tribune's
readers.

This postcard came from a Pakistani man who was
working as a taxi driver in New York City on Sept. 11, 2001.

A Chicago-area woman was in his cab when the Twin
Towers went up in flames. Neither of them knew what
was happening or what to do. He drove her home with
him to his Muslim neighborhood in the Bronx, and they
watched the terror on TV.

The day passed. The airports were closed. What was
she going to do? He drove her all the way back to Chicago.
After I wrote about their adventure, he sent me this card.

chapter 3

....

loss and survival

....

Julia Sweeney, Suburban Mom

Every day, even in the wind and snow, Julia Sweeney walks half an hour from her Wilmette house to Lake Michigan, and with an awe someone else might call religious, faces the sky and water.

She takes 10 deep breaths. How puny and impermanent we are, she thinks. How unlikely we are. Then she and her dog walk home.

"It's Pat!"

Nobody who sees her — a 50-year-old woman with a wide, lightly freckled face and cropped platinum hair — calls that out to her, but there was a time when strangers did.

In the 1990s, Pat, the sexually inscrutable "Saturday Night Live" character that made Sweeney famous, was almost as big in pop culture as Santa Claus.

But that was a long time ago, and maybe longer ago in Sweeney's mind than in real time.

Sweeney thinks back on Pat as an artifact of who she used to be, before she got, and apparently beat, cervical cancer.

59

She created Pat before she took care of a brother dying of lymphoma. Before she adopted a baby girl from China. Before she gave up God, turned all those occurrences into popular monologues and, last winter, stunned everyone she knew by leaving Los Angeles.

"I'm finally a suburban housewife," she said last week, sitting in Wilmette. "Honestly, it's my dream come true."

She laughed, as if to say she meant it, mostly.

That morning, Sweeney had come to a Wilmette neighbor's home to do a voiceover for the 30th annual variety show of McKenzie Elementary School, where her daughter, Mulan, is in fourth grade.

It's an amateur event put on by parents and teachers for the kids, but Sweeney went down to the basement studio, clamped on headphones and, standing erect at a mike, recited as enthusiastically as she would for a professional production.

"Is that cadence OK?" she asked. "Am I going too fast? I can do it again. I'll just do the whole thing again."

At one point, between takes and swigs of water, she said, "I used to do so much voiceover. I don't anymore. It makes me sad."

Sweeney seems pleased and a little perplexed by where and how she lives now.

Her LA life was full. She had contacts, jobs and friends, though those friends didn't include her old "SNL" pals.

After the death of former cast member Phil Hartman, she said, getting together was just too sad.

Sweeney was in her LA routine as a single working mother — the kind who put her daughter in the green room during her performances — when she got a strange fan letter.

The letter-writer had seen "Letting Go of God," her show about becoming an atheist after a lifetime of Catholicism. He told her she should marry his brother, Michael.

"C'mon," she thought.

Among other absurdities, the brother lived in Chicago. She married him anyway.

In December of 2008, Sweeney, her daughter and her new husband (Michael Blum, who runs a scientific instruments company) drove east from California in a minivan.

She had a few "Where-the-hell-am-I?" moments when she got to the North Shore, but she liked being in a place with old houses and big yards that was friendly to Mulan. It reminded her of Spokane, Wash., where she'd grown up with four younger siblings.

She'd thought she might get involved with Chicago theaters. Instead, she discovered a new desire. To be quiet and alone. No parties. No dinners. No big public life.

"Mostly," she said, "I just want to be in my house reading and writing."

Sweeney never gained the celebrity and power of some of her "SNL" colleagues.

The men, she said, were more skilled than the women at exercising their ambition.

"I don't have the temperament for it," she said. "Or maybe I wasn't funny enough."

But if those jokey guys — Adam Sandler, Mike Myers, David Spade, Chris Rock — have had a wider reach, hers has been deeper.

In her work, she has taken on the big themes — mortality, family, faith — and her opinionated uncertainty, her mix of funny and sad, that Irish-Catholic ordinary gal-pal thing, have won her fans.

When "Letting Go of God" premiered on Showtime in December, demand for the DVDs soared. She loaded a couple thousand copies into her minivan and drove them from Wilmette to the amazon.com warehouse in Indiana to be mailed.

But, just as she outgrew Pat, she has outlived her persona as "atheist girl."

"I'm not an activist," she said. "I'm trying to get off the whole atheist racket."

She also claims she's done using her life as her art. One reason: her daughter.

"Now she Googles me. 'Hey, I read your blog yesterday.'"

Sometimes, people ask Sweeney how, without God and church, she finds meaning and connection.

Family, she answers. Writing. Psychological exploration. The wonders of science.

And the sky and the lake, where every day, in her improbable new life, she can find peace in the thought of how fleeting and small we all are.

Kaia and Julia, After the Accident

To mark the first anniversary of the accident, Julia and Kaia rode the train south from Chicago a few days ago.

Nobody paid much attention to them as they sat on the train, pecking at their laptops while small towns and fields whisked past the windows.

Someone may have wondered why one of them, Julia, wore her left arm in a sling, or how the other, Kaia, got the scar that rippled from her forehead to her chin. But mostly they looked like ordinary college students, and only a person who got too close could have read the inscription in their identical blue rubber wrist bands:

We'll always have Faith. In loving memory. 4.23.92.

A year ago, Kaia Tammen, Faith Dremmer and Julia Baird were famous in the unique flicker of a way that comes with public catastrophe.

On March 24, 2010, all three — seniors at the University of Chicago Lab Schools, on a spring-break bike trip — were pedaling along a curve of rural road in southern Illinois, when a van driven by an 86-year-old man swerved across the center line. In the collision, Faith died.

Kaia and Julia, both severely injured, did their best to resume normal lives.

At the end of summer, Kaia moved from her parents' Hyde Park apartment into a U. of C. dorm. She brought with her a pair of Faith's socks.

Julia moved from her North Side home to attend Washington University in St. Louis. She brought along one of Faith's sweatshirts.

In the months that followed, the metal plates and screws in Kaia's right arm bothered her — picking up a backpack was hard — but the scars on her otherwise flawless face faded to a pale pink. She refused plastic surgery; the scars were a mark of the accident, and she never wanted to be embarrassed by the accident.

Julia's broken knee healed well enough that eventually she could run five miles four times a week. Unable to bend her left arm, she learned to open packages with her teeth. She learned to do sit-ups wearing a sling. The hardest thing to learn was how to accept help, like letting her roommate tie her shoes.

Julia and Kaia made new friends, but they talked often on the phone. Shortly before they left for college, they had met for falafel and agreed: We're a pair forever.

A pair with Faith in the middle.

When the anniversary of the accident approached, Kaia made a suggestion: Let's go back.

With a pinch of fear, they went.

Tony Cox picked them up at the train station in Carbondale. A local funeral home owner, he was the first person to stop on the road and tend to them after the accident. Every couple of weeks now, he emails Kaia just to check in.

The day after they arrived, Cox drove them to the three hospitals where they'd been cared for by doctors and nurses they didn't remember but were moved to meet.

"Oh my God, I remember you!" a nurse said when she saw Kaia. "You're that girl in the bike accident."

That afternoon, Cox drove them to the spot where Faith died.

It felt odd to be there, and empty, and important. They told themselves it was just chance that the sun vanished and the wind picked up.

They held on to each other and tried to remember.

Kaia remembered nothing of the accident except a flash of purple, maybe the purple of her bike.

Julia remembered only the time before it happened, and how hard the three of them laughed as they struggled up the hills.

They didn't remember Faith being hit. But here in the wind, next to the little white cross Cox had planted between the road and the field, they could feel her.

That night, they went to dinner at a restaurant, and over the Lenten special — fried fish and hush puppies — got to know some of the people who had helped them. A state trooper, a patrolman, a man who sat and comforted Julia.

All these strangers who cared for them that day, and still cared. For as awkward as it was, Kaia and Julia knew this was why they'd come back. This was the good to be salvaged from the loss.

"They wanted the best for us and they didn't even know us," Kaia said later.

"I owe them so much," said Julia.

In a bedroom in the Cox house, they stayed up most of the night, just the two of them, talking, listening to the Asian pop music Faith liked, asking themselves: What now?

Without an answer, they went home.

A month ago, a friend gave Kaia an old bike. She was shaky when she rode it for the first time. Now she rides all over Hyde Park. Julia hasn't gotten back on a bike yet but the two are planning to do a triathlon together next year, after they've recovered from the next surgeries on their arms.

On Thursday, the anniversary of the accident, Kaia went to see Faith's mother, Michele. She has been thinking about how to carry on her own life and how to honor Faith — not Faith the dead idol, but Faith the wonderful, imperfect friend she loved.

She took comfort in Michele Dremmer's words: "Faith isn't going to let you go. You move forward. She'll move with you."

SUNDAY, JUNE 24, 2012
....

Train Buddies

Another Monday morning, the Metra train to town. A routine 16 minutes from Oak Park to the Loop.

Karen Gillett boards the 7:51 and, as always, rides with her train buddies, train buddies being a particular category of friend forged in the constant commute from home to work and back.

The train pulls east, then somewhere, maybe right past Kedzie, a voice squawks from the speakers:

We have a medical emergency. Any medical personnel, please walk to the front of the train. We need your assistance.

Gillett, a nurse, looks at her train buddies.

"I guess I should go help."

Same Monday morning, same Metra train to town. A routine 22 minutes from Maywood to the Loop.

On her way to the Metra station, Cynthia Higgins drops off her two children at her parents' house.

"Have a good day and do good in summer school," she tells her son.

"I'm in a hurry, Daddy," she tells her dad. "Got to catch my train to work."

At the Maywood station, Higgins joins one of her train buddies, Shirley Gavin. The two women have ridden the train together just about every weekday morning and evening since they met on the platform four years ago.

On this Monday, they board the usual 7:45, in the usual first car and, unusually, sit face to face instead of side by side. They chat about the weekend. At Oak Park, the conductor takes their tickets.

"Good morning!" says Higgins, high-spirited as usual, to the conductor. "Happy Monday!"

Shortly after that, Higgins lays her head back on the seat. She goes silent.

"Cynthia?" Gavin says. She leans in. "Cynthia, what's wrong?"

She taps her friend's leg, then pats her face, stands up and shakes her.

"Get a conductor!" she cries. "Call 911!"

Karen Gillett, still athletic at 49, makes her way from the rear of the train all the way to the front. The large woman with her head back on the seat is so still, so apparently relaxed, that Gillett doesn't even notice her at first.

Then she searches for a pulse.

"What's her name?" Gillett asks.

"Cynthia," Shirley Gavin says.

"Cynthia, can you hear me?" Gillett asks. Over and over, she invokes this stranger's name.

Cynthia. Cynthia.

A man, a doctor, arrives, and as the train rumbles on, he and Gillett move Higgins to the floor. Gillett does CPR, pressing and pressing and pressing, never stopping though she is exhausted and worried she might break one of Cynthia's bones, wishing someone would offer her a rubber band to pull her hair off her face, thinking how beautiful Cynthia's cornrows are.

Gillett is still pressing when the train pulls to its final stop, Ogilvie Transportation Center. The paramedics arrive.

On board the train, one paramedic needs more light to see; Gillett provides the flashlight on her phone. Another paramedic wishes for some reading glasses; Gillett fishes in her backpack and pulls out hers.

Gavin grabs a cab to the ER, to wait there, while another of Higgins' train buddies uses Cynthia's cellphone to call the family.

Strange, Gillett thinks, how many people are snapping photos.

When Karen Gillett walks into the ER, Shirley Gavin is sitting there, hugging her chest, alone.

All of a sudden it hits Gillett: Oh my God. This really happened.

The two women sit next to each other, holding hands. Gavin cries, wondering what more she might have done to help her friend.

Gillett rubs her back and says she did fine, just fine, consoling Gavin the way she consoled the young woman on the train who had jumped in to administer mouth-to-mouth, then worried she wasn't doing it well.

Gavin tells Gillett about Cynthia.

Cynthia has a son (age 15), a daughter (age 10), a job as an administrative assistant at an engineering firm. She's president of the Maywood Park District's Board of Commissioners.

Listening to Cynthia's life, Gillett thinks about her own kids, and what it would be like to lose your mother, snap, just like that.

Then Higgins' parents, Albert and Shirley, arrive. Mrs. Higgins hugs Gillett, thanks her, asks for her phone number so she can call to update her on Cynthia.

Gillett, determined not to cry in front of the people who love Cynthia Higgins, demurs, says she needs to get to work.

And so she leaves, already knowing what an authorized person will soon come and tell them:

Cynthia is gone.

There may not be one person who rode Metra train No. 28 that Monday morning, June 11, who doesn't wonder if something might have saved Cynthia Higgins, a 46-year-old woman with parents, siblings, friends, a big smile and two kids she was raising alone.

Could something more have been done? Who might have done it?

Karen Gillett doesn't know if Higgins — who according to the medical examiner's report suffered from heart disease and died of natural causes — would have survived under any circumstances.

But, as a longtime nurse, she has suggestions.

Why doesn't Metra school conductors in CPR? And put defibrillators on the trains?

In fact, the only reason she was willing to talk about what had happened is because she hopes that Metra will see the need to be better prepared for such events.

"I want to make a statement about what Metra needs to do, not what I did," she said. "There's going to be a lot of other Cynthias on that train."

Putting defibrillators on Metra trains has been under discussion for years.

The issue flared in 2009, after a Barrington Hills man collapsed on a train then died, though it wasn't clear whether a defibrillator would have saved him.

The discussion may finally bear fruit. A Metra spokesman, Michael Gillis, said the agency is committed to putting defibrillators on every train by early next year.

In the meantime, Cynthia Higgins' mother lays no blame.

"I would just like to say thank you to everyone who helped," she said last week, headed to Missouri to bury her daughter in the family plot.

Since the morning Cynthia died, Shirley Gavin hasn't set foot in the Metra car where they always rode together.

"The ghost car," she calls it and rides one car back instead.

That's where Karen Gillett found her this past Wednesday, the first time they'd seen each other since the hospital.

Their eyes locked. They hugged. They cried.

"Is that the nurse-angel?" someone asked.

They rode on in to work, routine resumed.

Gillett will be remembered for a long time on train No. 28 as that woman who worked so, so hard to keep another passenger alive, a passenger who was memorialized Tuesday at Rock of Ages Baptist Church in Maywood, with a favorite train conductor in the crowd.

The obituary began like this:

"Cynthia Michelle Higgins, affectionately known by her family as Michelle and by her friends, co-workers, and political/community acquaintances as Cynthia or Cyan, entered this world on May 4, 1966, in Chicago. She transitioned from her mortal life to her eternal life on June 11, 2012, at Northwestern Memorial Hospital, Chicago, with her Metra train buddies standing by."

SUNDAY, AUG. 31, 1997

Saved by the Gettysburg Address

This is the story of a man whose life was saved by the Gettysburg Address.

His name is Dave Burgin. He was my first newspaper editor. He taught me half of what I know about the way words work, so it comes as no surprise that words would be his lifeboat. The surprise is only in which words.

"The stroke came on the 26th of July, a Saturday," is how he starts the story. "A stroke is not a bang thing. It's a long ordeal. You don't know what's happening, but something's happening to you. You figure out it's not a heart attack. And believe me, if you have a choice between a stroke and a heart attack, take the heart attack."

He laughs, weakly. "Anyway, I end up on the bathroom floor. I can't get up. My left side is gone."

Before long he's in the emergency ward at Marin General Hospital near his home north of San Francisco. He squints into the bright lights above his gurney, into a canopy of faces, sees looks that tell him he is dying.

"Keep him awake," says a doctor.

"You've got to hang on," says his wife.

She shakes him, shoves him, grips him by his golf shirt. He hears someone say that if he blacks out, he goes for brain surgery. If he goes for brain surgery, he figures, he's as good as dead.

"Then in walks a chaplain, a woman," he recalls, "muscles her way in. Says, 'Are you right with God?'"

The chaplain scares him most of all. He tells her to take a hike. He vows he will not die. But he's drifting toward someplace dark and far he doesn't want to go.

"Wake up," his wife, Judy, pleads. "Say something. Talk."

And so he begins: "Four score and seven years ago . . ."

He goes on, through every word and line of the Gettysburg Address, riding the comforting cadences he has known since he was a boy, until he reaches the final phrase: "and that government of the people, by the people, for the people, shall not perish from the earth."

"I can't follow that act," says the chaplain.

He starts again. "Four score and seven years ago . . ."

Next thing he knows, he is in intensive care, having escaped brain surgery.

"I owe it all to Abe Lincoln," he says.

If he'd had to predict his behavior on the brink of death, he would have guessed he'd be screaming for forgiveness, not quoting Honest Abe.

But his life has been oddly linked to Lincoln's since he was born in 1939 in Kentucky, Lincoln's home state, on Feb. 12, the date of Lincoln's birth.

"My grandfather, Elmer, was a schoolmaster in Bobtown, Ky.," he says.

"He was a Lincoln scholar, at least by the standards of Pulaski County, Ky. He was thrilled that his first grandchild was born on Lincoln's birthday. When I was two, according to family lore, I could do the Gettysburg Address, standing on a chair."

He didn't really understand what he was saying until he was 19 and visited the Gettysburg battlefield. And it was only a few years ago, when he dissected the speech phrase by phrase with the help of Garry Wills' book, "Lincoln at Gettysburg," that he could recite it without a hitch.

But he's carried it in his head for years — through all the newspapers he has edited, from Orlando to Dallas to San Francisco to Oakland — figuring that someday it would help him win a barroom bet or dazzle a cop. He's recited it at various social functions and never dazzled anyone.

Until the day he almost died.

"I'm not painting any miracles," he says. "I'm just saying, 'unbelievable.' Where did that come from? God, what you rely on in the strangest moments."

Over the phone, I ask him to recite it.

"You testing me?" he says. Then he recites.

His voice is weak, but I hear these words more clearly than I ever have, full of a passion that would make Abe Lincoln proud, uttered by a man for whom swallowing remains a triumph and walking just a dream.

"Tell all potential stroke victims to eat the cheeseburgers and have the beer," he says with a small laugh. "Just memorize the Gettysburg Address."

SUNDAY, JULY 16, 1995

Running With Bulls

We all tell stories of the crazy things we did in our 20s, at least all of us do who were lucky enough to have done crazy things in our 20s and luckier yet to have survived them.

From the safety of later adulthood, we reminisce fondly about the risks we took in those days, back when we were greedy for sensation and bold enough to seize it.

We shudder and chuckle over the risks, risks we wouldn't dream of running now, now that we understand that risk is really risk and not just an adrenaline rush topped off by a beer and a good laugh.

Looking back on those wild rapids, we marvel that we lived to tell the stories, which is why we love to tell them.

The rides we took as hitchhikers. The rides we gave to hitchhikers. The weird places we slept. The dangerous streets we walked alone. The strangers we accompanied to even stranger places.

These are our purple hearts of foolish courage, our badges of experience, cherished souvenirs. We are proud of the reckless things we did at 20, 21, 22, even though at this age we would be too smart to do them, or maybe just too scared.

Matthew Tassio was 22.

Fresh out of the University of Illinois, bound for an engineer's job at Motorola, he had a summertime to spare, and he decided to spend it on an American rite of passage, traveling in Europe.

For countless middle-class Americans, Europe is the free zone between the confines of youth and adulthood's traps.

Americans in their 20s go to Europe in search of risks. Out of the reach of parents and routine, they seek out epiphanies of food, wine, land-scape, sex, language, art, love. They go with heads full of myths and a fantasy of freedom, the kind of freedom that many suspect will come only once in life.

Do it now, a voice says, or you'll never do it. Life will soon lock you up for good.

So Matthew Tassio went to Europe, to Egypt, France, Italy, and finally to Pamplona, Spain, for the running of the bulls, a ritual two centuries older than the United States but unknown to most Americans until Ernest Hemingway romanticized it in "The Sun Also Rises."

Running with the bulls last week, Tassio was killed. In public. On film. At the age of 22.

The picture mesmerizes in the same measure that it sickens: a shining half-ton bull tearing into a brown-haired boy wearing shorts and sports shoes and a red bandanna.

In that awful picture, how many of us saw our own free-spirited, fool-hardy selves at 22? Thought of our own close calls and risky deeds and wondered, as everyone who knew Tassio surely has: Why him? Why was he the one who didn't survive the risks and get to turn them into tales?

Some will say it was a pointless death that came decades too soon and with uncommon cruelty. It was all those things.

But that isn't the main thing people who loved Tassio should remember.

What they should remember is the young man resourceful enough to do what many young people dream of doing but don't quite dare.

The young man curious enough about the world beyond Chicago that he vowed to travel until his money ran out.

The young man logical enough to be an engineer, but in whose heart stirred some passion that would lure him to a foreign continent and tempt him to run with bulls.

The 20s are a time when we test ourselves in ways we never will again. What you do in those years becomes the foundation for what you think you can do and who you think you are.

Risk is built into the tests. And while risk is a form of foolishness, it also is a show of hope, and the kind of exuberant, unfettered hope we bring to our 20s gets harder to summon as life goes on.

If you pass those self-imposed tests of the 20s, however foolish they may later seem, that knowledge and those experiences sustain you through dreary jobs and difficult relationships and all the mundane matters of the rest of life.

Unlike so many others, Matthew Tassio did not get to come home from Europe with a suitcase full of adventures survived and risks outrun, and the people who loved him will wish he never went. They can still admire the breadth of spirit that took him there.

FRIDAY, NOV. 20, 2009

Sharon and Wanda, a Love Story

Sharon Durling went to the morgue a few days ago to ID Wanda Jean Taylor's body.

Durling, a part-time writer with an MBA from Kellogg School of Management, lives in a house in Chicago's Lincoln Park. Taylor lived on the sidewalks, on the "L" or, lately, in a $585-a-month SRO North Side hotel with the inapt name "Chateau."

The two met when Sharon was 30 and volunteering at Deborah's Place, a women's shelter. Wanda, at 25, had a bed there. They played Scrabble — "She cheated like hell," Sharon says — and one day Wanda invited Sharon to a movie.

That was 22 years ago, the beginning of a friendship that Sharon learned was over when her phone rang on Monday, Nov. 9. She recognized the number: a psychiatric hospital where police had taken Wanda a few days earlier.

"Wanda," Sharon said into the phone.

Wanda, said the caller, was dead.

Sharon picked up Wanda's affairs, the things she'd been carrying when the police brought her in. They included seven orange medication bottles, an unopened bar of soap, a key chain with no keys, two Medicaid cards, six pens, a laundry card, three Starbucks cards and $1.84.

A hospital intake paper noted the reason for her admission: "impaired judgment."

None of that struck Sharon as strange. She knew Wanda. Wanda who stuck out her tongue at cops; who hit nurses with her cane; who was rumored to have stabbed someone; who'd been banned from several shelters; who took and dealt drugs before she got clean; who mixed up her meds; who sometimes called her friend Sharon "an effin' ho."

That was the same Wanda who always eventually apologized. The generous, gregarious Wanda who was wise enough to say, "Sometimes I have an evil mind." The Wanda whose poems had been collected in a couple of pamphlets and who scribbled constantly in notebooks.

A while back, Wanda had given Sharon one of those notebooks. The opening lines, in pencil: "Fear of my world. To my world I live in fear."

Over the years, Sharon had pieced together Wanda's life from scraps of stories. She was one of 10 children in a South Side family. A relative raped her. A neighbor raped her. She was bipolar. She'd lost all contact with her family, including the four children who had been taken away from her. The father of one of those children had bashed her head open with a brick.

During the early years of their friendship, the women met occasionally for a movie or a meal.

By the end, Wanda called Sharon almost every day.

She used Sharon's phone number on forms, so Sharon never knew when she might get a call from an emergency room, a psych ward or a jail.

"I've seen her in critical care in a coma," Sharon says. "But she had 29 lives. She had such a will to live."

Sharon had never met any of Wanda's family but introduced Wanda to her relatives, friends, boyfriends. Wanda wrote letters to Sharon's father. Her own father had died when she was 8.

Wanda had a life invisible to Sharon. One day last summer Sharon was riding her bike near Wilson Avenue and Broadway, where homeless people hang out. She spotted Wanda, who gave her a tour.

"It was like being with the mayor of a small town," she says. "Everybody knew that woman."

Through the years, Wanda spent a few nights at Sharon's house, but Sharon says they agreed that wasn't a great idea.

"I never had to establish boundaries with her," Sharon says. "She had already set them up for herself and never took advantage of our friendship."

She did let Wanda use her car trunk as a roaming chest of drawers, and Wanda, she says, thought of it as "their" car.

As Wanda got older, her maladies multiplied. Heart failure, strokes, asthma, epileptic seizures, vascular dementia.

Last year, when Wanda was declared unfit to care for herself, Sharon became her legal guardian. The judge looked skeptical.

"So you're just like a really nice lady who wants to help people?" she recalls him saying.

"No," she said, "I'm not."

"So why would you want to be her legal guardian?"

"Because I love her."

When word came that Wanda had died at 47 of dilated cardiomyopathy, just a few hours after her last phone call to Sharon, Sharon wasn't entirely shocked but she was bereft.

"It's not a one-way white-girl-helps-black-girl kind of thing," Sharon says. "I needed her. I miss her."

Sharon didn't really have to go to the morgue, but it felt right, so she did. She arranged to have Wanda buried and her lost relatives notified. On Wednesday night, she masterminded a memorial at Chicago Uptown Ministry, where Wanda recently had spent her days.

Eighty people came, Wanda's friends and Sharon's, black and white, well-to-do and not. One of Wanda's sisters, Mary Taylor, was there.

The only time she'd seen Wanda in years was on the "L."

She'd given Wanda her phone number then, but Wanda never called.

Sharon Durling can't say exactly why she and Wanda Taylor became friends. She's never had children and wishes she had. Maybe it was that.

Or maybe it was the simple mystery called love.

The Girl Scout Cookie Queen

Before she went to Stanford, before she was a cheerleader for the Chicago Bulls and before all the rest, Erika Kendrick was Chicago's Girl Scout cookie queen.

She was 9 the first time she won the crown, the first black girl in Chicago to be the top cookie-seller.

When she angled for her third straight title at age 11, I wrote a story about her, and every January when cookie season rolls around I wonder: Whatever happened to the cookie queen?

Here's what:

She walks into the Willis Tower Corner Bakery in a hip-hugging black skirt and shiny black stiletto ankle boots.

Buried in her big black bag, under the red-and-white pompons she carries everywhere like charms, is a copy of her novel, "Appetite," whose first page includes this:

"I whip my achy nakedness around to the crescendo of a bellowing snore. Yikes! A strange man is stretched out on the floor beside me entwined in half my sheet — clearly one of the puzzle pieces misplaced somewhere between the first Bacardi Mojito and last call's obligatory double shot of Patron."

This is not the geeky girl in braces I remember.

But at 35, Kendrick is still a Girl Scout. Really. Still pays dues. Teaches Girl Scouts. Says everything she needed to know in life — leadership, networking, teamwork — she learned as a Brownie.

"I'm a Girl Scout nerd," she says. "Forever."

Kendrick was visiting Chicago last week, and when I asked to meet, she suggested the tower she still calls Sears. As a girl, she loved to doodle it the way other girls sketch horses.

"This building," she says, "oh my God, has always represented, 'I gotta get the hell out of here.' My mom or dad would take me, or we'd go on a field trip, and being up at the top was, 'Oh my God, there's so much out there.' I lived in a house on the South Side, looked out at a tree."

Kendrick did get out, but the trail, as she describes it over coffee, has been hilly.

St. Ignatius College Prep to Stanford. Stanford to a Chicago hospital on suicide watch, diagnosed with bipolar disorder. Back to Stanford. Graduation. Then another collapse, more therapy. Then a year as a Luvabull.

"Dancing breathed new life into me," she says of her cheerleading days. "I thought, OK, I feel normal, whatever that means."

She felt normal enough to earn an MBA at the University of Illinois. Then the sadness sucked her down again.

"I felt," she says, "just very lost and empty."

She drank too much, smoked too much pot and finally went through rehab.

"I don't have an off switch," she says, "whether it's Haagen-Dazs or vodka."

Then eight years ago, Kendrick moved to New York. The moment she first stepped out of the subway, she cried. She felt happy.

Her breakdowns had taught her that she was most vulnerable when she couldn't express herself creatively. New York, she sensed, had energy big enough to match hers and would let her feel creative in a way no other place could.

So far, she says, it has.

Random House has published her two novels, "Confessions of a Rookie Cheerleader" and "Appetite." She's ready to embark on a college motivational speaking tour. She teaches writing and self-esteem classes to Girl Scouts.

"I'm always working," she says. "Unless I'm on a date. And even then I'm thinking about work."

She also teaches seminars on dating.

She says she no longer drinks, though. She eats no meat, meditates and plays basketball, all disciplines that, coupled with a creative life, have helped her manage her moods without medication.

"But that's me," she's careful to say. "I don't say meds are bad."

In every success story, there's a seed of trouble. In every story about trouble, there's a seed of better times. The former cookie queen has lived both.

And as for cookies?

"At 35," she says, "you've got to start watching the Samoas and Do-Si-Dos. But I sneak and eat them."

She flings her arms out like a cheerleader.

"My favorites are still the Thin Mints. Oh. My. Goodness."

The Famous Unknown Writer

He always writes sitting next to the window.

He likes looking through the trees and down toward Clark Street. The view makes his mind and his tiny apartment feel more open.

To the people on the sidewalks below — the Cubs fans, the shoppers, the carousers — he's nobody special. No one in his subsidized, senior-citizen high-rise knew much about him either until someone read a piece in The New Yorker magazine last year on the rise of Arabic fiction.

Now at least a few of his neighbors know that the short, smiling man in the plaid cap, the guy up on two, is a novelist with "a substantial and award-winning body of work in Arabic."

That little bit of respect buffers his solitude.

Once, a long time ago, he lived in a big house in Iraq, with a garden and a wife and two children. Now there's just him, and just enough space for a daybed, a smattering of chairs, a galley kitchen, and the computer by the window, where he writes and waits to be read in English and in America.

"I am like the player in Wrigley," Mahmoud Saeed says. "He has to play. I have to write."

He sits surrounded by Arabic books, some of them translated from English, including two by Danielle Steel. Setting down his teacup, he picks up his orange prayer beads and rubs them while he recounts his life.

When Saeed was a boy, the Arabic novel scarcely existed. Arabs wrote poetry, not fiction. But the library in Mosul carried Arabic translations of the great novels of Russia, France, England and the United States, and by his mid-teens, he had read them all. Tolstoy, Balzac, Zola, Dostoyevsky, Dickens, Hemingway.

Saeed's first novel was published on Feb. 1, 1963. On Feb. 8, the Ba'ath party, eventually led by Saddam Hussein, overthrew the government. On Feb. 14, Saeed was arrested and sent to jail.

"For a year and a day," he says.

Here in his Chicago apartment in 2011, he scribbles those dates on a legal pad. English is still hard.

When he got out of jail, Saeed fled to Morocco, but because his mother was sick he came back to Iraq, a country harsh on writers like him who refused to write propaganda for the regime. He taught secondary school, married and was periodically tortured in prison.

Through it all, he wrote stories. He hid them under furniture or in the refrigerator. He wrapped up a novel and stashed it in a water tank. The government destroyed whatever it found.

In 1981, after six months in prison, he began a novel about a mild-mannered teacher, much like himself, who was imprisoned and tortured. He smuggled the manuscript out, and years later it was published in Syria.

In the small Arab literary world, Saeed gained a reputation. Won awards. Published more. He moved to the safety of Dubai but sometimes returned to his family in Iraq. He refused the Iraqi government's offer to spy on Iraqis abroad, and on a 1995 trip home, he was again arrested.

"They put me in a room for one week," he says, "in a chair."

After that, he sold his Iraqi house for almost nothing, moved his family to Dubai and in 1999, broke but not broken, left for the United States, convinced that English was the only future for writers.

"I like Americans very much," he says. "I like Clark Street very much. Friday, Saturday night, it is very vivid?"

He looks toward his friend Allen Salter.

"Lively," says Salter.

Salter is an Evanston crime novelist who writes under the pseudonym Sam Reaves. He helped translate Saeed's most recent novel, and though he marvels that Saeed, who is 72, stays cheerful and productive, he worries.

Saeed's part-time job teaching Arabic literature and calligraphy at DePaul University vanished this spring. He has looked in vain for another job while he waits for his big publishing break.

"I keep telling him I've published 10 novels," says Salter, "and there's not much money in this."

In 2004, a British publisher released Saeed's 1980s novel, "Sadaam City," in an English translation by Lake Forest College professor Ahmad Sadri. It earned Saeed almost nothing. Six years passed before The New Yorker praised it, and praise doesn't pay the bills.

But not long ago, without telling Salter, Saeed submitted his new novel for the Arabic Translation Award at the University of Arkansas.

It won.

In "The World Through the Eyes of Angels," to be published this fall as part of the award, Saeed tells the story of a boy growing up in the 1940s and '50s in Iraq. The boy was poor, his life was hard, but his country was a place of beauty and harmony.

Saeed, who once resembled that boy, went back to Iraq this summer. Still afraid, he traveled around with a false name. He felt sick at the devastation everywhere. He said goodbye to his two surviving sisters, and came home to Chicago.

"Yes," he says, but only when I ask, "I feel very lonely."

He smiles. "But this is my life."

It's a writer's life, built on the hope that one day his stories will be known to the people on the other side of his window.

Just a Working Girl

The last time Ron Gagnier saw his daughter Keary Lea, she'd driven her Volvo up from her Rogers Park apartment for one of her frequent visits to her parents' home in North Barrington. It was quiet out there in horse country, where the Gagniers own three acres that include ponds, flowers, a creek and a calming view of marshes and savanna. It was everything Rogers Park — with its asphalt, apartments, cars, litter and stray people on the sidewalks — was not.

Ron Gagnier remembers sitting on the deck that late summer afternoon, looking down at the amber-eyed, brown-haired woman who had grown out of the little girl he used to call by the pet name "Gentle." She was in her favorite position, her long legs bare, her feet dangling in the fish pond, a glass of wine at her side, a book in her hands.

Keary Lea called this spot her "garden of contemplation." She liked it in part because it was there that just last spring the family had scattered the ashes of their old dog, Buzz, whom she'd knelt next to and held while the vet had inserted the needle that put him to sleep. No one could have dreamed that before long, her ashes would share that very ground.

On that Sunday afternoon, Ron Gagnier told his daughter, again, that he wanted her to get out of Chicago.

Keary Lea just laughed. Seven years after she'd left her parents' home for her one-bedroom third-floor walk-up, they still didn't understand why she loved the city. "Give it up, Dad," she said.

After dinner on the deck that night, Keary Lea drove home and, as she always did after visiting her parents, phoned to say she'd made it back safely.

She was 36 years old, but she knew her parents worried and she indulged their fear.

That was on Aug. 16. Four days later, on a trip to Minneapolis, Ron Gagnier had just lost a round of golf, and, fresh out of the shower, joined some buddies at a table at the country club to wait for his wife, Connie, to meet him for dinner.

"You had a phone call," one of the guys said. "Your wife. Said it was important."

Walking toward the phone, Gagnier thought about how many times in a life a person feels the dread of returning a mysteriously urgent phone call, thought about all the times it turns out nothing much is wrong.

His wife came on the line from the hotel. What she said made no sense. As he would recall the moment later, "Sammy Sosa could have taken my head off with a bat and I would have felt better."

What she said was this: "Keary Lea's been murdered."

Ron Gagnier's excursion through the bewildering terrain of grief had just begun.

He met with the police for the first time in a conference room at the station at Belmont and Western. A murder scene was sketched on the blackboard. Seven sympathetic cops filed in, sat down. They said the scene on the blackboard was not Keary Lea's. A weird relief: Someone else's murder, some other family's loss. Otherwise, the police said they knew little and couldn't tell most of what they did.

"A cop crosses his leg, and you see he's got a gun on his ankle," Gagnier recalls, "and you think, God, what a way to live."

This was no way he'd ever imagined he'd live. At 72, after a career in the hospital supply business, he was living a happy semi-retirement of golf, gardening and travel with his wife of 47 years. He was unusually close to his three children, including his youngest, Keary Lea.

Still, there were things he and Keary Lea didn't understand about each other. She would ask why he lived in such a big suburban house and belonged to the country club. He wondered why she lived in the city, unmarried, without children, how she shrugged it off so easily when her car was vandalized. She had boyfriends she brought home to meet the family. Some stayed in her life for a while, but things never quite worked out.

"She was a feminist," her father says, "all those things we may not have been. She was a modern girl, but she had old-fashioned values."

Keary Lea had been a good child, though not much of a student during her two years at Drake University in Iowa. She dropped out and took a job at the Crate & Barrel in Old Orchard. She eventually went to work as an executive administrative assistant for Rotary International, then for Ha-Lo, an advertising specialty company, and, finally, earlier this year, for Microtronic, a Northbrook microelectronics firm. In the meantime, she managed to earn a college degree at DePaul by taking night classes.

She lived like countless young people in the city. Cubs games at Wrigley, fondue at Geja's Café, trips to Lincoln Park Zoo. She liked long dresses and fancy shawls, loved Patsy Cline and Mozart, kept cabinets full of cooking and dining equipment that her father wistfully calls her "trousseau." In the summer, she often walked her beach chair and a book a block and a half to the spit of beach near her Pratt Boulevard apartment. She weighed 135 pounds and always wished she weighed 125. She recorded her fluctuations on a little chart taped to the bathroom wall.

The last person known to have seen Keary Lea, according to the police, was a Microtronic co-worker who told her goodbye about 5:30 p.m. on Wednesday, Aug. 19. The police calculate that if she left work by 6, she would have been home by 8. A friend called her at 8:30 but got no answer.

The next day, Thursday, a Chicago sanitation worker called the Gagniers' home in North Barrington. Their son, Terry, who lives there, answered. The city worker said he'd found several of Keary Lea's I.D. cards in a black garbage can in a Rogers Park alley. Terry called Keary Lea at work. She hadn't shown up that day.

A short while later, the police went to her apartment for a "well-being" check. The front door was bolted. The back door was ajar, unforced. In the ransacked apartment, a glass of red wine sat on a coffee table above the carpet Keary Lea had bought on a trip to China. Her VCR was missing. So were her credit cards. She lay on her bed, strangled.

For a long time, Ron Gagnier avoided media publicity about his daughter's death.

"The last thing I wanted was a Channel 5 or 7 truck parked in our driveway," he says.

But as the weeks passed, as the clues and the offer of a $2,500 reward led nowhere, he and his wife made a difficult decision. With the blessing of the police, he would go to the press in the hopes that publicity would help flush out whoever took his daughter's life.

"If it turns up one clue to catch the killer, hell, I'll dance on top of the John Hancock tower."

That's how it came to pass on Tuesday morning that he was sitting, in a pressed denim shirt, khaki pants and tasseled loafers, at Panini Panini cafe, a few doors east of the tan-brick courtyard building where his daughter died.

Imagine, he said, imagine one day someone called your father and told him you'd been murdered. He looked away, apologizing for his tears.

"Why her?" he said, "Why here?" He gestured past the plate glass windows, toward the passing cars and people, then shook his head. "Why not her? What makes us so much better?"

He was talking half to himself, answering questions he had not been asked. "Do I want to see him caught? Yes. Do I want to see him electrocuted? No."

Keary Lea's murder was not, contrary to the myth about women alone in the city, an ordinary murder. Most of the murders in the area, according to one detective, involve gangs or drugs. And it's rare for anyone anywhere in Chicago to be murdered at home by a stranger. Of course, maybe Keary Lea wasn't killed by a stranger.

The police are reluctant to reveal what they know, except to say that in the first couple days after she died, Keary Lea's credit cards were used to buy gas. A lot of gas. Far more gas than one car could use. Her cards turned up at service stations all over Rogers Park and at a couple West Side stations near Roosevelt and Pulaski.

"The thing that best describes this is, it's a mystery," said Chicago police Sgt. Tom Pufpaf. "The answer to a mystery could be anything."

Was she awake when it happened? Asleep? Did she jump from her bed when she heard the floorboards creak?

Gagnier asks himself the questions as he walks down the wet side alley next to his daughter's building. He turns left down the back alley, then stands behind her apartment, looking up. Maybe, he says, the killer watched his daughter open the black iron gate, walk down the narrow concrete path, climb the brown wooden stairs, enter her apartment. Maybe it was someone with a telescope from a nearby high-rise. Or a stalker who followed her home. Maybe it was someone sitting in that cafe.

He stands in the drizzle, a baffled detective, an aging man, a heartbroken father. He takes a deep breath, as if to swallow a sob. "She was just a working girl, trying to get along."

He holds a hand to my cheek, and as he turns without a word and walks away, I suspect it wasn't my skin he felt, but hers.

After the Quake I: 'The Only Child I Have'

Jean Alix Onelien opened his refrigerator door in Skokie Thursday morning and stared. So much food.

He closed the door.

Cereal? His wife prodded. Eggs?

He couldn't eat. Not as long as his daughter, who's almost 3, was living in a tent in Haiti, hungry.

"You eat something," his boss says.

It's Thursday lunchtime now, and Onelien is in a little room at Sunset Foods in Northbrook. His boss sets trays of croissant sandwiches, fruit and potato salad on the table, then pats him on the back.

Everybody wants Jean to eat, but since Jan. 12, when the earthquake hit Port-au-Prince, he has hardly been able to swallow. The waist size on his pants has dropped from 30 to 27.

He lays an e-mail on the table. It's from the Department of Homeland Security in response to his plea to get his daughter out:

"Your request for expedite processing has been reviewed and your case is currently being adjudicated. You should receive a notice of action within 45 days."

In 45 days, he knows, his daughter could be dead.

"My mom, dad, sister are on the street," he says, "but they are adult. You see your child like this and . . ."

He cries at home, too, but he goes into another room so his wife won't see.

If you met Onelien in the grocery aisles, he'd probably be smiling. Smiling is part of who he is. So is taking care of family.

He was 17 when he left his parents and four siblings and came to the United States alone.

After a couple of years in Miami, he bought a one-way ticket to Chicago. He'd heard there were more jobs here, and 11 years ago he got one at Sunset Foods. He graduated from cashier to assistant manager, became a citizen. On his two days off, he drives 14-hour shifts in a limo.

The people at the grocery store are the closest thing Onelien has to family here. His true family remains in Haiti.

He married a woman there, and after his last trip in June they left their daughter, Maulissa, with her sister so his wife could come learn English.

They hoped that by next month they'd have the paperwork that let their daughter come.

Then, the earthquake. Onelien learned about it from a note a customer left him at the service desk.

His phone call got through that night.

He heard the good news: his daughter's bed had flipped over in the quake, his sister-in-law had wrenched her out of it. The house collapsed behind them. He also learned one of his brothers had died.

Since then, his calls have been futile. All he can do is put money on his relatives' cell phone cards and wait for his phone to ring.

It has, twice. Once he heard about the gunfire, the stench of death and the crazy price of food if you could find it. Then he learned his relatives had left Port-au-Prince for the countryside, address unknown.

Nothing is worse, he says, than to not be able to take care of the people you love.

"How can you sleep at night when you don't know where your daughter's sleeping?" He touches his fingertips to his chest. "She's the only child I have."

Money? He'll pay. Travel? He'll go. Whatever it takes to get his daughter out.

Early Thursday, he got a call from the State Department asking about his case. He felt encouraged, better than he felt when he talked to his daughter Tuesday.

"Daddy," she said. She was coughing a lot. "Will you bring me candy?" He said, "Yes."

After the Quake II: 'So Much the Love'

As soon as he cleared security at O'Hare a few days ago, Jean Onelien went to the men's room to stash his money.

He hid $800 in one of his sneakers, $1,000 in the other. He tucked $400 into his underwear, the rest into his backpack and pockets.

Haiti has run on cash since the January earthquake, and he knew the only way to keep $3,200 safe was to split it up.

This was Onelien's second trip in five weeks to the island he left at 17. He is an American now, but he's married to a Haitian woman and has a Haitian child, and once again he was leaving his job at Sunset Foods in Northbrook hoping to bring his daughter, Maulissa, home.

I wrote about Onelien after his February trip failed. He had traveled for days, slept on the ground, smelled the rot, stood in long lines and ultimately hadn't been able to beat the bureaucratic tangle.

This time, he vowed, he wouldn't walk back into his Skokie condo, where his wife had joined him several months ago, without their daughter.

Maulissa was living in a tent. He had to get her out before the hard spring rains.

So once again it was O'Hare to Haiti. Once again dawn, a Monday, in line outside the embassy in Port-au-Prince.

Maulissa, who's 3, sat on his backpack and every time the line of hundreds moved, he scooted the bag forward.

"I have to be back to work on Friday," he told the woman in the embassy.

It didn't matter.

Maulissa didn't have a paper proving she'd had a physical exam. He'd have to get it and come back for a visa.

Onelien went to a place that does the exams. Twelve days minimum, they said. He went to another place.

By Friday, he had the paper he needed, but the embassy was closed.

Onelien called Sunset and said sorry.

Then another Monday, another dawn, another long, slow line outside the embassy. At 3 p.m., an official told him to come back March 24.

"Listen, I have to be back at work," he said. "I can't afford it. I work at a grocery store and . . ."

It didn't matter.

The next day, he was visiting a cousin in the countryside when his wife phoned his cell: "You need to check your e-mail."

He walked 20 miles to an Internet cafe. There, he read the e-mail he could barely believe: Be at the embassy Wednesday morning for Maulissa's visa.

Things happened fast then. The embassy, the visa, a rush to the airport for the Wednesday flight he'd booked days earlier unconvinced he and his daughter would be on it.

In the Port-au-Prince airport, he took off Maulissa's sandals and dressed her Chicago-style, in shoes and socks.

In Miami, after six hours in customs, he put his pack on his back and Maulissa on his shoulders and ran the long airport hallways, determined to make a connection to O'Hare. No luck.

But they made a flight Thursday. And there, like a mirage, stood his wife and a friend with flowers and a welcome banner. Maulissa took her first ride in a kiddie car seat. She wondered why the air was cold.

That night, Jean and Marie Maude Onelien stood next to Maulissa's new bed in her new home and watched their daughter sleep. He thought: This is joy.

The next day, he felt sick.

"Everything came through my stomach," he said on Friday.

He'd taken Maulissa to Sunset Foods that morning to meet the customers and co-workers who had cheered him on for all these weeks, but had left there exhausted.

I asked him what had marked him most in his quest to recover his daughter.

"All the response, the care," he said. "So much the love."

Then he needed to go lie down.

A Light in Iraq

At 12:30 Friday afternoon, Feb. 2, Paul Jepsen, an Oak Park police sergeant, got an e-mail from Kevin Landeck, a Wheaton soldier in Iraq.

"Mr. Jepsen," Landeck wrote, "I wanted to write you an email and let you know that the weapons light arrived to me the other day and it is awesome! Thank you and to all your fellow officers/friends who donated money for the light."

Jepsen had never met Landeck — a 6-foot-2 26-year-old with reddish hair who loved skiing and roller hockey — but any kid of his old high school friend Vicki's was a friend of his. So was any soldier.

It was only natural then that when word got around that Kevin was yearning for a special rifle light, the old soldier made sure the young soldier's wish was granted.

"I'm a Vietnam vet," says Jepsen. "I understand what it's like to spend your own money on good equipment."

He also understood what it must feel like for Kevin to be trying to do his duty in the pitch dark Iraqi nights, guided only by light from the sky, blind to what is just a few feet ahead. Without a good rifle light, he knew, turning a corner could feel like stepping into a black hole.

The light Kevin wanted resembled a big, heavy duty flashlight. It mounts on a rifle, has a high beam, a low beam and a safety device that keeps it from turning on unexpectedly when jostled.

"It's something every soldier should have when he's out at night," says Jepsen. "It's something the government isn't popping for."

At 54, Jepsen would have liked to go fight this war himself. He thought about taking a leave from his police job and from Kirsten's Danish Bakery, the Burr Ridge business he runs with his wife. The Army turned him down, so he looks for other ways to help.

Awhile back, he sent 135 used police vests to Iraq to be turned into makeshift armor inside military Humvees. He sometimes e-mails soldiers he doesn't know just to say thanks and recruits friends to do the same.

"I know what it's like to come home from war and be spit on," he says. "I'm thankful for what these guys are doing."

When he heard about Kevin's desire for a light, he wrote everybody on his regular e-mail joke list. Within 48 hours, he'd collected enough money to send a check to Vicki, Kevin's mom. The family found a Marine selling a light on eBay and shipped it off.

"I haven't had a chance to use it officially yet, busting into a house at night, but we still have 6 months of fun left and I will get plenty of use out of it," Kevin wrote Friday before last.

"Needless to say some of my buddies are jealous of my new toy and I brag how some great people back home chipped in to buy it for me without a second thought.

"I plan on sending something back to you from over here, I will let you know when to look for it. Thank you again, I can't say it enough."

Kevin added a P.S. "I'll send you some pictures through email of how it looks on the old pea-shooter!"

In the end, it wasn't lack of light that killed Kevin Landeck.

Eight and a half hours after he got Kevin's thank-you, Jepsen got a call: Kevin's Humvee had been blasted by an I.E.D., an improvised explosive device, the fancy term for road bomb.

The fate of the rifle light was the least of the Landecks' worries when they learned Kevin had been killed. But it mattered.

Before her son's death, Vicki Landeck had been so worried that Kevin and the troops didn't have sufficient equipment that she wrote a letter to Sen. Barack Obama's office.

"It's sad enough they have to be there," she says now, "but worse when they don't have the proper equipment."

Last week, when the family learned the light had been damaged, they made a plan. They would have it shipped back here, repaired and returned to Kevin's best Army buddy in Iraq.

FRIDAY, APRIL 5, 2013

Roger Ebert's Lesson in Dying

Roger Ebert was a hot trend on Google's top 10 trends earlier this week.

As of Wednesday, more than 50,000 people had searched for his name, an impressive display of his influence.

He wasn't quite as hot as North Korea or Jay Leno, but he was running neck and neck with Lollapalooza.

Ebert, the longtime movie critic for the Chicago Sun-Times, roused that interest simply by posting Tuesday night on his popular blog that he was taking "a leave of presence" while he was treated for another bout of cancer.

Despite a valedictory tone to his note, it didn't seem impossible that he'd be back, as promised, writing reviews, tending his website and preparing for his annual film fest. He'd seemed on the verge of death so often that why not believe he'd beat the odds this time?

He didn't.

Ebert's death Thursday — he was 70 — marked the end of a certain Chicago literary era. He had once hung out with the legendary likes of Mike Royko, Studs Terkel and Nelson Algren, trading stories while marinated in alcohol, until he gave up the alcohol. He was younger than the others, and less swashbuckling, but as long as he was alive, so was that literary moment.

Now that he's gone, he will be widely remembered as perhaps the most influential movie critic ever and as a member of a great vanished Chicago writing clan.

But Ebert deserves to be remembered for something more: dying with grace.

Some people die quickly, others a little at a time. Ebert faded slowly, dramatically, with a philosophical flourish.

In the past few years, doctors had cut out his thyroid, then part of his salivary glands, then a piece of his jaw. He could no longer eat, drink or talk.

A different person might have shrunk into despair. Ebert navigated his way out of the depths through writing, along with a connection to young people, a reliance on new technology and a humility that verged on bravado.

In a 2010 piece in Esquire — read it if you haven't — he allowed his ruined face to be photographed in close-up. His deformed jaw and permanently open mouth filled a full glossy page. His eyes still shone.

"When I am writing, my problems become invisible and I am the same person I always was," he said in that piece. "All is well. I am as I should be."

A while after that, he engaged in a political battle via Twitter with a conservative who gleefully mocked his cancer and his disfigurement.

Ebert tweeted back: "You want ugly? For that, you have to look at a mind, not a face."

I saw Ebert only once in his disfigured years, at a 2011 dinner hosted by the Chicago Public Library at which he received the Carl Sandburg Literary Award. He sat in an armchair onstage while the longtime newsman Bill Kurtis quizzed him. He answered questions by typing on his MacBook Pro, which channeled his words into an automated voice.

If he was in the least embarrassed, he didn't let it leak.

"In any other age, his illness would have isolated and largely silenced him," says my Tribune colleague Monica Eng, one of his close friends. "But with DVDs, blogs, Twitter and Internet, he could have one of his biggest reviewing years ever while cranking out nonstop Tweets, blog posts, essays and his autobiography. Instead of being silenced, he became more voluble than ever. In the purely physical world, he was largely hobbled, but in the world of words, ideas and wit he could still dance like Fred Astaire."

In his final blog post, Ebert talked of the work he would do next. He said he would write about the vulnerability of illness and about the movies that could transport him out of illness.

He didn't leave the public any further words, but he left a life that at the end said this:

When illness comes, don't hide. Stay connected to young people and to change. Find the strength in vulnerability. Hope even when there is none.

By Thursday evening, half a million people had searched for Roger Ebert on Google, making him the second-hottest trend in the nation, way ahead of Lollapalooza.

FRIDAY, MAY 21, 2010

Waiting by the River

Willy Castillo came back to the river Thursday morning with a sure feeling in his gut.

His son Cashmere, he was convinced, was buried beneath the mud, not far from where he'd slipped into the water Sunday. No way Cashmere had floated as far as the spillway, where the rescue workers had just resumed their search.

"I don't know if you believe in psychics, in the third eye," he said, standing next to the river on a spring day so bright and warm that ordinarily it would seem perfect. "We Asians believe that. And a friend told me my boy's body didn't pass the spill."

My boy's body.

In an ideal world, no father would ever have to utter those words. In an ideal world, no father would ever have to hear that his boy's body might have been found, only to learn later that it was just a sandbag, and that the search would go on, and with it, the wait.

In the past week, waiting for their boy's body has become a full-time job for Willy Castillo and his wife, Merrell, along with various relatives and neighbors. From early in the morning until late at night, whenever the search moves up or down the river, they fold up their lawn chairs and move too.

Thursday was Day 4 of the vigil.

Day 5, if you count Sunday night, when Castillo walked the banks until dawn, up a mile and then back again, over and over, alone, shining his flashlight across the dark, fast, cold water.

By Thursday, he had been waiting so long that he seemed too weary for emotion.

"I want to get my boy's body today," he said flatly. "Because they say it's going to rain tomorrow."

The river isn't really a river at the spot where Cashmere vanished. Where it flows through Eugene Field Park, it's more like a wide ditch, a stream with a concrete bottom that a little farther on, at the spillway, joins another channel and then moves toward downtown.

Whatever it's called, it supplies an unexpected charm to this Northwest Side neighborhood, which in many ways is Chicago at its best: ethnically diverse, friendly and filled with big old trees, well-kept old bungalows and children.

"Ninety-nine percent of everybody here has children," Castillo said.

And everybody gathers in the park.

On Thursday, groups of Hasidic Jews wearing big black hats strolled across the bridges. Three young women in Muslim headscarves cruised past in a convertible. A Mexican ice cream vendor pedaled his cart and clanged his bell.

A couple of old fishermen, poles in hand, stopped Castillo to share their river expertise and say they agreed: There was too much debris in that water for a body to get far.

Castillo, who is 37, moved to the neighborhood in 1991. In 1996, he married Merrell, a childhood friend from the Philippines, where he'd lived until he was 12.

"She came here, and life started," he said.

They had three children: Christian, 13, Cashmere, 8, and Carter, who is 1. They gave their children names associated with high fashion, he said, because "those are the things that last."

On normal days, Castillo leaves the house shortly after 4 a.m. and drives to Elk Grove Village, where he runs a machine that makes screws for automobiles. His wife works an overnight clerical shift in an office. In the early morning, when neither of them is home, his mother cares for their boys.

They've taken the week off work. Waiting by the river, for the body that will let them put their boy's soul to rest, is the only work that matters now.

"Look," Castillo said.

Morning had drifted into afternoon, and the rescuers had moved their search back up to where they started Sunday. Castillo and his family followed with their lawn chairs.

He leaned over the sagging 3-foot-high fence and pointed.

"You can still see the ridge from his flip-flops."

In the hardening mud lay evidence of his boy's life.

Cashmere had been playing tag Sunday when he stepped in a mud puddle. Castillo says that's why he clambered over the low metal fence, all 65 pounds of him, and maybe braced himself on the skinny tree, before inching his way down to the water.

Castillo had warned his son about the river, especially when he was playing ball nearby.

"I always told him, 'If the ball goes over the fence, don't go get it,'" he said. "'I'd rather buy you another ball than buy you a casket.'"

Cashmere was a kid with a big smile who loved baseball and "Guitar Hero." He wasn't irresponsible. On the contrary, he was in his school's gifted program. He worried every time his baby brother cried.

But he'd stepped in mud. He wanted to wash his feet.

On Sunday, the river here had been engorged and churned by recent rains. It was moving at 10 miles an hour, maybe 15, and was barely more than 50 degrees.

By Thursday, it was a different river. Lower. Slower. Still cold.

Castillo watched as divers from the Chicago Police Department's marine unit slipped in, insulated in black-and-orange vulcanized rubber, preparing to follow the river again.

One of them tossed a yellow harness down.

"Why wing it when we've got the harness right here?" he called to the diver in the water.

The divers had come back here because even with fancy sonar, the search farther away had been fruitless. For a while, with the sun glinting on the water, they trolled the old-fashioned way with poles, hands, feet.

They'd found a lot in the river in the last few days. Bicycle wheels. Tables. Chairs. Logs. Trash of infinite variety.

But not the body of a boy.

Some of the rescuers were volunteering on their days off or working extra shifts.

John Gana had started at midnight Thursday and 14 hours later was still on the job. He was trying not to think of his own kids, who are 6 and 8.

"You block out what you may be feeling," he said, "and do what you have to do."

But the rescuers, too, knew this was not ordinary duty. The body was a boy's. A boy was small, and in such cold water, not likely yet to float.

In these days of searching for Cashmere, the river has been many things to many people. A place to grieve and remember, a place to gawk or learn.

Cashmere's classmates have come to stand where he vanished. So have neighbors and strangers. One stranger brought his daughter to show her how accidents can happen in the blink of an eye.

Cashmere's brother Christian has been there, too, just as he was on Sunday.

"I think that maybe I'll just turn around and he'll just be standing there dripping wet," he said. He looked at the brown water. "I need to see him one more time because we never said anything to each other that day. He just slipped away."

Sometimes during his days of vigil, Willy Castillo walks a few blocks back to the family bungalow.

He can't sleep — "I keep seeing my kid's face" — but he walks into the house, unlatches the child's gate at the edge of the living room, latches it back and looks at the little bedroom he was renovating for Cashmere.

On Thursday afternoon, he stood at the bedroom door. The drawers had been taken out of the dresser. One drawer was filled with a boy's socks, another with his underpants.

For the first time all day, he cried.

Then he went back to wait at the river.

FRIDAY, SEPT. 9, 2011

Dominika Goes to School

Dominika Tamley started school Tuesday.

That morning, despite the fused shoulders that limit the range of her short arms, Dominika managed to shrug her 5-year-old self into her giant new backpack and set out for the brave new territory of kindergarten. The backpack, covered with Disney princesses, was pink and purple, a match for her glasses, her socks and her hearing aids.

> *What are those pink things in your ears?*
> *My hearing aids.*
> *Why is your face like that?*
> *This is the way I was born.*

Dominika's mother, Karen Tamley, had prepared her daughter to meet such questions in school. Be direct, she counseled, keep it simple, move on.

Tamley might have picked up this advice from the Chicago Mayor's Office for People with Disabilities, where she is the commissioner, but in fact, she learned it from her own childhood.

Why are you in the wheelchair?
Because I can't walk. It helps me get around.
Why can't you walk?
This is the way I was born.

A lifetime in a rolling chair has taught Tamley how to deal with the curious, the bold and the sometimes mean, and yet it couldn't entirely prepare her for the moment her little blond daughter, in a princess backpack, trekked into a classroom at West Ridge Elementary School and the teacher closed the door.

"It's on your mind wherever you go," Tamley said, "it" meaning the differences that make other kids stare at her daughter. "When you go to the playground or the pool. Or the first day of school."

In 2006, Tamley and her husband, Kevin Irvine, were applying to adopt through The Cradle in Evanston when they were told about a baby who had been in the nursery for five months. The girl had Apert syndrome, a genetic disease characterized by facial malformations, fused fingers and toes, and a skull whose plates bond prematurely so the brain has no room to grow.

The agency thought Tamley and Irvine would be the perfect parents.

Tamley was born with a rare disorder of the lower spine. Irvine was born with hemophilia, and in high school was diagnosed with HIV acquired from blood products.

They were both activists for people with disabilities.

Within a week, Dominika was home.

In her five years of life, Dominika has had 13 surgeries. Her fingers have been separated. Space has been made in her head to accommodate her growing brain. She has figured out how to swing on a swing set on her stomach; how to hold a fork and a pencil even though her fingers don't bend; how to improvise when she can't raise her arms high in her Tap & Twirl dance class.

"She was oblivious to kids staring when she was younger," says her father. "Over the past year, she has gained self-awareness. Self-awareness is a double-edged sword."

Sometimes, in her effort to figure out how to navigate her differences, Dominika looks at her parents and says, "Your toes are separated. Were you born that way?"

School is the place all kids face the wonders and cruelties of the wider world. It's where kids with disabilities get to know kids without, and where kids without meet those who were born a different way.

Tamley offers this advice on how to approach a child like hers:

If you have a kid without disabilities, let your kid ask the other kid questions. Let your child know it's good to engage.

If your child has disabilities, don't overprotect. Have high expectations. Help your kid figure out direct answers to the inevitable questions.

If you're a teacher, notice if a kid is being teased or isolated. Let the parents know.

To everybody: If you have a basic question (What are those pink things in your ears?) address the child, not the parent. And don't assume kids are mentally slow because they're physically different.

Dominika reports that her first few days of school have been good. Her parents, like parents everywhere, have posted Facebook pictures of her first day. The photos show an excited little girl, like a million ordinary girls, embarking with a princess backpack on the grand adventure called school.

TUESDAY, SEPT. 6, 2005

The Last Man in New Orleans

I was driving on a deserted stretch of Interstate 10 on Monday when I spotted what looked like the last man in New Orleans. On the street below, he was trudging waist-deep in water, dragging a canoe.

I parked on the shoulder and from an overpass peered into the liquid murk to shout a profound question, "What are you doing?"

I knew he couldn't be the last man. The radio had just said that though the city gets emptier every day, thousands were still water-locked, hiding or defiantly camping in their homes.

I also knew from the radio that in nearby Jefferson Parish, residents were being allowed back for the day, though with the warning: When you clean out your refrigerator, bury that putrid food to keep it from the maggots and the packs of starving dogs.

But from my post on the downtown overpass looking toward the sky-line, New Orleans looked abandoned except for this guy in his red shorts, Tulane T-shirt and sports cap. The freeway was empty too, except for crowds of plastic bags and bottles, a wheelchair, a stroller, a flip-flop, an abused Mazda, the assorted detritus of the hurricane homeless who had since been scattered to the outside world.

When asked what was floating in the water, the guy answered: "Dead bodies, sewage, rotting garbage, oil, gas, pesticides, household cleaning products."

So why was he wading in it?

The dogs, he explained. His two chocolate Labs, Cooter Brown and Orion the Hunter.

"I delivered them," he said. "They've followed me around since their eyes opened."

He couldn't leave until someone took the dogs, and he had heard about animal rescuers in a hospital a few miles down who might come get them. He had hoped to paddle, but the only paddles he could find in the flood were worthless plastic ones, so he lugged the boat behind him.

His name is Bill Peacock. He's 42 and runs the Wit's Inn bar. In the eternal week since Hurricane Katrina shredded New Orleans, he's lived upstairs in his aunt's house while his good paddles float in the cesspool of his downstairs apartment.

Peacock is not the stranded New Orleanian most featured in the news. He's white and not poor. But he's a typical New Orleanian in many ways, meaning committed to his home, accustomed to hardship and trained to believe that hurricanes, like the common cold, are always overcome.

When the 17th Street levee burst last week, he had been taking a shower after cleaning up Katrina's rubble. By the time he stepped out of the tub, Lower South Miro Street was an annex to Lake Pontchartrain.

In the past week, he's spent time talking to his one remaining neighbor — a retired African-American named Chuck — and reading Stephen Hawking's "A Brief History of Time."

"I finished," he shouted up from water, "but I'm still a little fuzzy on singularities."

He's learned other things as well. About, say, the refrigerator.

"It floats. Did you know that? So does a washing machine." And by the way, it takes half an hour to heat canned soup over a candle. And rubbing alcohol is a good cleanser after walking in toxic water.

Search helicopters drowned us out every few sentences, but except for the killer sun, there was no need to hurry. One of New Orleans' charms has always been to make the bizarre seem normal.

Peacock had been walking for hours, he said, his first venture into a demolished land he knew about only from the radio.

He finally saw his city now: Trees lancing houses. A roof that read: "HELP. NO FOOD. NO WATER. WIFE. MOTHER. SISTER. PLEASE." He knocked on the door. No answer.

If he can get his dogs and his aunt's miniature schnauzers out, he'll go too — for now. He hopes to talk his neighbor Chuck out too, but who knows.

Two things he would like right now, he said. A cold beer. And cell phone reception. He hadn't talked to his family in a week. He reached into a breast pocket and pulled out the phone. Punched it on just for fun.

It caught a signal, then died, but not before he had read a text message from a sibling: "Mom is going crazy. Are you alive?"

He grinned. "Hot damn." He snapped the cell phone shut and set off again through the water.

Back in the car, someone on the radio said, "It's not the beginning of the end, but it's the end of the beginning."

FRIDAY, MAY 29, 2009
....

The Last Man in New Orleans Dies

Bill Peacock dropped dead of a heart attack a few days ago in his Creole cottage in New Orleans. He was 45 and attended by his closest companions, two chocolate labs named Cooter Brown and Orion.

His sister Sandy sent an e-mail.

"We found your articles framed in his apartment," she wrote, "along with the letter from one of your readers and the first-edition [book] which meant the world to him. My family and I would like to offer our sincerest appreciation to you and your readers for their kindness after the storm."

The storm. It's such a small word for the hurricane, Katrina, that crashed into New Orleans in the late summer of 2005, leaving the levees ruptured and the city drowning.

Almost everyone with a will and a way got out, but Bill Peacock wouldn't go until he could rescue his dogs. I met him one broiling day when, standing on a freeway overpass, I spotted a big, sunburned man in red gym shorts pulling a Cajun canoe through the filthy waist-high water below.

At the time, Tribune readers flooded Bill with e-mails and encouragement. One sent him a first-edition book, a copy of one he'd lost when water rose to his ceiling. For the next two years, I periodically wrote about his recovery, which was a measure of the city's.

After Katrina, Bill moved to Colorado — he wanted to be high and dry — but he soon went back. Haunted as he was by the flood, by the sight of floating bodies, New Orleans was still his home.

At the time he died, his sister said, he was working two full-time jobs. One was managing The Alibi, an all-night bar that caters to French Quarter workers.

"He worked the graveyard shift because he was big enough to handle the strippers and the drunks and the dealers who followed the strippers in," his sister said.

By last summer, he had saved enough money to buy his own place, Station 8801, a restaurant and bar in an old gas station. An ardent cook, he specialized in crawfish boils, portobello mushroom sandwiches and a Cajun squash dish called stuffed mirliton.

Hurricane Katrina changed Bill Peacock.

"Post-Katrina," his sister said, "he was very minimalist."

He owned little beyond a sofa, a bed, some books. He no longer needed to collect guns or hunting gear, or had time to use them.

"He did like kitchen stuff," she said, "like his homemade pasta maker."

After Katrina, he made an effort to travel, especially back to Colorado, varying his route each time. Once an atheist, he had opened to the idea of a higher power. Rumor had it he was working on a novel.

Bill's friends and family held a celebration of his life on Sunday at Station 8801.

"It was full of salt-of-the-earth people," his sister said. "Strippers, policemen, bartenders, janitors, people who swept the streets, anybody that had something to add to a life perspective. He would sit and talk to anyone for hours if it gave him a different perspective."

One of the people who wept at his service was the young stripper he'd recently shepherded into rehab.

We don't hear much about New Orleans these days, but it's good to remember that people are still working to put their lives and their city back together. Bill Peacock did until his last day.

He is survived by his mother, a brother, two sisters, two nieces, many friends, and Cooter Brown and Orion, the dogs he risked his life to save after a hurricane.

Larry Comes Home

Larry Hull loved the sky, and he loved hazel-eyed Tyra Decker.

Tyra loved Larry too, and though, like most young people, they couldn't really imagine getting old, they liked the idea of growing old together. So when Tyra was 18 and Larry was 20, they got married in her hometown of Seminole, Texas.

Tyra wanted to be a teacher, like her mother. Larry wanted to be a pilot and follow his father into the Air Force.

"You should have seen the sky today," Larry would exult whenever he went flying, training for his wings. "You should have seen the sky."

The last time Tyra saw Larry was a rainy summer day in Lubbock, Texas, in an airport parking lot. The sky was gray, but she remembers blue: the blue of Larry's Air Force uniform, the blue of the car seats in the white Chevy Impala, the blue of the checked pants their 1-year-old daughter, Laura, wore as she sat between her parents on the ride.

"Don't come in," Larry said.

They stood in the drizzle next to the car and talked about paying the bills while he was away and about how long the mail would take from Vietnam, the kind of small, practical chatter that keeps the word goodbye from feeling like an explosion in a heart.

Then Larry walked off to war, and Tyra drove home with her baby.

On Wednesday of this week, Tyra Manning and her daughter, Laura, will fly from O'Hare to Hickam Air Force Base in Honolulu to collect the remains of 1st Lt. James Larry Hull, killed Feb. 19, 1971, when his small O-2A Skymaster plane was shot down over a jungle ridge in Laos a few hundred yards from the Vietnam border.

At the age of 59, Manning will bring back the bones of a 25-year-old man, laying him to rest in a casket she picked out on the day this summer that two military representatives came to her Highland Park home to confirm that Larry's remains had finally been excavated from a mangled plane on a Laotian hillside.

"I always hoped," she said last week, her voice still throaty in that particular Texas way. "But it was hard to always believe."

Manning — her last name is from a second marriage that didn't last — is a woman of some importance now. She directs the master of arts in teaching program at Dominican University in River Forest. Before that, she was superintendent of the River Forest elementary school district, which was where she was working in 1993, when she got the first specific clue to how Larry died.

She had come home from a night school-board meeting, punched on her answering machine and was hanging up her coat when a voice said: We have information about your husband. Please call.

A Vietnamese civilian, she soon learned, had stumbled on a crash site just across the border in Laos and brought back some bone and a dog tag. Larry's name was on the tag.

Later, Larry's mother donated DNA. The bone matched.

Reliving a goodbye

U.S. officials weren't allowed to cross the border to find out more, though, so Manning began her own search for information. It led her to Tom Yarborough, a retired Air Force colonel who had written a book that included an account of Larry's death.

She ordered the book from Barbara's Bookstore in Oak Park and the day it arrived sat down in a bookstore chair and started to read.

She had known that Larry flew missions over the Ho Chi Minh Trail, surveying the movement of Vietnamese troop supplies.

What she didn't know was that he had volunteered to be part of the secret "Prairie Fire" mission, assigned to scout the dense jungle for clearings where U.S. helicopters could land to deposit and pick up special-forces soldiers fighting in Laos, behind enemy lines.

Sitting there reading, Tyra saw Larry skimming over green treetops. Saw his plane shot down, watched it spiral out of the sky toward the A Shau Valley. Saw soldiers scramble to the wreckage and carry off the body of Larry's partner, who had been flung out of the plane.

And she saw Larry's body crushed inside. His buddies snared one of his dog tags but, in the heavy gunfire, were unable to take more.

Four days later, she learned as she kept reading, Yarborough flew over the valley and spotted Larry's plane, sitting upright.

Through Yarborough's eyes, Manning watched Vietnamese soldiers dipping under the grounded wings, pilfering the cabin.

Yarborough called for a recovery team then tried to mark the plane's location with a flare. In the mist that day, it was hard to see. The flare hit the fuselage and set Larry's plane on fire.

There in a suburban bookstore, half a lifetime later, Tyra told Larry goodbye again.

The years passed. Occasionally in those years, as in the ones before, Manning would open an olive-brown Samsonite suitcase.

She kept Larry's medals there, along with 21 reel-to-reel tapes he'd made from the scratchy records of fellow soldiers. Three Dog Night. Simon & Garfunkel. The Righteous Brothers.

The suitcase also held the cassettes Larry sent as letters. No more Kool-Aid in the care packages, he pleaded. Oh, and the military was going to let the guys grow sideburns!

And he would say, Tyra, keep working on that teacher's degree.

Larry's voice kept Tyra going long after he was gone. That's the romantic version of what drove her. There's a practical version too. She was a young widow with a baby daughter. What choice did she have?

In May of this year, after negotiations with the Laotian government, U.S. officials were allowed into Laos to seek the remains of Larry Hull and several other soldiers. In July, Manning found out they had found him.

Old friends emerge

Word started to get around. Larry was coming home. He'd be buried Nov. 13 at Arlington National Cemetery. Full honors. His Vietnam buddies started to call Manning and her daughter, to e-mail. One sent a photo.

The photo told her something she'd always wondered about Larry. Had he grown sideburns? He had.

Wars don't end when they end. They play on for generations afterward. We're in a new war now, but this old one lives on in families and in friendships, in the search for meaning and understanding and closure that never quite closes.

Recently, Manning ran across a carousel of Larry's photo slides. Slide after slide of clouds, cumulus clouds, cirrus clouds, thunderclouds, clouds at dawn and sunset.

Looking at those clouds, she thought about how much this young man loved what he did, and she thought about why he did it in a war: because he loved the sky, yes, but also because he believed in a country that believed in freedom. Freedom of the press. Freedom of protest.

That's as political as she gets, except to say simply, "I am so grateful that today in our country, we've learned to separate the warrior from the war."

SUNDAY, DEC. 15, 1996

A Writer's Final Story

Office No. 1418 at 6 N. Michigan Ave. is a tiny room at the end of a carpeted corridor near the fire stairs. The wooden door, unlike most of the others on the floor, bears no name, no number.

Behind that blank door, surrounded by bare white walls, a desk, a table, two computers and a file cabinet, Eugene Izzi wrote. And died.

Izzi, known to his friends as Guy, often arrived at the old brick-and-terra-cotta building around midnight, sometimes sweaty from jogging, head wrapped in a bandanna, occasionally stopping in the marble-walled lobby to chat with the security guard about old movies. He liked Jimmy Cagney and Humphrey Bogart.

If the guard said, "Nice day," Izzi was apt to say, "Nice day? It's terrific out there!"

From the recessed window of his little office, Izzi had a grand view of Chicago, the city that pulsed through his crime novels as both character and setting. He could see the red neon of Navy Pier, the gauzy blue of Lake Michigan, the silver and gray of skyscrapers, roads and train tracks. Michigan Avenue lay below, but he couldn't see it past the rooftop of the adjacent building. It would have been hard for Michigan Avenue passersby to see him.

Almost no one, in fact, ever saw Izzi at his office. His 14th-floor neighbors rarely ran into him, though they sometimes heard loud voices behind his door. The cleaning woman, according to the accountant across the hall, was instructed to exempt Izzi's office from her usual rounds.

But on the cold, sunny morning of Saturday, Dec. 7, a man glancing out a nearby window spotted Izzi.

Or, rather, saw his body hanging against the building's blackened yellow brick.

When the firefighters arrived, Izzi's door was locked. They broke in and found a rope running from the leg of his desk to his neck.

It looked like suicide.

It looked like murder.

It looked like suicide dressed up as murder. Or was it the other way around?

Chicago is accustomed to crime and death and deplorably hard to shock. But a man mysteriously hanged from a high-rise on the city's main street? That was a unique jolt.

In the days since Izzi died, at the age of 43, the truth about his life has proved as elusive as the truth about his death.

He was, if you can believe those who knew him and the reams written about and by him, a man of mismatched parts:

He was a friendly man who had few friends.

He was a private man who bared his private self in print.

He was a high school dropout who lived to write.

He was a man terrified of heights whose body was discovered dangling from the window of what was once the tallest building in Chicago.

The rescuers pulled Izzi's body — 6 feet, 200 pounds of it — in from the floor below. From his pockets, they pulled $481 in cash and what appeared to be transcripts of threatening phone calls he had received.

He was wearing a bulletproof vest. A .38-caliber revolver lay on the floor of his office. He also was carrying brass knuckles and a canister of Mace-like spray — just as a character in one of his novels did.

The only prop missing from what otherwise could have passed for a crime thriller movie set, one police officer noted, was the bottle of Jim Beam and the half-empty glass.

Forever running scared

Here are a few true things about Eugene Izzi:

He changed his phone number more often than some people change the oil in their car.

His last home address turns out to be not a home, but a Mail Boxes Etc. at Dearborn Station Galleria in the south Loop.

He once said he trusted only six people in the world.

He wasn't afraid to walk on the elevated tracks or to dash on foot across Lake Shore Drive, but he was always running scared.

"On more than one occasion," he wrote five years ago, "I have been heavily damaged physically by people who knew their business. . . . My wife sees me as paranoid because I am normally cautious. I know how things work and how easily they can break down."

Fear was at the core of Izzi's life, and there was a certain logic to it. Growing up, he was never safe.

"My earliest memories of my childhood," he once wrote, "are of my father beating my mother."

He grew up among the bungalows of Hegewisch, in the shadow of the steel mill smokestacks near the Illinois-Indiana border.

His father was a small-time thug, in and out of jail on charges that ranged from peddling illicit drugs to running a mob gambling business. His mother worked menial jobs to support her children. According to a 1994 Chicago Reader profile, Izzi has three sisters, one a twin, but as an adult he was estranged from all but the oldest.

Hegewisch was a war zone for the young and aimless, a place where a lucky boy would end up in the mills, a less lucky one was apt to wind up in a cell and the truly unlucky wound up dead. Izzi survived, but he was wounded.

He dropped out of high school at 16, joined the Army at 17, then came home to drink his way through off-and-on jobs at U.S. Steel.

It was from this life that writing would deliver him.

Writing as a rescue

Izzi learned to write by living. And by reading. He read Mickey Spillane and John D. MacDonald and Elmore Leonard, crime writers who turned hard-boiled prose into hard cash.

When he lamented to his wife, Theresa, that he, too, wanted to be a writer, she told him to stop talking and do it. So he did. But he also drank.

One night in 1981, he came home drunk and hit her hard. The next morning, he woke up to find her and his two sons gone. For three months afterward, he drank during the day and slept in a barbershop at night.

"I would stare, longingly, at the stropped razor blades on the back shelf, nestled there between the electric equipment and the combs, the brushes," he wrote in 1991. "Their sharpness appealed to me; the light glinting off them was my salvation."

He staved off the seduction of the razor blades, swore off alcohol and patched his marriage back together. Then he set to writing as if in a race for his life, or with it.

"Getting up before work to try to make that page dance," he wrote to a Tribune editor. "Staying up late, working weekends and holidays, seeing unemployment as a blessing because when I was out of a job I could devote full time to the important work."

Typing as much as 50 pages a night, he wrote seven novels no one wanted. At last, in 1987, "The Take" was published, followed quickly by "Bad Guys," "The Booster," "Prowlers," "Invasions," "King of the Hustlers," "The Prime Roll," "Tony's Justice," "The Eighth Victim" and "Tribal Secrets."

His setting was often the rough world of Hegewisch, and his heroes were typically echoes of himself, big-hearted tough guys at war with evil. His villains ranged from sexual sickos and mobsters to Lincoln Park yuppies.

The reviewers gushed — the next Elmore Leonard! The next Nelson Algren! Chicago's prince of darkness! — but Izzi himself shrugged off the praise. In his own eyes, he was "a two-dollar bum who got a break."

Success enabled him to buy a house in Park Forest, which he equipped with two burglar alarms and a vicious dog, and to dream of sending his sons to Harvard.

"He was so grateful to the reader, the prospective reader, the prospective buyer," says Judy Duhl, who knew him through his popular book-signings at her store, Scotland Yard Books in Winnetka. "He was in awe of the whole book process."

Perhaps most important, success gave the imprimatur of meaning to the hardships of Izzi's life. But success brought its own troubles.

In the realm of crime fiction, Izzi's books were better than most, and his best resonated passion and truth. But his worst were undisciplined and desperate for an editor, and by the mid-1990s he had been eclipsed by other pretenders to Elmore Leonard's throne.

"He needed success, recognition and esteem the way other people need oxygen," says Stuart Applebaum, a Bantam Books executive.

In 1992, Bantam published the highly autobiographical "Tribal Secrets." The novel, about a reformed alcoholic actor who escapes from Hegewisch to Park Forest, was to be Izzi's breakthrough book.

Bantam sent him to the American Booksellers Convention that year, where he was feted at parties, dinners and book signings. The publisher gave away 10,000 copies of the book to ignite a publicity "buzz."

The buzz was loud: The book was bad. Bantam canceled the tour, the ads, the talk shows.

The details of the feud that followed vary depending on who tells the story. Izzi dumped Bantam because he felt he had been lied to. Or his sales were so bad that Bantam dumped him. Or the two split because he veered too far from conventional crime novels into a proselytizing social agenda that turned off readers and editors alike.

He continued to write, publishing three novels under a pseudonym, Nick Gaitano, but Gaitano didn't stoke the critics' fires the way Eugene Izzi had.

The split with Bantam hurt Izzi psychologically and financially, though it's hard to say how much.

In 1993, he sold his Park Forest home for $54,000 and moved with his family back into the city. In June of this year, the IRS filed a $24,606 lien for his failure to pay his 1994 income taxes. He paid the lien.

He had cause for optimism. Avon Books had signed him to a three-book contract, the first of which was to appear next April.

"Beneath all the posturing and swagger, one got the impression that he was a very decent guy who was hungry to reinvent himself through his writing," Applebaum said.

"The books never really caught on and it made him crazy. It was as if his own background was being denied, his own opportunity for redemption."

Living the mysteries

A few more things about Eugene Izzi:

He talked about loyalty and honor as if they were food and air.

He always insisted on picking up the dinner check for rich publishers.

He didn't just write his books, he lived them.

"Fiction was part of journalism for him," says Andrew Vachss, a New York lawyer and fellow author whom Izzi referred to as his brother. "He believed, as I do, that it's the widest possible audience for social or political or psychological information."

That belief led him to live dirty and hungry on the streets to research the life of the homeless. It took him to therapy sessions with child sex abusers. And it allegedly took him inside militia groups.

Did a member of one of those groups kill him?

The evidence is scant, but some people think so. His family and his few close friends, who have designated Vachss as their spokesman, have been mum, but they are skeptical that this man — a generous man who despite difficulties with his wife called her his "angel," a man who kept on writing through all the unsung years — would intentionally abandon his dreams and the people he loved.

Vachss has discounted the militia theory, but he notes, "I know of no reason for Guy to have killed himself."

But even the people who knew Izzi best may not really have known him.

"Guy keeps everything separate, in compartments," his wife told the Reader in 1994. She added: "Guy gave up on himself a long time ago. He knows he'll never be happy."

Here is a final truth about Eugene Izzi:

You can add up all the small known truths about him, and the sum still could be wrong.

Some years ago when I was in the midst of some crisis or other — whatever it was, it's negligible now — my dear friend Sharman Stein sent me a little drawing of a bird fluttering above an alligator. She sent it without interpretation but what I saw in it was a message — that even when the world is snapping its jaws at you, it's possible to be that bright bird floating above it all.

I hung it in my Tribune cubicle the day it arrived.

A few years later, I texted a photo of it to Sharman. She was struggling with cancer. I hoped it would give her some of the courage it has given me.

She died soon afterward.

I'm choosing to think that her bright bird of a soul is out there somewhere fluttering above us, watching out for us.

chapter 4

family

Write Your Father

Write your father a letter.

You don't have to send it. He may not even be around to get it. But write it.

I wrote my father three times in his life. I wrote him four in mine.

The first letter I wrote him was in the summer after my freshman year in college, when I refused to return to the hot, tiny, rented Phoenix house where the other nine members of my family lived and, instead, went to live in my new boyfriend's big house on a hill in Santa Barbara.

I was the first of my siblings to leave home, and my refusal to rejoin the family for the summer infuriated my father, which is to say it broke his heart.

I remember sitting on that Santa Barbara sofa, with bordered stationery and a pen, white waves lapping on the beach below, while I told him why I could not come back. I hoped my explanation — I could take college courses, etc. — would protect him from the truth, that I preferred comfort and beauty to hardship and home.

He never answered my letter.

I wrote my father for the second time in my late 20s. He was concerned about the course of my life. In that letter, I tried to explain my choices and all the ways that he, and his values, still lit my route.

He never answered my letter.

I wrote him the third letter when I was living in Orlando, Fla., and had just been offered a job at the Chicago Tribune. I knew that, as an Iowa boy, he thought Chicago was the capital of the world, and this move would make him happy.

Three weeks later I came home to find a small white envelope, dropped through the mail slot, lying on my wooden floor. His letter was just a few sentences, in his big, neat penmanship, composed in the hospital. He said he was proud. He said his treatments were going well.

He died five weeks later.

Ten years after my father died, I wrote him a fourth letter. I was taking a literature class in which we were given the assignment of writing someone we loved, dead or alive, saying something we'd like to say.

In that letter, I told him that it took me six months to cry after his death, and that when I was done crying, I got mad. Mad about how unkind he was when he was drunk, mad about how he treated my mother. Mad, mad, mad.

Then I told him that when I was finally over being mad, I began to understand his hopes, his traps, his regrets over his failings. I told him that I loved him and that I'd never doubted his love. I said thank you.

Now, here's the weird thing. I had completely forgotten that fourth letter — in which I wrote about the other three — until several weeks ago, when the teacher emailed to say she still had it. I asked her to send it.

Rereading this letter my father never saw, I remembered it vividly and realized how pivotal it had been in helping me understand my relationship with him. I hadn't needed to remember it because the thoughts it occasioned me to articulate for the first time had, by now, become part of me.

There's a unique, clarifying power in writing down your thoughts and a unique, focusing power in directly addressing them to someone.

Write your father. Say something you've been meaning to say. Send it or don't. Either way, you'll be glad. It's easy to start:

Dear Dad.

A Not-So-Normal Christmas

Last Christmas Day my sister Gina and I went to her favorite coffee shop for dinner.

I mean coffee shop, not coffeehouse, the kind of place that's open 24 hours a day, serves as many free coffee refills as a truck driver can stomach and takes no reservations.

It's a place that doesn't typically come to mind when you hear the words "Christmas dinner."

Gina lives in a midsize Oregon town that buttons up for Christmas as tightly as a person might zip up for a blizzard. It seems to operate on the assumption that normal people stay home on Christmas Day, idling the hours away in the cocoon of family.

I arrived at Gina's early on Christmas afternoon thinking that's what we'd do. We had an invitation to a relative's.

She announced she'd rather stay home alone.

What she meant, I deduced, wasn't that she wanted to be alone. She just didn't want to be in a crush of family members, surrounded by yammer about politics, jokes she didn't understand, discussions of movies she'd never see, stories of Christmases she doesn't remember even if she was there. She doesn't remember anything before the age of 10.

Gina, who has struggled all her life with variously diagnosed challenges, lived with our mother until she died three years ago, and they always spent Christmas together. Now I go to see her at Christmastime.

"What if we go out for dinner?" I said last Christmas Day.

She brightened. "That sounds good!"

But this was not Chicago. In all the town, there appeared to be only one place open, a coffee shop whose claim to glory, along with pie, is that it never, ever closes.

In the damp air, under the gray sky, we set off in my rental car, down an empty highway, toward the outskirts of town, past the auto parts shops, the thrift store, the tattoo parlor, Burger King and Burrito Boy, all closed.

Then there it was, a squat box next to a parking lot, neon sign shining. There was a line out the door. An hour wait. At 4 p.m.

Who were these people? Why weren't they home on Christmas Day?

"Every dysfunctional family in town," I joked.

"You mean like us?" Gina said. We laughed.

Crowds make Gina anxious so we sat in the car while we waited for a seat, listening to Christmas music on the radio, watching people come and go.

An elderly man and woman, both on walkers. Single men. Solo dads with a kid or two. A couple of haggard but boisterous couples who looked like they'd been up all night and planned to be again. A few seemingly intact families.

I made up stories about them all. The old folks, with their kids far away, who didn't want to eat Christmas dinner at the nursing home. The men whose families didn't want them. The divorced dads who had the kids for the afternoon. The hard partyers. The families in which mom refused to cook.

I didn't know their true stories any more than they knew mine and Gina's, but it was clear we all shared something. We weren't normal.

Normal people would be sacked out on a living room sofa, setting a table, slaving over mashed potatoes. Home for the holidays.

The size of this crowd made it clear, though, that there are a lot of not-normal people on Christmas, all of us looking for somewhere to go, and most everybody here, as best I could tell, was happy as anybody else on Christmas Day.

Finally, we got a booth, next to two middle-aged men in camouflage gear who were talking about hunting rifles.

The restaurant was bright and noisy. Our waitress was robust and cheerful in the style of Mrs. Claus. Gina ordered the honey-glazed ham "feast" and I nibbled.

"This was a good Christmas," she said afterward.

It was. We plan to do it again this year.

In the social squeeze called the holidays it's helpful to remember: Things don't have to be normal to be good.

SUNDAY, JUNE 17, 2007

Joe's Daughter's Journey

On a Friday night this May, a month before she was to graduate from high school, my brother Joe's daughter stood in their kitchen and said: "Dad, I knew this day was going to come. I need to start my journey."

It was around midnight. She was wearing a backpack and a bedroll. She had just gotten a phone call from a boy, 17, saying he was in trouble. He was leaving town. Right then. She told him she was coming too.

"Dad," she said, when Joe protested and demanded to know where she was headed, "the only question you have to answer is, are you going to hug me goodbye?"

This is not the way a father imagines setting a child loose or himself free of children.

Joe's daughter is the last of his three kids. He had the first at 20. A few years ago, he and his wife divorced, but they remain close to each other and attentive to their two sons and their only daughter.

Now that young woman, whom Joe had spent a lot of his life ferrying to school and T-ball games, was on her journey.

Joe's a fairly strait-laced guy and strict, but he and his daughter, despite their arguments, have always shared an evident affection. In the time that she has lived with him, he has learned to live with her piercings, tattoos, veganism and memorable coiffures, like the spiked blue hairdo dubbed "Statue of Liberty."

Lately, though, when he comes home, nothing has moved, not even a bowl. For the first empty week, he lived in grief and dread.

His little girl was traveling around California, riding freight trains and panhandling, sleeping in parks. He knew these things because within 24 hours of leaving, she started texting both parents on her cell phone.

She wouldn't say where she was, but she called to apologize for leaving the way she did. She cried. He cried. She took to calling or texting every day or two.

She got sick at one point and needed a prescription she couldn't afford. Joe's ex-wife paid for it at their hometown chain pharmacy, and their daughter picked it up wherever she was, which they learned, when the receipt came through, was Sacramento.

Last Joe heard, she was in Wyoming with the boy; he's a long, separate story. They'd been pulled off a freight train by a security cop who later bought them dinner and paid for their motel room.

"BE WARY OF THE GOOD SAMARITAN," Joe texted back.

"Oh, Dad," she said when she called, "you're so cynical. You raised me well. I know."

He did raise her well. What he's learning now is that that is the most a parent can do.

"I'm not concerned about image the way I imagined I would be," he says. "So my daughter didn't finish high school with her peers. In some people's eyes, she's being a bad girl. Those things are meaningless now.

"You can have all your dreams and hopes and expectations for your child, but suddenly, when something like this happens, all those things you argue about and hope for, they just drop away and it comes down to: 'Are you safe?'"

He has been thinking lately about how young he was when he had kids, how all the choices he made as an adult were grounded in the need to care for them. Despite his fear and sadness now, he finds himself piqued by his daughter's sense of adventure and kind of admiring that she, a girl, is doing something that probably wouldn't scare or scandalize so much if she were a boy.

"By what I call her soft anarchy philosophy, she has challenged my lifestyle," he says. "And not that I'll really change it, but it makes me think: What am I doing now? Am I living just so I can pay the mortgage?"

Some of his friends tell him to cut off her cell phone: tough love. He says no: Love communicates.

On Father's Day, as on every day lately, he'll be listening for the text message beep.

He heard it at 1 a.m. recently and reached for his phone to find three small words on the screen: "LOVE YOU, DADDY."

SUNDAY, MAY 14, 2006

A Google of Mothers

If only there were a computer search engine, a Google, that let you access your mother's mind after she was gone.

That's what a friend of mine keeps thinking since her mother died.

If there were a Google of lost mothers, she would type "chicken" and with the click of a mouse discover what it was that her mother put in her signature chicken dish, a unique concoction now forever removed from the world's menu.

Using the lost-mothers Google, she could type "toothpaste" and discover why her family brushed only with Crest. Or type "typewriter" and rediscover which model it was that her parents had given her for her high school graduation.

And what about that shoe salesman, the guy at the store where they always bought her saddle shoes when she was little? With the Google of lost mothers, she could retrieve his name.

These are minor questions, she knows, but they seem oddly important now that they're impossible to answer, now that her mother, and the information she contained, are permanently unavailable.

"It's the minutiae I wonder about," she says, "the minutiae of life itself."

It's the minutiae only a mother would remember.

She could ask her father. He's still alive. But, she says, with a sigh, "fathers are useless for this kind of stuff."

Why didn't she ask her mother while she had the chance? Her mother was around for 73 years, receptive to interrogation, not particularly secretive, unless you count the fact that she never told her children her real maiden name, which her safe-deposit box revealed postmortem.

But the questions that nag at this friend now are things she didn't ask because she didn't know what she wanted to know until it was too late to find out.

She could have anticipated the big questions her mother's death would leave, the kind that articles in women's magazines encourage us to ask while there's still time:

Whom did you love? When were you happiest? What broke your heart? What were your parents like? When did you go through menopause?

But it never crossed her mind to wonder, as she did while sorting through her mother's belongings, what exactly did her family take out of their burning house when they fled the fire when she was 6?

She admits that many of the questions pressing on her now have more to do with her than with her mother. No need to apologize for that. That's one service most mothers offer — they notice you and remember you in a way no one else ever will.

A mother knows you first and often longest, sometimes best. A mother holds her children's lives from start to finish in her head. She's a living scrapbook. She remembers parts of your life better than you do. When she goes, so do pieces of your identity that existed only in her mind.

How much of you dies when her memory of you dies?

The images of you that lived in your mother's memory more vividly than in any photo — you as a baby, happy and sad as a child — those would also be available in the Google of lost mothers.

Listening to my friend talk about the questions she'll never get to ask her mother, I made one of those intermittent Mother's Day resolves that often dissolves a few days later: I would ask my mother more questions while she's still around.

But then I realized that's not the point. You can ask and ask your mother, talk and talk, and still not know which questions about her life, your life, her death will trigger.

I'm lucky enough to still have my mother, but I know that for many people whose mothers are gone, Mother's Day — like other days — comes with the frustration of these memories that can never be salvaged and mysteries that can never be solved.

If there were a Google of lost mothers, though, it would probably be like the real thing — you'd never learn all that there was to know.

The facts would be endless and they still wouldn't fill the hole.

Late-Breaking Marriage

My brother Michael is getting married today, Sunday, Sept. 17, 2000, an item of little interest to those who don't know him, except maybe for the fact that his is a late-breaking first marriage.

Michael is doing his first I do's at 44, an age when some of his peers are working on grandchildren and some are working on divorces and many can only dream of steering their battered but comfortably reliable lives into unknown channels.

He's not quite as old as Gloria Steinem, who recently married for the first time at the age of 66, but his tardy first marriage, like all such marriages, is distinguished from the median knot-tying by an unsettling, exhilarating whiff of mortality. It's a whiff that sneaks into the happiness, and in some ways makes it stronger, like a tart autumn breeze in the last hot days of summer.

The late-breaking first marriage isn't as strange as we often think, of course. My siblings and I — most of us notorious marriage delinquents — come from a tradition of late-breaking matrimony. Our father's mother didn't marry until her mid-30s. His only sister married at 40 (and more than 40 years later remains in the most stable, equal, romantic partnership I've ever been related to).

My generation grew up in a time when marriage was on the life menu as an a la carte choice, not part of a fixed-price meal that you ate in its entirety whether every item appealed to you or not. Marriage was a choice most people eventually did decide they wanted, but few of my friends, male or female, married before 35, and some waited even longer.

Still, a first marriage after 40 comes with a believe-it-or-not quality, a sense of the clock's hands moving from right to left instead of their proper way around, a sense of time tricked, of expectation defied, of a little miracle visited on the wary.

Like any marriage, the late-breaking kind is a kind of birth, a rupture of routine, a new direction. The 18th-century writer Samuel Johnson once famously remarked that marriage is the triumph of hope over experience; the late first marriage might more aptly be considered the triumph of hope over habit. Or hope over hardening of the arteries.

Unlike marriages that occur when both parties are young enough to believe that a diamond is forever, late-breaking marriages come with the realization that nothing is forever and that the things that matter most — love, health, family — could vanish at any moment.

Only a century ago, the typical man was dead at about the age at which Michael is embarking on his new adventure. This cheerful thought is not lost on Michael, who, though he looks as robust as an SUV with a full tank, has seen his share of health scare.

He has felt his heart play tricks on him, which is one reason he has worked hard to get as many of his seven siblings to his Oregon wedding as he can. He wants us all to stand on the banks of the McKenzie River to see him take this giant step, and all but one of us will be there.

But even more than he wants wedding witnesses, he wants a sibling party. He wants his far-flung brothers and sisters to come together one more time in a joyous ceremonial way, regardless of the ceremony. He cares not only that we're with him, but that we're with each other.

"This could be the last time when . . ." he said when I talked to him on the phone the other night.

"Don't say it," I interrupted.

"But it's true," he said. "This could be the last time we all come together for a ceremony that's not a funeral. And I don't mean Mom. I mean one of us." He laughed. "Could be me."

"Don't say it," I said again.

It seems impolite to talk of death in the same breath as a marriage. And

I wouldn't if he hadn't. But death is, inevitably, the undercurrent of life for people who've reached the midpoint of their own, and siblings know this about each other in a unique way.

Siblings are likely to be the most enduring witnesses of each other's lives, the ones likeliest to know each other's stories from close to the beginning until almost the end. They are the measure of each other's lives. One of you getting old is a reminder that you all are. And one of you doing something novel — like getting married for the first time at the age of 44 — is a reminder that you're all always young enough to try something different.

SUNDAY, SEPT. 23, 2012

A Place to Rest

My brother Bill and I are out for a drive on a sunny September Saturday when we pass the old cemetery.

Neither of us mentions the headstones whizzing past, but I sense them, the way you might sense a stranger's breath or shadow, as Bill says, "What's more common now? Burial or cremation?"

Not sure, I say, but I'd guess that most people still go the old-fashioned way, relatively intact and in the safety of the ground.

The cemetery, in Fort Collins, Colo., where Bill lives, stretches on as we drive, old stones under big trees, a graveyard that, like so many others, was once on the fringe of town only to have the town grow up around it, the incessant churn of new life pressing at its borders.

"Do you think about it?" he says. "What you want?"

"After I die?" I say.

Die.

Knowing Bill's long struggle with a cancer that won't quit, his past summer in and out of the hospital, I usually avoid the word when we're together. With the cemetery in the corner of my eye, the word is somehow easier to say without its being a renunciation of hope.

I tell Bill that, yeah, I keep thinking that I really need to make a will, need to figure out what to do with my belongings.

No, he says, he means a resting place. Or just a marker. Have I thought about that?

Until he asks the question, I haven't thought about it.

Thinking about the logistics of death is too easy to avoid. What's the rush?

But then an illness comes along — your own or someone else's — and the ultimate questions, the ones so far in the distance that they're ordinarily invisible, zoom into focus.

That's what hits me as Bill and I talk. Questions about our own death are there for all of us, all the time, not only for people who are sick or old. It's just that old age or illness accelerates, accentuates the need to answer.

We park by the Poudre River, get out and walk.

The sun is warm, the river sparkles and Bill's pain medicine is performing its daily miracle.

We keep talking.

About our father, how he's buried in a Phoenix cemetery, far from anyone who loved him. About our mother, whose ashes, at her request, we scattered in the Ocmulgee River in the Georgia town where she was born.

Shouldn't a husband and wife, a mother and father, be together in the afterlife? Shouldn't their children be near them? Shouldn't the souls of people who love each other stay assembled?

We talk about these questions even though neither of us is sure what a soul is, or where a soul might go when the body expires.

Bill asks me where my marker would be if I had one. Chicago? Georgia? I ask him where his would be. Fort Collins? Oregon?

Neither of us is sure.

How much easier these decisions were in a time when generations of families stayed close, when the local cemetery was the single destination, the cemetery as community with its roots in history and the land.

Now? Burial or cremation? An official marker? More than one? Here, there or somewhere else?

Along the river, Bill and I spot a bench. On it are inscribed a name, a date of birth, a date of death.

Now there's a good idea, we agree. A bench. An inscribed bench with a view. A gift to the living, a place where strangers and the people you love could sit for a while and rest.

I Miss My Brother

I miss my brother.

I've been staring at my laptop screen, trying to write something about what it's like to lose a sibling, and the only words that come clearly are those.

I miss my brother.

Bill was the first of my seven siblings, just a year younger than I am, the guy who elbowed me out of the center of our parents' universe. We grew up eating the same fried-bologna sandwiches, watching the same Captain Kangaroo, smelling the same Georgia grass, absorbing our mother and father from approximately the same angle.

We were different, though. I crooned along with the Bee Gees; Bill rocked to Led Zeppelin. While I was rehearsing with the pompom squad, Bill brooded over the charcoal sketches he made in the bedroom he shared with his four brothers. As I bought my first professional clothes, Bill grew his hair to his waist and moved to the Oregon backwoods to paint.

For years we rarely saw each other, and rarely talked, but shortly after I moved to Chicago, he called me one night.

"How would you feel about me moving there?"

Bill, the iconoclast? Wanted to live near me? He and his girlfriend, Eloise, found an apartment a block from mine on Roscoe Street. We had good times.

After that, our paths diverged again. He married Eloise, had two sons who are now in their teens, got a job on the website of a small Colorado newspaper. He worked long hours, lived in a small house, wore thrift-shop clothes and never found enough time to paint.

Then the cancer came.

Do you ever wonder who you would reveal yourself to be if you were dying? Watching Bill, I often wondered.

Would I be so gracious? So humble and tenacious? Would my first words to visitors be "How are you?" His often were, until he could no longer speak.

Bill hoped against the cancer until the end. He used it as incentive to make art, down in the tiny basement studio that no one was allowed to enter, painting even when his fingers were bloated and burnt by chemo.

After he was laid off a year ago, losing his income and his health insurance, he sought the sunny side: "Now I can call myself a full-time painter."

The cancer took him shortly after New Year's. He was at home. Eloise, who had nursed him as the disease stole more from him every day, held his hand as he died.

During my brother's dying, I came to see more clearly who he was. Through his final time, we talked about our parents, novels, TV, music, religion, his love for his wife and sons, the importance of staying connected to your siblings. Though he lived on intravenous nutrition, unable to eat, he taught me his elaborate routine for properly buttering toast.

In his absence these last few days, Bill continues to reveal himself. Paintings of his that I'd never known about have turned up, showing parts of him I hadn't glimpsed before.

The morning of his death, Eloise opened the door of his little art studio. Sitting on an easel facing the door was a surprise gift. A portrait, almost finished, of his younger son, the one he wouldn't live to shepherd out of high school.

I miss my brother, the one I got to know better as he died, and the one I'm still discovering.

At its best, this is what death offers, a jolt that makes you look at someone you loved and wonder more carefully than you ever have: Who was that?

FRIDAY, JUNE 28, 2002

Family Feuds

When I was young, I occasionally heard tales of sisters who hadn't spoken to each other in 20 years, or a father who hadn't spoken to his son in decades or someone's aunt who refused to speak to anyone in her gene pool because they had all, she felt, abused her in some way. Back then, those stories were more mysterious than fairy tales.

How could anyone reject a member of the family? How could anyone speak public ill of a relation? Estrangement among family members was the strangest possible notion, the warped luck of unreasonable people. Family meant love and love meant loyalty and loyalty meant you never let a fight escalate into a feud, certainly not one other folks could see.

Back then, I would have found it bizarre that, though they eventually called a truce, Eppie Lederer (Dear Ann) and her twin sister, Pauline Phillips (Dear Abby), didn't speak to each other for years. It would have seemed even more bizarre to me then that their daughters would continue in their mothers' feuding footsteps.

In case you missed the details:

According to Rick Kogan's story in the Tribune, Ann's daughter, Margo Howard, has accused Abby's daughter, Jeanne Phillips, of trying to "make hay" from Ann's recent death. Phillips, who has taken over her mother's Dear Abby column, appeared on "Larry King Live" Tuesday to express grief that her aunt had died. Her syndicate is also offering her "farewell letter to Eppie" to the media free of charge.

"This," said Howard, who writes an advice column for Slate.com, "is not about grief. This is about new clients."

Even 25 years ago, I would have found the transgenerational Ann vs. Abby duel entertaining, but primarily because it seemed freakish. Wow! Look! Relationship advisers toss tomatoes at each other!

And it is entertaining. But not because it seems freakish. Because it seems in its odd way universal.

The average family feud doesn't make the front page, but in most families, it seems, there's always somebody who's not talking to somebody. Several years ago, a member of my family cut off all normal contact with the rest of us, and I've almost — though only almost — given up on trying to get her back. At first I thought this made my family rare. But ask around.

"Do you have a feud in your family?" The answer is almost always, "Oh yeah."

One woman I asked told the story of her father's feud with his brothers. Another talked about her brother, who pulled out of the family because he felt disrespected. Another told of her husband's brother, who has withdrawn from family circulation on the grounds that he'll never be free of his emotional troubles until he's free of his family.

Most feuds boil down to a single question: Who got more?

Who got more love from mom and dad? Who got more attention? Who got more money for college or a car, more money in the will? If mom and dad aren't the source of all that beneficence or denial, it's the world at large. Who got a bigger salary, more success, more fame?

In short, who got more respect? And if the other person got more, can you ever feel you got enough?

Feuds rarely start as feuds. They start as fights, misunderstandings, wounds. A few weeks pass. Then a few months. A couple of years. Ten.

As time passes, insults, or imagined insults, accumulate. Silence compounds. Hearts harden. Like a roof that could have been saved if it had been fixed at the first sign of damage, the relationship moves beyond obvious repair. It's simpler and cheaper to move on.

And so whereas a fight has term limits, a feud can fester 'til death do you part. Sometimes it goes on afterward, carried forward by the next generation, as if by keeping the feud alive in the name of avenging the family honor, the offspring can keep the dearly departed breathing too.

It's these inherited grievances, these animosities passed down through families like chromosomes, that feed most wars today, from Ireland to Israel.

But when you're young, you don't understand all the long-term ways relationships tangle and unravel. Life's simple: You fight, you make up. And when you're not sure how, you just write Ann or Abby.

Uncle Cuyler's Alzheimer's

When my Uncle Cuyler was a boy in Macon, Ga., he was nicknamed Kiki in tribute to Kiki Cuyler, who was playing the outfield for the Chicago Cubs.

"Remember how Daddy called you Kiki?" my mother asked him a few days ago, sitting on his couch.

She looked for a long time into his blue eyes, congenitally tender and amused, eerily like her own.

"Kiki," she said again, the soft way you might call to someone in the dark.

Remember, she said, how you were such a short little boy, and how you used to hang by your hands from the magnolia tree next to the house and swing your legs, trying to get taller?

She smiled. He smiled. She looked at him, searching. He looked at her, offering no clues.

If only she looked long enough, she told herself, or smiled long enough, or summoned just the right detail from their childhood, he might remember something. Might remember her. She knew better than to believe it, but cared enough to hope.

We all know what Alzheimer's looks like by now. It's a theme of our modern age, a staple of prime-time dramas and news reports. But until it looks like someone close to you, and that person looks at you as if you were a stranger, you haven't really seen it.

I got my education last week when I took my mother to see her brother.

My mother's little brother is 74 now and 6-foot-2. He has a white beard and a fringe of white hair, and even in his New England home maintains the air of a courtly Southern gent.

He also rarely talks, shuffles when he walks, carries his fingers curled close to his chest, has grown afraid of stairs, balks at getting out of chairs, relies on others to feed him and to change his clothes and calls no one by name.

He was in his 60s when Alzheimer's staged its first small robberies. Words would vanish. Names. He'd be driving and forget where he was going.

My mother saw him one day in that early phase of the disease. They went out to lunch with other family members. He knew who they all were, but he walked away and sat alone at a table by the window.

She hadn't seen much of him in the years before that, and until last week, she hadn't seen him since.

Her brother left Georgia as a young man, married to his college sweetheart, Gayle, then made a very handsome living as an investment executive in Manhattan. Life took my mother in other directions, in every sense of the word.

But all those years of distance didn't matter in those four days last week. He was still her brother, the kid who always lost his cap when he went to school.

There are people who in huge ways know him better now, who have a greater claim. His wife and four kids cherish him, revere him, give him the finest care.

But children who come from the same place and the same seed, who grow up together, contain a piece of each other that no one who comes later can.

"It was his eyes that made me know he was my brother," my mother said when she got home. "And I hoped my eyes would let him know I was his sister. I felt in a way I didn't know him anymore but, in a stronger way, I did know him and he knew me. And then I reached a point where it didn't matter."

What mattered was that she got to touch him, to see he is well-cared for, to connect with both the old man and the boy who hung from trees.

Remember, she said, how you used to come down the stairs slapping the wall until one day you knocked a vase out one of the stairway arches? How you told Mother the wind had knocked it to the ground?

He stared. She put out her hand. He held it.

My Father Was a Common Man

My father was a common man.

That thought struck me for the first time shortly after he died a few years ago, and it hit me with the force of heresy. Fathers should be thought of as heroes. Fathers are supposed to be kings.

Like many men, particularly of his generation, my father believed his family was his fiefdom, a system defined by exclusive paternal privileges and obligations. His failure to meet those obligations as he perceived them broke his heart, though his broken heart was another thing I understood only after he was gone.

It was several years after his death, too, that I realized that life had taken him on a trip that could only have been baffling to a German-Irish Catholic boy raised in tiny Carroll, Iowa, in the 1920s.

He had never seen a black person until he entered the Army. Until the day he died, he believed that birth control was a sin. He felt the same about divorce. He believed he could be banished to hell not only for his sins, but for the sins of his eight children.

Yet he wound up married to a Baptist-bred Southern girl and lived in the small-town South until he went bankrupt and his gambler's instincts drove him west to the big raw city of Phoenix. There, he was mystified by sons who grew their hair long and daughters who were what he called women's libbers. Having hoped to breed priests and nuns, he instead got spiritual wanderers and skeptics.

He grew up in a place and time in which any self-respecting man wouldn't let his wife work, and in which a man could assume that if he worked hard, he could provide. He worked hard, and dreamed of a big house, cars, private schools. He died with $134 in the bank, owning virtually nothing but a white Econoline van filled with the buckets, brushes and rollers with which he earned his living.

Over the years, he had sold insurance and real estate, peddled Amway and encyclopedias door-to-door, ran a Norge Village laundermat and manned the H&R Block tax booth in the Los Arcos Mall, but in his final incarnation he painted houses, a boyhood skill he put to use after losing all his money a second time and moving his entire family into one room at the Motel de Manana on a seedy Phoenix avenue. He launched his final career by painting the motel to pay the rent.

For the next 15 years, he dressed every day in his painter's whites, right up until the last week of his life, when the cancer had eaten him down to 123 pounds and he no longer had the strength to stand on a ladder in the 112-degree desert days. When he could no longer work, he died, at the age of 60.

Until close to the end, he rose every day at 5:30 a.m., showered, shaved and went to 6:30 a.m. mass, no matter how much he had drunk the night before, which was always too much.

And when the day was over, he prayed again. Sometimes on visits home, I would see him kneeling there alone in his boxer shorts, elbows on his bed, hands folded, head bowed, praying, as he once told me, that the next night he would not drink so much, yell so much, hit the people he loved and who, though he didn't always believe it, never ceased to love him back.

How deeply he wished to change was another thing I also realized only after he was gone.

Trying to fathom your father while he is alive is like watching TV with your nose pressed to the screen. You're too close to see him clearly.

Now that we have some distance on our father's life, my siblings and I can make better sense of it. We trade scraps of insight and information as if they are puzzle parts.

My younger sister once showed me a rare four-sentence note that shortly before his death he had written to my mother, to whom he often was not kind, while she was away. He said that as the unliterary member of his literary family he felt self-conscious writing, said how much he'd missed her and concluded, "You are the closest person to God I have ever known."

In turn, I told my sister about her father as the young man I'd known before she was born, before disappointments led him to drink and drink led him to anger.

The details of my father's life are particular, but his life is not so unusual. Not long ago my mother said something about him that I suspect applies to many fathers: "He would have been happier if he'd believed his family would love and respect him even if he wasn't the kind of hero he thought he should be."

Making a Parent Make a Will

Several times while visiting my mother during the holidays, I had a vision of her 20 years from now, lounging in a living room chair, wearing a red necklace, sipping a glass of white wine and charming a wide-eyed kid reporter from the local paper with tales of how it feels to be 102.

In the meantime, I keep trying to get her to make a will.

"You don't have to call it a will," I said.

She listened.

"You could live another 10 years," I said, teetering along the crack between wishing and believing. "Twenty."

She smiled.

"Just make some document stating what you'd like to have happen on the off chance that you leave this earthly circus before we do. OK? Is there someone you think should have your old piano? Or the hutch you and dad bought when you got married? Nursing home? Burial? Cremation? Where? Tell us what you want, Mother."

She nodded.

"I'll make that a New Year's resolution," she said.

I believed her intention. I believed it last New Year's too. So this time I pulled out the sharpest weapon in the arsenal: If she didn't want to do it for herself, do it for us.

"Be kind to your children," I said. "Don't leave us squabbling like junk-yard dogs when you're gone."

One reason my mother hasn't specified the details, I imagine, is that she doesn't have much tangible to leave her eight kids. No house, no stocks, no car, no belongings that would sell on eBay.

Besides, though I sometimes fear we're capable of arguing like the offspring of millionaires, she thinks of her children the way we prefer to think of ourselves — as kind, rational people who would not go to war with one another on the occasion of our mother's death.

Our mother's death. My heart beats harder just looking at those words. Whose doesn't? They're among the saddest in the world. And I do think my mother's diminishing body will stay fortified for quite a bit longer by the anti-aging potion of generosity, curiosity and laughing.

But there comes a time when parents and children have to swallow the terror of such a terrible loss and talk about it. That's what the experts tell us, anyway: We must look into the void, then look back into each other's eyes and get ready.

That includes paperwork.

Some older people enjoy the clerical duties of arranging for their deaths. I had an aunt who filled idle time dotting all the "i's" of her funeral plan. I have a friend whose mother — living — has made après-vie preparations that include choosing her burial nightgown.

But more common are the stories like the one from the friend who was out to dinner recently with her parents when she edged toward the abyss.

"I thought, I'll take a shot at it," she says. "So I asked my folks — both about to turn 80 — whether they had any long-term care insurance. I also asked them where they had their important papers and whether they'd consider putting them in one place and telling me where they were.

"I prefaced it by saying that this wasn't about inheriting anything, that we just wanted to know where things were and what plans they'd made. Well, they looked at each other, rolled their eyes, smiled nervously and literally backed away from me. My dad said something like, 'Did you hear what she said?' And my mother (who probably did not literally hear it) just shook her head.

"I'm ashamed to say I haven't tried again because it was just too painful and awkward. And so I know there is going to be a mess of monumental proportions to clean up, both financially and emotionally."

The adult children I know don't want to be morbid or to badger. We understand why parents balk. Who wants their kids snooping and ordering them around, treating them like kids? And what parents want to contemplate how their death might not only break their children's hearts but fracture their families?

In the end, maybe the best both sides can offer and expect is that everybody abides by the one shared rule that always eases negotiations between children and their parents: Be kind.

When Your Father Dies

When your father dies.

Let the phrase settle for a moment. What words do you hear next?

For anyone whose father has died, finishing the sentence is apt to be easier than reciting the alphabet.

"When your father dies" is the opening phrase of one of my favorite poems, "Shifting the Sun," and it came to mind recently after a colleague's father died, just before Father's Day. It begins:

> *When your father dies, say the Irish*
> *You lose your umbrella against bad weather.*

In the next few verses, the poem, by Diana Der-Hovanessian, recounts how different cultures frame what's lost when your father's gone for good.

> *When your father dies, say the Russians*
> *He takes your childhood with him.*

That refrain — when your father dies — has been running through my head since I reread "Shifting the Sun" the other day, and I've found myself finishing the sentence in different, though less poetic, ways.

Like this:

When your father dies, it doesn't matter that other people's fathers have died, that fathers have been dying since human time was born. What matters in the moment of his death is that he was your father. Your one and only. Your loss is unique, profound, yours alone.

When your father dies, people say many things to you, much of it the same thing. Sorry for your loss. Condolences. May he rest in peace. You will not remember words. You will remember kindness.

When your father dies, if you weren't there with him, you will carry that knowledge forever like a permanent hole in your pocket. You will get used to it, but you'll always know it's there.

When your father dies, even if you were with him, you will think of all the things you meant to say, to ask, things you may have said and asked a million times but you'll want to say them just once more.

Thank you.

Sorry.

Why? What? When? Who exactly are you?

When your father dies, you will remember that time, maybe more than one, that he made you so mad.

When your father dies, you will worry about your mother, who, you are likely to learn, is more resilient than you gave her credit for. This assumes she's the one left behind, as mothers so often are.

And when your father's gone, you'll see your mother from a different angle. You'll see more clearly how your father helped her, hurt her, made her less and more than she would have been without him. You will see more clearly her power over him.

When your father dies, the small particulars of his life, the kind you barely noticed when he was alive, grow into revelations.

The smell of his after-shave. The style of his boxer shorts. How neatly he arranged his loose change on his bureau before he said his prayers at night.

When your father dies, even if he was grand, you realize how small he was, how human.

When your father dies, you will become more intrigued by the life he built from the childhood he was given.

When your father dies, you have to adjust your place in the world, in your family, your sense of who you are performing for. You wonder if you can. You can.

When your father dies, you discover how others — say, your brothers and sisters — saw him differently.

When your father dies, you start to know him better. "Oh," you think, a long time later, "now I get it."

When your father dies, you take to noticing how much you're like him. It's not all good, but it's how you keep him with you.

When your father dies, you wonder what he would be like if he'd lived longer, what he would think if he could see you now. You hope he would be proud.

When your father dies, you will grieve and then, one day you'll notice your grief has dried up. You may spend weeks with no conscious thought of the man who was once at the center of your universe. You will be relieved and your relief may feel like betrayal.

But every now and then, when the sky is a particular shade of blue, or you spot a man with a familiar build on the street, or you hear the chatter of a ballgame on the radio, you will feel a knot in your chest, and to no one in particular, you'll say, "Dad."

His Voice Lives On

Your father will talk to you for as long as you live. I don't mean for as long as he lives. I mean that even when his body is long gone, he'll trail you around chiding, guiding and otherwise commenting on your life and the world.

You'll hear him say things like, "How many times do I have to tell you? Glasses first, then plates, then silverware, then pots and pans!"

Those are the words I hear whenever I'm haphazardly washing dishes in the sink — a pot, then a glass, then a couple of forks — instead of in the order that keeps the dishwater cleanest longest. And when I do something even worse — wash dishes under a steady faucet stream instead of in a full sink — his ghost will cluck, "Didn't anyone ever teach you not to waste water?"

"You did, you did," I'll mutter and cut the water off.

My father, like most of us, had various voices for varying moments, but the voice of his that doesn't die, even though he died 18 years ago, is the one forever reminding me that I could be doing things better — more economically, more efficiently and cheerfully, with more attention to detail, more in sync in every way with the 10 Commandments and my potential.

"You are not a B student!" I hear him say when I'm trying to convince myself that it wouldn't be a crime to do a mediocre job on something just to get it over with.

"Put on your thinking cap," the dad voice says when I've made some silly error, or am about to. Or it simply says, "Pay attention."

When I walk out of a room and leave the light on, I hear my father remind me electricity isn't cheap, and so I walk back in and shut it off. When I'm reading in dimness, his voice will descend from the ether and command, "Put a little light on the subject before you ruin your eyes!" I'll get up and turn a light on.

Once when he was angry with me, he said, "What the hell are you doing with your life?" I still hear him ask that occasionally, and take a certain measure of myself based on whether I can honestly say what I said back then, which was, "The best I can."

We learn our attitudes and habits from many sources, but the instructors' voices apt to endure longest and loudest in our heads are those of our parents.

"One of my dad's evergreens was, 'Roll with the punches,'" says a friend. "Later in life, when we wrote weekly letters to each other, his closing was inevitably, 'Keep punching.' He would also say, 'Give 'em Truman.' This was his way of saying, 'Give 'em hell,' which was what Harry Truman used to say. He also liked to say, 'We'll muddle through,' and 'Keep a stiff upper lip.' Is there a theme here? Dogged endurance would certainly fit."

The theme of my departed father's continuing comments to me is that the good life lies not in how well you are rewarded but in how much effort, focus and proper conduct you invest in earning what you got. Another friend still hears his father advise him on patience.

"When I get frustrated with a task, or do it too fast," this man says, "I can hear my dad say, 'Slow down, take your time. And it will get done.' Or, 'If you just get up and get started, you can get it finished by the end of the day.'"

Of course, if other fathers are like my father, the lectures they gave and continue to give even when they're gone are lessons they didn't always apply in their own lives. Though my father did indeed live much of what he preached, he fell short of some of his own convictions, which, I now believe, is why he dispensed them so adamantly to his children. He didn't want us to be as good as he was; he wanted us to be better.

As a kid I was generally annoyed by my father's homilies on life. "I know, I know," I always wanted to say. Now I realize how much of what I know I know because he taught me, and still teaches me through that undying voice in my head.

I'm nevertheless glad to have finally bought a dishwasher.

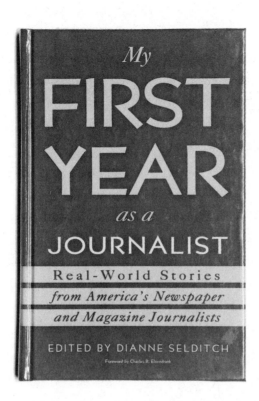

Clearing out the drawers in my cubicle, I found this book called "My First Year as a Journalist."

In it, I give an oral history of my first newspaper job, at The Peninsula Times Tribune, a small, scrappy afternoon newspaper in Palo Alto, California.

My chapter is called "Detail! Detail! Detail!" in honor of my first editor, Dave Burgin, who burned the value of detail into my psyche.

This was the early 1980s, at the beginning of the Silicon Valley tech revolution.

I didn't understand then that one of the best things that happened to me journalistically was to start at that small paper in that revolutionary place with an editor who held us to standards as high as any anywhere.

If I could change one thing about my time there it would be to more fully appreciate what the older female reporters — women around 50 by the time I got there — had accomplished in an era that wasn't friendly to working women. Now that I'm well past 50, I realize how little I understood back then about the lives of the women who came before me.

chapter 5

······························

taste of chicago

Royko

Mike Royko is not dead.

He will live on for a long time not only in the memories of his readers but in the columns of other columnists, in the sentences and sentiments of countless city chroniclers who at some point in their writing lives hoped for nothing more than to be like Mike.

He was the columnist of columnists, the rare writer who filled the greedy space day after day, week after week, year after year, come hell or high water or hangover. He was the guy who set the standard and the pace, a marathon runner in a field of rivals who often wound up wheezing on the second lap.

"Me and other columnists really have Royko as a role model," says Bill McClellan, who writes a city column at the St. Louis Post-Dispatch. "The way he looks at the world, many of us have adopted that."

It was the world view of the ordinary guy unafraid of power and pretension, who leavened common sense with wit, who anchored wit with guts.

Royko talked to you, not at you. He was a teacher but not a preacher. His aim was as straight as a ruler but he seldom rapped you on the wrists.

Sometimes he made you laugh so hard you hardly noticed you also were doing the harder work of thinking. Sometimes when the laughter stopped, you realized you were just the tiniest bit changed.

Mike Olesker, a columnist at the Baltimore Sun, calls Royko one of his "early inspirations." He remembers the day in 1967 when, while rummaging through a bookstore in Baltimore, he ran across Royko's first collection of columns, "Up Against It."

"I had never heard of him," says Olesker, who wasn't a columnist at the time. "I started reading and I thought, 'This is terrific.' I thought, 'I'm a city kid, I grew up in a housing project, I know Royko's kind of people.' Between reading Royko and Jimmy Breslin and Pete Hamill, I thought, 'I could do this for a living.'"

Royko belonged to a fraternity of men's men columnists — tough-talking, hard-drinking guys who knew the cops and the bars and the back rooms of the city — but he left his mark on women writers too.

Stephanie Salter, a columnist for the San Francisco Examiner, started reading him as a student at Purdue University. In that era, he wrote what she calls "one of the greatest feminist columns I ever read," in which, to mock the media's habit of describing the appearance of female politicians, he described the hair and clothes of Mayor Richard J. Daley and various Chicago aldermen.

"He became my hero," Salter says. "I loved him. That's the first relationship I had with a columnist."

Rheta Grimsley Johnson echoes the feeling.

"I don't know of anybody in journalism I have more respect for," says Johnson, a columnist at the Atlanta Journal-Constitution. "The body of his work is something that anybody who wants to write a local column has to look up to. If I could do it like anybody, it would be like him."

Johnson occasionally has referred to Royko in her columns, and within a few days always received one of his handwritten notes. The most memorable arrived after she wrote about trying to muster up the courage to introduce herself in a coffee shop during the 1984 Democratic National Convention.

"He was sitting with a newspaper but not reading it," she recalls. "I was afraid if he was nice, I'd be disappointed and if he was gruff, I'd be devastated."

So, as she explained in her column, she chickened out. She memorized the note — "one of my treasured possessions" — he sent in response:

"You should have spoken. I would have tipped my hat, bowed from the waist and pinched you on the ass."

It was the kind of remark that in later years would convince some people that Royko, champion of the little guy, whether the guy was black or brown or female, had changed. Royko would argue that he didn't change; the world did.

Either way, his work — 7,000 or so columns and too many words to fathom — stands above all his imitators'. Bill McClellan speaks for many of us when he says, "Royko influenced me in ways I don't even understand."

I hope he left knowing all the seeds he's sown.

WEDNESDAY, MAY 23, 2007

The Blue Bicycle

When the days grow long and warm, there's a good chance that some odd summer memory will surface in your thoughts, summoned by a slant of light or a rustling tree or the tender air.

But summer memories aren't all beaches and peaches, you know. Here's the one that out of the blue has been pestering me for two days, with an acknowledgment that it involves absolutely no news.

One night during my second summer in Chicago, when I was living on the top floor of a Lakeview three-flat, I came home from work and found my door ajar.

I was sure I'd locked the door that morning, but, oh well, maybe not. I closed it and was setting my keys on the table when bewilderment kicked me in the gut again: Where was my stereo?

My brain took an eternal, infinitesimal moment to retrieve the word "stolen." Then it raced on to a worse thought: "What if the thief's still here?"

I darted down the stairs.

My first-floor neighbors were a young couple with a baby. The woman worked long hours and I rarely saw her but her blond husband was often smoking on the stoop. He was an actor, out of work, and we'd had several pleasant chats. Once we talked about my 1923 Gibson mandolin, and I'd been glad to meet someone who understood what a precious instrument it was.

"I've been robbed," I said when he came to the door that night. Would he mind coming up and helping me make sure the burglar wasn't there?

We inspected every room and closet. The burglar was gone. So was my mandolin.

While I waited for the cops, my neighbor stayed with me. We talked about the perils of city life. When the police came, they said I'd probably never see my stuff again.

A few days later, I went down to the basement for my bicycle. A year or so earlier, my father had pulled me aside and said, "I heard you tell your mother you wanted to buy a bike." He handed me $100.

It was the most money he had ever given me, and he didn't have it to spare then either, but I took it because we both knew he was dying.

He did die, but he lived on in the $120 powder-blue bicycle that on a summer morning in Chicago, I discovered, was no longer in the basement.

My neighbor and his wife commiserated with my news, standing with their baby in their back doorway. We agreed we all had to be on the lookout. Who knew who was roaming around in the summer in the city?

The nights were hot, and I began to sleep fitfully, afraid of the next invasion. The days felt good, though, especially when I walked along the lake to work.

One morning, 15 minutes after leaving home, I turned around. I'd forgotten something.

When I stepped back into my lobby, I bumped into my neighbor. On the floor next to him was my guitar case.

I tried to shake off the fog — how did my guitar get down here? — while he explained that he'd heard a noise in the lobby and by the time he'd juggled the baby and gotten the door open, the thief was dashing out.

Again, he escorted me upstairs. Again, my door was unlatched. We puzzled over the burglar's m.o. until I said I had to get to work.

I was walking along the lakefront when the truth dawned, sickening, like the feeling of vitamins on an empty stomach.

I called the cops from my office desk: "I think my neighbor's robbing me."

The cops learned he had a small rap sheet, petty theft and forgeries for prescription drugs. Within a couple of days they arrested him.

He had been crawling in from the back porch through a window one of my houseguests had left unlocked, then exiting out the front, booty in hand. He went to jail for a while, and where he went after that I've never known.

The cops found my stereo in a pawn shop and my mandolin at a violin dealer's near the Howard "L" stop. They made me come to the station and play it before they'd give it back.

But they never found the bicycle, and every now and then, when the days get long and warm, I still see that shade of powder blue.

The Walls of William Walker

When Bill Walker didn't answer his phone Monday evening, Jon Pounds drove to the Minnie Riperton Apartments.

Walker lived alone in the South Side public housing high-rise. His best and perhaps only close friend, an elderly woman who had recently moved to a nursing home, hadn't been able to rouse him by phone that day either, so Pounds wanted to make sure he was OK.

Pounds knocked. No answer. A building employee inserted a key in the door.

William Walker, one of the great street mural artists, had passed away, at 85.

"I was sort of relieved for him," says Pounds, a public arts advocate who has spent decades trying to keep Walker's work alive, "because I knew he carried sorrow as much as he was a joyful man."

If you've ever admired a mural on a public wall in Chicago, you owe it in part to William Walker. If you've ever walked into a school and seen images of African-American heroes on a "wall of respect," you're seeing Walker's influence too.

"Fifty years ago, there was no such thing as a community street mural movement," says Olivia Gude, an art education professor at the University of Illinois at Chicago. "Now we take it for granted. It's hard to understand what Bill Walker — and the great Chicano artists of that era — created. They created a new art form."

That era was the 1960s. All over the United States, black Americans were striking back at laws and customs that treated them as inferior. In the tensely segregated city of Chicago, this new art — by the people, for the people, about the people and on the public walls — became a tool of the revolution.

Walker, who had studied art, was working as a mail sorter when, in 1967, he had the idea to paint a wall on a grocery-and-liquor store at

43rd Street and Langley Avenue. In bold colors on white brick, he and an artists' collective created a mural of more than 50 African-American achievers.

Miles Davis. Malcolm X. Billie Holiday. W.E.B. Du Bois.

Such a public montage of black faces was radical in a time when black faces were rarely seen in textbooks or on TV.

It was called the "Wall of Respect." A movement was born.

"You can go to Boise, Idaho," says Pounds. "You can go to Ireland. And you will see people inspired by this idea that artists' work should be public, tell stories and inspire people. It all goes back to the Wall of Respect."

Walker was shy, humble, even reclusive, though if you got him going, he would talk passionately about the devout and devoted grandmother who raised him, an only child, in a shantytown in Birmingham, Ala., before he came to Chicago at the age of 11 to join his mother, a seamstress. He never knew his father.

In his later years, if you could track him down at his favorite Starbucks or JJ Fish, he might talk about the violence that drained the neighborhoods where he painted. His work depicted that trouble. It showed guns, drug dealers and prostitutes, along with people of different colors holding hands.

He painted all the afflictions of his community, along with all his hope for it.

After he stopped painting, in 1988, too old to climb scaffolds, he hung around courtrooms, watching gangbangers' trials, seeking to understand why they did what they did.

Over the years, most of Walker's two dozen or so murals were whitewashed, painted over, torn down. The "Wall of Respect" vanished after a fire. Pounds, who runs the Chicago Public Art Group, has worked to keep and restore the four Walker murals that remain.

"Come out and paint with us," Pounds would sometimes coax.

"No," Walker would say, "it's past my time. It's the time of these young artists now."

Occasionally he showed up, picked up a brush, hopped on the scaffolding. Sometimes he watched, barely noticed.

Olivia Gude tells a story: It's 1 a.m. She's painting a mural on a viaduct wall at 56th Street and Lake Park Avenue, using a light projector.

"And all of a sudden I'm aware that there's this man standing there and staring. The figure steps forward through the light of the projector.

I recognized him. William Walker. Emerging into light in the middle of the night. It was a mythic experience."

A few years ago, Walker moved into the spare, one-bedroom apartment where he died, and there, he sometimes drew, always figures on black paper. Before that, he lived for a while in the home of the late Margaret Taylor-Burroughs, the co-founder the DuSable Museum of African American History.

His one luxury seems to have been his Cadillac Seville.

Walker died without immediate known family. He had a daughter from a long-ago marriage, but no one around him knows where she is.

"Family is the greatest thing in the world," he once told Jeff Huebner, a Chicago writer who is working on a book about him. "I would imagine it's a wonderful thing."

But, really, he said, it was a thing he hadn't had since childhood.

"Whoever befriends you," he said, "that's your family. Whoever is kind and considerate to you, that's your brother and sister, that's your family."

The family of people who loved William Walker and the art he gave Chicago will hold his memorial sometime soon, knowing that they never really knew him.

SUNDAY, JUNE 27, 2010

Up on the Roof

One June a few years ago — recent enough that the memory still makes me want to nap — three college students moved into the condo below mine and set to enjoying their idea of the perfect Chicago summer.

I live in a six-flat building that real estate people refer to as "vintage," which is a fancy way of saying that it's a century old, the rooms are small and the mortar crumbles during thunderstorms.

But for all its vintage annoyances, our building has one perfect feature: a rooftop deck with a skyline view, and when the new downstairs neighbors saw it, they heard a call to action:

Party!

On their first day in the building, without asking the other residents, they moved a bar table and high stools up on the roof, along with a couple of lounge chairs, ashtrays and a beach umbrella.

That night, under the prairie sky, next to the strutting skyline, they threw their first bacchanal.

Talking. Shouting. Laughing. Cursing. Singing. Barfing. Beer bottles crashing down onto the gangway.

The rooftop revelry filled the air until dawn. And they did it again the next night.

All summer, with a cast of friends and family, the new neighbors partied overhead as if the roof were their private paradise. They persisted despite the polite pleas, then the stern warnings, then the 3 a.m. 311 calls of neighbors.

Whenever we objected, the rooftop revelers looked at us blankly, as if to say: But isn't that why God made roofs in Chicago?

I wasn't entirely unsympathetic.

A Chicago rooftop is an intoxicating thing. In the heart of the city, where ground is in short supply, rooftops serve as backyards for a lot of us. They're a place to relax and retreat, a hypnotic, elevated dreamland where it's easy to lose track of time and exactly where we are.

Up on the roof, released from winter and Polartec, we can watch the sun set and the moon rise and witness this astonishing city light up one window at a time.

In summer, rooftops are as much a part of Chicago's social topography as stoops and alleys.

Hotels brag about their rooftop bars, and tourists argue over which is better: the Wit or Trump Tower?

Restaurants tout their rooftop farms and gardens. The Harvest restaurant at the Marriott Downtown Magnificent Mile raises bees on the roof and uses the honey to make Rooftop Honey Wheat beer. Watching a Cubs game from a Wrigleyville rooftop is the stuff of Chicago legends.

And then there are the home rooftops. Some are lavish, appointed with clean hammocks and polished teak, and ready to be photographed for a Crate & Barrel catalog.

The one I share with my neighbors is humbler, especially now that the noisy neighbors have taken their bar stools and beach umbrella elsewhere. We have a couple of wobbly plastic tables and some plastic CVS chairs, but that's all a Chicago rooftop needs. The rich view makes up for the cheap furniture.

To me, a rooftop isn't a place to make noise, it's a place to escape it. There's nowhere better suited to a solitary reverie or a quiet conversation or a glass of wine at the end of the day.

And yet I understand that one person's place of peace is another's place to party. Up on the roof, we have to indulge each other.

But as we enter rooftop season, a gentle plea from the rooftop peace lovers to the rooftop partiers: Not at 3 a.m., OK?

Daley Was the Dad

Daley was the dad.

Good dad. Bad dad. The man we've loved to hate and the one we've depended on more than we like to admit.

Go ahead, curse him. It's fashionable, and often deserved.

He throws tantrums. He plays favorites. He is not cool. He has screwed up some things big-time. Disobey him at your peril.

But for years, all we've had to do is look around the neighborhood — Detroit, St. Louis, Cleveland — to see that we've been lucky to have a guy like him running our household.

While other cities stumbled and fumbled into the new millennium, Mayor Richard M. Daley led.

He led Chicago far and fast, and if he did it for pride and power, he also did it for love.

He hasn't done it alone, and he certainly hasn't done it perfectly, but in his 21-year tenure, Chicago has turned into the great city it used to only think it was.

I say this as someone who has lived many other places and lived here for 25 years. When I arrived, Chicago was dirty, viciously racist, tired.

Under Daley, and in important ways because of him, the city got better. It seemed, physically and spiritually, to get brighter.

It's no surprise then that when Daley announced Tuesday that he wouldn't run again, you could practically feel the tectonic plates shift beneath the Loop.

"Simply put," he said at a news conference, "it's time. Time for me, it's time for Chicago to move on."

He's right. It's time, for him and for the rest of us.

He's 68. The city budget is a shambles. His popularity is down. His wife, Maggie, who stood next to him Tuesday, leaning on a crutch, is living with cancer.

He seems to have sensed, in the words of the old Michelle Shocked song, "The secret to a long life is knowing when it's time to go."

Opinions quickly fell into two camps.

One: Good riddance.

The other: OMG. What now?

Even the "good riddance" people have to be worried about what now.

Today's college freshmen weren't even born when Daley took office 21 years ago.

They take for granted the gleaming skyscrapers, the clean streets, the green roofs, Chicago's prominence in the world.

And if they also take for granted the troubled schools, the gangs and guns, the cronyism and corruption, it's important to remember that Daley's failure wasn't inventing those, it was failing to fix them.

Go ahead, argue. That's part of living in this vast, messy town. Chicago feels like family. We argue, loudly.

And one reason Chicago feels like family — I've lived in cities that don't — is that for 21 years, the same guy has been head of the clan, like his father was before.

In deep, subtle ways, the fact that Chicago has been a family-run operation has provided a sense of connection and security. I don't mean security in all its forms; we all know the unemployment rate and the crime stats. I'm not arguing that patronage is good.

But Chicago feels grounded in a way few cities do, connected to itself in a rare way, in part because it has been run by someone who has the city in his history and his bones and his heart.

Cities, like people, go through phases. This has been a good phase for Chicago. We may not appreciate how good until later.

SUNDAY, JULY 13, 2008

The Swimming Twins

When Jennie and Julie Papilli turned 12, their father gave them a little birthday money, so Julie said to Jennie, "Let's buy a bathing suit."

They went to Montgomery Ward and picked out matching one-piece suits, shiny and canary yellow. Then they went to the library and checked out books on how to swim.

As the books suggested, the girls started by floating on their faces. They advanced to conscious breathing. They moved their arms around. Within two weeks, the identical twins in their identical suits were gliding through Lake Michigan.

Julie and Jennie went to the lake to swim every day that summer of 1946. They went every day the next summer, and the one after that, year after year, as Chicago got bigger and they got older.

High-rises went up near their beach at Grand Avenue; the water went down. They moved their daily swim up to North Avenue, and there, on almost any summer morning in 2008, they can be found climbing down ladder No. 1 and plunging in.

The twins, as they are known, are quiet legends of Chicago's lakefront. All the dawn swimmers at their ladder know their routine.

Julie puts her flip-flops on one side of the ladder, Jennie puts hers on the other. They swim a mile south to Oak Street and return, side by side, always with a backstroke. Even in the cold months, they never wear wet suits. They are described as very shy and — a word not commonly applied to 74-year-olds — buff.

"I swim 100-plus miles a year there," says David Olive, known as Diver Dave, "but they always have me beat because they swim every day."

Every day except in rain or lightning, they said when I met them Thursday, their red suits still dripping. And every year since the age of 12, except one.

"It was 2001," said one of them. I was having trouble telling them apart, even though they'd untucked their matching auburn hair from their matching white swim caps.

"No," said the other, "2002."

Whatever year it was, it was the year they both had herniated disks in their necks, and that swimless year, they agreed, was terrible.

Jennie and Julie, who stand 4-foot-11, lived in rural Indiana until the age of 12. Their speech still hints at the fact that they spoke only Italian until they got to school.

"We were living in the country and came to the city," Jennie said, explaining what it was like for rural girls, daughters of a tool-and-die maker, to arrive in busy Chicago with its mystical, vast lake.

"When I first started swimming," Julie said, "there was another aspect to the world."

"I felt something," said Jennie, "something . . ."

"Opened up," said Julie.

"Opened up," said Jennie.

The twins swam through their college years at Roosevelt University, swam through their years of jobs in real estate, accounting, key punch, substitute teaching, selling clothes at Sears.

After-work traffic persuaded them to switch their swims to dawn. And not just summer dawns. They're always out by May, sometimes April. One year they swam into December.

"Remember one day," said Jennie, "we went swimming and then went to McDonald's, and you looked out and said, 'Do you know it's snowing?'"

Jennie and Julie moved in together when they were 40 to take care of their mother.

They remain close to their younger sister.

They agree on politics (Hillary) and food (vegetarian), but they differ on swimsuits.

"I like two-piece," said Jennie.

"I like one-piece," said Julie.

They alternate, but always match.

After they swim each day, they take care of several properties they own. Julie does plumbing. Jennie does electrical.

It's the swimming, though, that shapes their bodies and their lives. Though Julie had arthroscopy on her shoulders and Jennie survived a torn rotator cuff, they have never, they say, been sick.

Occasionally they've swum other places. Once in the Dead Sea. Once, not happily, in California.

"Salt in the eyes," said Jennie.

"I couldn't stand it," said Julie. "It was so hot."

It's this Midwestern lake they love, the cold unsalted water, some days calm and some days not, always different and every day since the age of 12 making them slightly new.

SUNDAY, NOV. 16, 2008

Sam Cooke's Brother

L.C. Cooke was sitting at home on Election Night watching his big-screen TV when he heard Barack Obama quote his brother Sam.

"It's been a long time coming," Obama told the Grant Park crowd, "but tonight, because of what we did on this date in this election at this defining moment, change has come to America."

Pretty soon the phone in L.C.'s Calumet City two-flat was ringing. Old friends from Texas, Detroit, New York. Did you hear that, L.C.? It's been a long time comin'. That's Sam's song.

"It shows you the longevity of Sam," L.C. said when I phoned him Friday. "One thing about Sam's music, Sam's music don't get old."

Obama's rise has resurrected Sam Cooke, the Chicago singer and songwriter whose 1964 hit, "A Change Is Gonna Come," became an unofficial anthem of Obama's campaign.

I'm sure I'm not the only person prompted lately to go back and listen to some of Cooke's other songs — "You Send Me," "Chain Gang," "Wonderful World," "Twistin' the Night Away" — and be struck by how good they still sound and how much American history is embodied in Cooke's life.

None of Sam's reclaimed fame surprises L.C., who's 75.

"Sam," he said, "was a visionary."

Had he seen Sam in the pro-Obama video on YouTube?

"I heard about it."

Sam and L.C. were practically twins, born 11 months apart, carried as babies by their mother on the Greyhound from Mississippi to a new home in Chicago. Their father, a minister, organized them and three of their six siblings into a group called The Singing Children. Sam sang tenor, L.C. bass.

As boys, L.C. and Sam made the rounds of back porches in Chicago's Bronzeville. Sam crooned while L.C. passed a hat. They wrote songs together.

But Sam, said L.C., was always a little ahead of everybody else.

"He had a little stack of books. He read every single day. And he was the first one started wearing his hair natural. Black people, you know, used to press their hair. He told me, 'L.C., now one day all blacks are going to have their hair natural like mine. You'll know who started that trend.'"

Sam was a singing success by 19, famous by 26 and dead at 33, shot by a hotel clerk who claimed it was self-defense. People still argue over exactly what happened and why.

In the years since, L.C. said, he's been able to live pretty well thanks to his brother.

"Mostly Sam's manager takes care of me," he said, "very good care of me. Right now, I've got an '09 Lincoln sitting in my garage. I don't have to do nothing but rest and dress."

L.C. lives with his wife, father-in-law and his wife's cousin in a neighborhood that was populated by whites when he arrived two decades ago. He's especially close to his next-door neighbors, among the few whites who stayed. Occasionally, he writes songs or goes out to sing.

"I sing for Aretha," he said casually, as if we all know Aretha, which anyone who has read this far probably does.

His new Lincoln has a talking jukebox that holds 2,400 albums, but mostly he plays Sam all day every day.

"What would you like to hear?" the jukebox asks, and lately he often answers, "Sam Cooke's 'A Change Is Gonna Come.'"

For people who want to hear more of Sam's songs, what recording would he recommend?

"One Night Stand," he said. "He made it in Harlem. Sam was really at his best."

Sam's ex-driver called L.C. the other day with news. He was taking L.C. to the inauguration, which would be the closest L.C. has ever been to Barack Obama.

"I'm going to make it my business to meet him," he said.

He's not sure how he'll make that happen, but when it does, he'll say hello on behalf of Sam, his visionary brother who believed in change long before most people could.

Living on a Street of Ghosts

I'm living on a street of ghosts.

From my front window, I see a couple of the ghosts every day lately. They're sisters, old women, though sometimes I see them as little girls, playing outside the house across the street, where they had lived for most of the past century.

The house is gone now. So are the sisters, except as apparitions in the construction zone I overlook from my living room.

One day last summer, some big machines snorted down the street. As fast as you could rob a bank, they tore that house to rubble.

I assume the sisters were gone by then. I hadn't seen signs of life over there in a while. I'd heard one had died; she was around 100. I'd been told one was deaf, and she was still alive. There had been three, though all of this is neighborhood hearsay and not totally reliable history.

According to the hearsay, the sisters had been born around the early 1900s in the wood frame home across from my brick three-flat. They'd grown up here back when the Near North Side was the pastoral fringe of young, raw Chicago.

Their house looked both rambling and modest, in the way of an old farm place. Between the main house and a smaller one in the rear lay a yard.

I never met the sisters, though when I first moved onto the street, I'd sometimes see a white-haired woman pad outside in a housecoat to pick up the morning paper.

One of the sisters, maybe two, had had kids, I was told, but still they stayed in the house where they themselves had grown up. And now that house has vanished as thoroughly as the century it occupied.

My street and the ones around it are like a lot of Chicago streets these days. Not only are the old residents dying or otherwise moving on, their homes and histories are disappearing, replaced by new palazzos that span not just one city lot but often two, sometimes three or more.

The palazzos have Greekish columns, gothic gargoyles, chateauish roofs, an assortment of architectural ruffles reminiscent of fabulous vacation destinations. The new homes climb high and spread wide, extend from front sidewalk to back alley. There are few yards.

When friends come to visit, they ask in awe to take the tour of the new palazzos. I also show them the ghosts.

There, I say as we stroll, that palace used to be a little house where a guy sat outside on his stoop with a radio that always seemed to be playing "Volare" or something by Sinatra.

And there's Ray. Or, rather, that's his old place, waiting for a grander reincarnation. Ray's passed on, but he was the street historian, a lanky guy with a little gray ponytail. He kept detailed maps as property changed hands and peasants were replaced by princes.

I met Ray one summer night when I was out walking. He recognized me from the paper, introduced himself and said, "I thought about calling you the day the last Puerto Rican moved off the block."

Now, though I never saw the last Puerto Rican in real life, I occasionally spot his ghost on the corner.

There are other ghosts, too, old people I used to see ambling on the sidewalks. Occasionally the ghost of one will appear for no apparent reason except to say, "Hey, you hadn't even noticed I was gone."

They're right. Walking past the palazzos I can't always remember what was there before, or who.

But I still clearly see the sisters' house, even though the land is now a concrete pit.

The dirt lay idle through the fall and winter, but recently the machines chugged back. Almost every day now, they shudder, grind and ding, dig, pour and dump, while men scurry around with jackhammers and wheelbarrows.

This is the nature of city life, the business of prosperity. You tear down. You build up. You forget.

At least for now, and though I knew them only from half-baked legend, I remember the sisters. I miss them and their house, and I miss the part of the neighborhood's life that left when they did.

FRIDAY, MAY 27, 2016

Walking Man

His name is Joe.

Who knew?

Not most of the people who for years have watched him walk the streets of Chicago, up near the Hancock Center, south near the Willis Tower, next to the river and across the bridges, occasionally in more far-flung precincts.

To most of his fellow downtown pedestrians, he was just "Walking Man," or "Walking Dude," or "Walking Yanni," a familiar, tall, mustachioed guy who loped around town in a V-neck T-shirt and a kerchief tucked in the breast pocket of his suit jacket, going who knew where.

Occasionally, he'd stop to comb his flamboyant hair, which through the decades faded from black to silver, while his long stride got a little shorter and slower.

Could he talk? If he could, it was rare to witness. Walking was his thing, mile after mile, alone.

Walking Man has been one of those people commonly called a character, a word that shrinks a human being into an amusing story, but the speculation he incited usually seemed friendly.

"I saw Walking Man!" people would report to each other. His followers would post surreptitiously shot photos of him on Facebook, videos on You-Tube. His mystery was part of his allure.

Now an act of violence has given him a real name, a family, a past.

On Tuesday morning, a homeless man attacked Joseph Kromelis, 69, with fists and a bat on Lower Wacker Drive, sending him to the hospital with leg injuries and his eyes bloodied.

Ordinarily, a fight between people who live on the streets wouldn't make news. But this was Walking Man, and his assault has inspired not only media attention but a rush of sympathy, outrage and offers of financial aid.

"A quiet wandering soul," one person wrote on a comment board.

"He makes my day better whenever I see him," said another.

"A familiar face in a city full of strangers," wrote one.

Of course, to most of us, Walking Man is a stranger too. But he has been one of those strangers who, seen so often and for so long, come to seem like friends. That's why his attack has touched a collective nerve and felt somehow personal.

We don't know him, but we feel we do. We project stories onto him. One of the stories — true — is that he's the kind of person who makes Chicago a more interesting place to be.

All of this has come as a surprise to his sister-in-law, Linda Kromelis, who says she knew nothing of his stature in Chicago until now.

"No, no way, nope," she said Thursday. She added that she doubted he knew either.

"He doesn't do computers," she said, "and he doesn't have a cellphone. We tried to get him one."

She acknowledges, however, that there are a lot of things about him she doesn't know.

She said that when his parents moved from Chicago to Michigan in the mid-1960s, he stayed in the city but regularly came to see his mother, until she died in the mid-1980s. After that, he visited only periodically, but when he did, he talked.

"Oh, yeah," she said, "he's a big talker, especially when he was here with his brother. They liked to argue."

The family worried about him, she said, especially after he lost his long-time apartment a couple of years ago. They tried to persuade him to come to Michigan, but Chicago was home.

"It's just his way of life," she said. "He liked the city, liked walking, liked selling jewelry on the street. There's nothing wrong with him. But we worried about him."

Joe Kromelis' brothers are all dead now, along with one of his sisters. His remaining sister didn't want to talk. But his sister-in-law passed on a photo from a few years ago that shows him with his family, on a deep-green lawn surrounded by trees.

For people who have known him only as the solitary Walking Man, to see him that way is startling and comforting.

On Thursday, police charged Kromelis' attacker with reckless conduct, a misdemeanor, a charge so light it incensed a lot of the strangers who think of Walking Man as a friend. But police say they couldn't charge a felony unless Kromelis was willing to sign a complaint. They say he refused because it's the code in the homeless community not to rat someone out.

In his conspicuous way, Walking Man has always seemed like a very private person. The violence done to his body has cost him some of that privacy.

But maybe what he has lost in privacy will be partially made up for with the knowledge of how much affection and concern he has inspired among his fellow city-dwellers.

Chicago sends you its best wishes, Mr. Kromelis.

FRIDAY, SEPT. 7, 2007

Death at Montrose Harbor

Doug Nishimoto recalls a time a few years ago that the regulars at Montrose Harbor had gathered with their kids for some family smelt fishing only to be confronted by a group of troublemakers.

"Like skinheads but more redneck," he recollected Thursday. He was sitting near the blue lake while the masts on the bobbing white sailboats clanged in the September breeze.

"These guys were cussing and one of the fishermen, one of the Spanish guys, says, 'Hey, can you tone the language down? We've got kids here.'"

The troublemakers hurled back a variety of multiethnic insults — "to incite us, like they're daring us" — then one drew a cross in the grass and lit it on fire.

"That's when the Spanish guy, the whites, blacks, Asians, everybody unified," Nishimoto said. "Started throwing beer cans at them, charged them."

The troublemakers fled. Peace was restored. Nishimoto doesn't remember anything like that happening again, and he tells the story as proof of how well people usually get along out in this united nations of a harbor.

It's precisely because Montrose Harbor seems so far from the ordinary hustle and bite of the big city that Du Doan's death last week seemed more than ordinarily disturbing.

A small, 62-year-old Vietnamese man, fishing alone at dawn, Doan must have looked like serenity incarnate at the moment when, out of the blue, allegedly, a 31-year-old guy he'd apparently never met shoved him in the back and into the water.

He couldn't swim and quickly drowned.

If you live in Chicago, you expect a certain amount of violence. On the streets, on the L, in the alleys and the bars.

But a harbor? The word implies safety.

At Montrose Harbor, the lake ripples east to the horizon; the skyline shimmers 5 miles to the south; big trees shade green grass berms; Lake Shore Drive is a soft, invisible whoosh in the distance.

Here, it's possible to believe in harmony. Of people with different kinds of people, of city people with nature. Anybody with patience and a pole is welcome to engage in the ancient art of catching fish.

"You get away from the rat race," said Nishimoto, 52, who has been fishing for perch, smelt and salmon here since he first rode his bike over from Uptown at the age of 10. "Get away from the horns. The idiot drivers."

That's not to say that everybody loves everybody all the time. Some Chicago-born fishermen, like Nishimoto, get upset at the immigrants who catch more than their legal limit.

Fishermen of all sorts get irked with the boaters, who have been known to ride blithely over fishing lines or spray fishers with lake water as they zoom toward shore.

"The boat owners are kind of arrogant," Nishimoto said. "They think they're better than us."

But mostly the harbor regulars look out for one another. Out here, Nishimoto said, people know each other by face, though not so often by name.

When the fishermen see somebody climbing over the gates to the boats, they call the cops. Strangers may help one another net a fish or pull a dog out of the water.

And yet the harbor can be more dangerous than it looks. Winds change. The currents run strong. Waters can swiftly suck a body under or out into the deep.

Other treachery, too, can lurk in the darkness and the dawn, the tranquil hours when the fishing is the best.

"We've always looked over our shoulder," Nishimoto said. "We keep our eyes open."

He's looking over his shoulder a little more now. Police are calling Du Doan's death "random" and "senseless." They say it's not, as they first suspected, a hate crime.

The linguistic distinction is small comfort to Nishimoto. He's angry that as an Asian he feels just a little more vulnerable here in the place he loves. Still, he's been out fishing every day since Doan died, and he'll be back.

"This is Chicago," he said.

This is Chicago. I heard that line several times from the fishermen I talked to Thursday.

Translation: Bad things happen. And you keep on fishing.

Studs Turns 90

"I'm deaf as a post," the birthday boy warned, cheerfully prepared to answer questions anyway.

How do you manage to look so good at 90, Studs?

"Orneriness," he answered, in the kind of voice that makes you smell a cigar and think about ordering a martini.

One true thing you've learned in these 90 years?

"I've learned about the vulnerability of all of us."

Of all the interviews you've done over the years, do you have a favorite?

"A former grand cyclops of the Ku Klux Klan," he said, cozying up to a story as familiar to those who know him as the red-checked shirt and rooster-red socks he wears every day. "It'll take about five minutes, if you'll let me."

Five minutes? A couple of the reporters who'd gathered at the Chicago Historical Society Thursday glanced at their watches. Five minutes is a century in media time. But it wasn't every day a man has a 90th birthday party, and Studs Terkel wasn't just any old man, and so he got to tell his tale about the Ku Klux Klansman, the kind of redemption tale he loves.

There's not much that Studs Terkel hasn't been asked over the years and seemingly not too many of his stories he hasn't already told. But he brings fresh vigor to every old tale, and that passion for stories that tell us who we are and were has turned him into the closest thing Chicago has to a living city symbol.

Back in the 1960s, however, Studs hadn't acquired the polish of a civic icon, if polish is a word that applies to an impish guy whose tufts of white hair can't resist doing the hula on his head. Back then, he was a civil rights activist, a pro-union rabble-rouser, a thorn-in-the-side. The first Mayor Daley could hardly have dreamed that the next Mayor Daley would declare May 16, 2002 "Studs Terkel Day in Chicago."

Even now there are a few curmudgeons who view Studs — and everybody calls him Studs — as nothing but an old leftie with a great press agent, namely himself. And yet mostly these days Studs is seen as the revered incarnation of Chicago as it likes to see itself: down-to-earth, rambunctious, egalitarian, hopeful, adaptable but principled, and in for the long haul.

You may have heard the synopsis of Studs' life: Grew up in his mother's working-class Chicago hotel. Studied law at the University of Chicago. Became an actor, a radio DJ, a master interviewer, oral historian, champion of blues, gospel, folk and jazz. Wrote books that captured the voices and times of so-called ordinary Americans, the most recent, "Will the Circle Be Unbroken?," published just last year. Never learned to drive, still takes the bus.

All of this was celebrated Thursday on stage at the Chicago Historical Center.

David Schwimmer, star of TV's "Friends," told the audience how he recently watched old episodes of Studs' TV series, "Studs' Place," afraid he'd discover that this man so accomplished in so many realms might also be a fine actor. What a relief to discover he wasn't.

Garry Wills, star of books, mentioned that it takes forever to take a walk in Chicago with Studs because everybody wants to talk to Studs and Studs will talk to anybody.

Sydney Lewis, a local author, recalled seeing Studs practicing his pitches a few days ago in preparation for tossing out the ball at Friday's White Sox game. He was muttering to himself, taking on a ballplayer's persona, the same quality of empathy that has made him such a good interviewer.

"It's what everybody wants to be," said Garrison Keillor, star of radio's "A Prairie Home Companion." "Ninety years old and still have the lights on upstairs."

Studs has made a life out of words, and many words were spent in his honor Thursday, words that paid tribute not just to who he was, but to who he is, a man still at work, still wondering, still asking, still being heard.

But it was during a bittersweet song by folk singer Jamie O'Reilly that I felt his full measure. He sat on the stage watching, listening, enraptured, quiet, a 90-year-old man entitled to be proud, brave enough to admit a few regrets, his small body filled with all those other lives, lives that will live on long after he's gone because he had the curiosity and courage to capture the stories on paper and tape.

FRIDAY, JUNE 22, 2001

Chicago Thunderstorms

On one of those thunderous Chicago nights not long ago, when the wind was so wild it set hundred-year-old brick three-flats to swaying like trees and threatened to send hundred-year-old trees flat to the sidewalk, I woke up, switched on a lamp and picked up the current New Yorker magazine to read a story about Chicago a century or so ago. It was by E. L. Doctorow and was called "A House on the Plains."

Reading in the dim light, while the windows whistled and the night sky flashed, I came across this passage:

"Chicago to my mind was the only place to be. . . . I above all liked the city because it was filled with people all a-bustle, and the clatter of hooves and carriages, and with delivery wagons and drays and peddlers and the boom and clank of freight trains. And when those black clouds came sailing in from the west, pouring thunderstorms upon us so that you couldn't hear the cries or curses of humankind, I liked that best of all. Chicago could stand up to the worst God had to offer. I understood why it was built — a place for trade, of course, with railroads and ships and so on, but mostly to give all of us a magnitude of defiance that is not provided by one house on the plains. And the plains is where those storms come from."

You know how sometimes you stumble upon a sentence in a book, or a scene in a movie, that clarifies for you who you are, how you think, what you want or where you live? How until you've read or seen it, until this vision or notion exists in someone else's words or pictures, it doesn't quite exist?

This short passage had that effect. In the middle of that stormy night, I saw Chicago's thunderstorms through history, saw their emotional effects, recognized how fundamental thunderstorms are to the identity of this place.

And later, brimming with the rapture of discovery, I assaulted a longtime Chicagoan with my thoughts on thunderstorms. He shrugged.

"You grow up here, you don't think about 'em."

But you should, because thunderstorms are as essential and startling a part of Chicago life as the skyscrapers, the lake and the relentlessly flat land. They are a measure, in Doctorow's inspired phrase, of this city's "magnitude of defiance."

I grew up with thunderstorms in the South, but forgot their power and pleasure during years in California. Only when I moved to Chicago did I realize how much I'd been subconsciously yearning for those old storms, for the heart-rattling comfort of the rowdy angels bowling.

And Chicago has delivered, especially at night, with all the theater a lover of thunderstorms could wish for, with shows that are even more thrilling because these are big-city storms. In Chicago, thunderclouds dwarf skyscrapers and bring both into relief. Lightning does what starlight rarely can, which is to pierce the city's electric glare.

Thunderstorms bring the prairie to the city, reminding us we're not so far removed, in either place or time, from nature and raw land. When city and storm meet, we can see each of them differently.

"In the Midwest, we get a unique breed of thunderstorm because you've got a jet stream nearby and there are imbedded disturbances in the jet stream that draw the air aloft with even more intensity than in the South," confirmed Tom Skilling, the passionate weathercaster, when I called searching for some scientific heft for these ramblings. "It makes for a particularly vigorous breed of thunderstorm."

For the sake of those of us who think jet streams are RVs, Skilling added: "I look at these things in something less than poetic terms."

But poetry has a place for numbers, and he supplied a few on Chicago thunderstorms:

Annual thunderstorm days: 37.9

Average in June, July, August: 6, 6, 6

Height of a Chicago thunderstorm cloud: 10 to 12 miles

Annual thunderstorm days in Honolulu: 6.7

It's easy to dismiss thunderstorms as inconvenience. They ruin your cookout, cancel your flight, flood your basement, shut your power down. But the next time one blows through, remember that they're also part of the soul of where we live, defiantly if a little wet.

SUNDAY, JAN. 16, 2005

Rod, Before the Fall

You don't have to be an English major to know that the feud between our governor and his father-in-law is the stuff of literature.

"Literature?" snorts a guy to whom I float this thought.

Sure. Think how many Shakespearean and Greek tragedies recount the unraveling of family power alliances.

"This isn't tragedy," he says.

Not yet. No murder. No madness. No downfall. So far.

"More like 'Dynasty,'" he says.

Not a huge difference. Greek tragedy. Schlock "Dynasty." The drama of Dick and Rod. The costumes may be different, but the themes are the same.

From truth to fiction, in old Shakespeare plays and in modern potboilers by authors with names like Nora Danielle Susann, nothing makes better stories than power struggles within families, especially when the tale's enemies were once friends.

We romanticize families as sanctuaries, but we love stories about families as shark tanks, partly because we fear that darker truth.

"The rivalries in family are intense," said David Bevington, a University of Chicago English professor, when I called to ask what literature shows us about power in families.

In literature, he said, "competition is often fatal, and the temptations to commit crimes against members of one's own family prove irresistible. One could turn to King Lear."

Poor Lear. He's the old king in Shakespeare's play who'd hoped to keep the peace by dividing his kingdom among his daughters. But he banishes the virtuous daughter, the one who truly loves him, when she won't flatter him the way he wants. He's left to rely on the two conniving others until, enraged, he stalks onto a stormy heath, where he goes mad.

It gets worse from there.

Then there's Richard III, another Shakespearean leading man. He has one brother murdered, bumps off a couple of princely nephews and gets himself declared king, only to have the kingdom rise up against him.

Or travel back to ancient Greece and Aeschylus' story of Agamemnon.

"Agamemnon is a man," in professor Bevington's summary, "who sacrifices his own daughter to appease the gods and has to face his wife, Clytemnestra, who murders him. The son in that family, Orestes, has the painful obligation to avenge his father's death, which is to kill his mother."

Ouch.

None of those stories would be so painful — or so compelling — if the heroes and villains weren't relatives. These tales warp our sense of safety by battering conventional notions of family trust, loyalty and obligation.

That applies to the saga of Gov. Rod Blagojevich and Ald. Dick Mell. If they weren't family, their falling-out wouldn't be front-page news.

And if the drama of Dick and Rod lacks classical tragic depths, it certainly has the components of a bestseller by Nora Danielle Susann. Imagine her summary:

A young ambitious man (Rod) marries the daughter (Patti) of a wily powerbroker (Dick). The older man grooms the young one in the ways of politics, opening wallets and back rooms to his protege, sharing in the glory of the young man's rise.

But the young man has independent designs on power. He's wily too, 21st-century style. As he ascends, he pulls away. The puppeteer loses hold of the strings.

The old man fumes privately. Until one day, the young man, with moral fanfare, closes down the business of a relative. (In reality, the business is a landfill, but in a Nora Danielle Susann novel, it would be a nightclub.)

The old man takes the closure personally. He strikes back. Publicly. Says the kid is tearing up the family. Accuses him of campaign misbehavior. In steps a woman to investigate, a tough lawyer with her own clout connections.

Meanwhile, through it all, trapped between the men is another woman — wife of one man, daughter of the other.

OK, it's not quite Shakespearean. But the ingredients and the lessons aren't all that different.

Power shifts. So do allegiances. Rivalries play out for years. Everything is to be continued.

Did You Ever Smoke?

One of my favorite parlor games of the past few years is asking: Did you ever smoke?

This is a mother lode of a question, rich with revelations of a person's past, dense with stories of late nights, love affairs, study habits, work habits, parents' habits, body weight, seedy bars and twitchy nerves. It also includes the assumption that you're not insane enough to smoke now.

Obviously, many people still smoke. I know, like and admire some of them. But most of the people I know who once smoked look back on it as a crazy compulsion they were lucky to escape.

"I stopped smoking the day I got married," says one friend, now disgusted by the smell of smoke, "because I was too busy to go get cigarettes."

These stories seem quirkier and quirkier, tragicomic and anachronistic, as more and more people understand the hazards of cigarette smoke and smoking.

Remember when you didn't think twice about sitting all night in a bar or restaurant that smelled like a five-alarm blaze? Remember how you didn't even notice that your clothes stank, and your hair?

And nobody noticed you stank because they reeked too?

And really, were you ever so desperate or deluded that you thought it was dandy to kiss the Marlboro Man after he'd sucked back another pack?

How about ashtrays? Remember ashtrays? Once found in every living room, office and restaurant, often with a whiff of someone else's fumes, they now seem almost as quaint as rotary dial phones.

As for lighters? I'll confess I miss lighters. They made the perfect little gift. Now we're stuck with photo frames and too much fancy soap.

The evolution of our attitudes toward smoking has been one of the lifestyle revolutions of my lifetime, right up there with understanding that drunken driving isn't just a lark and seat belts really do save lives.

When I was growing up, kids were raised to think cigarettes were as natural as bread and butter. "You have the steady hands of a Camel smoker," my father would commend me as I polished two-tone shoes. Years later but still young, he would die of smoking, with steady hands but no voice box.

His death was part of my evolution, but before that happened, I smoked, or pretended to. I was living in France, where you could more easily refuse baguettes than cigarettes. I did not inhale — yes, Bill, I believed you — but I liked the flourish of the cigarette in the air, the pleasure of someone else's match setting it on fire, the little crunch the butt made when it was squashed. The ritual made me feel more French, "French" being shorthand for "sexy and profound." Plus, my accent seemed better when I was blowing smoke.

Like many people, I was lucky that my cigarette flirtation never graduated into addiction. But even people who've had to struggle against tobacco's grip are apt to be nauseated by cigarette smoke once they're not living in it. Once they stop producing smoke, they learn how sickening it really is.

Given how much so many of us have changed, it's all the more startling how many people haven't. People like Mike Ditka.

Ditka argued to the Chicago City Council this week that smoking should remain legal in the city's bars and restaurants. Deprived of the pleasure of smoking while drinking, he said, smokers might not go out to eat at all.

That hasn't been the case in New York. And remember how the airline industry was going to collapse if puffers weren't allowed to pollute the air from ORD to LAX? Smokers, it turns out, are adaptable.

And smokers should remain free to smoke. Just not in the space cohabited by the growing number of people who've grown out of thinking it's OK to breathe pollution.

Until you stop breathing cigarette smoke, you may not fully realize how bad it makes you feel. But once you stop gulping your own or someone else's, there's no going back.

There will come a time when there's no smoking in Chicago's bars and restaurants. And years from now, we'll shake our heads and say, "Remember when you could? Isn't that weird?"

Power Reveals

"Power," said Adam Galinsky when I phoned him Thursday, "doesn't corrupt. Power amplifies. It accentuates. It reveals your truest tendencies."

Everybody's got a theory on the charges against Rod Blagojevich, on why he taunted the feds and fate by, allegedly, cutting unsavory deals even as he was under investigation. I'd like to toss a few of Galinsky's ideas into the mix. Even if they don't fully explain the governor, maybe they'll explain your boss.

Galinsky teaches at Northwestern University's Kellogg School of Management. Along with studying negotiations, organizations and ethics, he studies power, and he believes that power has a couple of important effects.

One is to let a person's true nature emerge. At the same time, it alters a person's neuropsychological processes.

In one experiment, Galinsky designated participants as managers or subordinates and then sent each one to a private room where an annoying fan was blowing. The managers were twice as likely to move the fan or shut it off.

OK, so that may not sound like an experiment that requires Galinsky's Princeton PhD, but it illustrates how power liberates people to be more assertive.

Here's another experiment, not one of his: A researcher gave a group of subjects some cookies. The people who had been told they were "high-power" were much likelier than the "low-power" people to eat messily. They were also likelier to take the last cookie.

Power, said Galinsky, makes a person more optimistic and less inhibited, more prone toward illusions of control and less attuned to the perceptions of others. Unbound by ordinary constraints — the boss doesn't have to ask permission — a powerful person loses certain psychological restraints.

So the big guy is apt to take risks. To think he can get away with things. To lose sight of being watched.

"To be in power means more eyes are focused on you," Galinsky said, "yet people in power psychologically feel invisible."

Someone like that might not think it was bizarre or perilous to try to auction off a U.S. Senate seat.

Galinsky isn't saying that low-ranking people always behave well at work, just that they behave badly for different reasons.

"Low-power people would be more concerned about getting caught, and more aware of the possibility," he says. "Even when high-power and low-power people take the same risky behavior, high-power people do it out of pride, low-power people do it out of fear."

The desire for power, he said, comes in two forms. There's the Plato model, in which you gain power to do good for others. And there's the Machiavelli model, in which you gain power to help yourself.

Powerful people, like the rest of us, work within systems. Systems can encourage or discourage certain aspects of our personality.

The way Galinsky sees it, Blagojevich's natural "narcissism" was perfectly potted in the corrupt soil of Illinois politics. The system didn't entirely make the man, but it allowed him to flourish.

It's a cautionary tale for anyone in charge. When you're in power, you're not as dependent on the ordinary rules or the perceptions of others. Your true self — whether it's selfish or selfless — is revealed. And you may not know how far out of bounds you've gone until, to your surprise, but no one else's, you get caught.

SUNDAY, MAY 31, 1998

Jordan Made Us Talk

In her entertaining new novel, "The Short History of a Prince," the Wisconsin writer Jane Hamilton describes a reunion of an extended suburban Chicago family at the family's longtime summer home.

"It was remarkable," thinks the book's main character, "that the collection of people around the table had very little in common but their phantom forefathers, years of shared summers in one place and their pleasure in Michael Jordan."

It's a fleeting remark in the book, but the kind of perceptive detail that marks a good novel. And it raises the question: After the eventual day Michael Jordan leaves the Chicago Bulls, what will we all talk about? What will we agree on?

Year after year after year, Chicagoans have been unified by the pleasure we take in Michael Jordan. He has been the social glue of fractious families and offices in every pocket of this city. He has been a bridge over troubled waters, spanning gaps in race and politics and lifestyle. He has supplied an uncommonly common point not just of reference but of agreement for people who otherwise don't agree or even speak.

We've come to rely on Michael Jordan, not just as someone to watch, but as someone to discuss. He is our great conversation equalizer. We all have a stake and stock in him, and we like to talk about it.

Pakistani cabbies, Schaumburg soccer moms, Gold Coast socialites, Uptown activists, wizened old women with support stockings rolled at the knees and shirtless frat boys in backward baseball caps. Black and white and other, we can converse like pros on the topic of Michael Jordan.

Particularly this time of year, as the NBA playoffs rev tighter every night, Michael Jordan is our social lubricant, endowing even the conversationally clueless with easy subject matter. He and his team are the oil that can grease any social interaction, from a cocktail party to an "L" ride.

I'm normally too shy to talk to strangers, but when the Bulls are playing, I can strike up a conversation with anybody.

The other night, I walked past a homeless man sitting on the Michigan Avenue sidewalk. From the radio he held to his ear, the bellow of the United Center trickled out in a low buzz. Normally the man might have called, "Spare a dollar, Miss?" Normally I might have looked away. Tonight we were friends and teammates.

"Who's winning?" I asked.

"Pacers are up," he said, "but it ain't over."

We chatted for a while. Could the Bulls pull off another championship? It was debatable, we agreed. But there was always Michael Jordan. Never underestimate Michael Jordan.

We both nodded, residents momentarily of the same happy place in the universe, before he returned to listening to the game, too absorbed in Michael's miracles to ask for the dollar I gave him anyway.

The Bulls, thanks largely to Jordan, have turned even those of us who don't give a bleep about sports into sports fans. People who think Soldier Field is a war memorial, people who know Wrigley only as a chewing gum, people who don't give a puck about hockey can recount the Bulls' last game and Michael's plays in excruciating detail.

Meanwhile, other perfectly interesting, talented city leaders can't excite more than two sentences of conversation between strangers.

Next time you're on a bus or in a cab, try striking up a conversation about, say, Paul Vallas or Forrest Claypool or Terry Hillard. The conversation will be over in the time it takes to accelerate from zero to 30.

That does not reflect poorly on those fine leaders of our town. It simply reminds us of Jordan's unique power to make people connect and converse.

Part of Jordan's appeal as a conversation topic is that while he inspires discussion, he doesn't provoke dispute.

Have you ever heard anyone say, "Jordan? I dunno. The guy's not as good as he's cracked up to be"?

Michael Jordan has become as much a staple of Chicago conversation as the weather. In some ways, he has been our weather, as reliable as the sun, his success the source of a kind but invigorating civic climate in which we all get to bask. Thanks to him, everyone in the Second City gets to feel first-rate.

And when he leaves, whenever that day comes, he'll leave us a little less talkative, and nostalgic for the time we could all agree on something.

FRIDAY, APRIL 6, 2012

Opening Day

If only every day were opening day.

The blank slate. The fresh buzz. Hope as sweet as a baby's burp.

I'm not talking only about baseball, but let's go there first, up to North Clark Street, just before the Cubs game on Thursday.

The blue mob surges north under the chilly sun, past the pulsing bars and purring cars, in a blur of happy shouts and chatter.

Anybody selling tickets?

Programs, score cards! Only a buck!

Please stay on the sidewalk!

Cubs hats, Cubs shirts, Cubs sunglasses and pajama bottoms, the full pledge of allegiance is back on parade. It's a carnival of fans, hucksters, police, hangers-on, and nobody mad, yet.

There's a guy dressed like a goat, wearing a "Reverse the Curse" T-shirt. There's a beggar with a big, hand-scrawled sign — WHY LIE? I NEED COLD BEER — who collects a few dollars before a friendly cop hustles him away.

Anybody got two?

He wanted to come, but he's too fat for the seats.

Will you take our picture?

Please! Stay on the sidewalk!

In the crush, Rich Callow sells peanuts.

"Who needs peanuts?" he calls. "Get your peanuts! Six twenty-five inside! I got 'em for five!"

Callow is a year-round, lifetime Cubs fan. "Big-time," he says. "See this tattoo?"

He shifts his collar off the back of his neck to reveal a bear inside a big C, big-time stamped into his flesh.

But Callow, who's 47, doesn't like dealing with the fans on the street, especially the drunks. So many drunks, and they'll be twice as loud, he promises, after a couple more drinks.

That's why he sells peanuts only on opening day. Ten straight years of opening day peanuts, and there's no day like it.

"It's a new beginning," he says.

Opening day.

All you have to do is say the words and you feel the shutters thrown wide, the room air out, the light pour in.

In baseball, no other day is so pure with possibility. No scores yet, no losses, no blame or disappointment. No hangover, at least until the game's over.

On opening day, the past is not proof of the future.

"Every opening day is special," says Ted Butterman, 77, who with his Chicago Cubs Dixieland Band has performed at every one since April 9, 1982.

The band is there on this Thursday — clarinet, trombone, trumpet, banjo, tuba — dressed in blue, under the red Wrigley Field sign, five white-haired men old enough that they're reluctant to give their ages.

Most of the opening day crowd is too young to name most of their songs. A man, maybe 25, steps up as they finish a spry rendition of "Give My Regards to Broadway."

"Hey," he says. "Were you guys around the last time we went to the World Series?"

It is not clear whether this is a joke.

It doesn't matter. It's opening day. Everything's good, at least before the ninth inning.

We need opening days, not only in baseball, but in the rest of life. They're the days we feel we're starting fresh. It's why we celebrate New Year's Day. It's the theme of Easter. It's the appeal of the first day of school or summer.

Opening day is any day when you can believe that the past doesn't count against you, that the future is yours to make.

But in baseball and the rest of life, as the Cubs proved Thursday, with a losing score of 2-1, the real test is how to find that energetic optimism when opening day is over.

Goodbye, Tribune Tower

If you've ever moved out of a home, you've probably had to remind yourself of some vital truths while you're packing:

You are not the house. The house is not you. You are not your stuff. Your stuff is not you.

No matter how much life occurred in those rooms, no matter what tales those walls could tell, the walls and the floors and the stuff in the drawers are not you. You can leave it all behind without losing yourself.

The same principle applies to a newspaper:

A newspaper is not a building. A building is not a newspaper.

Many of us at the Tribune have been reminding ourselves of that truth as we pack in preparation for Friday's departure from Tribune Tower, a building that exists only because this newspaper does.

Without the Chicago Tribune, there would be no Tribune Tower, but the grand neo-Gothic building, completed in 1925 to house the paper, belongs now to people who plan to turn it into condos.

Already, the Wikipedia entry for Tribune Tower says it "was" the home of the Chicago Tribune.

But my colleagues and I are still here, making peace with the past tense as we clear out our workspaces, shrinking the material stuff of our work lives into plastic orange crates, one per person.

In its way, our shedding is as communal as a barn-raising. While we're also putting out the paper, we dig through drawers, flip through half-remembered folders, excavate shoes from underneath our desks, share our discoveries, seek counsel.

"Anybody want this?"

"Should I keep this?"

"Oh my God, I'd completely forgotten I had this."

To keep or not to keep? Over and over, that's the question.

Packing up a place, especially one you've occupied for a long time, stirs up memories and moods as surely as wind kicks up dust. It can be as true in an office as in a home.

A desk may be small, but like a house, it's a nest. We feather it with papers, photos, cherished objects that mean nothing to anyone else.

That vial of white-out — is it junk or a collectors' item? What to do with the mysterious undeveloped roll of film? The unidentified computer floppy disk?

Will I ever need these notebooks and documents again?

And, by the way, how did I wind up with a middle desk drawer full of nothing more useful than grimy pennies, swarms of paper clips and three half-used tubes of toothpaste?

As I've rooted through my cubicle over the past few days, I've encountered hundreds of letters readers have written me over the years. I've paused to reread a few, grateful to everyone who took the time to write. Well, almost everyone.

Many are kind, encouraging, smart, funny. A smaller but notable number are gleefully insulting, even obscene. I've answered a lot of them, but others have landed in the "good intentions" pile.

What happens to them now?

What happens to the little Tribune news box piggy bank? The exquisitely crafted letter Eudora Welty typed me rejecting my request for an interview? To the poems, many of them sent by readers, that I've tacked to the cubicle walls?

How about the books I'll never read again or never got around to reading but whose presence connects me to the ideas in them?

Every object presents a choice, and every choice is hard. Value is in the heart of the beholder.

One way I've handled our tower departure is by posting photos of my cubicle artifacts on Facebook and telling a short story about each one. A story, I've learned, is good preparation for letting go.

Tell a story about something and it lives on even after it's gone.

Some of my colleagues are also using story therapy.

Louisa Chu, who reports on food, has resolved to write a short chapter about leaving Tribune Tower each night this week. She started Monday.

"Yesterday morning," she said on Tuesday, "I was surprised by the loss I felt, like the morning after you lose someone. I've purged and packed a lot in my lives before here, so I have a few rules: Do I need it? Is it valuable?"

How she answers the questions will guide the story she writes.

Those of us who work for the Tribune — and the thousands who have in the past — have been lucky to work in a building that stood with such symbolic pride in the great city of Chicago.

But a newspaper is not flying buttresses and arches and limestone. It's a living, breathing, changing thing. What matters most is the life and work inside the building.

When we unload our orange packing crates in the new office at Prudential Plaza, we'll keep doing the work we do, exploring and explaining where and how we live, trying to make it better.

We're leaving a building. The newspaper still stands.

June 6.

6 Juin.

The anniversary of the D-Day invasion of Normandy by American soldiers in World War II.

I always register the date because in 1984 my editor at the Orlando Sentinel dispatched me at the last minute to cover the 40th anniversary celebration.

I hustled to Washington, D.C., got a quickie passport, hopped a plane to Paris, went immediately to some French office that was dispensing a special journalists' credential, then rented a car and headed toward the Atlantic Ocean.

Every day for a week I wrote a story, one of them after sitting on the windswept bluff next to Pointe du Hoc as President Ronald Reagan delivered his famous "These are the boys of Pointe du Hoc" speech.

I met old soldiers who, I know looking back, weren't all that old. I came to understand something about World War II that I hadn't before, and, as a result, something about my father, who, like so many soldiers of his day, came home and never talked about it.

chapter 6

travel

A Leap of Faith in Rio

I am terrified of heights, of falling. I get queasy on bridges, balconies, department store escalators. As a child I dreaded nothing more than to be forced onto a swing set or the monkey bars, with the earth a lost paradise miles below my lonely feet.

And that is why not long ago I went hang gliding off a mountain in Rio de Janeiro.

"OK," I told my Brazilian friend Regina as we bounced up a mountain road in the backseat of a blue Volkswagen bug, our hang glider strapped to the hood, our eyes just inches behind the bronzed shoulders of our driver, Pedro. "If I die . . ."

"You're not going to die . . ."

"If I die in my ridiculous yuppie pursuit of conquering my greatest fear . . ."

"You're not . . ."

"If I do, I want you to tell our friends that it was in the arms of a young Brazilian man."

I had found Pedro through a guidebook that had assured me that hang gliding was one of Rio's more tantalizing adventures. It was certain to be less frightening than strutting on the sands of Ipanema in a thong.

"I have two rules," said Pedro once we had disembarked on our forested mountain top, actually a plateau that was part of a former coffee plantation. He was assembling the metal bars and wings that would carry us to our deaths. "The first rule . . ."

I wasn't listening. I was transfixed by the chipped turquoise paint of a wooden plank anchored in the ground at the mountain's edge. I tiptoed closer. Gagged. This was where I would make my death march, out onto these weather-beaten boards that jutted at a 45-degree angle into the void far above the tiny distant blur of Rio.

"Never stop running," Pedro was saying, in his charming Portuguese accent. "That is my first rule."

He explained that once we were strapped to our suicide machine, I would fling an arm around his shoulder and together we would run, run, run down that wooden plank. Our survival depended on my making a leap of logic that said it was indeed better to jump off that plank than it was to do what everything in my life until now had prepared me for, which was to dig in my heels as the edge approached and lurch back screaming, "No!"

"Second rule," said Pedro. "Never touch my bar."

He used the metal bar to navigate, he explained, and navigation apparently is not aided by crazed women clutching for a pacifier.

Then there we were, my arm around his shoulder, his hand on his bar, the wind swirling around our wings, me and Pedro standing at the top of the death plank.

"Are you scared?" said Pedro.

"No," I lied.

"Are you ready?"

"Yes," I lied.

"Run!"

We ran. We ran and ran, legs synchronized across the plank, and then all there was was air.

Later Regina said, "You made the most incredible sound when you hit the air." A sound like a thunderclap. I didn't remember. What I remembered was what felt like my entire life surging through me, every person I had loved, every grief I had known, every moment of consequence, plus some absurdly minor details, condensed and vivid, surging through and out. I was electrocuted.

As we flew, I felt the contours of my body against the sky, felt how much more solid than sky I was, but how much smaller and more fleeting. More than I ever had, I loved my tiny temporary collection of blood and bones and yearnings. I had only one clear thought and it was this: "This is my life in the middle of my life."

And through it all I cried.

I cried as we sailed on in the silent air, above the deep stretches of green forest, down away from the stone obelisks that ring the giant sweating city, out toward the roofs and highways of Rio de Janeiro.

I cried as we drifted on invisible currents toward the long curve of tawny beach, toward the beach's white rim of waves, toward the blue-green Atlantic Ocean that rocked toward Africa.

Poor Pedro. Stuck mid-air with a weeping woman.

"Are you afraid?" he said.

"N-n-o."

"Are you sad?"

"N-not really."

"Are you happy?"

"I don't kn-know."

"Look at the trees," he said. "Aren't they beautiful?"

I cried for a minute more. And, abruptly, stopped. Everything that had ridden through me — not memories, but life, my life relived in real time at breakneck speed — had vanished into the endless sky. I was on the other side of something I couldn't name. No past, no fear, no struggle. An empty vessel. Just a girl, a body, in middle age. Flying.

Like most of life's greatest pleasures, this one passed without my noticing enough of the details. Birds swooped past. From these heights, the trees seemed as densely packed as broccoli and Rio's endless high-rises looked as puny as dandelions. The air was more welcoming than silk.

I could have flown forever if Pedro hadn't said, "We'll be landing soon. Remember, you must land standing up."

Standing up? Was the man a maniac? We'd breezed out over the ocean, but now he cornered the glider hard, we swung around, and we began our kamikaze dive toward the beach.

Just when it occurred to me that panic would be a rational response, our feet were grazing sand. We made a few gentle hops, and then we were standing, still and straight and safe, shielded from the killer noontime sun by our lifeless wings.

We walked up to the sidewalk, to one of the kiosks that line Rio's beaches, and ordered two agua de cocos. The guy in the kiosk whisked a machete through the top of a coconut. We plunged straws inside and sat in the heat sipping the coconuts' cold water.

Maybe this was just the self-indulgence of an American willing to pay $80 for the thrill of being terrified. But whatever the sociology or psychology of the moment, I had never felt so relaxed, so clean, so resurrected.

Flying in the quiet breeze above Rio, I had briefly died. At least I had come as close to dying as you could come without meeting the undertaker. If the whole world went hang gliding every morning, felt the ordinary world from that distance and perspective, there would be no war, no divorce, no graffiti and no lawyers.

That's what I was thinking when Regina, who'd driven down from the mountain, finally sauntered up.

She grinned. "You're alive."

The Night Betty Grable Died

Thirty-two years ago this weekend, Betty Grable died. She was a famous World War II pinup girl, and this story has almost nothing to do with her. Almost.

It's a summer story, a summer story being one that bakes into you a memory that helps define your summers ever after. You probably have one. Will you indulge one of mine?

The summer after my sophomore year in college, I was a waitress at Tuolumne Meadows Lodge in Yosemite National Park. One day, my co-workers Blythe and Phil said, "Let's go on a cross-country hike."

Hiking was new to me, but I had gear. I put on a bikini top and short-short denim cutoffs. I filled my day pack with a bag lunch; a tube of zinc oxide; some moleskin for my blisters; some toenail scissors for the moleskin; and a copy of Ernest Hemingway's "The Sun Also Rises."

Thus equipped, I plunged into the High Sierras.

Cross country meant without a trail, but no problem. I had a road behind me, a mountain in front of me and a man with a topo map by my side.

A couple of hours later, my blisters had swollen to the size of water balloons. So when Blythe and Phil announced they were going up a mountain, I announced that my blisters and I would wait. I ate. I read. My skin burned. I swatted flies and got antsy.

Finally, I ripped my brown lunch sack open, anchored the edges with rocks and with letters I'd cut from moleskin left my comrades a message: WENT HOME.

I set off the way we'd come.

Have you ever been lost? In the wilderness? Alone? It will teach you to pray.

Based on the crusting blood on my socks, I'd guess I'd walked for three hours when I realized I was not headed home. Somehow I'd wound up in a forest, not a mountain in sight, not a creek within earshot, the sun just glimmers beyond the dense treetops.

I walked in circles then. Circles within circles. I began to weep. To scream. To cut deals with God faster than you could cut cards.

Get me out of here and I will never again snap at my mother. I will eat more broccoli. Get me out of here and I will believe.

When I finally found my way into a meadow, the sun was dipping behind the mountains. I looked left. Right. I heard a voice: God? No, Phil. Earlier he'd said: "The Gaylor Lakes are right over that ridge."

I was about to learn that in the mountains "right over" does not mean "right over." But I'd been to the Gaylor Lakes. Find them, and I was saved.

I began to walk toward that ridge. And then to run.

The sun went down. The moon came up. A moon that lit the ground as I climbed and scrambled and panted, rock scraping my hands raw, and my thighs. Stupid cutoffs.

I reached the top of a ridge. But not the ridge. Every time I reached what felt like the top, a previously unseen top loomed higher. A metaphor for life.

The night got colder. I sweated harder.

And then they were there. Way, way down there. From high on some rock, I saw black circles in the moonlit ground. The Gaylor Lakes.

I had my first true ecstatic experience right then. Fear transformed into power, mind released from body, the self became just a spirit in space. I ran. When I fell, I got up and kept running.

It was 1 a.m. when I pounded on the window of the tiny Tioga Pass ranger hut, the only artificial light for miles. Inside, listening to the radio, was a legendarily eccentric park ranger named Ferdinand.

Ferdinand opened his window. Inspected me as if I were just another toll-paying car. He said:

"You must be the one they're looking for."

Then "There's bears out there."

Then "Betty Grable died tonight."

That's why I've never forgotten the night Betty Grable died. It was the night I didn't. The night I learned the ecstasy of being lost and found, almost dead and yanked through to life. The feeling we could wish for from every summer.

SUNDAY, JULY 4, 1999
....

The Need to Get Away

The deepest universal need among us human beings is not for sex or love or food. It's the need to get away.

I hadn't fully realized this until I visited the tiny village of Gambell, Alaska, on St. Lawrence Island, a lonely patch of tundra and gravel beach in the Bering Sea. I arrived, unwittingly, the day before Alaska Day, to find the village, pop. 650, oddly quiet. The central store was closed. So was the sole deli. The place felt as dead as downtown Chicago on the 4th of July.

"Where is everybody?" I asked the young Yupik Eskimo woman who greeted me.

"It's a holiday," she said. "People had to get away."

Get away? From what? And where? The only ready way off the island was on a tiny propeller plane that whirred across 200 miles of choppy sea to Nome. The island's only other village wouldn't be easily accessible until the snow came and the roadless terrain could be conquered by snowmobile. There were no cars.

"Oh, lots of people are at their camps," my hostess said, and by camp she meant tiny settlements without water, lights or the faintest whiff of luxury. "Sometimes life in the village is just too much. People have to get away from the phones and the TV and the stress."

I might not have given a second thought to getaways in Gambell if a couple months later I hadn't gone to Chatham Island, pop. 750, at the opposite end of the globe. It was the week of New Year's and Chatham's wind-blown plains seemed even emptier than usual. I was soon informed that many of the locals had taken advantage of the holiday to — yes — get away.

But once again, I wondered: Get away to where? And why?

New Zealand, to which the island technically belongs, was 600 miles west. As it turned out, many of the island's fishermen and ranchers had retreated to their primitive encampments down by the vast lagoon, blissfully removed from phones, faxes, showers and, as one local explained, the stress of all those sheep.

The lesson in those trips was that from the North Pole to the South Pole, no matter where you live, you sometimes need to leave it. You don't have to go far, but you have to go far enough to escape your routine and your usual responsibilities.

Middle-class Americans take getaways for granted this time of year. The summer vacation or the three-day travel weekend is almost as common as the ice cream cone.

Sometimes a getaway means simply escaping the office. Home can be a getaway for the worker who spends too much of her waking life at work. But trains, planes and automobiles have made it easy for us to travel, and so in weeks like this one the roads and airports are packed with Americans getting away from it all.

Well, not all. In her new book, "Working at Play: A History of Vacations in the United States," historian Cindy Aron says that Americans have always felt torn between their devotion to work and their desire to play.

She writes that vacations as we know them didn't even exist until the middle of this century. A hundred fifty years ago, when the word "vacation" came into vogue, vacations were primarily the privilege of the rich, who escaped to springs and seaside resorts. Not until the 1940s, when paid vacations became a standard benefit for peons as well as bosses, was the average American able to indulge in the real getaway.

Aron notes that we still haven't shaken our Puritan work ethic. Too many of us remain afraid that if we get away from work too long, we won't have work to get back to, and so we pack the laptop with the beach chair.

Still, a getaway's a getaway. It's a change of scene and of routine. When you change what you see and smell and hear, you're bound to change, if only for a while, how you think and feel. Change the patterns of the day and you can't help but change, if just a little, the patterns of your heart and mind.

So when I'm escaping to some island, the islanders are escaping to somewhere else on the island. When Chicago is overrun with tourists fleeing Ohio, Chicagoans are getting away to the dunes of Michigan. One person's home is another person's getaway.

But one thing's the same all over the world, and that's the urge to pack up and go.

Never Travel With Anything You Love

Never travel with anything you love.

This is an important lesson, particularly in vacation season when millions of Americans load their lives into their luggage and embark on trips from which their luggage may never return.

I repeat: Never travel with anything it would break your heart to lose.

You may have heard this handy travel tip before. If you are normal, you have disregarded it. You continue to pack your favorite things, determined to be prepared for every possibility.

Who knows? It's possible you will attend a formal dinner dance at a five-star resort, meet with influential members of your profession at a downtown business lunch, go swimming at a balmy beach, take a hike on a snow-capped mountain and down a few beers at the local juke joint.

You pack for all these possibilities even if your ticket indicates you are merely going to Mom's and Dad's house in Toledo.

What is it about packing that makes so many travelers' imaginations run wild? What makes us imagine that on a 10-day trip we must take six months' worth of underwear and a year's supply of razor blades? That we must have earrings to match every outfit, outfits to match every mood, shoes to match the earrings and books for every whim?

Whatever it is, get over it. Or you could wind up as I have, bereft of half of my belongings, including my three favorite dresses, most of my underwear and all my running socks.

"It'll probably show up on the next flight," said the nice young man at the Skywest Airlines counter the day my suitcase was hijacked somewhere between San Francisco and Ontario, Calif.

He filled out a form and checked the box next to "Delayed Baggage Report."

Delayed. A genteel, hopeful word. A word that hints that your suitcase had a little unexpected business to finish, got caught in traffic, didn't quite make the flight but will catch up with you in time for "Letterman."

Delayed. My suitcase was delayed six days ago. The more appropriate box, it now appears, would have been the one for — they really call it this — "Pilfered Baggage."

There is nothing like losing a suitcase to teach you how much even a small suitcase can hold. What once seemed like the highest virtue of my trusty bag proves to be its tragic flaw: Though it appears barely bigger than a breadbox, it is actually big enough to hold a grand piano.

My piano was virtually the only thing I own that wasn't in it.

Losing your belongings is only half the agony of losing your suitcase. Equally awful is the realization that someone somewhere is sniffing through your life.

A suitcase is as private as your bedroom. Its contents reveal your tastes and habits, good and odd. Strangers are not entitled to know what size anything you wear.

"Did you have tags from any previous trips on your suitcase?" asked the Skywest agent.

Probably.

Suitcases lead adventurous lives, and mine had been on many odysseys. It had journeyed to dozens of states, to Mexico, France, Japan. Once when I went to Seattle, my suitcase went to Hawaii. That time, like so many other times it was "delayed," it managed, like Lassie, to find its way home.

"We've run this through our universal tracking system," said the Skywest agent. "All the major airlines in 60 cities have a description. No one seems to have it."

The agent brightened. "We'll check Ontario, Canada."

I'd like to imagine my suitcase is simply on Canadian holiday. The sad truth is that someone somewhere right now is riffling through a smokey-blue soft-sided vinyl suitcase that contains lavender sprigs from a garden near Tomales Bay, three Size 6 dresses, a letter from some man, a pure boar bristle Kent of London hairbrush, a black sweater, a clock, running shoes, sandals, black suede pumps, an old retainer case containing three pair of earrings and a wilting bridesmaid's bouquet of snapdragons and white orchids.

These are just things, but things once they are lost become more than things. They become memories. They become money. The next time you pack, calculate what it would cost you to replace each item you put in your suitcase. Ask yourself if these things can be replaced. You will be inspired to lighten your load.

My one remaining hope is that the pilferer at least reads that copy of Annie Proulx's novel "The Shipping News." It's right on top of the toiletries bag.

SUNDAY, JUNE 21, 2009

Mama Goes to France

My mother needed to go to Paris before she died. She had never talked of it that way — Paris as a stamp on her passport to the afterlife — but every now and then when one of my siblings and I talked about the years each of us had spent living in France, she would muse, "I'd love to go to Paris someday."

As my mother got older, the idea bubbled up more and more; in other words, as it grew less and less likely that she could physically make the trip. By her mid-70s, she was leaning on a cane for simple jaunts from her front door to the mailbox. I couldn't imagine how she'd make it through the Charles de Gaulle airport.

Still, the notion nagged. Of all the people I knew, no one would soak up the unique beauty of Paris as ecstatically as my mother.

During most of the 32 years of her marriage, my mother hadn't gone far beyond the church and the grocery store. She'd flown on a plane only two or three times. She did, however, remember traveling before she was married, and loved to tell the stories.

There was the time in the late 1930s when she, her mother and sister rode a train across Canada. There was the time, circa 1945, when she and a friend drove her two-door Dodge sedan from Macon, Ga., to Boston, charming men with their Southern accents all the way up the Eastern seaboard. There was the bicycle trip through Quebec, the one she and her college roommate Martha would have taken if Martha's parents hadn't said young women had no business bicycling alone. When I was growing up, my mother told these stories as if to show that she was someone else — not Mrs. Schmich but Mary Ellen, an independent woman, enigmatic, bold — before she was the mother of eight who could barely afford gas for the station wagon.

When my mother was 61, my father died. A loss, a liberation. My siblings and I began to take her traveling.

She flew by herself to see my brother Chris, who was living in Moscow. She flew alone to see my brother Michael, who was living in Hiroshima, Japan. With my other brothers, she toured New Orleans, the coast of Oregon, the Colorado mountains.

I drove her once from Phoenix to Chicago, and once from Chicago to Boston. We saw the Painted Desert, Canyon de Chelly, the marshes of Cape Cod. Except for her inability to speed-read a map and her tendency to do dramatic oral readings of road signs — "Gas, food, lodging 3 miles!" — she was the ideal traveling companion. She greeted every new place with delight and curiosity, talked to everyone, ate anything, slept anywhere.

Time, as it does, passed. She stayed ever ready to pack her bags and explore worlds she had never seen, but by the time she was 77, she was stooped by osteoporosis and hobbled by bad feet, barely able to pick up even a heavy purse.

Paris? In her physical condition, it might as well be the moon. Then I had a thought.

"Mama, how do you feel about a wheelchair?"

At the time, talking to my mother about a wheelchair felt to me like asking about her casket. I had met elderly people who would rather shut themselves inside their homes for good than be seen outside it in a wheelchair. A wheelchair to them was at best a hassle, at worst a humiliation, infantilization, the defeat of the will to walk.

"A wheelchair?" my mother said. "That's a wonderful idea."

And so we went to France.

The wheelchair, as it turned out, was a ticket to the express lane and respect.

At customs, the wheelchair attendant whisked us past the parade of rumpled, yawning fliers. At the taxi stand, we were waved to the head of the line.

At the Musee d'Orsay, the grand railroad station turned museum, we checked out a wheelchair in the cloakroom and were granted access to the paintings before they opened to the mob.

South of Paris, in the Loire Valley, we used one of the wheelchairs supplied by the chateau of Chenonceau and rolled merrily through the long tiled corridors, across the River Cher, out into the gardens of the kings and queens.

"This is how to get the royal treatment," my mother said. "Get a wheelchair."

We couldn't get and didn't want a wheelchair everywhere. In the streets of Paris, as long as she could lean on a cane or someone's arm, my mother could walk a few blocks. In truth, she walked farther than she did at home. Beauty is therapy.

One day we drove north to Mont St. Michel, the Gothic abbey that rises like a dream on a cone of rock in the middle of a bay. I told my mother I was going to hike the 900 or so steps to the top while she sat in a cafe. I was sorry she couldn't come, but there were no elevators, no cars, no wheelchairs.

"Maybe I'll walk just a little ways," she said.

Slowly, we climbed the first few stairs. She held my arm with one hand, the stone banister of the ramparts with the other. We stopped to rest, the bay glittering below.

"Just a few more," she said. Another stair, then two, four, 10. She had to sit down.

And then — I still don't know how this happened — she decided to crawl. And somehow, a few hundred steps later, she was at the top.

If I were a certain kind of person, I would call what happened that day a miracle, that a white-haired woman, stooped by time and tired bones, made it, on her feet and hands and knees, to the top of one of the wonders of the world.

My mother's 86 now. A few months ago someone knocked her down and broke her hip. She uses a wheelchair in the grocery store and a walker just to get from the bathroom to the bed. One of my brothers had been promising for several years to take her to Scotland, her ancestral home, but all the miracles and wheelchairs in the world won't make that happen.

There comes a time in most lives when travel truly is impossible. But that time may not be as soon as you imagine. If you can, give your parents the gift of travel. It will be a gift to yourself.

Mesdemoiselles de la 'Cuisine'

My old friend Diana was in town recently for a reunion at Lake Forest High School and just before she stopped by to visit, I rummaged through a drawer and pulled out an ancient typewritten letter addressed to the two of us. It began:

> *Mesdemoiselles,*
>
> *Thank you for your letter received this morning, concerning the trip we propose onboard my 40 foot sailing yacht "BOUCANIER" from La Rochelle (or Bordeaux) to the Mediterranean.*

The letter requested that we meet at the Cafe de la Paix in Paris to discuss the trip. It was signed by a Commandant Jacques Dore.

Diana Goulding and I met on a semester abroad in France and as the program ended, eager to stay on, we answered a small ad we'd found on a Parisian bulletin board asking for American female cooks for a yacht cruise.

We knew nothing about this Commandant Dore or his two "mates," described in the letter as a jet pilot and the general manager of a prestigious Paris hotel, but we went to the cafe on the appointed evening. We smiled. They smiled. We got the job.

Diana was 19. I was 20. We were innocents.

Soon — this was long before tourist barges crowded the Canal du Midi — we were bobbing over the Atlantic Ocean toward the 17th-century canals that run through the French countryside out to the Mediterranean. We'd barely made it to the first canal lock when it became clear that our employers expected more than cooks.

Diana and I — plus our friend Pam, who'd come along — were astonished. So were the three middle-aged men: Had we really thought cooks meant cooks?

To make matters worse, they really did expect us to cook, which we'd assured them we could. In truth, we knew nothing, though just before departure I'd bought a pocket paperback called "La Cuisine Francaise."

Within a few days, our mismatched crew had a routine. Diana, Pam and I helped navigate through the locks, pausing while the wrinkled peasants who lived on the canal banks slaughtered our daily chicken, picked our vegetables and brought us local wines.

Our employers taught us to make coq au vin and a good vinaigrette, then, in the warm evenings, with food and wine and cigarettes, we explained why we could not concede to their sexual wishes.

The jet pilot, Pierre, got off in Toulouse, muttering. "Not the vacation I planned."

The rest of us cruised on, however, in a tense truce that grew into a kind of friendship.

The Commandant, a jowly man in his 50s, made light of his miscast cooks by writing out a daily "ordres de service." I still have the paper. It begins with reveil, petit dejeuner and travaux maritimes, directions we followed.

It concludes with the services we refused: education sexuelle (theorie) and education sexuelle (pratique).

Things could have gone terribly wrong for Diana, Pam and me on that journey. But they didn't, and when we reached the Mediterranean and chastely told our employers goodbye, the Frenchmen cried.

"Oh my God!" Diana screamed when I showed her the letter the other night. "Can you believe we did that?"

Hardly. And that's the beauty of it. We were too young to be afraid, naive enough to take a risk that would become one of our great steps toward adulthood.

Diana and I live far apart now and rarely see each other, but that trip bonded us for life. It also taught us the difference between an adventure and a vacation.

A true adventure is an event that makes you think afterward, "I can't believe I did that."

WHITE HOUSE

POOL

Name
Affiliation
Date

THE TRIP OF
THE PRESIDENT
TO
**Corpus Christi, Texas
Beeville, Texas
Houston, Texas &
Montgomery, Alabama**

**December 27, 1989-
January 1, 1990**

MARY SCHMICH
NAME
CHICAGO TRIBUNE
AFFILIATE

PRESS

WHITE HOUSE

0999

Mary Schmich
Name
Affiliation: Chicago Trib.
Date

POOL

Credentials. They're the souvenirs of a reporter's life. I hate wearing them. I like saving them, though until I started clearing out my cubicle I hadn't looked at mine in ages.

A couple of presidential inaugurations, the L.A. Olympics, a papal tour, the NASA space center after the Challenger explosion, some political conventions, a ride on Air Force One to Texas with the first President Bush.

They remind me of the excitement and exhaustion of those assignments, which usually involved bad food, too little sleep, logistical calisthenics and brutal deadlines. I loved 'em all.

chapter 7

the world we live in

The Discipline of Optimism

We're going to miss Barack Obama's voice.

"We" isn't everybody, I know, but it's the millions of us who have really liked listening to that guy talk for the past eight years.

What we'll miss is not just the melody of his voice but his words, words that even in the worst of times helped us believe that with work, generosity, humility and courage we could make this country better for people of all kinds.

On Tuesday, he's coming home to Chicago to give the last speech of his presidential life. One more time we'll hear that eloquent voice speaking to us, and one more time, if the past is a prediction, he will summon us to what I think of as the discipline of optimism.

The discipline of optimism.

Obama rose to power preaching the audacity of hope but in the past few years, it's this other phrase — the discipline of optimism — that comes to my mind whenever he speaks.

Twenty children and six adults shot to death at Sandy Hook Elementary School. Nine black parishioners gunned down by an angry white man in a Charleston, S.C., church. Five police officers shot and killed by a black man in Dallas. Forty-nine people dead in a gay club in Orlando, shot by a man who claimed allegiance to Islamic terrorists.

After each new atrocity, Obama was summoned to find the right words, and every time, in addition to his anger and his calls for justice, he summoned us to optimism.

Optimism isn't quite the same as hope, no matter what the thesaurus says. To my ear, hope is a fluffier thing, that pretty flower that springs spontaneously from the dirt, no gardening skills required.

Optimism, on the other hand, is hard. It can take work. It demands focus in the face of contradiction. It's a habit of mind, and like all habits it can be difficult to cultivate, easy to lose.

Optimism is tested every day by reality. Bad news flies at us from every direction, like bullets, a constant spray of anger, violence, hatred, loss, fear and insult.

That's where the discipline comes in.

The discipline of optimism asks you to believe that — with focused effort — things can get better, even when times are bleak. It asks you to look up and forward when you're tempted to look down and back.

At the 2015 funeral for the slain pastor in Charleston, Obama spoke of the event as a moment of grace. Maybe, he suggested, it could help the country mend its racial divisions.

It was a chance, he said, "to find our best selves."

At the 2012 prayer vigil for the victims shot at Sandy Hook, he called for us to "find the strength to carry on and make our country worthy of their memory."

In Orlando, after the nightclub shooting, he said, "You can't make up the world into 'us' and 'them' and denigrate and express hatred towards groups because of the color of their skin, or their faith, or their sexual orientation, and not feed something very dangerous in this world. So if there was ever a moment for all of us to reflect and reaffirm our most basic beliefs that everybody counts and everybody has dignity, now is the time."

The discipline of optimism doesn't ask us to believe that everything is OK. Everything is not OK. Obama's optimism often comes with a blast of righteous anger. He sees injustice and names it.

But still he calls on us to be our best selves, even when others don't follow the call.

The way our leaders talk to us infuses how we talk to ourselves and to other people, how we think and act. Obama did his best to help us see what is good and how what is wrong can be made better.

"We do a disservice to the cause of justice by intimating that bias and discrimination are immutable, or that racial division is inherent to America," he said at the 50th anniversary of the civil rights march in Selma, Ala.

"If you think nothing's changed in the past 50 years, ask somebody who lived through the Selma or Chicago or LA of the '50s. Ask the female CEO who once might have been assigned to the secretarial pool if nothing's changed. Ask your gay friend if it's easier to be out and proud in America now than it was 30 years ago. To deny this progress — our progress — would be to rob us of our own agency; our responsibility to do what we can to make America better."

This optimism is one of Obama's great parting gifts to us. It's up to us to find constructive ways to use it.

FRIDAY, MAY 11, 2012

The Gay Marriage Evolution

The first gay person I ever met was surely not the first gay person I ever met.

But until the day one of my best college friends told me he was gay, I wasn't aware of knowing any gay people. This was in the early 1980s, when "coming out" was a term still typically associated with debutantes.

A few weeks before David made his revelation, we had met for dinner in San Francisco, and afterward he suggested we take a walk. Our stroll took us to the noisy bars on Castro Street, and David suggested we stop for a drink.

I had never seen so many men unbuffered by women, or seen men enthralled with each other. I had never felt so different from everyone around me.

I don't remember exactly what I said, just that my remarks were slightly defensive and slightly derisive and that David didn't reply.

I later suspected that David was trying to sense my attitude toward homosexuality. The truth is, I didn't have a clear attitude, beyond some vague uneasiness I'd inherited from the general culture. I didn't need to have an attitude. As hard as it is to believe now — in the age of "Modern Family" and Rachel Maddow — there was no wide public discussion of gay people, much less of gay marriage.

And I didn't know any gay people. Until David let me know I did. He was the beginning of my evolution.

When President Barack Obama came out in favor of same-sex marriage this week, he referred to his evolution on the subject. Politics being the cynicism factory that it is, the doubters howled.

Evolution? Right. Better to call it a flip-flop. Or a flip-flop-flip, since he supported gay marriage before he renounced it in the service of his political ambition.

Evolution, though, is a plausible word.

Evolution implies progress, slow progress. One dictionary defines it as "a gradual process in which something changes into a different and usually more complex or better form."

When Obama talked Wednesday about his evolving thoughts on gay marriage, he focused on his relationships with gay people — neighbors, staff members, soldiers, the same-sex parents of his daughters' friends.

For him, as for so many straight people, it's those ordinary relationships that have added up, one by one, to a conviction: Gay people deserve an equal right to marry under the law.

Most revolutions are actually evolutions, shifts that gather force day by day, person by person, thought by thought, until they burst into broad view and are labeled change.

In the case of same-sex marriage, the change is not just in what Americans have come to believe, it's not only in what we feel free to say — it's in what many of us feel obligated to say.

Obama would have waited longer to exercise his obligation if Vice President Joe Biden hadn't done it first, in a Sunday TV interview, but part of Obama's evolution, even if it was spurred by politics, is knowing that it was time. Time not just to think the right thing, but to say it.

The number of Americans who favor legalizing same-sex marriage rises. Polling shows supporters now outnumber those opposed. The support is stronger among the young.

Support will never be unanimous, but even more people will eventually acknowledge that allowing gay people to marry is the American way. The change won't come primarily through argument. It will come through a more persuasive power — relationships — and it will one day be fortified by law.

Viva la evolucion.

Is There a Heaven?

A few days ago a friend who's very sick asked, "Do you think there's a heaven?"

She was lying on her couch. I was sitting beside her. We were holding hands.

I said, "No."

It's the blunt answer I would have given if we'd been sipping wine at dinner and discussing the Meaning of Life, the kind of philosophical conversation she and I have had over and over for years. We've called them our MOL discussions and figured we'd be having them for a long time to come.

But all of a sudden her time is running short and in the same instant that I said no, I registered that this wasn't just another ruminative, self-entertaining MOL talk. Her question was urgent, and my answer felt wrong.

But what was the right answer? The right way to answer?

After former first lady Barbara Bush's recent death — coincidentally three days after my friend asked me this question — her husband, George, the former president, issued a statement saying, "We have faith that she is in heaven."

Her son, George W., echoed his father's faith.

"She truly believes that there's an afterlife," he said, "that she'll be wonderfully received in the arms of a loving God and therefore did not fear death."

It's a comforting belief. My mother had it. At least I think she did, though in the final weeks of her life, she seemed to be seeking enlightenment beyond her familiar religion.

One night toward the end, when I was lying next to her as she drifted off to sleep, she mumbled, "Honey, can you explain Buddhism to me?"

I assured her, regretfully, that I was not qualified.

Is there a heaven?

Stephen Hawking, the legendary physicist who recently died, called it a fairy tale, and he was a genius. All I know is that I'm not convinced there is, and it would have violated the spirit of my relationship with my friend to start lying to her now just to comfort her.

But I did want to comfort her, so as soon as I'd said no, and heard how bleak it sounded, I said something else I think is true:

We don't know what this life is, so how can we know what comes after it?

Think of every flabbergasting thing we've seen and learned in our relatively short lifetimes. Who could have imagined that one day people would speak into a tiny, untethered machine called a cellphone and have their voice transmitted across the planet? Or type into that same tiny machine and send written words across the ether? Or consult a thing called Google and learn, in the time it takes to type "heaven," how every religion in the world defines that word?

Think of our constant discoveries about bodies and minds and the universe, discoveries that reveal our vast ignorance of almost everything.

Maybe, I suggested, the best we can hope for is the consolation of mystery.

"That's a good way to think of it," she said, and closed her eyes.

I've been with several people toward the end of their lives and every one of them talked about what came afterward. A couple seemed certain there was some happy new place. A couple of others, like my brother, saw only doubt on the horizon.

We, the living, hope that the people we love die without fear, but no matter how peaceful they seem, how can we know?

A couple of days after our discussion of heaven, my friend, lying in bed, asked a different version of the question. We'd been talking about many other things — work, love, family, memories, that trip we took to Paris right after she got married — but it circled back to this:

"What do you think happens to us after we die?"

I still didn't have a good answer, the answer I wanted to offer as pain reliever. But I told her what I could honestly say, that as the people I love vanish from my physical universe, I'm drawn, in defiance of my beliefs, to the images conjured in songs and stories of the dead who have gone not to heaven, but to that otherworldly place called "home," who have crossed a mythical river to some mythical "other side" where their loved ones are waiting with a welcome banner.

I managed to muster the wisest words I know on the subject, the lyrics to a song by Iris DeMent:

> *Everybody's wonderin' what and where they all came from*
> *Everybody's worryin' 'bout where they're gonna go*
> *When the whole thing's done*
> *But no one knows for certain*

And so it's all the same to me
I think I'll just let the mystery be

"Let the mystery be," she said.

And then, unable to turn my back on her, I backed out of her bedroom, both of us knowing that, absent a miracle, we had just had our last discussion of the Meaning of Life.

Just Because She Didn't Report It

I was ashamed, confused, afraid.
I knew no one would believe me.
I knew no one would help me.
I knew I'd lose my friends.
I didn't know what to say.
I didn't know who to tell.
It would have ruined my reputation.
It would have hurt his family.
I thought it was my fault.
I thought I was tough enough to deal with it alone.
He was my pastor.
He was my stepfather.
He was my boss/my teacher/my brother/my co-worker/a cop/my dad's
    best friend.
He was my husband.
He said he'd kill me.

Anyone who has been reading the flood of recent tweets under the #WhyIDidntReport hashtag on Twitter has read some version of all of the above. The testimonials are depressingly similar, despite the differences in details.

A man assaults a woman, or in some cases a man. The person who was assaulted tries to move on. Moving on means keeping quiet, hoping to be spared the added trauma of suspicion, mockery, humiliation.

For many years, according to Christine Blasey Ford, moving on meant telling no one about the night in the 1980s, when, she says, a 17-year-old boy named Brett Kavanaugh, now a nominee for the U.S. Supreme Court, assaulted her at a party.

Blasey, who was 15 at the time, recently told the Washington Post that she didn't report the attack because she feared her parents would punish her if they knew she'd been at a party where teenagers were drinking.

I remember those parties. I remember the fear that my parents would find out I was there. Do not underestimate fear of parents as a reason for a teenager not to reveal an assault.

But Blasey's explanation of why she didn't report her allegation back then hasn't satisfied many people, most notably the president of the United States, whose tweet on Friday morning triggered the Twitter backlash.

"I have no doubt that, if the attack on Dr. Ford was as bad as she says," he tweeted, "charges would have been immediately filed with local Law Enforcement Authorities by either her or her loving parents."

I have a lot of doubt that Dr. Blasey, as she prefers to be called, would have done any such thing.

When a woman — or a man — alleges sexual assault, it's only fair that certain questions be asked, certain information solicited. If the allegation comes a long time after the assault, it's fair to ask why it wasn't reported sooner. In this case, it's fair to ask Blasey to say more about her claim and fair to ask Kavanaugh what he remembers.

What's not fair — what's ugly, demeaning, downright abusive — is to assume that because an assault went unreported it didn't happen.

Sexual assaults are hard to count. According to the Rape, Abuse & Incest National Network (RAINN), a nonprofit organization that deals with sexual assault, only 310 of every 1,000 rapes are reported to police. Of those reported, only 57 lead to an arrest. Only six perpetrators end up incarcerated.

Those figures suggest another reason a woman may be reluctant to file a legal report: The perpetrator is likely to go unpunished, so why endure the ordeal of coming forward?

But whether or not she tells anyone, a woman who has been sexually assaulted may carry the memory around for years like a stone in her heart.

The boy who raped her at a party. The relative who repeatedly molested her when she was 9. The neighbor who exposed himself to her when she was just a girl. The stranger who broke into her house and raped her at knifepoint. The boss at her college job, a man twice her weight and age, who pinned her on the floor and groped her for a long time while she struggled.

All those situations I just listed? They've happened to women I know, all except the last one, which happened to me.

The day after it happened, I told my college roommate but no one else. I was embarrassed. I felt sick. I was a good girl and felt bad I'd gotten myself into the mess. What if my parents found out? And, honestly, I wasn't sure how to name what happened.

One of the most moving entries under the #WhyIDidntReport hashtag on Friday was one that said: "No one ever taught me what sexual assault was so when it happened to me I didn't even know."

Too often assault is dismissed as horseplay, rough-housing, boys being boys. You can't report what you can't properly name.

In the next few days, we may hear more facts on what happened on the long-ago night Blasey has described. But we don't need more facts on that situation to be clear on this fact: The failure to report an assault doesn't mean it didn't occur.

According to RAINN, the number of sexual assaults has fallen by more than half since 1993. Given the murkiness of sexual assault statistics, it's hard to know exactly what that signifies, but it feels like progress. It's progress that comes because women and men continue to tell their stories and people continue to listen, hoping to understand.

And to those who testily ask: Will we ever stop talking about sexual assault and harassment?

Don't worry. We will.

As soon as it stops happening.

SUNDAY, DEC. 2, 2001

George Girls

Nobody was a George girl, at least no girl I knew. You were a Paul girl. Or a John girl. Or, if only because you liked his name and wanted to stand out in the screaming crowd, maybe you were among the two or three Ringo girls on the planet.

But George Harrison didn't stir the teenybopper heart to manic highs and desperate lows back in the Beatles' heyday. For the necessary teenybopper fix of unrequited yearning, a girl needed the more ebullient boys in the band.

Oh, that Paul. He was so darn cute and cuddly. When that mop top flopped, a girl's goose bumps did the twist-'n'-shout.

And John. Moody, manly, engaging John. His whiff of danger was as seductive as patchouli oil.

And Ringo. What a lovable goof.

But George?

The news stories about George's death Thursday called him "the quiet Beatle." Maybe that appealed to a few dozen mature girls in some hidden corner of the globe, but to the teenyboppers and pre-boppers I knew, quiet just meant boring.

Certainly to me — a Paul girl, I'm sorry to say — George seemed wooden and remote. Where Paul was light and airy, George was dark and dense. While Paul's bubbly persona teased the girls with a "Come on, come on," George exuded a silent "Let me be." Even his smiles often seemed forced.

It's not surprising that in death, as well, George didn't make a splash, except to the extent that the death of any Beatle lands like a cannonball in the pop culture pond. There was no high tragedy or distinction to mark his transport from this world. He would be outlived by Paul and Ringo. He'd be eternally upstaged by John, whose 1980 murder by a crazy fan keeps him forever fascinating.

George died, quite ordinarily, of cancer. He wasn't sufficiently old to die, but not heartbreakingly young either. He was just a man in late middle age stolen by the same common criminal that takes millions of people whose names you've never heard.

And yet, even to many of us who were never George girls, his death matters some.

A band is a symbol of its generation. When the bands that defined your youth break up, you realize, maybe for the first time, that you're getting old. When the band members start to die — not of anything as theatrical and premature as suicide or drugs but of the common afflictions that eventually hijack us all — you realize you weren't old when they broke up; but you are ancient now.

Or, in the case of George, you realize that you've grown up.

When I heard that George had died, I realized that over the years, probably like many other former teenyboppers, I'd become a bit of a George girl without noticing. His songs, which in their infancy were the ones that caused me to stomp over to the record player and lift the needle to the next groove, grew over time to seem intriguing, complex, appealingly melancholy in ways that a 13-year-old rarely understands.

"Something," "While My Guitar Gently Weeps" — these weren't the easy singalongs that made the Beatles famous, but when I hear them now I ride some deeper tide than I do with "She Loves You" or even a song like the ultimately sweet "Yesterday."

A teenybopper wasn't likely to recognize it at the time, but Harrison's sitar helped "Norwegian Wood" feel somehow more adult, more potent, edgier than many Beatles songs of that time, despite the fact that his sitar guru, Ravi Shankar, thought his playing on that recording stank.

Looking back on George's life, it's easy to see that he was in some ways the most free-thinking Beatle. He was a seeker who explored Eastern music and mysticism. He introduced the band to transcendental meditation. All these years later, Western culture has followed him down that path. The benefit concert he organized for Bangladesh was the precursor for a generation of celebrity fundraisers.

On Friday when I heard that George had died, I pulled out a battered Beatles songbook and plunked out "Here Comes the Sun." It's my favorite Chicago winter song, and it never would have existed if he'd never lived.

So he's gone, but the songs remain, and anyone who sings them is a George girl after all.

FRIDAY, MAY 9, 1997

The Days of Driving Drunk

Oh, to be young and having fun, to be young and foolish, to be young and driving drunk.

I remember the days. And it's a miracle I'm here to recall them.

How many of us recollect with shame and horror the too many times we climbed behind a steering wheel and cruised into the night on an overdose of alcohol and luck?

What a thrill it sometimes was — shooting over a dark road with the windows rolled down, the music cranked up, someone's warm hand on your knee, the world wide and wild and entirely negotiable for as long as the ride and the buzz lasted.

Nothing like a car and one drink too many to make you feel as infinite as the universe, as invulnerable as God. Nothing like a car and one drink too many to make you stupider than a pit bull, and just as dangerous.

"I'm amazed I didn't kill myself," half the people I know now mutter, recalling their drinking-and-driving days. "I'm amazed I didn't kill somebody else."

Nobody I knew talked blood-alcohol levels in those days. Driving in a haze of drink was a cross between a romance and a right.

Besides, we weren't sloppy drunks, slurring drunks. According to the laughably liberal law, we may not even have been drunk. Drunks were cartoons and jokes and sad sacks. Drunk was Red Skelton staggering through a comedy routine. We, on the other hand, were just having fun.

And how else were we going to get home after the party?

But the world changed, and a lot of us changed with it.

Age worked part of the conversion. Somewhere between say, 25 and 40, the body that could drink until 2 a.m. upped its closing time to 9. The metabolism that could process three drinks, four drinks, five, took to sputtering to a halt at two.

But it was more than just age that persuaded some of us to avoid the car when we'd been drinking. It was the public campaign against drunken driving.

Don't drink and drive.

Friends don't let friends drive drunk.

These slogans became refrains that anyone who stepped into a car after a few drinks couldn't help but hear. And honest drinkers knew they became unfit to drive well before they'd reached the legal limit.

Now the campaign has gone even further, aided by the bite of law.

In North Carolina, a jury just sentenced a man to life in prison without parole for killing two college students while driving drunk.

Illinois, meanwhile, is just a governor's signature away from a law to reduce the blood-alcohol level that constitutes driving under the influence. The law's opponents have fought a long, hard fight, arguing that it would hamper social drinking.

Hamper social drinking? Probably. It will also hamper drunken driving.

Fifteen years ago, I visited a friend in Sweden. Birgitta was blond, personable and the hardest drinker I have ever met. I can still see her in a routine pose — raising a tiny glass of vodka to her lips, nodding slightly and saying, "Skol!" I can see her doing this at breakfast.

My first night there we went to a disco. Birgitta ordered mineral water. I gaped in dismay.

This wasn't like the United States, she explained. Drink and drive in this town, even once and even just a little, and you could spend some serious time in jail. The threat of legal punishment sobered her right up, at least when she was on the road.

A few years later, I decided I'd no longer drive if I'd had more than one drink. By that time, I rarely drove after more than two, but I knew that even two was an invitation to an accident.

Now I bum rides, pay for cabs, don't go to the party or go and hardly drink. I still curse the inconvenience of the resolve every time I obey it. But it's like buckling your seat belt. Once it becomes a habit, operating any other way seems like the path to suicide.

Yes, refusing to drive under the influence hampers your social drinking. But driving is a social activity, too, one that carries obligation. Someday we'll look back — not just as individuals, but as a society — and shudder at how readily we tolerated drunken driving.

Tougher laws will make it likelier we'll survive the road. Better that than the old-fashioned routine of relying on raw luck.

SUNDAY, OCT. 26, 2003

Rape Is Not Amusing

Rape is so totally, like, trendy, you know?

You can hardly turn on the TV in prime time anymore without being assaulted by a supposedly entertaining story of another woman violated.

Here, for example, is the official episode synopsis for this season's premiere of "Law & Order": The discovery of the body of a raped and mutilated teenaged girl in an alley sends Detectives Briscoe and Green tracing the victim's last hours in the hope of finding a suspect.

Here's the official synopsis for last week's "Law & Order: SVU": When a young woman is found brutally murdered after a violent sexual assault, Detectives Benson and Stabler rest their hopes on the only witness to the crime, the woman's young son.

How about this one for last week's "Las Vegas": Inundated with sci-fi geeks and girls in bikinis hoping to enjoy the last few weeks of summer,

Danny and Ed hunt for a sexual predator preying upon unsuspecting women.

And here's another one: One suspect, eight attacks!

OK, so that last one was really a local newscast's recent teaser for the story of a real-live rapist stalking Chicago, but it was delivered in the same professionally gasping tone used for prime-time drama ads. All that was missing was the catchy theme song.

Without a doubt it's significant news that since August eight women on Chicago's North Side have been raped or otherwise assaulted by, it seems, the same twentyish, shortish, dark-haired creep.

I live just a few blocks from a couple of the attacks and I'm glad to be alerted by the media, glad in ways that have nothing to do with voyeurism and everything to do with self-protection, concern for the women assaulted and anger on behalf of all the women left walking their neighborhoods in fear.

And yet whenever real rapes make big headlines, I can't help but notice how much we rely on rape as amusement. And, though we tell ourselves we know the difference between fact and fiction, relying on rape as amusement is bound to warp how real rapes are perceived and portrayed.

It's hardly new and not necessarily perverse to be fascinated by rape. It's natural to wonder why some men are driven to abuse women through this most intimate of intrusions. It's reasonable to be interested in how women individually and collectively, physically and psychologically, combat the enduring threat of sexual violence. You could even argue that prime-time rape entertainment has shed light on all those things.

But for every bit that TV crime dramas have illuminated and destigmatized rape, they've also glamorized it. Sexual assault on TV comes packaged with snappy dialogue, hip clothes, sexy stars, rock 'n' roll. Like Quentin Tarantino-style violence, TV rape almost always comes across as kinda cool. And that's kinda sick.

How quickly rape has gone from being taboo to being trendily explicit. TV watchers are now routinely treated not only to grisly scenes of violated women — on beds, in alleys, in Dumpsters — but to white-smocked lab techs talking breezily about swabbing sperm from one or another of the assaulted woman's cavities.

I cringe at the crudity of the previous sentence. But that's the lingo of TV rape and the tone encouraged by TV and popular fiction — clipped, detached, explicit, pseudo-clinical, the raped woman reduced to plot twist.

If sexual assault were eliminated as a prime-time TV plot device, a lot of TV writers would be out of work. Writers have lost the knack for — or can no longer get paid for — exploring mysteries of human behavior that don't involve sexual aggression.

More and more, in books as well as on TV, suspense depends on violent sex. Whodunit now means who done the rape. "Women in peril" has long been a Hollywood staple. Some TV type once told me that we may as well face it — women in sexual jeopardy are simply more interesting than men in any kind of jeopardy.

That's no excuse for our increasingly casual use of rape as entertainment. Rape is real. It's not a show. It's not amusement. It's an outrage.

FRIDAY, DEC. 5, 2003

Going to Ground Zero

On Monday I went to see Ground Zero. The December day was brisk and sunny, the air alert in that way unique to New York City. I walked from Greenwich Village down Hudson Street, past people with coffee cups, newspapers and dogs, past swarms of shouting schoolkids, on past the shops and lofts of Tribeca, toward the bustling suits and briefcases of the financial district.

After a while, I spotted a chain-link fence, a couple of bulldozers, a detour sign and a big hole in the relentless pavement. Was that it? The battle ground, the burial ground? My heart thumped.

It wasn't. I squinted at my map and kept on walking. Funny how the mere suggestion that I was witnessing Ground Zero could stir the imagination and the blood.

Even two years later, there's a lot in New York City to incite remembering and imagining. If you haven't been there since that famous Sept. 11, you might be startled by how startling it is just to see the skyline.

The night I arrived, the city from a distance was its usual thrilling cluster of lights against the dark sky, and yet it all looked different. It was like seeing a friend who'd survived a trauma since you last saw her, a trauma you hadn't fully understood because you weren't there. Now here she was, looking vulnerable and bruised, proud and strong, familiar but changed.

"Remind me," I said to the taxi driver as we crossed the bridge into Manhattan. "Where was the World Trade Center?"

He pointed left, and I saw the twin towers shimmer into view, then crumble and vanish. Suddenly that hole in the sky was as visible as a hole in the ground.

Before I left Chicago, I hadn't thought about whether I'd make the pilgrimage to Ground Zero. Once in New York, I realized how odd it would be not to.

"Are you going to go see Ground Zero?" New York friends asked, hinting it was important that I did. Talk of Ground Zero filled the radio and newspapers every day. The subway station at the site — a soaring new monument of white metal — had just reopened. And once I found it, there was no mistaking that vast pit where two of the world's tallest buildings once stood.

It's always strange to see in real life what you've seen on TV. You know the place, and yet you don't have a clue. So while throngs of New Yorkers hustled by without a glance, to-ing and fro-ing from the busy shops and offices nearby, I joined other map-clutching tourists and stood there gawking.

Peering into the pit, occupied by construction workers and machines, I tried to envision what had happened, what had vanished, what's to come. I sniffed in search of the notorious smell that gagged the neighborhood for months. It was gone.

So were most of the scrawled tributes to the dead. Here and there, fresh bouquets were tucked into the viewing fence, but signs warn that anything placed there will be taken down pronto. A remarkable job had been done of cleaning up.

Recently a New York friend asked how much Chicagoans think deeply about Sept. 11. He seemed surprised when I guessed, "Not much." Only in seeing Ground Zero did I understand how alive that day remains for many New Yorkers. It's not that they obsess about it. It's more as if that day's events, which have become peripheral for so many Americans, have become a piece of their routine, as half-noticed but as basic to their lives as breath.

As a glimpse of history and resurrection in process, Ground Zero is a good place to visit. And as one New Yorker told me, it's good to go now.

"Can you imagine what it'll be like when it's rebuilt?" He rolled his eyes. "It'll be the biggest tourist attraction in town, and they'll be hawking every tacky souvenir you can imagine."

Which will make it just that much more American.

The Curse of Options

Give me limits, please.

Give me boundaries, no-entry signs, expiration dates. Tell me the offer is good only while supplies last. No rainchecks, please, no infinite possibilities. Don't talk to me of endless options. Tell me the end's the end. Promise me that's all there is, folks.

Do not, do not, do not tell me I can have a baby at the age of 63.

Wait. I don't mean that.

Wait. Yes, I do.

Possibility is confusing, isn't it?

Last week, possibility suddenly swaggered in front of women like an unexpected suitor — irritating and irresistible, exhilarating and exhausting, tantalizing and terrifying. To women who thought they'd seen the stop sign just up the road or in the rear-view mirror, this Don Juan whispered, "Hey, hon, how about that 63-year-old California gal? You know, the oldest woman in the world ever to give birth? How about it, babe? Wanna take that ride?"

Funny, but Don Juan's voice sounds a lot like the devil's.

If this woman's postmenopausal foray into motherhood had been Mother Nature's whimsy, it would be a different, safer story. If it had been a once-in-a-millennium event, it would have been an aberration, not an option.

But her pregnancy was no freak of nature, it was a feat of science. What technology hath wrought can be wrought again, and that, for many women, is the awful news.

No, it's not awful that this particular woman had a baby. May she and her infant give each other joy and sleep-filled nights.

Nor is it awful that other so-called "older" women might follow her down the high-tech trail. Older women can be perfectly good mothers, even if their bunions hurt.

And we are not, despite the alarmists' cries, on the threshold of a world in which members of AARP will be stampeding to fertility clinics like shoppers to a Marshall Field's sale.

In fact, women who choose to become mothers late are apt to do so after long thought, even agony. And that's the awful part.

The hard questions childless women now face in their late 30s and early 40s — Should I or shouldn't I? Will I or won't I? — can now last a couple of decades longer.

Menopause will no longer mark the pause between one phase of life and the next. It won't even be a coffee break. Out of the blue, one of life's few certainties has — zap! — become uncertain.

A locked door has been thrown open to a world of vast possibility. And too much possibility makes you dizzy, even crazy. Options wear you out.

I have a friend who calls this the pantyhose problem.

You go to the store to buy a pair of pantyhose. This should be slightly easier than flossing. But standing in the hosiery department, you are attacked by possibilities.

Control top or not? Reinforced toe or no? Opaque or sheer? Taupe, tan, brown, beige, black, off-black, white, off-white, blue, navy blue, pearl, cream, Givenchy, Hanes, Christian Dior, Calvin Klein or L'Eggs?

You spend an hour making a decision that would have taken 20 seconds if your only choice had been one-size-fits-all nude. And whatever you choose, you're haunted by what you didn't.

The pantyhose problem is just one symptom of a modern plague — the plague of possibility. The entire 20th century has been a march toward options and more options.

The car, the phone and the airplane opened up the continent, the globe. Should you live in Chicago or San Francisco, Tampa or L.A.? Should you vacation in Michigan or Paris? Anywhere is possible.

Technology and medicine tore down nature's barriers. Should you grow old naturally or should you bleach and tuck, suck and trim and replace a body part or two? Anything is possible.

And which of the 2,000 options should you choose for your checking account?

There is a war in most of us. We yearn for a certain certainty, we crave possibility.

The news that childbearing remains a possibility years longer than we ever dreamed will satisfy that craving for some women.

For the rest of us, it's a reminder that "option" is just a polite term for something new to worry about.

Hillary Didn't Quit

Thank you, Hillary Clinton. Thank you for not quitting before it was time.

Clinton has driven a lot of people nuts by staying in a contest they decided should be over because they wanted it to be. They wanted her out before the vote in Indiana. Before the vote in West Virginia and Kentucky. Before Puerto Rico, Oregon, Montana, South Dakota.

And every time I heard the self-appointed umpires try to end the game while Clinton had a plausible chance, even a small one, I thought of a story one of my sisters told me a long time ago about running high school track.

Because my sister was fast and strong, the coach sometimes made her run with the boys. Girls running with the boys may not sound like a big deal, but in those days it was almost as noteworthy as a woman running for president.

So my sister ran with the guys. But whenever she reached the last stretch, she slowed down, which meant a boy always beat her.

One day the coach called her over and pointed it out. Girls had a habit of doing that, he said, but don't. Don't quit early.

Whether we've all consciously recognized it — and a lot of people haven't yet — it was important that Clinton not quit early.

For her candidacy to matter as much as it might, for it to genuinely advance the possibility of a woman as president in some year before the ice caps melt, she needed to keep the pace all the way to the finish line, even if she didn't cross it first.

Has Clinton been the perfect female candidate? There's no such thing, not if perfect means a woman who can command the votes and respect of everyone, or of every woman. Women are just like everybody else: We vary. So do our political tastes.

So, no, Hillary has not been a perfect candidate; some of what she's said and done has made even her supporters wince.

What she has been is a tough, smart, energetic, passionate campaigner who attracted almost 18 million voters and ran neck-and-neck until the very end.

That's as amazing and inspiring as the fact that she was outrun by Barack Obama, the son of a white Kansas mother and a black Kenyan father.

This week CBS News released a poll on Clinton. It showed that seven in 10 voters think her candidacy will make it easier for other women to run for president.

Seventy-six percent of Democrats said it would. So did 63 percent of Republicans. If she'd quit the race before now, those numbers wouldn't be so high.

"I think she changed forever our understanding of the possibilities of leadership," Gloria Steinem, quoted in the Boston Herald, said this week. "She showed such courage in the face of a media that was trying constantly to get her out of the race and all the misogyny. . . . She put up with that with grace. She enlarged my vision."

And then Steinem — a famous feminist who had ardently backed Clinton — said she's going to campaign for Obama.

That's good sportsmanship and good timing, the spirit Clinton should display on Saturday, when she's scheduled to officially step out of the race and endorse Obama.

But if Clinton had gotten out much sooner, we would have spent a lot less time thinking and talking about women's place in politics. Although that would have suited a lot of people fine, we're better off for the discussion.

From here on out — absent some astonishing plot twist — two men, as usual, will be running for president. May the best man win.

But let's give some credit to the woman who broadened our vision, who showed us that girls don't always quit early.

The Governess Myth

Watching the 30th anniversary broadcast of "The Sound of Music" on NBC Sunday night, I was struck by a giant cultural shift that has occurred between the film's spectacular debut and its descent to the tiny screen:

In these 30 years, we have witnessed the quiet demise of the governess myth.

Our stories are of nannies now, and the nanny of modern myth is not the governess of old, even though both supply the hand that rocks the cradle and both have a way of insinuating themselves into a household's heart.

The governess of the old myth accumulated power through her

innocence and goodness. The nanny of the new myth does it by scheme or wisecracks.

The governess was a heroine. The nanny, at least in her worst incarnation, deserves to fall to an early death from an 80-story building.

But in its long-gone glory days, the governess myth was a seductive force, especially for us reading girls. We knew that through governessing, plucky girls without rich parents could find money, love and freedom.

Jane Eyre followed this path, as did scores of lesser heroines, young women with whom I became intimately acquainted at the age of 13 while reading potboilers in the bathtub.

These women were at once bold and demure, wise but unworldly, keenly intelligent but smart enough not to flaunt it, and possessed of a smoldering sexuality disguised by competence and simple cotton frocks.

In romances by such writers as Victoria Holt and Mary Stewart, awed young readers learned that as governesses with a good attitude, we could conquer a world that was so often unkind to smart, headstrong women without rich daddies.

The governess myth tended to go like this:

Act I: Plucky poor girl takes governess job for man with demon kids. Man is wealthy, arrogant and fond of the company of wealthy, arrogant, sexually ripe women. His wife is either dead or crazy.

Act II: Plucky poor girl tames demon kids, capturing heart of man, who is only too ready to have the promise of his squandered past redeemed by female virtue.

Act III: Governess marries guy and lives happily ever after, with a fabulous new wardrobe.

Nowhere was this myth more gloriously told than in "The Sound of Music."

The movie is the embellished real-life story of plucky, poor Maria, who leaves the convent to take care of the seven children of a rich Austrian aristocrat whose heart has been hardened by widowhood.

Maria is a governess on speed. She sews the children playclothes from her curtains! She bikes! Canoes! Teaches the kids to sing in harmony!

In the standard governess myth, the wealthy, arrogant man has a wealthy, arrogant ladyfriend who is always the first to notice the passion swelling beneath the man's broad chest and the governess' pretty, covered bosom.

In "The Sound of Music," this role is played by the blond baroness, whose obvious sexual savvy is a counterpoint to Maria's purity.

"Where's that lovely little thing you were wearing the other evening when the captain couldn't keep his eyes off you?" coos the cool and catty baroness.

"Couldn't keep his eyes off me?" chaste Maria says, blushing and astonished.

After Maria and the children have staged a singing marionette show, the baroness purrs, "My dear, is there anything you can't do?"

No. That is the essence of the governess of myth. She is indomitable. And she shows us that simple, honest ways will triumph over monied sophistication. This was a message of hope to all us plucky poor girls.

In real life, of course, the governess life was not so glamorous. The mythical governesses bore as much relation to reality as do the nannies of newer tales.

And the governess myth, seen in the harsh light of modern sensibilities, looks suspiciously like a standard rescue fantasy, in which a woman awaits a rich man who will sweep her into paradise.

Still, watching "The Sound of Music," it was nice to recall the governess myth — and even better to realize that these days plucky poor girls can dream of other ways to get ahead.

WEDNESDAY, JAN. 21, 2009

Emma and Obama

The past always rides with us into the future, and the public is always personal, and so all through Barack Obama's inauguration Tuesday I thought of Emma.

The last time I saw Emma, my sister and I were on a road trip, passing through Macon, Ga., where we'd lived as children in my grandfather's house. My grandfather was long gone, but Emma and her husband, James, still lived down on Dannenberg Avenue, in a bungalow set on cinder blocks in a neighborhood where white people didn't go.

We hadn't warned Emma we were coming, but she didn't look surprised when we knocked. She wiped her hands on her apron, flung the screen door open, hugged us and then said: "James died this morning. Can I fix you something to eat?"

We sat at Emma's kitchen table, and she shelled peas into a metal bowl while she told us how two hours earlier in the hospital James had said, "Kiss me, Emma," and she'd kissed him and then, just like that, he died.

"Won't you let me fix you something to eat?" she said again.

In the three years we lived with my mother's father, in the late 1960s, Emma was always around, friendly, efficient and a little mysterious. She had cooked and cleaned for my grandfather for two decades, and then, because my father had lost his money and we'd lost our home, she helped care for me and my seven brothers and sisters.

Once, as I sat on a stool next to her ironing board, she told me she'd dropped out of school in 6th grade — my grade — to pick cotton.

She showed me her palms, tough as tree bark. Cotton hurts. She said she wished she'd learned to read and write as well as I did.

I never heard Emma mention politics and so never thought of her as political — until that day almost 20 years later when James died. On her living room wall, near photos of her daughter and one of me and my siblings, hung a poster of John F. Kennedy and a portrait, framed in plastic flowers and Christmas garland, of Martin Luther King Jr.

In that instant, I glimpsed Emma Wise whole. I sensed the dreams and disappointments, imagined the resentments, that she kept secret from white people, and I saw more clearly than ever how the country in which we had grown up had permanently divided even blacks and whites who loved each other.

Later that day, when Emma's pastor showed up to help her mourn, she introduced my sister and me: "These are my white children." I still ponder the complexities of that statement.

Emma died about 10 years ago. I learned just recently that after my grandfather's death, one of my uncles had helped her buy her house, and that she'd wanted to move into a white neighborhood. Various people counseled her against it. Her vision, it seems, was too wide for her moment.

Emma would have been close to 100 if she'd lived to hear Barack Obama marvel to the vast inaugural crowd on the Washington Mall that a man "whose father less than 60 years ago might not have been served at a local restaurant can now stand before you to take a most sacred oath."

I never saw Emma cry, and I don't know if she would have Tuesday. But I cried for her, wishing she'd been around to witness her country, with all its troubles, continue to repair itself.

The Peril of Mental Labels

My youngest sister was 3 when she was diagnosed as severely mentally retarded. She didn't walk or talk until after that and now, as an adult, says she remembers nothing before age 9.

When she was in her 20s, after a childhood boxed into school programs for the retarded, after her identity and destiny were shaped and branded by that word, her mind was given a different label.

She wasn't precisely "retarded" after all. She was "mildly autistic," then a newly fashionable diagnosis more congruent with her huge vocabulary, impeccable spelling and ability to solve word-search puzzles.

Later, after she took to screaming at supermarket clerks, fellow bus riders and cops during her ambles around town, "borderline personality disorder" was thrown into the mix.

Through these years, as the labels for my sister's troubled mind have changed, so have her medications, a slew of pills that, like the diagnoses themselves, never seem quite right.

My sister comes to mind because the American Psychiatric Association is revising its Diagnostic and Statistical Manual of Mental Disorders.

If the proposed changes happen, "intellectual disability" will replace "mental retardation." Sex addiction will be termed "hypersexuality." Some children who would have been diagnosed with "bipolar disorder," and medicated accordingly, will fall into a new category and be treated in a new way.

Some of these proposed new labels have stirred no trouble. "Mentally retarded" has certainly outlasted whatever purpose it ever served.

Other changes are controversial. In a shift upsetting to some, the behaviors now termed "Asperger's disorder" will be subsumed into "autism spectrum disorder."

To anyone whose life isn't immediately touched by mental abnormalities — is there anyone? — these linguistic tussles may seem trifling. But mental labels are serious business.

How we label the mind's activities shapes our world: our laws, our schools, what drugs are made and marketed.

Little words — retarded, autistic, disordered — help steer a person's fate. They shape how a person sees and treats herself, how others see and treat her.

Get the labels wrong, and a life can head in the wrong direction.

And the labels will always be at least a little wrong. Labels are a product of their time and culture. What one society calls sadness and treats with prayer, another calls depression and treats with Prozac.

In a recent New York Times essay called "The Americanization of Mental Illness," Ethan Watters wrote:

"Some philosophers and psychiatrists have suggested that we are investing our great wealth in researching and treating mental illness — medicalizing ever larger swaths of human experience — because we have rather suddenly lost older belief systems that once gave meaning and context to mental suffering."

Think how different "suffering" sounds from "disordered."

We all want explanations and solutions for the troubled mind. Labels promise both. You name it, you tame it. At least that's the dream.

We dream, too, that our understanding of how the mind works is always advancing. If it is, what we know now, and how we label it, is guaranteed to wind up looking wrong and outdated.

My sister's mind isn't normal, but I no longer find it as strange or limited as the labels make it sound. More and more, I see how faint the line is that distinguishes her mind from mine, and I wonder how her life would have been different if her troubles had been given other names.

More Wrinkled Women, Please

We need more wrinkled, jowly, white-haired women in power.

We lost one of the very few last week when Sandra Day O'Connor quietly made her resignation official, ceding her U.S. Supreme Court seat to Sam Alito, a guy destined eventually to join the big, old club of wrinkled, jowly, white-haired power-toting men.

Don't read wrinkled, jowly and white-haired as insults. They're not, certainly not as applied to O'Connor, who remains plenty handsome.

But she's a woman who looks her age, who looks, as the saying goes, "good for her age," but that's a fully seasoned 75.

I'd never fully registered that fact until I saw a candid photo of her several months ago.

In the photo, her wayward hair lapped over the rim of her black judge's robe. Her chin did what most chins do with time. If she wore makeup, it didn't conceal the fact that her skin had seen its share of sun and years.

She looked like she'd been so busy working she hadn't made it to the salon in weeks. She looked — dare I say it? — like Ted Kennedy.

And that was beautiful.

It was beautiful because it was so shockingly rare. How often do you see a publicly powerful woman past 70? Past 60? A woman whose very age invests her with authority even as it pads her midline, an older woman who's the equivalent of the power male found in Shakespeare plays, corporate boardrooms and the newspaper front page?

Pop culture's idea of a powerful older woman is Madonna. Or Oprah, who looks younger with every monthly magazine cover.

And if the majority of Americans have come around to believing a woman could be president, it still happens only on TV. Even there it happens only if she looks like Geena Davis who, let's face it, needs a firmer chin line than Martin Sheen to survive in prime time.

Looking at that recent photo of O'Connor unaided by stylists or lighting specialists, I saw something I hadn't seen until then: She not only served the cause of women by becoming a justice, she served it by aging realistically in the job.

When President Ronald Reagan chose her for the court, he deliberately chose a woman. Her appointment opened closed minds and job slots.

It gave women a new realm of realistic aspiration and robbed men of old reasons to shut women out. O'Connor's success as a judge helped many women become judges.

That's what role models are for: Look, Ma, a girl can do it too.

What you can see is easier to imagine and to wish for.

I came of age when the very idea of role models for women was still new. Girls had to reach deep into history to find stories of women who led public lives. Once you'd polished off the skinny school-library biographies of Susan B. Anthony, Betsy Ross and Madame Curie, you were left with Nancy Drew.

Now loads of women lead lives that within my lifetime were once considered unavailable to us: sports stars, politicians, company executives.

But we're still short on powerful older women whose lives send the message: Look, kids, old girls can do it too.

Look at the front page of the newspaper on the average day. Count the men in power. Count the women. And notice that when women do appear, they rarely, for example, look like George Ryan.

In this allegedly post-feminist age, it's deemed somehow pouty and retro to mention that women are still unfairly underrepresented in the spheres of public power. But they are. And in those domains, older women barely exist at all.

When Sandra Day O'Connor joined the court, lots of people couldn't imagine a woman there. We not only learned to imagine a woman there, but a wrinkled, jowly, white-haired one, exercising full authority. That's part of her legacy.

It's nice to think, to hope, that as more younger women come into power, more women will grow old in power.

Too bad that for a long time to come, except for Ruth Bader Ginsburg, women will have to look for models somewhere besides the United States Supreme Court.

SUNDAY, OCT. 14, 2018

Who You Callin' Elderly?

A couple of days ago, a colleague mentioned that her mother was turning 73, and I responded with a small exclamation — along the lines of "whoa" or "oof" — as if to suggest that, wow, 73, that's really getting up there.

Then I paused. Why had I reacted that way? No doubt because, however subliminally, I've been conditioned by the social messages that from the time we're young tell us that 70 is old and being old is regrettable.

But the older I get, the younger 70 seems. So I revised.

"Seventy-three's not old," I said.

But it's not middle-age either, my colleague said, so what would you call someone of her mother's age? She thought "elderly" was an accurate term. I disagreed.

No doubt about it: There is a new phase of life that begins after, oh, 60 or so. I say this from the perspective of 64.

By the time you're in your 60s, you probably have at least one friend or sibling who has died, and your own mortality has moved from the far reaches of your peripheral vision a little closer to center view.

By then, your appearance has begun to shift toward something the culture constantly suggests should be hidden or repaired. You've abandoned whatever delusion you may have clung to in your 50s that you — you alone in the history of humankind — would not succumb to the hazards of time. You haven't memorized the lyrics to a new pop song in a while.

Does all that make you elderly?

Aging well involves aging honestly, and it's good to embrace the truth of getting older, no matter how vital and engaged you remain as you do. But we don't have good language for aging, a lack that reflects our culture's underlying discomfort with it.

Google the word "elderly" and the first definition that pops up offers these as synonyms:

"Old, mature, older, senior, hoary, ancient, senescent, advanced in years, in one's dotage, long in the tooth, as old as the hills, past one's prime, not as young as one used to be, getting on, over the hill, no spring chicken."

Clearly, while "elderly" may be used with clinical detachment by doctors and social service agencies, its broader use is often, if unintentionally, demeaning.

But who cares? A word is just a word, right?

If only it were so.

Words reflect and shape our prejudices and expectations, and as the anti-aging activist Ashton Applewhite, who is 66, puts it, ageism is "the last socially sanctioned prejudice."

With the wrong words, we reinforce prejudice. With the right words, we begin to dismantle harmful, ill-conceived notions. Many of us — I include myself — carry those biases without realizing it.

After my conversation with my colleague, I posted a question on Facebook: When you hear that someone is "elderly" or hear the term "the elderly," what age or age bracket comes to mind?

The question quickly spurred more than 200 comments. The majority said it started around 80, but many said 90. Only a few commenters, typically under 40, thought it started sooner.

One man in his 30s cited 72 because it was the age at which his grandmother died. Someone replied that when her mother died at 78, she always told people her mother died young.

"Touche," he wrote.

Another man, who is 40, pegged "elderly" as "Whenever you start complaining that it is drafty."

A few other comments:

To me, it seems that elderly now is only applicable with those who need a lot of assistance to get by day to day.

For some time now, I have noticed that my concept of "old" is 20 years older than my parents. When they were 40, 60 seemed old. When they were 50, it was 70. And now, believe it or not, I think of old as 90!

I'm a very active, vital man of almost 63, in the midst of building my second career. Yet I'm certain if I were ever mugged or in an accident, a newspaper would describe me as an elderly Chicago man.

Not our newspaper, I hope. The AP Stylebook says "elderly" should be used carefully and sparingly:

"It is appropriate in generic phrases that do not refer to specific individuals: *concern for elderly people, a home for senior citizens,* etc.

"If the intent is to show that an individual's faculties have deteriorated, cite a graphic example and give attribution for it. Use age when available and appropriate."

A lot of people like to say that "You're only as old as you feel," a well-intentioned sentiment but false.

Age is real. Time runs out. We can't wish that truth away, but we can broaden how we talk and think about it.

In certain yoga traditions, the life cycle is divided into three phases: sunrise, midday, sunset. That pleasant division skips too quickly from noon to 7 p.m.

I'd say there's a phase between midday and sunset, one that would include the age of 73. Call it late afternoon, a beautiful moment in the day, with plenty of time to get things done, even though it's obvious the light is fading.

A Cell Phone Photo Says It All

Shortly after my brother's cancer flared up again, after a long time in hiding, I started texting him photos from my phone.

A Chicago sunset. Light rippling on the morning lake. The skyline swaggering. Wrigley Field on opening day.

Bill used to live in Chicago, so I like to think these are scenes he'll enjoy, pictures that silently say: "Hey, look, life! Beauty. Right here. Right now. Things change, things endure. I love you."

I don't spell any of that out with the photos I send. All I type is an explanatory word or two, caption-style, and he usually texts me back something equally pithy, like "Pretty" or "I needed that."

Should I be writing about this?

Even as I do, I wonder because the whole point of the photos is that they are not writing, they are not words.

No quest for the right verb, adjective, punctuation. No platitudes. No questions.

What a relief and liberation that is, a chance to communicate and connect, instantly and often, without having to speak or write or expect words in return.

On a routine day, the image says everything that needs to be said.

Not so long ago, it wouldn't have occurred to me to communicate through the silence of photos, especially when it involved something as important as an illness. Nor would it have been possible.

But we're living in a time when photos have become not just an addition to words, but in many ways, a substitute for them, not only in the public media but in our personal lives.

It didn't take Facebook's billion-dollar purchase of Instagram this week to make that clear, but Instagram's success makes the trend even more apparent:

We want to take pictures, everywhere. We want to share pictures, fast. We want pictures to do more of the work we've long relied on words to do.

Before Instagram and Facebook, of course, people snapped and shared photos. What's changed, and keeps changing, is how many photos, how quickly they're exchanged and for what purposes.

Instagram, which calls itself "a fast, beautiful and fun way to share your life with friends through a series of photos," captures the change in its very name. The pictogram meets the telegram meets the age of instant everything.

Point. Click. Share. Presto. Message accomplished.

Instagram is just one example of our growing reliance on photos to express ourselves, whether it's to a big circle or one-on-one.

A cellphone without a camera seems as quaint as a camera that uses film. And remember the jokes about how Facebook was nothing but a collection of status updates on morning coffee? That's so 2007.

Now Facebook users are likelier to post a photo of their coffee cup — and get a lot more response. It's easier to look than to read.

We still need words, and we'll always use them.

Words communicate in ways photos never will, which is why my brother and I talk and email some too.

But it's the photos that provide the easy, regular conversation and sometimes tell a better story. When he was in the hospital a couple of weeks ago, his wife, with whom I also trade photo texts, sent me one of him in his hospital gown, sitting with one of his teenage sons.

When he got out, she texted me again.

The photo showed Bill, his face in close profile, next to a pond in a park in the evening light.

She sent it without a single word, and all I needed to say in reply was "Beautiful."

WEDNESDAY, DEC. 6, 2017

The Year of the Reckoning

Today I nominate the word "reckoning" as the 2017 word of the year.

Forget "complicit," the word that Dictionary.com recently anointed as the year's top word. While "complicit" has certainly run rampant this year, it's not a word most people, even those who should, would apply to themselves.

Everyone, on the other hand, is part of the reckoning.

In the past few weeks, as one sexual misconduct scandal has followed another in a breathtaking cascade of allegations and apologies and denials, the word has been everywhere.

A few recent headlines:

What Hollywood Could Learn from Wall Street's Sexual Harassment Reckoning (The New Yorker)

Trump May Face a Reckoning in Case Brought by Female Accuser (The Washington Post)

Reckoning with Bill Clinton's Sex Crimes (The Atlantic)

A Reckoning on Sexual Misconduct? Absolutely. But How Harsh, Women Ask. (The New York Times)

The reckoning has touched people high and low, male and female, from LA to D.C., from Michigan to Alabama, straight, gay and other.

It has forced us to ask ourselves more starkly than ever before: How have we allowed this degrading, predatory, shockingly widespread behavior to go on for so long?

Like most words, "reckoning" comes with a range of nuance. One dictionary defines it mildly as "a settling of accounts." A more biting definition calls it "the avenging or punishing of past mistakes or misdeeds."

In a reckoning, the past catches up with you. It's the moment the bill collector stops calling and instead breaks down the door.

It's when you learn the delayed cost of what you took for free or for granted, or by force.

A reckoning compels you to look in the mirror, no turning away no matter how much you dislike what you see.

In a reckoning, the truth is set free.

Only a few months ago, "reckoning" wouldn't have been a contender for the year's top word. Then came the stories of movie mogul Harvey Weinstein's alleged assaults on women in the film industry, quickly followed by other names in other domains, the whole mess colored by the fact that the president of the United States stands accused of sexually predatory behavior.

The timeline of the 2017 reckoning may, in fact, have started during the president's campaign, when he was caught on tape making vulgar remarks about women, but it took all these other stories to give this moment its momentum.

A reckoning, in part, is consciousness raising, a term popularized during the women's movement of the 1960s and '70s.

Women gathered in consciousness-raising groups to talk about their lives, and together learned they weren't alone. Together, they began to understand the common experiences and social systems that shaped them and consigned women to an inferior status.

Only then — together and aware — could they force social changes that began to elevate women toward equal standing.

In the reckoning of 2017, Facebook and Twitter are the consciousness-raising groups. Through social media, women and men have been able to share experiences, an exercise that has made us reckon with how widespread sexual misconduct is, and how damaging.

It's a double reckoning, really. We're dealing with the problem on a grand social scale but also reflecting on it in our private lives.

Like most women I know, and some men, I've had many "aha" experiences during the past few weeks, thinking back on unpleasant things men have done to me, reflecting on why I didn't publicly protest, or protest at all. Men I know have told me they've been examining their own behavior and wondering where they may have transgressed.

Not everyone is so reflective — a spin through Twitter will prove that — but there's no escaping the conversation.

And that's why "reckoning" should be the word of the year. More than any other, it captures the zeitgeist.

It's not over either. A reckoning of this magnitude isn't a short event. It's like an earthquake that won't quit. It demands argument and self-interrogation, and it goes beyond examining or avenging the past.

A true reckoning helps to light the way forward. Once we can see the past, in all its ugliness, we move to the next question: What do we do now?

We need to get clearer on the appropriate consequences for sexual misbehavior. We need to connect the dots from sexual predation to all the other ways sexism plays out in our workplaces and our lives.

The year of the reckoning will last longer than 2017.

SUNDAY, SEPT. 11, 2011

The Day That Changed a Decade

What exactly are we remembering today?

That it was a Tuesday. Morning. We begin by remembering that, and how the sky, in New York and in Chicago, was a deep September blue.

We remember where we were.

I was in my car. I casually flipped on the radio, and there was some announcer saying something that made no sense, something about passenger planes and the World Trade Center.

Remember that? How at the beginning, we simply wondered what the hell was going on?

For hours that bled into days, we watched the unwatchable on TV: Monsters of ash chasing tiny humans through Manhattan's streets. Tiny humans jumping from high shattered windows. In replay after replay, those homicidal, suicidal jets gliding past the mighty skyline of New York with perfect aim.

Who was doing this? Why?

And because we didn't know, because the horror unfolded one shock at a time — a tower in orange flame; then its twin in black smoke; then a plane into the Pentagon; then another in a Pennsylvania field; and the skyscrapers, falling — we knew this mutilation, this humiliation, could continue anywhere at any moment.

So we were nice to each other. Remember that? How bewilderment and terror and fury made us nice? We looked for the goodness in others and in ourselves. For a few days, subdued in the rubble of the broken fantasy that our land was safe from foreign attack, we were a united nation.

The day soon had a name. Nine eleven. Nine eleven would shift the course of the next decade. We're remembering that decade today too.

The 9/11 decade came with its own vocabulary, words we had rarely or never heard: Ground zero. War on terror. Gitmo. The Patriot Act. Anthrax. Abu Ghraib. Homeland security. Orange alert. Waterboarding. Freedom fries.

Most of us had never heard of al-Qaida either, or of sleeper cells or Osama bin Laden. When American soldiers, barely out of high school, went to Afghanistan to rout the 9/11 mastermind and his terrorists from their caves, we took out our maps. Where?

And soon we were studying the map of Iraq, arguing over a war that might or might not have something to do with the terrorists, a war that could also be called an American invasion.

We would be at war, and at war about war, throughout the 9/11 decade.

Today we remember the dead.

On the deadly day the decade began, most Americans knew little about Islam, or how to distinguish the essential religion from al-Qaida's violent brand, or how the tangle of international politics fed the terrorists' hate.

We weren't aware of how many Muslims lived among us — how many Muslims were us. American Muslims then lived largely on our social fringes. In the 9/11 decade, in the name of security, too many would be treated as foreigners and as suspects in their own country.

The years passed. We shed some of our ignorance, much of our conspicuous fear.

Remember how we knew we'd never fly again? How we didn't want to shop but did, out of patriotic duty? How we knew we'd never laugh in the same way?

Shortly after Sept. 11, Lorne Michaels, the producer of "Saturday Night Live," stood on stage with Rudy Giuliani, the mayor of New York.

"Can we be funny?" Michaels said.

"Why start now?" the mayor deadpanned.

It was a relief to laugh, though in the new decade, we laughed a little differently. The national taste in humor turned from the exuberant triviality of Jerry Seinfeld to the political bite of Jon Stewart.

We went back to the airport.

Shoes off! Laptops out! Arms up! Our minds downgraded the intrusions of the new security into a tolerable nuisance. Entrepreneurs found a market in 3-ounce travel bottles.

We forgot about survival kits.

We resumed our almost ordinary days. Got married or divorced. Had a baby, lost a parent. Bought or lost a house. Got or lost a job.

If a certain uncertainty was the new status quo, the insecurity was mostly about money. We came to fear more for our livelihoods than our lives.

Then faraway, but as close as Twitter, young Arabs rebelled against their tyrants. American soldiers killed Osama bin Laden. New terrorists hatch new terror, but so far, in the grand scheme, we've stayed safe.

On the average day, we worry less about terrorists than about how Facebook and Google invade our privacy.

Now here we are. The 10th anniversary. Trying to figure out what those 10 years add up to.

The answer may be revealed, a long time from now, only to those too young to remember.

This summer, I went to see the new skyscraper rising out of the hole that once held the World Trade Center. The streets were happy and mobbed by people from all over the world. Passing a tour guide, I stopped to listen.

The guide talked about what happened 10 years ago, here and in Washington, D.C., and in Pennsylvania, and how those nearly 3,000 deaths rippled through the world.

His audience was junior high students. A couple paid rapt attention, but most talked, laughed and played with their cellphones. You can't remember what you didn't live.

The past is designed to fade, and there's no point in mourning that. Those students brought to mind a poem by the Polish poet Wislawa

Szymborska. It's called "The End and the Beginning," and it's about the aftermath of war. Here are its final verses:

> *Those who knew*
> *what this was all about*
> *must make way for those*
> *who know little.*
> *And less than that.*
> *And at last nothing less than nothing.*
> *Someone has to lie there*
> *in the grass that covers up*
> *the causes and effects*
> *with a cornstalk in his teeth,*
> *gawking at clouds.*

EUDORA WELTY
1119 PINEHURST STREET
JACKSON, MISSISSIPPI 39202

Dear Miss Schmich,

Thank you for your letter, and if I could
do so I'd like to give the interview you ask.
I appreciate your interest. But this is the
most crowded sort of time for me, and even if I
felt I could give an interview (I don't very
often any more, since I try to work as much as
possible) there wouldn't be any chance at all.
I'm sorry. My home town has plans covering both
weekends before my birthday, and though it
is wonderful of them, I am not quite certain
how well I'm going to come through it all.
You'll understand, I feel.

                              Sincerely,

I spent five years as the Tribune's Southern correspondent,
based in Atlanta. In 1989, when the legendary Mississippi
writer Eudora Welty was about to turn 80, I wanted to
interview her.

I'd heard she rarely did interviews and wouldn't answer
her phone so I FedExed her a plaintive, sycophantic, but
entirely sincere request. This is the note she wrote me
back. It's the finest rejection I've ever received.

chapter 8

·····························

reading and writing

·····························

'On Writing Well'

Of the four books I kept on my desk at my first newspaper job, the one I most enjoyed having a drink with was William Zinsser's "On Writing Well."

The other books — a dictionary, two manuals of writing rules — were useful, but, like certain co-workers, not fun to consort with after hours.

Zinsser's book, on the other hand, was good company anywhere, any time, and my memory of the night I first read it is more vivid than my memory of my first newspaper assignment:

Nine p.m. A dim cafe. The book open on the table. Yellow highlighter in one hand. Glass of wine in the other. Bliss.

Go easy on the exclamation marks? OK!

Hold the adverbs? Boldly, firmly, zealously, I would try!

As a newcomer to the newspaper life, I was alarmed yet validated to read that "there is a kind of writing that might be called journalese, and it's the death of freshness in anybody's style."

That was a long time ago, but I recalled that night this week when I learned that Zinsser had just died, at the age of 92. He'd had glaucoma for a while, but into his 90s, people came to his New York apartment to read their work out loud. Practically blind, he helped them revise by listening to them read their writing.

"Good writers of prose must be part poet," he once advised, "always listening to what they write."

On Thursday, I went in search of my old copy of "On Writing Well" and, to my surprise, found it, not my original wine-stained edition but one of the several reissued versions.

Leafing through it, I winced to realize all the ways I don't live up to Zinsser's standards, but I was also struck by how many important ideas his book had planted in me.

He's hardly the only writer to preach clarity and concision, but he preached it more clearly and usably than many.

In a chapter called "Clutter," he warned against frills, cliches and jargon.

"Don't dialogue with someone you can talk to," he wrote. "Don't interface with anybody."

In a chapter called "The Lead and the Ending," he emphasized the importance of the last sentence in each paragraph: "Try to give that sentence an extra twist of humor or surprise, like the periodic 'snapper' in the routine of a stand-up comic."

He liked short paragraphs.

As I perused the book, I realized that I had internalized many of his prejudices. He rejected the term "senior citizen," and to this day so do I, even when, unable to find a good substitute, I use it.

By the way, the word "internalize" in the paragraph above? He probably would have thought it had an unpleasant corporate odor.

And he might have sniffed at "perused," on the grounds that it's not a word I use when I talk.

"Never say anything in writing that you wouldn't comfortably say in conversation," he advised. "If you're not a person who says 'indeed' or 'moreover,' or who calls someone an individual ('he's a fine individual'), please don't write it."

Zinsser's book is practical — it breaks writing into components that can be analyzed and improved — but the reason it has sold 1.5 million copies, I think, is that it goes beyond the technical.

He talks to writers about their psyches as well as their verbs. He knows that writing means wrestling not just with words but with fear.

This week, The American Scholar reposted his 2006 essay on how to write a memoir: theamericanscholar.org/how-to-write-a-memoir.

It's the best piece I've encountered on the topic, and I often recommend it. Like "On Writing Well," it's practical and motivating, filled with advice like:

"When you write your own family history, don't try to be a 'writer.'"

"Your first job is to get your story down as you remember it — now. Don't look over your shoulder to see what relatives are perched there. Say what you want to say, freely and honestly, and finish the job."

"Think small."

In the years since I discovered "On Writing Well," I've accumulated other books on writing, some good but none better at instilling the most vital thought that sticks with me from that night in the cafe, the thought that every person who sits down to write needs every single time:

I can do this. I can do this. I'm not sure how yet, but I can do this.

Alice Munro's Nobel

When the news came Thursday that Alice Munro had won the Nobel Prize in literature, only the 13th woman to earn that honor, a lot of her admirers reacted like football fans whose small-town team had freakishly, though deservedly, won the Super Bowl.

Really? Not Philip Roth? Or Bob Dylan? Or Haruki Murakami? Go Alice!

As one of those astonished admirers, I cheered out loud at the news, and, like countless other cheerleaders, I posted it on Facebook, where an acquaintance promptly responded, "Someone who writes so incredibly well as to win the Nobel Prize, but I've never heard of her. How is that?"

There are good reasons you may never have heard of Alice Munro.

She has been widely praised and reviewed since she published her first story collection in 1968; such well-known writers as Jhumpa Lahiri ("The Lowland") and Elizabeth Strout ("Olive Kitteridge") cite her as a major influence.

But Munro, who's 82 and Canadian, doesn't do big book tours, never has. Her short stories don't feature an ace detective, graphic sex, adorable dogs, guns, dystopias, vampires, self-help aphorisms or Ivy League graduates brooding and having affairs in Brooklyn and Manhattan. She doesn't clobber you with edifying facts or politics.

Munro's writing is a quiet seduction. There are no literary pyrotechnics, only the feats of clarity and concision, suspense grounded in ordinary emotion, surprise endings that spring from plausible twists of fate.

For almost half a century, Munro has written mostly about women, typically young women who want to live beyond the strictures of their Canadian farms or small towns, who set out into the wider world in search of love, sex, drama, purpose, meaning.

These young women find themselves duped or duplicitous or both. They make choices that lead them to unexpected and often unhappy places. They grow up, grow old. They remember and forget. They learn to make peace with the life that, one choice at a time, they've built.

Munro's titles alone suggest the nature of her stories and the emotion they evoke. To name a few of her 15 books:

"Friend of My Youth." "Open Secrets." "The Progress of Love." "Too Much Happiness." "Runaway." "Dear Life."

Munro grew up in rural Ontario and lives there today, and in some ways resembles the characters she creates.

"I was brought up to believe that the worst thing you could do was 'call attention to yourself' or 'think you were smart,'" she told a New Yorker writer, in a recent, rare interview.

She took to writing anyway. The first writers who moved her deeply, she once told the Paris Review, were women from the American South. Eudora Welty, Flannery O'Connor, Katherine Anne Porter, Carson McCullers. They showed her she could write about small towns, rural people, the marginal.

"The mainstream big novel about real life was men's territory," she said. "I don't know how I got that feeling of being on the margins, it wasn't that I was pushed there. Maybe it was because I grew up on a margin. I knew there was something about the great writers I felt shut out from, but I didn't know quite what it was. . . . I was often disturbed by writers' views of female sexuality."

Me too.

It's that quality of "me too," coupled with stories that take us to new places, that so many readers respond to in Munro's work. Her settings and situations may be nothing like our own lives — that's part of the appeal — but the deep, subtle emotions she evokes are ones we recognize.

If you've never read Munro and want to start, I'd suggest her 2004 collection, "Runaway," or her last collection, "Dear Life."

After the publication of "Dear Life," Munro said she was retiring from writing, and the final four stories in that book are, she says, as much as she'll say about her own life.

The last lines of the last story offer a taste of how much complexity she can pack into a few simple sentences:

"I did not go home for my mother's last illness or for her funeral. I had two small children and nobody in Vancouver to leave them with. We could barely have afforded the trip, and my husband had a contempt for formal behavior, but why blame it on him? I felt the same. We say of some things that they can't be forgiven, or that we will never forgive ourselves. But we do — we do it all the time."

You'll Understand, I Feel

I never met Eudora Welty. That fact is the gift she gave me, the gift of a lesson, one we all should learn.

Welty — Miss Welty, to be proper — was legendary for longer than most Americans have been alive. When she died Monday at the age of 92, near her home in Jackson, Mississippi, she had won almost every literary prize that can be won. Her short stories had been anthologized and taught in schools. She had even inspired the name for a popular e-mail program, Eudora.

Though her writing wasn't to everyone's taste — too slow and quiet for some, too much like a Southern summer afternoon — she not only depicted the South from which she came, she incarnated it. She lived through almost a century of the South's complexities and changes, from its racial atrocities through its modern boom times, and from childhood until old age she recorded her place in words.

In Jackson, where she spent most of her life before and after a couple of years at the University of Wisconsin, Miss Welty was venerated as both saint and celebrity. Ordinary folks liked to mention they'd spotted her at the grocery store, or on the sidewalk, or outside the Tudor house on Pinehurst Street where she had lived since high school. Naturally, any reporter covering the South wanted to meet her.

So in 1989, when I was covering the South for the Tribune and her impending 80th birthday was being ballyhooed around the region, I wrote and asked if I might come see her. I'd been warned that lately she considered interviews an intrusion on her waning writing time; she particularly hated being interrupted by the phone.

So I FedExed her my request, a letter I was sure contained an irresistible balance of abject flattery and naked wheedling. On the occasion of her 80th birthday, I pleaded, readers in Chicago needed to hear from her.

Three or four days later, a small white envelope arrived in my mail. On the white sheet inside, Eudora Welty's name and address were embossed in tiny blue letters. On it she had typed the following and signed it in blue ink:

"Dear Miss Schmich,

Thank you for your letter, and if I could do so I'd like to give the interview you ask. I appreciate your interest. But this is the most crowded sort of time for me, and even if I felt I could give an interview (I don't very often any more, since I try to work as much as possible) there wouldn't be any chance at all. I'm sorry. My home town has plans covering both weekends before my birthday, and though it is wonderful of them, I am not quite certain how well I'm going to come through it all. You'll understand, I feel."

You'll understand, I feel.

I read that line over and over, my heart swelling with the music of a perfect sentence, four words and a comma that made the ultimate grace note. Being told no had never felt so good.

"You'll understand, I feel" made me complicit in my own rejection. It said, "I want to give you what you want, and if I could I would. Alas, I can't. Not everyone would understand, but you, a sensitive, discerning soul, will feel my predicament. You, a kindred spirit, would make precisely this decision in my place. I know this because just as you feel me, I feel you. We will be honorable together, though we never meet."

Ever since, I've been trying to bamboozle people with that rejection formula, in which the graciousness of the rejector compels the graciousness of the rejectee, in which graciousness leaves no room for argument. Because I don't speak with the gentility common to Southerners of Miss Welty's vintage, I've tried revising the formula to fit my own speech, only to discover that phrased any other way, the sentiment loses part of its grace and power.

"I think you'll understand." "I know you'll understand." "I hope you'll understand." "I trust you'll understand." They're better than nothing, but they still don't accomplish the full feat.

So from time to time, looking for the perfect way to say no, I go ahead and say it Miss Welty's way — You'll understand, I feel — and smile at the thrill of having learned the art of rejection from a master.

Warm Regards

An epidemic of warm regards has erupted recently in my e-mail box.

"Warm regards," wrote a public relations person eager for publicity on some blogger's book about relationships.

"Warm regards," wrote someone who was peddling construction materials from somewhere in Asia.

"Warm regards," cooed someone promoting a revolutionary diet book by a legendary author I'd never heard of.

Warm regards? From strangers looking to do a business deal?

Every time I read that closing salutation, which seems more often all the time, I long for the days when the conclusion of business correspondence required nothing more emotive than "Sincerely."

"Sincerely" seems stodgy these days, like a formal bow after a dance, but I prefer it to the fumes of phony friendship.

And yet I know how hard it is to find the perfect way to wave goodbye at the end of an e-mail. Finding the right final flourish has perplexed writers since the invention of the letter.

"Sincerely?" "Respectfully?" "Yours truly?"

Even when the options were fewer, there were hard choices to be made. Now the options seem as boundless as the Internet, and we all correspond more than ever. The conscientious e-mailer can stare at the computer screen for a long time, straining to find the one or two words that perfectly suit the relationship.

Obviously, business letters and personal letters present different challenges. But the line between personal and impersonal has blurred ("Warm regards, stranger!"), and whichever type of e-mail you're writing, you don't want to be too familiar or too formal, too warm or too cold.

It would be simpler to forgo the final salutation altogether. Say what you have to say, then sign your name. (Your full name? Your first name? Initials?)

But a concluding salutation is to an e-mail what WD-40 is to a door.

It's the grease that allows a graceful closure. And so the search goes on, often in foreign languages:

"Ciao?" Never great, now passe.

"Bisous?" Too cute unless the recipient is French.

"Hasta la vista?" You can do better, baby.

"Gra mor?" A guy I know, who would never write something as squishy as "Big hugs," uses the Gaelic equivalent with friends, and he can get away with it because he's as Irish as a Dublin pub.

I'm embarrassed to say how much time I've spent, in personal and business e-mails, backspacing and deleting as I switched closing salutations, searching for the proper vibe.

"Cheers?" It's common and can work for personal or some business e-mails, and yet . . .

"Always?" Only if it's true love.

"Love?" You'd better mean it.

"Thank you" works in many cases. But should you write "Thank you?" or "Thanks?" "Thanks much?" "Thanks very much?"

When this topic came up among some of my friends at a party, several agreed that the best option when writing strangers or mere acquaintances was "Best." I use it sometimes when I'm stumped, but it feels stilted.

When I asked a woman in her 20s for a solution, she looked puzzled. "I don't e-mail. I just text. That's not relevant."

For her generation, the problem may be solved. For the rest of us, the quest goes on.

"Peace?" A lovely sentiment, but not one I'm comfortable writing.

"Be well?" I'm occasionally guilty of this one, but even as I type it, I hear treacly massage music.

"Your humble servant?" Only to the boss.

Don't Lend That Book

One of the rudest acts a person can commit is to lend a book to someone who didn't ask to borrow it.

Lending a book unsolicited is different from merely recommending it. A book loan can be an act of aggression posing as goodwill.

One day you show up at work, for example, and there on your desk chair is a loaner book that interests you about as much as the latest treasury report. The lender has paper-clipped a note that says, "Enjoy!"

Or you're at a party, gazing at the books just to avoid the chit-chat, when the host seizes a volume as big as a microwave and insists you take it home.

"Let me know how you like it," he chirps while you blink back teary visions of the piles and pounds of guilt that already nag you in the form of loaner books you will never even open.

From bedside tables, living room shelves and car floors — You never even took it out of the car, you lazy wretch? — these loaner books mock, goad and wag their fingers.

So you prefer that best-selling trash to a serious book like moi, slacker? Don't have the guts to read me or to return me, wimp?

A friend of mine tells this story:

"I met a friend — let's call her Jane — for lunch one day, and she was carrying a historical novel she had just finished. 'Read this,' she commanded. 'It's not very good, but you should read it.'"

My friend told Jane no thanks. No time to read. Too many books already on the nightstand, etc.

"Oh, take it," Jane insisted.

Soon afterward, my friend got a call from another of Jane's friends, who was about to take a trip; Jane thought she should take the book along. Could my friend get it to her?

My friend was not happy to drive across the city to deliver a book she'd never wanted in her possession, but she was delighted to ditch this dog.

Awhile later, she met Jane again for lunch. Here, said Jane — and again she presented the dreaded novel. Exhausted, my friend took it, knowing that, again, she wouldn't read it.

"I love books," she says. "But I'm not interested in wasting my precious reading time on completing someone else's reading list. And I sure don't want to feel responsible for someone else's property."

Lending books unsolicited is a way of sharing pleasure. It's also a way of exerting power.

"I do not ask to borrow books, nor do I offer to lend my books," sniffs one avid reader. "Books are like underwear, in my view: intended for use by one person only. I exclude library books, which I suppose are more like bowling shoes."

Reading a loaner book can be a burden. Returning it unread can be as bad.

"Is it better to keep it until they ask?" frets another loaner hater. "Or is it better to just fess up that you couldn't find time?"

Sometimes she reads snippets of the book to create the appearance of caring and trying. And once in a while, an unwanted loaner surprises her.

"I can think of one such book that I loved so much that I then went on to foist it as a recommendation on all sorts of poor victims," she says.

I am a perpetrator as well as a victim of bad lending behavior. A colleague recently asked me for book suggestions. I didn't just recommend. Unrequested, I lent. Not just one book. Two.

She quietly set both books on my desk a few weeks later. She'd really liked one of them, she said; her command of the details indicated she wasn't bluffing. Tactfully, she didn't mention the other at all. Tactfully, I didn't ask.

If you must lend, at least do it gracefully. If you ask, "Would you like to borrow this?" and the person declines, back off.

Better yet, spare both of you the awkwardness of "No." Instead, say, "If you'd like to borrow this sometime, let me know."

And if in your enthusiasm you lend some book unbidden, always say, "Please feel free not to read this." Then say, "Please feel free not to read this." Then say it one more time.

My Marriage to Kurt Vonnegut

At the time my life got strangely linked to Kurt Vonnegut's, the only specific thing I remembered from the books of his I read in college was the word "karass."

To this day I'm not sure I interpreted the word quite the way he intended it in "Cat's Cradle," but from the age of 19 on, my version of his idea helped shape the way I saw the world.

A karass, to me, meant a group of people to which you belonged not by a fluke of common blood or nationality but because you shared some spirit, some purpose, some sensibility toward life. You didn't know who the members of your karass were until, unpredictably, you met them, but when you met them, you knew.

Back in college, it never occurred to me that Kurt Vonnegut might be a member of any group to which I could belong, or even anyone I might ever see up close.

He was, as his obituaries said last week after he died at age 84, a voice of a generation, famous in a time when fame was more like an Olympic gold medal than just another penny anyone could pick up off the street. He seemed too grand for any karass that might include us ordinary mortals.

Then 10 years ago, a column I wrote rocketed around the Internet misidentified as a graduation speech Vonnegut had given at the Massachusetts Institute of Technology. It became well-known as an Internet hoax and was turned into a CD, loosely known as the sunscreen song, by the Australian moviemaker Baz Luhrmann.

Vonnegut's name gave my words a life beyond the newspaper archives where they otherwise would have gone to die, and he became a permanent presence in my life.

By the end of his life, the sunscreen piece surely didn't cross his mind, but every few weeks, even now, I get an e-mail from someone asking, "Was that you or Vonnegut?"

I sometimes wondered if he minded that his name had been so indelibly inscribed on something he didn't write, but in our few encounters, he was kind, a graciousness I appreciated even more as I read his obituaries.

One quoted author Tom Wolfe: "There was never a kinder and, at the same time, wittier writer to be with personally."

Another quoted author Gay Talese: "He was not a mean man. And boy, that says something for writers."

Another quoted one of Vonnegut's main characters: "Hello, babies. Welcome to Earth. It's hot in the summer and cold in the winter. It's round and wet and crowded. At the outside, babies, you've got about a hundred years here. There's only one rule that I know of, babies — 'God damn it, you've got to be kind.'"

Reading about his kindness, it was hard not to compare him with the social commentators in vogue today. He could be acerbic without being bitter, ironic without being snarky. He could hit harder with a single clever sentence than a shock jock does with a thousand vulgar barbs.

Still, it should be said, his view of life wasn't sweet. The obituaries also mentioned melancholy, pessimism, despair. He once tried to kill himself.

For all his kindness to me, I tried to keep a respectful distance. I never wanted to seem I was trading on the association, although, with a teenage awe, I also kept tokens of proof that it existed. For years, I held on to a funny, sweet voice mail he left me, until one day I inadvertently killed it by pressing 7 instead of 9.

I still keep a letter he typed on a manual typewriter that begins, "Dearest Mary . . . We are married, whether you like it or not, and we have this dreadful child who, in one of a thousand different disguises, likes to yell at me, 'Hey, Vonnegut! You wearin' sunscreen?'"

I liked to think that the dreadful child amused him some, played to his refined sense of the absurd.

I'm still not sure we were legitimately in the same karass, but our shared absurdity will live on for me as proof that there are forces beyond our knowing, connections we can't anticipate or understand, and that in the face of the mystery, the surest thing is to be kind, damn it.

SUNDAY, MAY 31, 2009
....

Elizabeth Strout in the Toad Hole

Elizabeth Strout, who recently won the Pulitzer Prize for her novel "Olive Kitteridge," compares her life as a writer to the life of a toad.

"Because I grew up in Maine and played in the woods, I played with toads." It was Friday noon, she'd just gotten off a plane, and we were talking by phone while she ate a sandwich in a cab.

"Toads live under pine needles. It was so cozy, to see the little toads in there, breathing. I think of that in terms of my work. That's where the work takes place, underneath the pine needles, where the earth is dark and rich."

Publicity and prizes, she went on, arrive like flashlights to flush the toad out, which is fine, as long as the toad makes it back to the hole.

Strout, who is 53, has spent a lot of time lately outside the toad hole. On Thursday, she collected her Pulitzer — a Tiffany paperweight — at a luncheon in Manhattan. On Friday, she had just flown into Charlotte, N.C., to teach a writing class at Queens University.

Next Sunday, she'll be in Chicago for a discussion I'm moderating at the Printers Row Lit Fest, which was why I'd tracked her down.

Strout has been writing since she was a girl, scribbling the day's events into notebooks her mother gave her. To this day, she writes by hand, usually on lined paper with holes on the side, which may help explain why her sentences are uncommonly clear and fluid.

"Sentences," she said. "I love them. I love the sound of them. I love finding the right rhythm. There's no detail that's too small for attention. Somebody told me four or five years ago, 'Why bother to write a good sentence anymore? Nobody notices.' I don't believe it. I believe that people don't know they need good sentences but they do need good sentences."

When Strout moved to New York with her husband 25 years ago, she briefly joined a writing group. She dropped out because she felt the members came mostly to read their work aloud and be told it was fine. She remains ambivalent about writing programs, even though she teaches in them.

"I didn't go to one and it wouldn't have been for me," she said. "It's not my nature to let people see my work."

In writing programs, writers get pummeled with opinions, conflicting opinions. Strout has relied on the same female friend for years to be her main reader and critic.

For many of those years, she wrote without telling most people that she did. She'd spent six months as a lawyer — "oh my God, the most awful time of my life" — and when she couldn't find a publisher for her novel "Amy and Isabelle," she considered becoming a nurse.

Then "Amy and Isabelle" turned into a sleeper hit. "Abide With Me" followed. Now "Olive Kitteridge," a collection of connected stories that add up to a novel, is on the best-seller list.

All good novels are in some way about secrets, about the things people hide from one another or themselves. "Olive Kitteridge," the book, reveals its secrets one story at a time. Olive Kitteridge, the woman, is never exactly the person you've decided she was.

A retired 7th-grade math teacher, Olive is imperious, cantankerous, tender, harsh, philosophical, frank, deceitful, emotionally frozen and alive with desire into old age. She's an unapologetically difficult wife and mother who sometimes, but only sometimes, tries to do better.

In some of the stories, she's a minor character, seen only in passing by other inhabitants of her small Maine town.

"I grew up in Maine with a lot of elderly relatives all living on the same dirt road," Strout said. "She's a compilation of many relatives who were of a certain New England style. And yet, she kind of rose off the page as herself."

Strout considers herself a self-taught writer, but she offers these tips for other writers:

Read good writing, for example Alice Munro, William Trevor, Anton Chekhov: "So your mind is getting filled with good sentences, not bad sentences."

Tap into a deep urgency: "You have to write something that makes you feel if you don't write it, you'll die."

Be wary of praise and criticism: "You have to learn to listen deep down inside yourself."

Revise. Revise. Revise the revisions.

Be prepared to stay down in the toad hole.

WEDNESDAY, OCT. 28, 1998

A Discount Ticket to Everywhere

Not long ago I visited Frost Junior High School in Schaumburg to talk to an English class about reading. The teacher, aware that persuading video-era kids to read requires special tactics, has been inviting a variety of adults to his class this semester to talk about their reading habits.

How much do you read? I was asked. What do you read? Why do you read?

The first two questions were easy, but to the last — Why do you read? — I offered up a tedious, meandering response that not until one day last week did I realize could have been summed up in two words: To travel. I read to travel.

This obvious response came to me, oddly, on a flight to Nome, Alaska. The plane was crowded with Eskimos headed home to their remote towns and villages after the annual Alaska Federation of Natives Convention in Anchorage.

Two Eskimo women, on their way to the town of Kotzebue in the icy plains north of Nome, sat down in my row. The 11-year-old daughter of one of the women took a seat in front of us.

We chatted briefly, but once the plane was in the sky, we all set to reading.

The Eskimo woman by the window sank into the final chapters of a Danielle Steel novel, a tale of megabucks and megalust set in Beverly Hills.

The Eskimo woman at my left elbow perused the Alaska Airlines magazine, an issue full of information on Palm Springs desert resorts, a Seattle wine auction and pumpkin celebrations in Half Moon Bay, Calif. The Eskimo girl — about the age of the pupils I met at Frost Junior High — was engrossed in a book about a girl who survived the Holocaust in World War II Germany.

I, meanwhile, was reading about Eskimos.

There we sat, each of us in our private reading bubble, traveling to worlds far from our own, the Eskimos to lands of wine and war and pumpkins, me to a land of whales and walrus. The vehicle that took us to these exotic places — places we might otherwise never even imagine — had no engine, required no gas. It was simply the printed word.

In one of my books on Eskimos, I ran across a quote from an Eskimo named Anders Apassingok: "What you do not see, do not hear, do not experience, you will never really know."

In some measure, that's true, of course, but reading — if the writing's good — lets you see and hear and experience as if you were really there. Reading can take you places as distant and exotic as any airplane can and to places no airplane ever could.

It can take you places that exist only in the writer's mind and places swallowed up by time.

Reading allows you to visit the bacchanals of ancient Greece as well as the house at Pooh Corner.

And reading can enable you to see more clearly the places that you visit in body as well as in your imagination. As any Chicagoan who's read Studs Terkel, Gwendolyn Brooks or Saul Bellow knows, reading lets you travel deeper into the place you live. It introduces you to customs, ideas, people and emotions you might otherwise never meet.

After the plane landed in Nome the other day, I had the strangest feeling on the short taxi ride into town: I've been here before. The wide dusty main street, the saloons, the barren ice fields — they were eerily familiar even though I'd never seen them. Through reading, I'd come to know this place even before my eyes and ears physically arrived there.

We all yearn for other worlds, and reading opens up vistas of otherwise invisible realms of geography, mind and feeling. I was reminded of this yet again when, after Nome, I flew west to an Eskimo village on the tip of St. Lawrence Island on the Bering Sea. What was there, spitting distance from Siberia, in a frigid land without paved roads or even trees? An Eskimo woman reading a subscription copy of Ladies' Home Journal, devouring recipes, homemaking tips and tales of Christie Brinkley.

Look around on any given day, on the bus or on the "L" or in a park. People of all kinds are reading all kinds of material. Whatever they're reading — a newspaper, a textbook, a comic book — all of them are traveling.

That's what I should have made clear to that class at Frost Junior High School: Reading is a discount ticket to everywhere.

WEDNESDAY, APRIL 22, 2009

'Rain Light'

One day last March, when I was flying home from visiting my mother, afraid she might not live much longer, I stumbled on a poem in a magazine.

The poem, by W.S. Merwin, was called "Rain Light" and it seemed to drop into my lap like an oxygen mask. It began:

> *All day the stars watch from long ago*
> *my mother said I am going now*
> *when you are alone you will be all right*
> *whether or not you know you will know*

I ripped it out, a raggedy-edged square of 12 printed lines, brought it home and tucked it under a magnet on the refrigerator.

On Monday, Merwin won the Pulitzer Prize, his second, for "The Shadow of Sirius," a collection of poems that includes "Rain Light." Most people probably missed the news. No Pulitzer is more obscure than the one for poetry.

When I called a couple of bookstores on Tuesday looking for "The Shadow of Sirius," neither of the clerks had heard of it and neither store had it in stock.

The Pulitzer board cited Merwin, who is 81, for his "luminous, often-tender poems that focus on the profound power of memory," but that doesn't quite convey "Rain Light" or why I keep it on the refrigerator. I like it because it looks grief in the eye and nods and doesn't turn away.

Once, after it fell off the refrigerator door, I picked it up, put it on the counter and later realized I must have swept it into the garbage. I dove in, past the soggy coffee filters, retrieved it and posted it, coffee-stained, again.

> *All day the stars watch from long ago*
> *my mother said I am going now*

In the year since I put it there, my mother has carried on, but the mothers of a couple of my friends have not, and I've sent the poem to them. Its dozen lines say more than a sympathy card, more than a self-help book, about the solitude that follows a parent's death.

> *when you are alone you will be all right*
> *whether or not you know you will know*

I'm rarely sure I've read a poem "correctly," by which I mean read it the way the poet intended. I don't care. It helps, in this case, that Merwin has said even he doesn't know exactly what "Rain Light" says.

"What is it about?" he mused in a December interview on NPR's "Fresh Air." "What happens as you face the fact that the entire world is slipping, literally dissolving, around you. Around us. We have that feeling about our civilization, about our species and everything else, [that] it's all endangered. And indeed it is. And we either face that as a recognition — that that's our moment — or we sort of groan and dread it, which is a waste of time."

After all that, he concluded, "This is not a rational poem at all."

It may not be rational, but it makes total sense. It says, but says it in a more compelling and nuanced way, something we all know but may be helped by hearing: Someone you love dies, and the stars go on. There is something beyond each of us that endures even when, as the poem's last line says, "the whole world is burning."

The 'Peanuts' Grind

When Charles Schulz announced last week that he was retiring his classic comic strip, "Peanuts," a wail of loss sounded across the nation. My first thought, on the other hand, was, "Whew! The end of 50 years of @$%!^ comic strip deadlines!"

A comic strip deadline is a peculiar critter. It's the deadline that repeats itself into infinity. One deadline is met only to be replaced pronto by another, week after week, year after year, decade after decade, as relentlessly as the tide comes in.

The comic strip takes no vacation. It's there in your newspaper every day, come rain or shine or apocalypse. You will never open your paper and find empty panels where a story or a gag should be. You will never — or almost never — see an announcement that the cartoonist is "taking the day off" or "on assignment" or "ill." That's a perk reserved for wimpier forms of creative life, such as columnists. And comic strips rarely enjoy the relaxation of reruns.

Theoretically, a comic strip creator can go on vacation, but such escape requires discipline. No vacation benefits come with the job. Any cartoonist who gets a break must be in such command of the work that he gets the work done early, which is why many a cartoonist can be spotted at the seashore or in some hotel or on an airplane cartooning his vacation away.

I say this from sad experience. I've spent the past 14 years vacationing with "Brenda Starr," the comic strip I write. I have stood in line in the rain for a French pay phone to call a week of dialogue into the artist. On a trip to Japan, I spent a lot of time looking for business centers where I could employ my most fluent Japanese sentence: "Do you have a fax machine?"

How thrilling it was to learn this was not a private pathology but a common flaw of the species. I had that epiphany one day when I ran into Tribune cartoonist Jeff MacNelly in the convention hall at the Democratic National Convention in Atlanta — and he was rushing off to FedEx a last-minute week of his comic strip, "Shoe."

"There tend to be two beasts," says Amy Lago, Schulz's editor at United Feature Syndicate. (By "beasts" she means mild-mannered cartoonists.) "One is the one who works a little better under the pressure. And then there's the one who likes to get ahead."

There is? And how nice of her to imagine that procrastination is a sign of working well under pressure.

Lago has had to put up with many cartoonists who "work a little better under the pressure." She recalls the cartoonist who filed his last-minute strip from Paris, and the one who dashed into the syndicate to finish inking his strip before receiving a comics award that night.

"My favorite story of all time," she says, "is running into a cartoonist — who was not one of mine — at a convention and seeing him standing at the business center waiting for the fax machine. I looked at what was in his hand, and I said, 'I know what those are — and you're late.' Actually, that was Garry Trudeau. And he didn't laugh."

Trudeau is one of the few cartoonists with the courage and clout to take a break. Schulz surely could have, but he didn't until the age of 75, when the syndicate offered him a five-week vacation — one week for every decade he has been in syndication.

"He was thrilled," Lago says.

It was uncharacteristic for a man who, in anticipation of heart-bypass surgery some years ago, wrote eight weeks of "Peanuts" ahead of schedule so that he could fully recover without a lapse in the strip.

"He always wanted to be ahead of his deadlines," Lago says. "His ability to be ahead of deadline was always a source of pride to him."

In fact, at the end of each year, Schulz used to routinely return his annual schedule from the syndicate, with all the deadlines crossed off and a quip like "What now?" or "Another year down."

"I used to put it in my office as a nice reminder that there are people out there who turn in their stuff ahead of time," says Lago, "and whose stuff is really good."

Despite the interminable deadlines, any reasonable cartoonist will admit that writing a comic strip is a privilege. As work goes, it's luxury.

"Even though Mr. Schulz feels that deadline pressure like a gray cloud over him," says Lago, "this is what he's always wanted to do. He feels really blessed to be able to do it."

We've been blessed that he has. May he now relax.

How Not to Write

Before the folks at the Off-Campus Writers' Workshop in Winnetka invited me to come talk about writing Thursday, I would have advised them, or anybody else, "Don't give your work a title before you've written."

Writing the title before the text is like building a box before you know what's going in it. Do you really want the box to determine the size and shape of the contents?

But they demanded a title. So I gave them a title: "How Not to Write." What did that mean? I didn't know — until I started to cobble together what follows, a short list of notions that help me write. Whether you write for a class, simply for your own pleasure or in the hopes of getting published, maybe they can help you too.

1. Do not try to write like Ernest Hemingway. Or Nick Hornsby. Or Molly Ivins. And absolutely never try to write like Dave Barry. What works for them is apt to make you look foolish. On the other hand, feel free to do what one famous writer did early in her career, which is to type out pages of her favorite writer's writing to feel how he structured sentences. Or keep good writing handy — I particularly like poems for this purpose — and when your brain is locked, read for a while. Feeling other writers' words and rhythms can loosen up your own.

2. Do not wait for inspiration. You don't need inspiration to write. You need a deadline. If you write only when you're inspired, you'll have dust-free floors, a gleaming toilet, mounds of clean underwear — and a blank computer screen.

3. Do not wait for "perfect" writing conditions. By the time you've perfected your writing environment, it'll be happy hour. On the other hand, if you need a short voodoo dance before you write — making another cup of coffee, mating your socks, clipping your toenails — indulge in your warm-up jig. Getting ready to write is part of writing. But remember, as some famous writer once said, that the secret of writing is staying in the chair.

4. Topics to avoid: Antics of your adorable children. Your revelations about life while on a luxury vacation. Your dead dog. They've been done, and only rarely well.

5. More topics to avoid: Your love affairs and your mood disorders, unless you can be painfully honest or really funny.
6. One more topic to avoid: Anything that makes you think, "Hey, this is cute." Cute is for kids.
7. Avoid cliches like the plague.
8. Sugar. It's a lousy muse. That Snickers bar won't give you more than three good sentences.
9. Coffee. Ditto. Two good sentences, and that's only for the first cup. More than one just makes you even more nervous about your worth as a writer.
10. Alcohol. One good sentence. And even that won't look very good when you wake up from your nap. Take a walk instead.
11. Don't think you have to know what you're going to write before you write. Writing is an investigation. Writing teaches you how to think and what you think. What you think may surprise you.
12. Don't write as a way to make people love you. Some people may love your writing, but that's not the same as loving you. And remember that someone will always hate your writing.
13. Don't be afraid of offending people with what you write. But be aware that if your writing is in public view, you'll eventually offend somebody. Is it worth losing a friend just to tell that funny little story or make that flip remark?
14. Do not think your first draft is good enough. But don't hide from criticism with interminable "polishing." If you wait for it to be perfect, it will never be done. As we say in the news biz, "Push the send key."
15. Don't quit your job to write just because your friends who receive your holiday newsletters have said, "You should be a writer." But if you burn to write, then write. And write. And write. Until you get published or can't stand the heat of rejection anymore.
16. Don't invent your title first just because you're desperate to see words on the page. But when you don't have a clue what to write about, try it. Sometimes it's fun to build the contents to fit the box.

Szymborska, My Companion

Wislawa Szymborska was my constant companion.

I never actually met her, but for years I've carried her poems in my mind the way you might carry worry beads in a pocket, reaching for them in times of trouble or sometimes just for fun. I fantasized that one day I'd knock on her door in Krakow, Poland, to tell her so, and once I even checked the plane fares.

She died Wednesday, though, at the age of 88, and now what's left are the poems. Poems about new love, old love, war, the loss of a mate, the suicide of a friend, the mysteries of the sky, the writing of a resume, the astonishing, amusing, hopeful sadness of it all.

She wrote about our ancestors' short lives:

> *Few of them made it to thirty,*
> *Old age was the privilege of rocks and trees.*

She wrote about the impermanence of everything:

> *Nothing can ever happen twice.*
> *In consequence, the sorry fact is*
> *that we arrive here improvised*
> *and leave without the chance to practice.*

Long popular in Poland, Szymborska was scarcely known in the United States before she won the 1996 Nobel Prize for Literature. That's when I discovered her, and since then I've returned often to her poems for comfort, birthday gifts and examples of how to turn complex thoughts into a few clear words.

On Sept. 11, 2001, her poem "Hatred" popped into my mind with the force of a prophecy remembered:

> *See how efficient it still is,*
> *how it keeps itself in shape —*
> *our century's hatred.*
> *How easily it vaults the tallest obstacles.*

Szymborska's voice was easy and familiar — like the voice in your own head — but also unique. In one poem, she imagines what Lot's wife was thinking when she turned to look at Sodom and doomed herself to turn to salt:

> *They say I looked back out of curiosity,*
> *but I could have had other reasons.*
> *I looked back mourning my silver bowl.*
> *Carelessly, while tying my sandal strap.*
> *So I wouldn't have to keep staring at the righteous nape of my husband*
> *   Lot's neck.*

"She was the most unusual person I ever met," said Northwestern University professor Clare Cavanagh, one of her longtime translators. "She was the most enchanting, unexpected person. And funny. Frat boy funny."

Before the Nobel, Cavanagh said, Szymborska ("a hard-core, dedicated introvert") lived in a one-room Soviet-style apartment. After the Nobel, when she could have lived lavishly, she moved to a four-room Soviet-style apartment, decorated largely with wacky gifts from friends, like the barbed wire toilet seat that was, fortunately, encased in Lucite.

"She was so suspicious of great people," Cavanagh said. "She never thought of herself as one."

Not everyone in Poland loved Szymborska, despite her popularity as a poet.

"A lot of people programmatically hated her," Cavanagh said, "because she wasn't a practicing Catholic; the love of her life was a married man; she was a member of the Communist Party when she was young."

Szymborska's life is over now, but the poems endure, and anyone who loves them is apt to feel, in Cavanagh's words, "I will never see the world the same."

The best poets, like the best artists of any kind, frame something — maybe your own thoughts — for you in a new way. They read your mind and expand it. That's what Szymborska did, and her bequest is double-edged lines like these:

> *Why do we treat the fleeting day*
> *with so much needless fear and sorrow?*
> *It's in its nature not to stay:*
> *Today is always gone tomorrow.*

Quote Culprits

"Hell is other people at breakfast," as the French philosopher Jean-Paul Sartre did not say.

Many people would agree that the above quote is a deep existential truth, but it's also true that, contrary to widespread belief, that is not what Sartre said.

His famous words were actually "Hell is other people."

What Sartre did not say about people, breakfast and hell has caused a small online stir in the past few days, thanks to a blogger named Dan E. Bloom, who sent me his post on the subject.

Bloom was provoked to protest the common misattribution after spotting it recently in a New York Times Weekly supplement tucked into a Chinese-language newspaper in Taiwan, where he lives.

"The fake quote has now taken on a life on its own," he wrote, "thanks to the speed at which people read online and the power of the Internet to spread false facts and quotes."

Bloom's lament over the faux Sartre quote is a good excuse to pause and take stock of how we use quotes of any kind in an online age.

Got a speech to give? A paper to write? A love missive that could use a rhetorical boost?

How simple and tempting it is to fire up Google then snag whatever quotable quote pops up on whatever site.

Quote culprits come in many forms: school valedictorians and principals, businesspeople, students, journalists, ad writers. Let he who is without sin cast the first stone, or whatever, as the Bible, or maybe Stephen Colbert, once said.

Quoting makes us feel smarter, wittier, more authoritative. It makes us feel we've studied hard and done our research. The Internet makes such borrowed brilliance easy.

So it's inconvenient to acknowledge that most online quote sources aren't reliable, even if many of their quotes are right.

"When something wrong gets out there today, it's like spilling red wine onto a white carpet," says Charles Lipson, a University of Chicago professor who trains students in academic honesty. "You never get it out. And somebody keeps spilling more wine on top of it."

Lipson says the most reliable quote source is "The Yale Book of

Quotations," so I called its editor, Fred Shapiro, who immediately offered his first, only slightly exaggerated, quotation rule:

"Any time you see a quote attributed to Mark Twain, figure that one is false. Similarly with Yogi Berra and Benjamin Franklin."

I'll admit that I'm interested in accurate quotes in part because I've had words mangled in the online quote factory.

For example, a line from one of my 1997 columns — "Do one thing every day that scares you" — is now widely attributed to Eleanor Roosevelt, though I have yet to see any evidence that she ever said it and I don't believe she did. She said some things about fear, but not that thing.

Meanwhile, on Twitter and assorted websites, including QuoteMyDay .com, my name is attached to this profundity: "Loved you once, love you still. Always have, always will."

I never wrote that. Maybe Eleanor Roosevelt did?

The key to discerning the accuracy of a quote, Shapiro said, is to look for when and where it was said. If you don't know, be very wary.

That means be wary of online quote sites, which rarely offer such information. (One of my editors also recommends "The Quote Verifier," a book compiled and researched by Ralph Keyes.)

If a quote is good, why should we care whether it's correct or who really said it? I asked Shapiro.

"Because generally," he said, "the truth is better than error."

SUNDAY, APRIL 9, 2006

Art Buchwald on Depression

Ten years ago when I was in a period that I would look back on as "the tunnel," the famous funnyman Art Buchwald made me weep, for which I've always wanted to tell him thanks.

Art who?

If you're under 39, you probably don't know Buchwald, unless you've run into him these past few weeks, when dying has resuscitated his name and fame.

Buchwald has recently appeared on CNN and MSNBC, in The New York Times, purposefully cheerful as he repeats his self-proclaimed mantra: "I've put death on hold."

His name even popped into my e-mail inbox last week, on a local press release recommending a hospice story tied to his decision to renounce dialysis and count down his mortal days in a Washington, D.C., hospice, where he has been receiving guests, reading mail and knocking out a few last columns.

Art Buchwald. In his heyday, that name was as big as Jon Stewart's is today. His medium was newsprint, back when that wasn't a cause for anxiety.

By the time I started reading him regularly, in the '80s, he'd been writing for three decades; to me, he already seemed crotchety and old.

The little picture that ran with his column showed a good-humored, broad-faced guy, not handsome, behind giant black glasses. What really popped off the page was his voice, more stand-up comic than Washington pundit — short paragraphs, sharp quips, a simple style that's harder than it looks.

He wrote wittily about important events and important people without acting self-important. Occasionally his writing just seemed silly — an occupational inevitability, I now understand — but when he chose to shoot to kill he had perfect aim.

Categorized as a humorist and satirist, he protested the Vietnam War, mocked Watergate, and won a Pulitzer Prize in 1982 for columns compiled in the book "While Reagan Slept."

It's hardly breaking news, though, that humor's dark twin is melancholy, and Buchwald lived through two profound personal depressions.

That's what he was talking about the day 10 years ago that, during a hard time in my own life, I flicked on the radio and heard him speaking at the Harold Washington Library in Chicago.

It was 1996, shortly after the publication of his memoir, "I'll Always Have Paris," and he was talking in front of a live audience to WBEZ's Mara Tapp.

Self-deprecating and charmingly gruff, he told stories of his childhood in an orphanage and foster homes, his gala days of living and writing in Paris, his divorce after 40 years from his wife, who died in 1992.

He made the requisite wisecracks. But he was serious when he talked about his periods of depression.

I don't remember his remarks verbatim, but I remember the voice coming out of the radio like a shaft of light shooting into my tunnel when he said: I want to tell anyone who is going through this to hang on. You will get through. You will be OK.

Is that exactly what he said? Maybe not. But that's what I heard. And I said out loud to the radio: Thank you. Thank you. Thank you, Art Buchwald.

There was nothing poetic in his words that day, and the same words coming from other people sounded like platitudes. Why did they sound different — believable, persuasive — coming from, of all people, Art Buchwald?

Probably because he so clearly understood that life is funny and sad, usually both at once, sometimes only in alternation. And because he extended hope not with a therapeutic coo but in a crusty Queens accent. And because he was old and a guy and famous and yet unafraid to be so exposed.

And because his words were so simple.

Occasionally since then I've wondered how many other people were listening that day, how many others he helped to hang on, to get through.

More than one, I bet. We all owe him a thank you. So do all the people who have found encouragement in his frank approach to death.

As he once said, "Whether it's the best of times or the worst of times, it's the only time we've got."

FRIDAY, JAN. 29, 2010

In Honor of Holden

If you really want to hear about it, the first thing you'll probably want to know is whether I liked "The Catcher in the Rye" during my lousy childhood and all that kind of crap that people are talking about just because some famous writer died, but I don't feel like going into it, if you want to know the truth.

In the first place, I didn't even read the whole book, and in the second place, I was not totally bawling when I heard about J.D. Salinger. Am I supposed to commit suicide or something because an old guy died?

And if you're not sure why I'm writing like this, go read the first page of "Catcher in the Rye" and you'll figure it out.

Anyway, to tell you the truth, I was a little sad about Mr. Salinger.

I'm always sad when artists die because it's like they create this secret world in your mind and when they're gone, a little of your world — your moment in the world — dies too.

Another reason I'm sad is because I missed out on this big "rite of passage" thing the obits keep boring me with.

I'll tell you more about that in a minute, but first let me say that if you don't know what I'm talking about, you must be wasting your life thinking about Leno and Oprah.

Talk about phonies. The whole "Tonight" show thing makes me puke, and don't get me started on John Edwards.

Anyway, this guy, J.D. Salinger, wrote this book, "Catcher in the Rye," which almost everybody since 1951 had to read in school, except in the schools that banned it — and those kids especially wanted to read it.

And then Urban Outfitters makes it into a T-shirt, which is phonier than Jay on Oprah but still better than just selling lava lamps.

Anyway, "C in the R" is about this cynical adolescent named Holden Caulfield, and he writes sort of like this, only better, and he's a poor role model due to his vulgarity, blaspheming and sexual stuff, which is why he's an icon of teenage rebellion.

Not that you care, but I've been reading amazon.com and Wikipedia, which is where I stole "cynical adolescent" and "teenage rebellion." Totally phony terms.

Personally, when I tried to read this book in high school, I hated it. Holden reminded me of my little brothers, and I did not need any more of that gross behavior. Another thing is that he went to prep school, which was so not my life.

But when I hear people talk about this book as a rite of passage, I get it, even though that phrase is also phony.

I respect any book that puts into words stuff you didn't even know you were thinking or didn't think you should think, or reveals weird stuff you didn't know anybody else but you was doing.

I know some girls who liked "The Bell Jar" or Judy Blume books better, but who cares?

I heard this one guy Thursday wonder how a miserable recluse like Salinger could write such great stuff. Personally, I think 95 percent of great writers are probably jerks because writing, especially writing the truth, is kind of anti-social, which is another thing that makes me sad.

Anyway, even if Mr. Salinger was the worst boyfriend ever, it is damn hard to write something that 59 years later is loved equally by people who are 16 and people who are 60.

You don't have to adore the man to admire the thing he left behind.

A Lesson From Elmore Leonard

During a radical book purge several years ago, I got rid of my Ernest Hemingway but kept my Elmore Leonard.

This struck some of my friends as a shocking literary crime, but it felt right to me. Plain and simple, I preferred Elmore Leonard, the man and his work, to the master from whom he learned.

Last week, in commemoration of Leonard's death at age 87, I plucked the books from the shelf for the first time in a long time. They're tiny, lightweight paperbacks, all from the 1980s, before the peak of Leonard's fame, and the yellow pages have taken on a musty, geriatric odor.

Even so, when I picked them up, I could feel the dazzling novelty of early Elmore Leonard, remember how reading one of his books felt like a major discovery you couldn't wait to share with everyone you knew.

Opening "LaBrava," a 1983 thriller set in Miami Beach, I instantly landed on a paragraph that helps explain his appeal:

"*I have a feeling you might be in danger.* All the next day he would hear himself saying it. The tone was all right, not overdone, and he believed it was true she was in danger. But it didn't sound right. Because people who were into danger on an everyday basis didn't talk like that, they didn't use the word."

Those lines come from the mind of one of the book's characters, but you can also hear Leonard talking to himself about his writing:

Got to get the tone right. Got to find the right word, the everyday word, the word people really use.

As last week's obituaries noted, an ear for common speech was at the heart of Leonard's success, an approach summed up in what may be his most quoted sentence: "If it sounds like writing, rewrite it."

But I think Elmore Leonard knew that his writing prescription wasn't meant for every writer. He was talking about what had worked for him, and his genius lay in knowing that what worked for him grew out of what he had the skill to do.

I learned this firsthand when I spent a day with him many years ago at his home in a wealthy suburb of Detroit. He had just written "Killshot," the first of his books with a woman in the lead, which had inspired an editor at Vogue magazine to deploy me on a freelance assignment to talk to him about writing female characters.

In most respects, he was nothing like his imaginary gallery of cops, cons and dames. He was a small man, gentlemanly, cerebral. He insisted on picking me up at the airport and he arrived in a cashmere coat, leather driving gloves and white Reeboks. James Bond meets suburban grandpa.

"I'm not going to sweep anybody away with my poetry," he said that day, sitting next to his manual typewriter, puffing on a True menthol.

He explained that he had developed his style by reading Hemingway, listening in the streets and respecting his creative limits. He wasn't good at description so he learned not to do it. He wasn't a master of plot, so he worked to master what he could: character, dialogue, mood, place.

And he wasn't good at women, not to begin with, a fact that he attributed in part to an education in an all-boys Jesuit school. His early female characters were dolls and molls, cliche cutouts from the noir tradition of earlier male crime writers. But by the time of "Killshot," he was moving beyond cliche.

"My women are getting better," he said. "They'd better be. I'm working hard enough at it."

He credited his second wife, Joan, for the improvement. He would read her manuscript pages at night and she would respond: A woman wouldn't talk like that, think like that, do that. He would rewrite.

Elmore Leonard — it just feels better to call him by both names — spawned countless imitators, which may be why his books, filled with mayhem, don't appeal to me as much as they once did. In books, movies and TV, mayhem has taken over as story currency, and it gets tiresome.

But I'll always love my Elmore Leonard books. And I'll always appreciate what his life teaches about writing, which, in a word, is discipline.

He had the discipline to give up alcohol. The discipline to listen. The discipline to write day after day, year after year. And the discipline to know what he would never master, then work on what he might.

FROM
THE
DESK
OF

Mary
Schmich

In 1994, the Ms. Foundation invited a group of girls from Chicago's Cabrini-Green housing project to the White House for Take Our Daughters to Work Day. I went with them. The girls were part of a club run by Lue Ella Edwards, a longtime Cabrini resident. The trip was overseen by Pastor Chuck Infelt, who ran Holy Family Lutheran Church, a true place of sanctuary and salvation next to Miss Lue Ella's red-brick high-rise.

After that trip, I got to know Miss Lue Ella and Pastor Infelt better and it's thanks to them that I got the access and insight to write intensively about Cabrini for the next 20 years.

I remember this day as bright and beautiful and how excited the girls were to be there. I wish I had more photos of them — this was pre-cellphone camera so I don't — but I'm glad someone captured this photo of me paying no attention to that gray-haired guy in the background.

chapter 9

cabrini-green

Crossroads of Change

I am standing on the corner of Sedgwick and Division, at the crossroads of a blighted past and something still to come. Already it's hard to remember what was here not long ago.

There are bulldozers now, and cement trucks and dump trucks, rasping and rumbling all around the neighborhood, exterminating and creating and coughing clouds of dirt. This is the machinery of change.

On the south side of Division Street, against the backdrop of the downtown skyline — Marina City's scalloped cylinders, the glinting black Sears Tower — Cabrini-Green is dwindling. And like so many people for whom Cabrini isn't home, I've watched it shrink and yet not fully noticed.

Cabrini's notorious high-rises still pop up here and there, but a couple have been demolished and others have gone blind, brown plywood covering their windows. Next to one vacant lot, a tattered white sheet hangs from the back stairway of an old three-flat. In giant black letters, the sheet says: Stop Urban Cleansing.

I've passed this spot for years, so it's strange to realize, staring at the vacant lots, with their mounds of dirt and clumps of purple wildflowers, that I can't quite summon the memory of buildings past.

What was over there, across the fresh asphalt of Division from Cabrini? Men in hard hats — yellow, orange, white — dig and trowel and hammer, lift and saw and measure in the vast dirt field.

Whatever was there, what will be there by September is a Dominick's grocery store. "Prairie style," explains Sam Furman, an architect involved with the building who just happens to be cruising past in his shiny Mazda on this cloudy Thursday morning. "Not to say this is a Frank Lloyd Wright building, but it's the same flavor."

Imagine that. A supermarket, one with a fancy architectural flavor, in the land of fast-food joints and shabby liquor stores.

Old Town Square they call this now, giving the gloss of venerable age to the new construction in a part of town once so dangerous and decrepit that cabbies hated to drive through. "Old Town Square" is what the sign outside the Dominick's says. It's what the sign just across Sedgwick Street says, too, the one by the row of new townhouses "starting from $356,900."

Imagine that. Townhomes starting from $356,900 across the street from a housing project where 7 percent of the residents are employed.

It's all part of a makeover of this coveted patch of the Near North Side, a change that in a perfect world will benefit the rich, the poor and the in-between. The plan is to bring new people in and mix them with the old and create a happy new blend of colors, incomes and lifestyles.

With luck, it will happen as the utopians hope. But right now it feels like a place trapped in time, a mystery, neither what it was nor what it will be.

I ask several passersby what used to be on all these newly vacant lots. Some can't quite remember. They pause. They shake their heads. Was it an Oscar Mayer plant on the Dominick's lot? Or was that over by the new townhouses?

Deante Jones, on the other hand, remembers. He is 12 and has lived all his life in Cabrini.

"It was a basketball court here," he says, pointing to the Dominick's lot. "And across the street," he says, pointing past Division, "was a little red church and a club where people go and party. Then there on the corner was a pizza place called Chester's. And next to that an Arab place where the taxi drivers came. There was a cleaners and a Chinese food place. I liked the shrimp-fried rice."

He also remembers the years growing up when he sat in his apartment playing Super Nintendo because he was too afraid of gunfire to go outside. He remembers it all, and he hopes what's coming will be better.

It will certainly be better for some, though for whom and how many won't be clear until the legal wrangling and other work is done. But the one sure thing right now is that this neighborhood as Chicago knew it is gone. And there's an odd danger in that.

Cabrini made poverty visible to people in the city's affluent heart. It was a daily reminder to those who don't live in need that there are those who do. How tempting it will be to forget that for too many years too many people lived in such poverty and isolation, and that there remain parts of the city where they will continue to live that way. It's so easy, and convenient, to forget what you can't see.

SUNDAY, JUNE 4, 2000

The New Dominick's

Daryl Benton, lifelong resident of Cabrini-Green, has recently become a specialist in the culinary habits of well-to-do white people.

"White people," Benton says, sitting in the cafe of the Dominick's on Division Street, "they buy like the chutney, and olives from over there in the deli. They buy like the hummus and stuff in Aisle Five. That's our world import aisle. And they buy the water crackers. Black people don't buy the water crackers."

Benton has been exposed to all kinds of cultural novelties since he took a job changing light bulbs and sweeping floors at this Dominick's in the heart of the Cabrini frontier. The same could be said of just about everybody who shops or works here.

Walk through the store's doors — with Cabrini and the downtown skyline at your back — and you're also walking into a social test kitchen. Rich people, poor people, black people, white people — from produce to poultry to pantyhose, this is a collection of classes and colors rarely seen in Chicago. As the formerly derelict neighborhood undergoes a drastic makeover, this market is a measure of how well the new mix will work.

When it opened a year and a half ago, the store's success was hardly guaranteed. Would the wealthy whites flooding into the neighborhood's new homes really shop across the street from the notorious Cabrini-Green?

Sure they would. If you gave them ample parking for their Lexus sedans and SUVs. If you drove panhandlers off the lot. If you gave them five security guards instead of the usual one. If you gave them water crackers.

Now this store is growing faster than almost any Dominick's in town. And just as it benefits from the changes around it, it's changing the neighborhood.

For the first time, Cabrini residents have a supermarket — and a major job source — within an easy walk.

"Thank God for this store," says Justin Thomas, who works dumping garbage and washing pots. "This store is a school. This store right here's giving a whole lot of people a chance who wouldn't have a chance."

Almost all the employees here live in Cabrini. Some have never worked. Some decide work's not worth their while for $5.65 an hour. Too many don't show up when they should and then are stunned when they're fired.

And they will be fired. Strict standards are one reason the store is a success.

"I'm not going to baby 'em cause they had a worse life than me," says Todd Mich, one of the managers. "We're all professionals."

Mich, a white 30-year-old from Chicago's Northwest Side, has been frustrated by the attitude toward work he's encountered in many employees. He's also been pleasantly instructed.

"I was expecting more employees to be meaner, rude, less interested," he says. "Maybe it was because of all the bad things I heard about Cabrini-Green. The way they were raised is different from me, but you give them the respect, they'll give you the respect back."

That attitude permeates this Dominick's. There's a sense here that everybody — customers and staff alike — was expecting something worse from people of the other color and are hugely relieved to be wrong.

"I don't see any prejudice in this store," says Justin Thomas. "It just blows me away."

He confesses, however, that he had his own prejudice.

"Being black, you would assume the focus is on the white customer," he says. "If a white customer asked me where something was, I would have shown the white customer the aisle. I'd just tell the black customer, figuring they wouldn't report it."

He's had that attitude schooled out of him. The managers here work hard to convey a simple principle: Every customer is equal.

Occasionally problems flare. Sometimes white customers seem unnerved by more boisterous customers from Cabrini. Not long ago, members of two rival gangs bumped into each other while shopping; security was called.

Yet there's a strong feeling in this store of being somewhere new, somewhere better. Interracial interactions that on the street might seem risky seem safe in the cereal aisle.

I think most of us yearn for more connection to people who aren't like us, for glimpses into cultures different from our own. In its small way, this grocery store in this changing neighborhood allows that.

The other day, for example, Daryl Benton got curious enough about the oddly popular water crackers to buy some. "They're good," he says.

FRIDAY, JAN. 26, 2001

This Is Deep

The wrecking ball arrives like an alarm clock, before sunup, six days a week. In his third-floor Cabrini-Green apartment, Wence Edwards wakes up and listens, knowing that the whirring, whacking, rumbling, beeping and drilling of the demolition machines will last all day and sometimes into the night.

Later, almost every day, Edwards goes down for a while to watch the Bobcats and the wrecking ball bite into the neighboring red-brick high-rise. On these breezy winter days, the demolition dust gusts in waves across the nearby dirt and asphalt.

"This is deep," he said, standing there one bitter morning while a wrecking crane wheeled in the bright sky. "It's deep. I'm just looking in amazement. It's over. Before this, people believed they had a chance."

For all the talk of tearing down Cabrini-Green to make way for a mixed-income community, and for all the new stores and houses that recently have popped up just beyond its borders, it had been five years since a residential building here actually met the bulldozers. Then just before Christmas, with a long-standing legal blockade lifted, the work crews arrived at 500-502 W. Oak St.

They hunted down the rats and roaches with super-strength poison.

They bricked up the lower floors. They "trashed the building out," ridding the abandoned rooms of sofas, stoves, refrigerators, all the assorted junk of the departed lives that once made this place a home. Finally, the motors of the wrecking machines clicked on.

Now the back-yard racket reminds the residents of Edwards' building that the end is near for them as well, and sometimes, as the building shrinks to bigger mounds of rubble, they reminisce about the old days.

Remember when?

Remember when that building was called The Castle, in tribute to its status as a center for the money, drugs and crime of the gang known as the Vice Lords?

Remember when Dantrell Davis, 7, was shot right outside as he walked to Jenner School?

Remember the prayer vigils in the entryway? The snipers' nest above?

Edwards, 31, remembers when his family lived in 500-502, before moving just across the way to Larrabee Street. He remembers much later when the tenants were evacuated and he worked on the Muhammad Ali Foundation crew that boarded up the windows.

He also remembers the occasion when some gun-toting Vice Lords chased him between that building and his own.

"That was my gangbanging days," he said, standing in the cold sun all these years later, "when I was in good form."

He pointed to a scar in his right jaw, then a dent in his left cheek.

"That's not a dimple," he said, "it's a bullet hole."

Cabrini is an eerie patchwork these days of new and old. There's the giant new police station waiting to be unveiled just up the block. The gleaming new Jenner Academy of the Arts. And everywhere are vacant lots and ancient ghosts and stories.

"Right there," said Edwards, pointing to the sidewalk behind him, "that's where my little sister got shot."

Edwards belongs to one of Cabrini's most famous families. His 14-year-old sister, Laquanda, was shot to death in 1992 when she stepped outside to buy milk. His mother, Lue Ella Edwards, was a Cabrini leader, once honored at the White House, who died of heart failure three years ago at age 51. Her son has her broad, friendly face and manner and still lives in her apartment with three of his brothers.

But for how much longer? Knowing that the building next door will have vanished by March, he wonders.

But then so much of his Cabrini has disappeared already.

His mother. His sister. The Vice Lords who once chased him.

"And the guys I grew up with is gone," he said. "Dead. In jail for murders."

He counts himself lucky. He's alive. Out of the gang. "I saw the light," he said. "Gunshots hurt. Jail is crazy."

This week he has an interview for a job in a mailroom.

"Four hours a day," he said. "I gotta start at the bottom. Not the CEO spot. I gotta make a move."

And though he says some days it's hard just to leave the apartment, the wrecking machines are always there now to wake him and his neighbors up, in more ways than one.

Who Will Be Saved?

At nightfall, just down Larrabee Street, women in stiletto heels and men in suits sit cocooned by giant potted fronds at the new riverside restaurant Japonais. They're fingering wine goblets and nibbling edamame.

A block and a half up, here in Cabrini-Green, men play chess beside the liquor store, women push baby strollers and a few crack addicts huddle near a weedy lot. Cop cars crawl by, scouting for trouble.

"Hey, white girl," someone calls.

It's a friendly call, curious. White people live all around Cabrini now, but except for the occasional bicyclist or jogger, rarely cross the border.

I've come because for the past few weeks I've been exploring the radical change in and around Chicago's most famous housing project, a change long in the air, slow on the ground and now, finally, unavoidable even to those who have hoped it wouldn't happen.

"This community is like a wounded animal trying to survive," says Ronald "Silky" Crosby, who's out on the lively summer sidewalk with his two young sons.

Before long, I'm surrounded by residents eager to talk about their neighborhood.

And Cabrini is a neighborhood, not just a public-housing complex, a neighborhood more neighborly than most. It's a place where generations are bound by blood and church, by hardship and struggle, by an old-fashioned reliance on each other. Now they're losing the ground they once thought of as theirs.

"This was a gold mine right here," says a man who prefers to be called simply D'Nice. He gestures toward the downtown high-rises, all those jobs Cabrini people might have had, though mostly they didn't. "But it's over. It's over."

No doubt that the teeming Cabrini-Green of yore — 15,000 people, many who rarely left the property — is just the stuff of stories now. But on this pulsing summer night, Cabrini-Green obviously is not quite over.

Or should I say, "the notorious Cabrini-Green?"

Run a computer check of news reports on Cabrini and you'll find story after story unable to resist that label, as if Cabrini's name began with "Notorious."

Notorious for the field where in 1970 Cabrini snipers shot two police officers to death and notorious for the apartment where in 1981 Mayor Jane Byrne lived briefly as a call to stop the violence.

Notorious as the place where in 1992 a 7-year-old boy was shot to death while walking to school holding his mother's hand.

Notorious as the place where in 1997 a 9-year-old girl was raped and left for dead in a stinking stairwell.

Notorious for a trilogy of plagues that during the complex's six decades of life have fused into a single pestilence: gangsgunsdrugs.

Cabrini has been so notorious that, along with Chicago's other less-iconic public-housing high-rises, it's being razed and resurrected as a community where the rich, the poor and the in-between will live as neighbors and mingle up the street at Pottery Barn.

"Cabrini's still there?" you may be thinking if you've heard such forecasts of Cabrini's imminent demise for years.

It's there.

It's there against the photogenic backdrop of downtown skyscrapers, in walking distance to the shops of the Magnificent Mile, the mansions of the Gold Coast and Lincoln Park, the sparkling lake.

It's there, kept on life support by tenants with hope and lawyers, tenants for whom Cabrini is not just a notorious housing project and a great chunk of real estate but community, culture, history, home.

It's there, but not for long.

So far, not a single new building has risen on Cabrini property, but the first phase of construction is set to begin within a year. Already, new developments — on the big surrounding swaths of rezoned barren or industrial land — squeeze it on all sides.

Just feet from its borders, construction cranes wheel against the clouds, hammers bang and jackhammers shudder, and every day, it seems, more luxury lofts, penthouses and town homes shimmer forth into a neighborhood that not so long ago taxis avoided.

Now Mercedeses, Saabs and Volvos parade down Larrabee Street, a happy detour from the gridlocked shopping corridors nearby. And out their windows — usually rolled up tight — the passersby can see the Cabrini that remains:

Seventeen high-rises and mid-rises still standing but slated for demolition.

Vacant lots where five buildings have come down.

Boards on the windows of hundreds of emptied apartments. Or giant holes where vandals have ripped the boards off and stolen the pipes inside.

Rowhouses, the only part of Cabrini destined to survive.

Still, there remain in Cabrini 1,300 officially occupied apartments and who knows how many occupants. Four thousand? Five?

Squatters live in many supposedly vacated units. Leaseholders share rooms with countless unauthorized friends and relatives, among them the officially relocated who have unofficially come back.

Some return because they couldn't cope outside public housing, even with the government rental vouchers they were given when they left. Too many rules, utilities to pay.

Some return because they miss their friends, their family, the solace of what is known.

One day, theoretically, many Cabrini leaseholders can come back. Go, the city said. Go so we can redevelop, and if you want, we'll try to find you a new or rehabbed unit back here. Many residents have been flat-out guaranteed new homes in the neighborhood.

But thousands of tenants were forced out years ago, and barely 200 new public-housing replacement homes have been built, all in developments around, not in, Cabrini. Hundreds more are planned, but there will never be enough for everyone who leaves.

"You can't save everybody," Crosby says on this summer night on the Cabrini sidewalk. "Everybody don't deserve what they dishing out."

You can't save everybody.

It's a stark thought. And it's realistic, despite the hype about Cabrini's "transformation" remaking Chicago for the good of all.

So who will be saved?

It's too soon to be sure. Hard to know what kind of city will emerge from this extraordinary mass movement of people, this tearing down and building back on a scale rarely seen except after war.

For those who have left, the signs aren't good.

For better or for worse, the adventurous have divorced themselves from their old Chicago web of relations — both the trouble and the support — and headed north to Minneapolis or Milwaukee.

Some have gone back to the South, the place so many black Chicago families left half a century ago looking for a better life, only to wind up poor and isolated in Chicago's misbegotten public housing.

Most, though, have gone a few miles up to Rogers Park, out to the West Side, down to remote suburbs, to scattered places with one shared trait: They're as racially segregated as Cabrini, and if all aren't quite as poor, they're nevertheless estranged from the opportunities of the new old neighborhood — the jobs, the supermarkets, the frequent buses, the new parks and library, the beauty and promise of Chicago.

Still, the world being constructed in Cabrini's place is, at its best, an audacious act of hope. It's a world in the process of becoming, still so undone that with some vigilance, it could bring a better life to many different kinds of residents.

It could break the famous "cycle of poverty" for thousands. It could introduce the well-off and the poor to each other as neighbors. In the process, it could demolish Chicago's reputation as the country's most racially divided city.

Whether it — whether we — succeed depends, in the end, on people.

In the last few years, I've written a fair amount about Cabrini's changing neighborhood. For the next couple of weeks, I'll be writing more, about a few of the people guiding this vast change and a few whose lives are changing as a result.

"There's a story here, a lot of stuff to tell about this neighborhood," says Crosby, who wrote four plays about Cabrini the last time he was in prison.

A few yards away, lights are twinkling from the scores of new luxury lofts.

"This fixing to be history, you know what I mean?" he says.

History in both senses of the word.

The Gangbanger

He was born into the power days of Cabrini's gangs. Those were the days when gang members were the titans of Cabrini's high-rises and the shabby towers strutted against Chicago's skyline with fancy nicknames like The Castle.

They were the days when in the silence just before the shooting started, mothers knew to call their kids indoors and kids knew to hit the ground. Those days were just life when this man was a boy.

He's 19 now, tall, solid and fierce, wounded, tired and scared. Now, the gang business is staffed by grown-up boys like him.

But the freewheeling power of Cabrini's old gang days has vanished, gone on the gusts of redevelopment. Police have turned up the heat. The old alliances have fractured as gang turf has shrunk. In the hallways, stairwells and other trading posts of this dying housing project, suspicion and a mood of doom are as prevalent as crack.

"Money's getting short," says this young man, who's got too much trouble with the police already to let his name be used. Standing in the high caged breezeway of the building where he has lived all his life, he looks down 15 floors, past the withering old Cabrini, out to the blooming new neighborhood.

Can't he see a place for himself down in that luxuriously remodeled world on the turquoise lake, a place better than this cage up here?

"Yeah," he says. "I can see a place. Death. Hell."

Cabrini's gradual demise has forced change on everyone who lives here, but the change for the gangs has been unique. They're losing not just their homes, but their incomes, their status, the place they worked their illicit business. In the words of another gang member, redevelopment is "corrupting the street organizations," and however startling that use of "corrupt" is, it's precise.

To corrupt: break down, mix up, cause to deteriorate, alter from the original.

Now, this young man explains, as Cabrini buildings are closed and residents are shuttled to different buildings, you don't know everybody anymore. The guy who just got evacuated from his building into yours? For all you know, he killed your brother.

Now, he says, you see an old friend and his pocket is bulging with dollar bills while yours is empty? You get jealous. Mad.

"They're putting people together," he says. "Making us fight."

Kids flit past him in the busy breezeway as he talks. He gently ruffles their hair. Without a word, one man shoves by, toward the stairwell, and passes him a small brown paper sack stained with grease. A small paper sack stained with grease is the way a bag of crack is disguised to look like fast food.

The young man says that once pegged as a gangbanger, it's hard to escape the identity. Or the cops. The cash. Cabrini. He tried.

He tried pumping gas, shoveling snow. At 15, he left school and moved to Milwaukee, but it cost too much to stay. "Rent," he says. "Rent was kicking my hair out."

He came back. At 17, he swore off gangs and drugs. He spent 15 months as a janitor for his building. He volunteered at the nearby Y.

"That was more pressure," he says. "Everybody knew I was doing good, and then —"

He stomps on the concrete, miming the extermination of his best intentions.

Then one payday, when his hours had been cut and he got his paltry check, he had a revelation. He thought of a book he had read. It was about how the government planted drugs in the projects to destroy the poor and how those same powers now want those neighborhoods back.

He thought about the 20 or so family members — siblings, nieces, nephews, his mother — who rely on him for money. He thought of the $375 a week he could earn selling drugs.

"It just keep calling," he says. "I can work hard, but when it don't pay off, I'm cheating myself."

So he stepped back into the quicksand, where he has been sinking since even before he dropped out of high school.

Why'd he drop out?

He studies the dirty hallway wall. "I had no patience."

No patience for?

He looks back, his brown eyes hot and close to tears. "Life."

Not long ago, he was arrested for stealing car parts. Presto — he was another Cabrini guy who could apply for a job not just as a dropout but as a felon.

Given all his trouble here, wouldn't he like to try life somewhere else?

"Like to?" he says. "I'd love to. I'm not getting nowhere." He raises a hand above his head and tugs. "Got a string tied around my neck."

But he's on probation so he can't go far enough to escape the old troubles and seductions. And on a minimum-wage job, even if he could find one, he couldn't afford to take his family with him, and he won't go anywhere without them.

"I got people that love me here," he says. "My family keeps me alive."

One of those people is his 15-year-old brother, whom he has vowed to keep out of the gang and its business.

"Because I'm hurt, I'm hurt, I'm really hurt," he says. "He'll have a better chance to leave."

This man's life makes an argument for tearing down the old Cabrini, though it's naive to think that lives of gang members will change just because Cabrini will. Gangs are merely transplanting to other neighborhoods.

And yet there's an opportunity in Chicago right now, say those who know the gangs. In the few months between leaving the housing project and rooting somewhere else, many could be weaned of gang life. Liberated from the old identities, obligated to find new ways to work, they could be helped. If help were there.

But it rarely is. So because they have records instead of resumes and work habits that don't count as job skills, they settle into a new life that looks too much like the old one.

FRIDAY, JULY 16, 2004

The Dogwalkers

Before he moved out of Cabrini-Green, Deshaun Pughsley, who's 12, was more terrified of dogs than guns. He'd see a dog coming and he'd shriek, maybe hide behind a garbage can.

The Cabrini dogs he knew were fight dogs, dogs egged on to violence by a chorus of sideline gamblers.

Then Deshaun's family moved into North Town Village, the biggest and most mixed of the mixed-income developments to rise so far in the remodeling of Cabrini and its neighborhood. Here, on the sidewalks outside the spotless red-brick homes, well-groomed residents promenaded well-groomed dogs on leashes, scooping the aftermath into little plastic bags.

So one day, recounts Deshaun, "one of our neighbors, he was walking his dog, I ain't knowing him at first, I asked could I hold his dog?"

Not long after, Deshaun asked if he could walk the dog after school. For pay.

"He's asking for a job," the neighbor's wife whispered. The neighbor said OK.

Sibling rivalry can be the mother of enterprise, so when Deshaun's brother Andre, 10, spotted a woman moving in next door, he instantly marched over and announced, "We walk dogs."

Soon, a family business was born, and all five Pughsley kids were out escorting Abby, Dude, Maverick, Samantha, Pepe and Zoe, from whom they've learned that dogs, and life, can be different outside Cabrini.

Out here, it's rules that bite.

"You always have to pick up their poop," said Deshaun, sitting in the new living room where his mom had built a cardboard fireplace from a kit and flanked it with wall sconces topped by candles, as yet unlit.

"We can't have them off leash," said Andre, "or we'll get a fine."

In the long run, if the mixed-income makeover of Cabrini-Green is going to keep its promise of making Chicago a better place, it has to open new lives to the kids. To kids like these:

Andre and Ashante, 10, broad-faced twins who shout and wave "Hi" and "Bye" with the exuberance of actors accepting Oscars.

Deshaun, 12, the dapper, watchful entrepreneur.

Darian, 13, the one who keeps to himself.

Kentrell, strong-bodied at 14, with a gaze that can be frank or hooded, who preaches to his younger brothers the most valuable thing Cabrini taught him: When somebody tries to fight you, walk away.

There's another child on the edges of this family too. A child so famously, heart-rendingly slain that his name survives on a street sign in the housing project he helped make legendary: Dantrell Davis.

A dozen years ago as Dantrell, 7, walked to school, a sniper's bullet hit him in the head. His father, no longer living, was the father of Kentrell, Darian and Deshaun.

"If he was over here," said Deshaun of the big brother he lost when he was barely born, "he'd be, like, meeting everybody. He'd be glad and happy."

Not that the Pughsley kids are always glad and happy. North Town

Village rules bar them from riding bikes except to enter and exit. Guards shoo them off common-area lawns and sidewalks. Playing is considered loitering.

"Managers follow them," says their mother. "Sometimes it's harassment, really."

Deneen Pughsley is 33 and, like most Cabrini women, she raises her kids alone. But she's a strict mother and was an employed one too, until a few months ago when she lost her maintenance job in the Cabrini row-houses. She does side jobs now — painting, fixing lights or ceiling fans — but, like many Cabrini crossovers here, struggles with the unaccustomed obligation of paying utility bills.

Still, Pughsley calls her four-bedroom town home "my dream home." It was worth the drug test, the credit check and the housekeeping inspection required to qualify. And though North Town Village sometimes feels unfriendly to Cabrini people, she likes the vistas the dogs have opened to her kids.

"My dog sits at the window and waits for them," said Jennifer Hallett, a 35-year-old attorney. "When she sees them, she starts crying."

Hallett was about to move to the suburbs and have a baby, but she said she would miss how the Pughsley kids refreshed her middle-class perspectives. She recalled the time two ex-Cabrini mothers broke into a curbside screaming match over a fight between their sons.

Would mothers in her new neighborhood fight like that, the kids asked?

"Sure," Hallett laughed and told them. "But they'll file lawsuits instead of the moms coming out on the street."

The vision for the new mixed-income Cabrini is a grand, fragile and elusive one, but for a little while each day, the Pughsley kids live it. Dogs in hand, they cross the chasms of class and color, enjoying new liberties and learning from new rules.

"My brothers don't do the things they did in the rowhouses," said Ashante, who was reclining now — against regulations — on a lawn while Andre and Deshaun tossed toys to the dogs. "They used to, like, fight a lot."

"Some of the people that we know here," said Deshaun, "they're, like, our friends."

On this warm afternoon, the three kids then wandered with Dude, a bichon frise, to the black, spike-topped wrought-iron fence that separates the back end of North Town Village from Cabrini's white high-rises.

They pointed through the rails. There was a drug raid in that building.

And a killing over there. One time, they said, Cabrini kids stood on top of that school and threw rocks at them. Jealousy, maybe.

Then they looked up, toward the clouds. Deshaun detected a duck. Andre imagined a fluffy airplane.

"Is it true," asked Ashante, "that when someone dies and it shines in the clouds, it's somebody's spirit shining through?"

A while later, a property manager would rebuke them, again, for something involving the dogs, but for now life was pretty good, with Cabrini across the fence, under the same sky, a lifetime away.

SUNDAY, JULY 18, 2004
....

Cabrini in the Year 2020

By the year 2020, the scariest thing in the neighborhood once known as Cabrini-Green will be gridlock.

In that big reborn patch of Chicago's Near North Side, the thousands of lofts and town homes that today seem so unrooted and so raw will have shed their construction dust and settled in as naturally as trees. Their occupants will shuttle in new cars through clogged streets to nearby downtown jobs, to restaurants that prefer reservations, to stores that rarely use the term "discount."

That's part of the future I imagine after two months of exploring the new neighborhood rising around Cabrini-Green and the past couple of weeks writing about it.

And I imagine this:

By 2020, the area will have been rechristened something pastoral and charming. Riverside? Westlake? Lincoln Park South?

The notorious name Cabrini-Green, already expunged from real estate promotions, will have vanished even further. It will live on primarily in the memories of those old enough to remember the decades when "Cabrini-Green" signified the project — once home to 15,000 people — that convinced the world that Chicago public housing was brutal, corrupt, tragic.

By 2020, the majority of people who once lived in Cabrini will have vanished from view too. At least from the view of well-to-do Chicago.

They'll be raising children and grandchildren in poor, segregated, job-starved outposts of the West and South Sides. Gangs will still thrive, though today's gang members will have handed off the crime and violence, like a relay baton, to the young.

And yet some people who once called Cabrini home will still be in the new old neighborhood on Division Street. They'll be the ones who had the will and the skill to adapt, and some help doing it. They'll be the ones — far fewer than originally advertised — who learned to find jobs, keep jobs, pay utilities, be quieter.

By 2020, the children of those lucky few will have finished high school, probably had at least a little college. They'll have steady jobs and decent teeth. For them, life after Cabrini will be a better life, though they'll never know their neighbors as comfortably as people knew each other in the vanished world.

That's my prediction. It's rosy for the neighborhood. It's not so bright for the neighbors who are leaving.

I'd like to have a different picture of the future, a picture that lived up to the new Cabrini's billing as a truly mixed-income community, as a "transformation" for everyone involved.

Believing in the promise

And sometimes in the past few weeks, as I've talked to scores of people in and around Cabrini, it's been possible to believe in the promise of this vast change.

When Peter Holsten, the developer of the neighborhood's biggest mixed-income projects so far, talks frankly and passionately about how to repair his mistakes as development proceeds, it's possible to believe.

It's possible when Rev. Chuck Infelt, the white pastor of a Cabrini church for three decades, tells his black congregation that this change is a chance, finally, to live Martin Luther King's dream of integration.

It's possible to believe because the neighborhood's alderman, Walter Burnett, grew up in Cabrini and hasn't forgotten his personal stake in the welfare of its people.

And because Cabrini leaders like Carole Steele have fought to preserve for themselves a piece of the ground they think of as their history and home.

The dream seems doable when you listen to new residents like Chris Johnson, a hotel manager whose family moved into a mixed-income development. He likes the diversity and responds to the tensions that sometimes flare with the useful phrase, "Patience is the key, truly."

The five kids of Deneen Pughsley, a single mother who left Cabrini and moved close to the Johnsons, offer hope too. Her kids — who've started a dogwalking enterprise in their new mixed neighborhood — have a better shot now at learning to behave in ways that will make them welcome in the wider world.

And yet watching Deneen Pughsley's trouble finding a new job and her struggle to pay utilities — a struggle that keeps many people from surviving outside public housing — I had to wonder.

I had to wonder when I met the five smart kids of Amelia and Rick McKnight. Those kids are still in Cabrini, dreaming of a new house where neighbor kids won't beat them up, but their parents haven't yet figured out the finances and logistics of getting out.

I had to wonder when I listened to a 19-year-old drug dealer say that the only future he saw outside Cabrini for himself was "Death. Hell."

And I had to wonder as I talked to many Cabrini residents who obviously wouldn't pass the credit check, the criminal background check or the housekeeping inspection required to qualify for the new developments.

And I really had to wonder on the day in Cabrini when a man approached Ald. Burnett with a request: Could Burnett help him change his parole to Texas? He'd just spent some time there.

"I did things I ain't never done before," he said.

Like what?

"Got a job."

Two jobs. In Texas, he said, employers didn't hold it against him that he had a Cabrini address and a prison record. He swept his hand through the neighborhood. "There's nothing for me here."

Can the dream be saved?

Moments like that could make anyone wonder: Can this dream of "transformation" — for public housing, its residents, the neighborhood, the city — be saved?

I took the question to Sudhir Venkatesh. He's an expert on Chicago public housing who, after years as a University of Chicago researcher, now teaches at Columbia University in New York.

His answer?

"I feel really sad," he said, speaking not only of Cabrini but of Chicago's citywide plan to convert public housing developments into mixed-income. "I'm not saying it's a failure, but we've missed an opportunity."

Then he backtracked. There's still time to make it work, if the city takes its time to solve some problems.

For example, he said, many of Cabrini's strongest families left soon after the announcement of Cabrini's "transformation plan," in the mid- to late-1990s, before the whereabouts of those who left were reliably recorded. Those people aren't likely to come back to the new neighborhood, though many of them, unable to pay utilities, have already lost their rental subsidy vouchers and are doubling up with friends and relatives.

So now Chicago is left with a volatile, unbuffered mix of the very poor (mostly black) and the well-to-do (mostly white). To keep that mix from exploding, the city needs to draw more African-American working folks into the new developments.

"When we look nationally at the mixed-income developments that work," he said, "the upper working class or lower middle class have been very important as anchors, as stable families. There's not a lot of effort to do that in Chicago."

What's more, if the poorer members of the mix are going to survive, they need neighborhood stores they can afford. Pottery Barn, Restoration Hardware and Whole Foods don't qualify.

And if rich and poor are going to integrate, they need schools that attract both. Despite the proliferation of luxury homes around Cabrini, the public schools remain the province of poor African-Americans.

Venkatesh worries too that in converting its public housing neighborhoods to mixed-income, Chicago is making a mistake to expect developers and property managers to provide social services to public housing transplants.

"Property managers aren't caseworkers," he said. "We don't want to expect developers to help families with mental illness."

Churches and other agencies need to be more heavily enlisted for that work.

Then there are the gangs. In the first year after leaving the housing project, said Venkatesh, gang members could shed their gang identity and dependence — if they got help that most aren't getting.

"We have a chance to turn these youth around," he said. "We're missing a real chance at crime prevention."

Left unattended, these problems will turn the place once known as Cabrini not into a mixed-income neighborhood, but once again into a single-income one. This time, though, because the neighborhood is endowed with such a rich location, the income will land at the high end of the scale instead of in poverty's sub-basement.

Half a century ago, when Cabrini and Chicago's other public housing high-rises were built, the city failed to anticipate the problems it was building for everyone who lives here. We're trying to correct those terrible mistakes now. Before we go any further, we have to ask: What are we failing to see and do now that will haunt us later?

WEDNESDAY, DEC. 1, 2010

'This Land'

The last residents of the last Cabrini-Green high-rise trickled away on Tuesday, except the ones who wouldn't go. It felt like an undercover operation, even in the cold gray light of day.

"You can't be in here," said a guard when I stepped into a dirty, narrow elevator, past a mover and a mattress.

I'd just like to talk to some residents, I said.

"You can't be in here," he said. "Per CHA."

He waved me away, toward the parking lot, where several moving men huddled in the rumble and fumes of the orange Midway trucks.

"They told us, 'Don't talk to them,'" a mover said, "'some of them are going to be emotional.'"

The residents of 1230 N. Burling St. thought they had until Jan. 4 to find a new place to live, but the Chicago Housing Authority had warned that if the occupancy dropped too low, they'd have to go sooner.

Some residents said they learned last week that sooner meant Tuesday. A few said they didn't find out until Monday. When the moving trucks pulled up Tuesday morning, some resisted.

One resident sent out a news release: "Residents demand the right to spend their holidays in their community, according to the terms of CHA's own relocation agreement."

But on this biting November Tuesday, others knew that it was over.

While the rest of Cabrini's high-rises were torn down as part of the transformation of Chicago's public housing; while thousands of Cabrini residents scattered; while the Near North Side neighborhood made way for condos and young professionals, the Burling building and its last residents hung on.

Now residents left, calmly, one at a time, rolling their suitcases, shopping carts and babies out into the wind, past the security guards, the police officers and the movers.

"It's stressful," said Tamika Smith. She reached into her stroller and tugged a blanket over her 2-year-old daughter. "I never been down there, always over here. There's always a lot going on down there."

By "over here," she meant north of Division Street, where the highrises known as "the whites" once stood and where she has lived all of her 21 years.

By "down there," she meant the Cabrini row houses just south of Division, where she and other Burling residents will live, until those apartments close too.

By "a lot going on," she meant shooting. People displaced from other Cabrini buildings move in and out all the time now, and tensions stew.

At midafternoon Tuesday, when I found out the Burling building was closing, rumor had it there were four or five families still there. No one who knew for sure would say. Per CHA.

Every now and then, someone who looked official hurried past, avoiding eye contact and my polite "Excuse me's."

The light faded. It got colder.

"Two," said one of the movers when I asked how many families were left. He asked if I wanted to warm up in his cab. I hopped in. One of the officials walked over, glared, gave the driver a signal. I hopped out.

A man from the contracting company pulled up in a silver car. He was there to help seal the building and make sure a fence was installed that night. An empty building is a lure to the homeless.

"A lot of homeless around here," he said.

A few snowflakes were falling when Dwayne Landry walked out of the building. In his right hand, he held a shopping bag that bulged with towels, a box of Swiss Miss and his fishing rod. In his left hand, he carried a small case of forks, knives and spoons. He and his mother, Velma, were taking the minimum to the row houses.

"So many memories," he said. He looked up at the singed walls of 1230 Burling. "Good, bad, sad. It was like a monument in a way."

There were still a couple of families left at that point. The CHA planned to go to court Wednesday to force them out if they didn't leave.

Velma Landry came now, though, a little wobbly, without a cane. She wore a stylish brown coat, pink Crocs and silver rings on all her fingers.

She is 82. She has lived in Cabrini-Green for 53 years, in the white high-rises, the red high-rises and, beginning Tuesday, the row houses.

"When I go to sleep tonight," she said, "I will have slept in all three parts of this land."

This land. This is how Cabrini-Green has felt to those who lived in it, on it. It was not just home, it was land, homeland.

Velma Landry handed me her cell phone.

"Will you take my picture?"

I did. She looked at it, snapped the phone shut, got into her son's car, with the duct tape on the window, and rode toward her new bed.

FRIDAY, DEC. 10, 2010

The Last High-Rise

The end began.

Rose Ricks rolled her suitcase, a carry-on decorated with Route 66 road signs, out of 1230 N. Burling St. and into Thursday morning's icy wind.

The cameras and reporters surged.

Where's your mother? Is she coming down soon?

In the last few days, Rose's mother, Annie Ricks, has become modestly famous as the last resident of the last high-rise in the infamous Cabrini-Green.

When other families left nine days ago, Ricks held on, not because she loved this old building, with its caged gangways, dirty walls and smelly elevators, but because she felt a promise had been broken.

She thought she'd been told that her new place would be in the neighborhood, in good shape and safe.

"She's upstairs," said Rose, clutching a Dunkin' Donuts coffee cup, "making sure they don't break our trophies."

How does it feel? Where will you go? Will you wave goodbye to Cabrini for the camera?

Rose, who is 17, waved and smiled, and then an older sister politely hustled her away.

"Y'all freezing my sister."

No such media fanfare marked the disappearance of the rest of Chicago's public housing high-rises.

In the past decade, as the city tore down public housing to make way for mixed-income neighborhoods, most of the other high-rises vanished without publicity. Their demise gets noticed chiefly in the consequences, namely the violence that stings the far-flung neighborhoods where many displaced residents have landed.

But the closing of 1230 N. Burling was different.

Even though some of its small row houses remain open, Thursday marked the end of Cabrini-Green, and Cabrini was special.

Cabrini, with its history of murdered cops and slain children, was the housing development that came to symbolize the squandered hope of them all. It was a Chicago name known to the nation. It was also unique, sitting as it did on prime land near downtown and the city's wealthiest neighborhoods.

The fact that Annie Ricks and her family were the final residents was incidental, really, but it made a convenient story.

On Wednesday night, Rose Ricks reported, they blasted the music in Apartment 1108. No neighbors, so why not? Rose let her nieces and nephews hop on her pogo stick. They jumped rope and played with the hula hoop. Everybody shared memories: schools, friends, family. Good times, even in the bad.

Then morning and the moving truck arrived. While the media waited for Annie Ricks, moving men trudged up and down the truck ramp. Boxes, mattresses, a TV, a grandfather clock.

Deonta Ricks, 25, carried the trophies out himself, treading cautiously on the ice. He had taken the day off work, as a salesman for a security company, to help his mother.

A year ago, he said, when the family had to move from a nearby high-rise into this building, the movers broke a lot of the trophies. His mother kept them in a trophy case in the front room, proof of the accomplishments of her 13 children, several of whom still lived in Cabrini.

By media request, Deonta reached into a box and pulled out a U.S. Cellular stay-in-school trophy. He estimated there were 100 trophies. Baseball trophies, basketball trophies. Trophies for perfect attendance and citizenship. One for a valedictorian. They are his mother's prized possessions.

"It's like she seen us do so much stuff they say we couldn't do, but we did," he said.

In Cabrini's heyday, 15,000 people lived in its white high-rises, red high-rises and brick row houses. Born as a hopeful haven for the poor, it devolved by the 1970s into an oasis of poverty in which guns-gangs-drugs melded into a single demon.

Things had to change. There's no arguing with that.

Whether life has changed for the better for the majority of people who have moved out remains a question, but the neighborhood is clearly better.

That's why Annie Ricks wanted to stay. Cabrini had been her home for 20 years, and now it's a safer neighborhood than the ones where so many Cabrini residents have gone. Even the Burling building was safer than the West Side or the Cabrini row houses, where the Chicago Housing Authority had proposed to move her.

Finally, a few days ago, she agreed to move to Wentworth Gardens, a rehabbed public housing complex on the South Side.

Around 11 a.m., the movers slammed the truck door shut. Annie Ricks emerged. The cameras pressed in on her as if she were a movie star.

How do you feel? What's it like to be the last person in the last high-rise? To go to an unfamiliar neighborhood?

"I feel hurt," she said, and didn't say much more.

By February, the high-rise at 1230 N. Burling is likely to be rubble.

Rose Ricks, who said she was excited by the change, will ride public transportation north to Lincoln Park High School to finish out her senior year.

Annie Ricks will put her children's old trophies in her new living room.

And soon, like the other former residents of the place once known as Cabrini-Green, she will be largely forgotten.

Ollie's Last Stand

When the history of Cabrini-Green is written, the murder of Ollie will mark the day Cabrini really died.

Ollie's full name was Bassam Naoum, and since Saturday night, when he was shot to death in one of his two small stores, he's all anyone in Cabrini seems to be talking about.

The elderly women pulling shopping carts, the men sitting on plastic buckets, the cops who roam the sidewalks, the people of all kinds who mill outside his stores to weep or testify:

"When I went into the hospital, he offered to take me."

"I had to get my zoo zoos and wham whams there. It's going to be hard for me to go anywhere else."

"I hope they get the (expletive) what did it and burn his ass up."

Early Parker, who's 66, was playing chess over by the Cabrini row houses a little after 9 on Saturday night when somebody ran past and said somebody got shot.

Over on Orleans. At Munchies. It was Ollie, Parker's boss. Shot repeatedly. In the back.

"He gave me a job," Parker says. "An older guy like me."

Ollie gave jobs, and chances, to people no one else would. He went to his customers' homes when they were sick, to their funerals when they died.

"He didn't care what color you was," Parker says. "Green, purple, polka dot. You were a human being to him."

As a young man, Naoum left Jordan for college in Alabama, and after earning a business degree from DePaul University, set up shop on Larrabee Street, Cabrini's main drag. It was 1993, during the wars.

That's how Cabrini people remember those days, as "the wars." Gang snipers in high-rise windows, kids leaping under classroom desks for gun drills, a 7-year-old boy shot to death on his way to school.

Why would an outsider open a store there?

"Probably because he thought the people needed a store," says his son, Farris, who is 20.

That was Ollie.

If you truly needed it, you got it. Pampers. Bus fare. Breakfast. Bail. Pay him back later. He might reach into a pocket for a fat wad of the bills he carried and peel one off for you.

But don't steal from him.

Once, shortly after he opened Ollie's, he chased a thief all the way into one of the red-brick high-rises. He got his money back.

"Ollie wasn't no pushover," one resident says.

Naoum loved spending time with his wife, daughter and son, and maybe watching a little Arabic TV, but business occupied most of his life.

Morning after morning, he got up at 5, drove north from his Hyde Park home, flicked on his store lights at 6, opened the door at 7, came home a little before midnight.

"He never spoke of being afraid," says his son, who even now holds no grudge against Cabrini. "The people there loved him so much and he loved them."

Ollie's prospered. He opened a second store, Munchies, on the fringe of Cabrini.

He shuttled between the two, sometimes in his Range Rover, often on foot.

People greeted him as he walked past the red high-rises and the row houses, past corners where, in Cabrini's heyday, you could buy the best cocaine and heroin in Chicago.

"I have a story about what he done for me," says Deborah Hope, who grew up in Cabrini. "Hopefully I won't cry on you, OK?"

May. Two years ago. Hope wanted to throw a peace party. Ollie helped her get free food for more than 500 kids. And when yet another of her relatives was shot, Ollie listened.

"And I was telling him, 'I'm tired of Chicago. I want to run away.' He said, 'No, Deborah, that's what the enemy wants you to do is run. You got to stand.'"

Ollie stood. He kept his stores, which were also social centers, even as the Dollar Store, the liquor store and the grocery store moved off Larrabee to make way for the shiny new neighborhood. He stayed even as the tall red-brick buildings toppled, replaced by weeds and bulldozers.

He stood until Saturday night. When police arrived, he was still wearing his Rolex. Cash was still in the register.

Rumors ripple through Cabrini about who did it, and why.

"It was a case of people wanting the land and killing Ollie for it," said a woman Tuesday, standing outside Munchies, where the night before, hundreds gathered to mourn him.

More likely, says a cop who works Cabrini, it was a teenager, one of the "displaced" people who recently moved from a closed building into the row houses, where tensions boil as Cabrini shrinks.

Ollie survived the worst of the wars, only to be gunned down at the moment Cabrini was almost gone. To the Cabrini people who loved him, that fact is ludicrous, bitter, proof of the end.

How did he survive so long? I ask the cop.

He answers: "Strong will, good heart."

When that strong will and good heart vanished, so did something at the very core of Cabrini-Green.

FROM
THE
DESK
OF

Mary Schmich

A h, "Brenda Starr."

In 1985, I was asked to take over the strip, created by Dale Messick in 1940. This is one of her first drawings.

When I think about weird things I've done in life, this is near the top.

Like many girls of my generation, I grew up on "Brenda Starr, Girl Reporter," spreading the big colorful funny pages out on the floor on Sundays, lying on my belly to read, entranced by this adventurous, independent, working woman in an era when such images of women were rare in pop culture.

Beyond that I knew nothing about writing a comic strip.

"What makes you think you can?" asked the editor who offered me the job.

"I just know I can," I said, one of the few times in my life I've had the guts to bluff.

And for the next 25 years, while doing my newspaper work, I wrote her adventures and misadventures, which were brought to visual life by two remarkable artists, Ramona Fradon first, and then June Brigman.

chapter 10

·····································

the seasons

·······································

Winter: Chicago vs. New York

It seems indecent to mention winter just as spring has finally poked through the gray, and the birds are again yakking before dawn, and it grows more plausible by the day that someone in Chicago will witness a leaf on a tree.

But I have to get something out of my system. New York.

I was in that great city a few days ago and something happened that happens every time I'm there.

"Chicago?" said a woman I met at a social event when she learned where I lived. "It's so — " she shuddered "cold."

How, she asked, could I stand it?

OK, fine, on some winter days every reasonable Chicagoan wonders that, but on this April Sunday the Manhattan sky was grimmer than a funeral, the temperature was in the 40s and the wind hacked through my coat with the zeal of a killer on crack.

It was 64 and sunny in Chicago.

I've made many trips to New York only to have the weather there be

285

nastier than what I left in Chicago, and yet New Yorkers continue to act as if they live in Key West. A good friend refuses to visit me from November to June.

"You come here," he insists. "I can't deal with Chicago in the winter."

I might pity his winter wimpiness if he lived in L.A. But he lives in Brooklyn. It's like the gelato calling the popsicle cold.

"New Yorkers always act as though Chicago is in the icy zone and they are in the tropical zone," said the novelist Jeffrey Eugenides when I reached him by phone in New York. "They act like Chicago is Nome, Alaska. The way they act about Chicago weather is the way they act about the city in general. They want to dismiss it."

Eugenides, the author of "The Virgin Suicides" and "Middlesex," has been teaching at Princeton University in New Jersey since last fall, but he spent three recent winters in Chicago. Having once heard him bemoan how New Yorkers dis Chicago weather, I phoned him to corroborate my complaint.

When he moved to Chicago, he said, he took to "obsessively" comparing the weather with New York's in hopes of proving New Yorkers wrong.

"I've had this conversation numerous times," he said. "It doesn't matter what I say. You hit a wall when you try to tell New Yorkers Chicago can have warm winters."

He even considered investigating meteorological records and making a comparison graph. He never got to it, but I recruited Tom Skilling, the Tribune's weatherman.

"With the cold Atlantic sitting next to NYC," Tom e-mailed, "the snail's pace at which warming occurs in spring there is not one of that area's more stunning meteorological attributes."

Yes!

"If you think cold Lake Michigan haunts us with lake breezes, you ought to see what an ocean can do in delaying the onset of spring's warmth."

Yes!

"I lived 13 years in Westfield, New Jersey, as a kid so I experienced those interminably cool springs there."

Yes, yes, yes.

"But . . ."

But? That little word is often an ill wind.

"We are, by almost any measure, the colder of the two locations — and pretty definitively. Here are some comparative stats."

Average number of days each year when the high doesn't top 32? New York: 19. Chicago: 42. With at least 1 inch of snow on the ground? New York: 21. Chicago: 50. Subzero temps? New York: 0. Chicago: 9.

But I'd like to point out that the mean annual temperatures aren't all that different. New York's Central Park: 55. Chicago Midway: 51. And at the moment of this writing, it's 74 in Chicago and 72 in New York.

And, please, New Yorkers. Don't get started on how it's so much hotter and more humid in Chicago in the summer.

Yours Is Itty Bitty

The friends from out in L.A. call,
They purr, "Oh, aren't you freezing?
Why here it's sunny, bright and warm
No coughs, no itch, no sneezing."
In Tucson, Scottsdale, Palm Springs too
They think our weather's frightful:
"We're wearing sandals, shorts and thongs
The desert sun's delightful!"
Miami pals pick up the phone,
They chortle, "We've been boating!
The water's clear, the sky is blue . . .
No, honest, we're not gloating!"
"Are you OK?" they phone to ask,
"Is everyone surviving?
Oh, by the way, too bad you missed
Our great day scuba diving."
The front page of the New York Times
Cries "Windy City Freezes!"
As if in Brooklyn and the Bronx
It's all Fijian breezes?
What's wrong with all these tepid fools?
Yeah yeah, Chicago's chilly.
It's winter, guys: Chicago's cold
And, duh, the Alps are hilly.

We live for winters just like this
We love to moan and suffer.
So all the wide wimp world can see
Chicagoans are tougher!
Sub-zero winters heat our hearts
In our book, bitter's better.
Who wants to live in places where
You're warm in just a sweater?
We want our Gore-Tex, fur and down
We want to brrr and shiver.
We want to tell the world that they
Are softer than chopped liver.
You citizens of lukewarm spots
You don't know what you're missing:
Saliva freezes on our lips
Each time we're winter kissing.
Our hair's afly with static cling
We fatten like a turkey.
Our thighs get raw from scratch-scratching
Our skin's just like beef jerky.
And everywhere the city streets
Are looking kind of squalid.
Our cars are sporting coats of salt
The dog poop's frozen solid.
Our feet are ice, our faces stone
Our noses always dripping.
But even though we freeze outdoors
Inside we're always stripping.
We dress, undress and dress again
"Too hot, too cold," we mutter.
"These bleeping boots and gloves and muffs
Have turned my life to clutter!"
The air bites like a mangy dog
It claws worse than a kitten.
We trail the dirt and slush inside
We've always lost one mitten.
The gas tanks crack, the car doors stick
The water pipes are clogging.

But even when it's 10 below
We're not afraid of jogging!
Sometimes we dream of someplace warm
We're sipping cold martinis.
Beneath a gently swaying palm
And wearing French bikinis.
But, no, we're proud, we won't give in
We won't be weak and whiney.
The winter fortifies our souls
While freezing off our hiney.
And if the lake's a glacier now
And wind is like a dagger,
Well, folks, that's why we love this place
It gives us cause to swagger!
Yes, friends in all those balmy climes
We do not need your pity!
Our winter's big as winter comes
While yours is itty bitty.

SUNDAY, MAY 25, 2003

Summer Ticks Away

Set your summer clock today. Press the countdown button. Go.

If you lived in some chronically toasty place, this weekend wouldn't be the beginning of the summer countdown. If you lived where the gardens grow all year and the sun beams as relentlessly as an interrogation light, you could laze around for a few more weeks before launching into the work of making summer summer. You'd know you could still be skinny dipping in October.

But you don't live in California, Arizona, Florida, in any of those places where summer is so year-round that those sun-fried souls don't really know what summer is. You live here, on the windswept Northern prairie, with your sun-starved skin and your sandals lying fallow, and you know exactly what summer is:

Short.

Summer in Chicago is a season that defies the equinoxes, lasting not from June through September but from Memorial Day to Labor Day. That's 14 weeks. Or if 14 weeks sounds too short, you can make yourself feel better with the knowledge that you have 98 days. Or here's a way to make yourself think that the summer larder isn't as skimpily stocked as it really is: You have 2,352 hours to squeeze summer from your life, or into it.

What are you going to do with that time? Watch reruns?

Unfortunately, a Chicago summer starts before the weather has noticed the word "Urgent" penned on the calendar. The savvy Chicago summerer knows that summer rhythms must be established early or you never get into the groove, yet it's hard to get in the summer groove while your teeth are still chattering.

Stop complaining and repeat after me: The sun is out. At least the sun is out.

And then repeat: Short. Summer is very, very short. If I wait for the weather to behave in full summer fashion, it'll be winter again.

Summer is so short in Chicago that the lake barely has time to melt before the autumn wind sails back in.

Summer is so short that it seems hardly worth the trouble of moth-balling your wool clothes. Take it from the owner of too many moth-eaten sweaters: It's short but not that short.

How short is a Chicago summer?

Summer in Chicago is so short that if you wait to buy that bicycle on sale in August, you'd better buy a Polartec jacket to ride in.

It's so short that if you don't plant your flowers right now, today, they'll come into full bloom the day before the first frost. Get to Home Depot pronto.

But it could be worse. We could live in Fairbanks, Alaska. I recently was visited by a friend who does. We were strolling through a May day, shivering, and I was apologizing for the cold, as if it were as subject to my control as the quality of the guest bed.

"Cold?" she said. "This would be a wonderful summer day in Fairbanks."

I checked, and yes, summer weather in Fairbanks hovers around 60, give or take a degree or two. It's 48 in May, 45 in September. Fairbanks makes Chicago feel like Key West.

But just because summer is shorter somewhere else doesn't mean it's not short here. Speaking of shorts, fish yours from the musty bottom of the drawer. Put them on. No, the goose bumps aren't attractive, especially on your winter-puffy legs, but how many times do you have to be told:

Summer's here. You've got to act the part before you're suffocating in Gore-Tex again.

So gas up the grill. Open the windows. Buy sunscreen.

Make a list of all the things you meant to do last summer and the one before, only to look up, your fun undone, to discover it was snowing:

Canoe? Go to the farmers market? A baseball game? Swim in the lake? Nap on a bench in the middle of the workday? Learn to make a decent summer salad? Get some sandals you can actually walk in? Play hooky on one of those perfect summer afternoons that remind you not only that summer is short but that life is?

It's easy to curse the brevity of summer in Chicago, but some of the best things in life are short: good songs, witty remarks, certain kinds of love affairs.

One reason to love a Chicago summer is that its fleeting nature calls on you to wake up and do things. Now.

Hear that ticking?

FRIDAY, AUG. 12, 2005

When the Cicadas Stop

At some point every August — about this point — a summer-lover begins to wonder when the cicadas will shut up.

When the dog day cicadas stop, a Chicago summer-lover knows, it's over.

"It" is shorthand for heat, light, the fantasy that time can be stretched beyond its ordinary, strangulating, suffocating, life-annihilating boundaries. "It" contains sunflowers, fresh corn, naked toenails and assorted other opportunities that if not seized immediately will be gone for the eternity called winter.

"Summer's almost over," said Mrs. Kwon, my dry cleaner, when I stopped in the other day.

"It is not," I spat, knowing perfectly well it almost was. It's one thing to know something unpleasant, it's another thing to have to listen to someone say it.

Mrs. Kwon, on the other hand, didn't seem to mind summer's passing, because she'd just spent three days in her cramped dry-cleaning shop with a broken air conditioner.

But as long as the cicadas are still alive and shrieking, summer and the hope of summer carry on.

"Summer's almost gone and I've ridden my bike twice," I heard a woman mourn on Sunday.

No. Let me repeat. The cicadas. Listen. Those guys — and I do mean the guys — still are shaking their maracas. The females still are answering the call. If the cicadas still can roust themselves, so can we. We must do our best not to know that this ruckus is just the party before the funeral.

We live in a noisy city. Sirens, jets, air conditioners, drunks on the side walk at 3 a.m. Noise presses in on us like cement. But the cicada noise is different. It reminds us that Chicago is just a prairie in disguise, that we are more than just the sum of our expressways and skyscrapers.

The cicadas evoke time beyond the present, and that's the essential job of summer, to bring us completely into the here and now while simultaneously, like a train in the distance, reminding us that the here and now never stands still.

"Can you believe summer's gone already?" mourned a friend at yoga class, who obviously has not learned the yogic principle of living in the moment.

To which I could only repeat my tiresome platitude: Listen to the cicadas. In Chicago, summer comes late but we lament its passing a little too early.

Listen to the cicadas rev up in the afternoon. It's nature saying, "Go ahead, take a nap." Cicadas are the perfect white noise for a siesta.

Listen at 8 p.m., when they're out there in full throttle, harping: "Cut the TV off. Come outside. Remember 8 p.m. in January?"

Objectively, the cicadas are way too much like cockroaches for my taste. And objectively, the song of the cicadas should be as annoying as the hum of a refrigerator. Or the grind of a power saw. These guys aren't Sting or Frank Sinatra. They're not singing timeless melodies. Musically, their drone is only slightly better than a mosquito's.

But when I hear them I feel the same melancholy thrill I get listening to Sting sing "Fields of Gold" or Sinatra sing "It Was a Very Good Year."

Cicadas stir memory and longing as surely as the best songs. And, like the best songs, they leave you wanting just a little more.

"Late August, early September," Ron Wolford, an urban gardening educator, said when I called the University of Illinois extension to find out when the cicadas would stop singing. "They're at their peak right now."

Hearing the words "early September" gave me chills. Early September is a lovely time, but it's when you feel a meaner season riding toward you, winter chasing with a whip.

But there's still time, as long as the cicadas sing. Don't think too much about the fact that the peak of anything is always the beginning of the fall.

Look on the bright side. The cicadas come out of the ground in summer, they mate and then they die. They will never see another August. Most of us will, though in January that will be very hard to believe.

WEDNESDAY, NOV. 10, 2010

Indian Summer

In the morning, you lie in bed and sense the world is out of order.

Too much light sifts through the curtains. That extra blanket was so hot it wound up on the floor. The birds are too loud for November.

You get up, pad toward the bathroom or the kitchen, and still the world's a few shades off. The sky's too blue, the air too mild.

You open a window you thought would be closed until baseball season. On the branches of a shedding yellow tree you could swear that you see buds.

This isn't the way November is supposed to happen, not at Chicago's latitude. Up here, November means wet roads, cold gusts, snow on the gray horizon. One of the first years I spent in Chicago, November's claim to glory was 29 days with no sun.

But there's no cold wind now, and even though the buildings drown in shadows by 3:30, the sun is out, the leaves are bright and snow seems as remote as Nome.

"Can you say Indian summer?" says a friend when I do. "Is it politically incorrect?"

I think it's OK. And no other words quite get the mood of these warm days that arrive like a dessert it didn't even occur to us we could order.

Just when we thought we'd had our last summer meal, ice cream and raspberries show up with a note: November has been postponed.

Meanwhile, in California, the LA Times reported Monday: "Gusty winds, frost on tap for the Southland."

Chicago better in November than Malibu? The world is out of order.

Places like Malibu rarely get the pleasure of a true Indian summer, the sense of summer gone then reappearing, of time lost and then found, of a romance unexpectedly revived.

A true Indian summer is that freakish burst of autumn warmth after the first frost. It presumes frost in fall. It presumes the hardship of a real winter.

No one seems sure where the term came from. I asked WGN forecaster Tom Skilling. His answer:

"The term may have come into use because of gatherings of settlers and Native Americans after the autumn harvest in which the bounty of the year's harvest was shared, often in periods of warm weather that were among the last of the fast-fading warm season."

Even if that's not the real origin, it expresses the mood: warmth and bounty in the middle of the end.

Whatever you call it, these warm November days bring a peace destined to expire.

"A 65-degree day after some 40s brings out the panic that winter is coming," says a friend. "I panic to use that day to its fullest before warmth drains away and I end up welded to my couch."

One day recently, he walked along the I&M canal trail in Will County and watched freight trains fly by.

"Simple things," he says, "all outdoors, trying to suck as much outdoors in my lungs as I can."

A lot of us have done things like that in the past few days, gone out just to be out, aimlessly soaking up the sun with its unfamiliar angles.

On Tuesday at midday, the sun shone at such a slant that I could see the tips of my eyelashes and the veins of the dying leaves.

The shadows of trees and porch railings were different too, shadows as sharp as the things themselves.

This grace period won't last long. Brevity is what makes it grace. But is it too late to put the cushion back on the porch chair?

SUNDAY, SEPT. 25, 1994

On the Lakefront

The season of equal opportunity has come to an end in Chicago. Once again, open air democracy shuts down for the winter.

For a few months every year, from June through September, Chicago, at least along the lakefront, becomes a different kind of town, a place where people of all classes, colors and styles of exercise gather and miraculously do not riot or slit each other's throats.

Along the lakefront, everyone is equal. The water doesn't judge. Open access for all. Tolerance triumphant.

So it was melancholy to walk the lakefront Friday morning and to see that right on schedule, on the first day of fall, the city's most egalitarian season had concluded.

Overnight, a curtain dropped. Bang, the show was over. Everything blue had dimmed to gray. Wind-whipped waves beat the concrete shore. At Oak Street, the dollop of sand that passes for beach was bare except for a few lonely birds.

A man clutching a plastic Jewel sack napped on a bench. Two women in sweaters pushed a baby stroller. A solitary pair of chess players stared at their game. A bicyclist zipped past, in an ominous rain poncho.

The most lamentable thing wasn't the weather, though. It was that, except for these few, everyone had gone home, back to their separate neighborhoods, back behind their usual walls, back to lives that rarely meet certain kinds of other lives without the lake as an excuse and an invitation.

There may be a few more sunny days, but it will be another three-quarters of a year before rich people and poor people, black people and whites, jocks and slobs, suburbanites and cityphiles routinely and so amiably share territory.

Walking along, I recalled the hot bright day I met three 10-year-old boys from Cabrini-Green on Oak Street Beach. They wore swimming trunks and shirts of sand. The lakefront was their summertime back yard.

Every morning, they walked the mile from their cramped apartments to the lake, to build mud castles, to paddle in the water, to watch, enthralled, as volleyball players with well-oiled pecs and muscled thighs lobbed a ball across a net. Every day, they stayed until dusk to avoid going home.

Then there was the 4th of July. With an out-of-town guest, I drove to Calumet Park on the far southern end of the city's lakefront, through a world of shabby bungalows and stark streets that eventually opened into a festival.

Hispanics, blacks, some whites. Salsa music, rap. Every inch of grass and sand was covered with tablecloths or towels, barbecues or boom boxes, and everybody had a view.

Another day, I took another guest on a bike ride on the lakefront trail, up past Fullerton and Belmont, Irving Park and Montrose, past tinkling boats and swimming dogs, past Koreans playing soccer and a mariachi wedding band.

Throughout the summer, I took several guests on these lakefront cultural diversity tours. All of them were amazed.

It wasn't just the water that stretched almost to Canada that astonished them, or the silhouette of the city glinting on a curve of shore.

It was the people, the variety, that impressed them most. People of so many different kinds, with equal access to turquoise water and bicycle trails and shimmering skyline views.

Inevitably they would say, "We don't have anything like this back in . . ." Fill in the blank: Philadelphia, New York, Baltimore, San Francisco, Atlanta.

It's hard to imagine how much more discontent would rumble through this city if a hundred years ago Montgomery Ward hadn't fought to rid the lakefront of shanties, garbage, old freight cars, railroad sheds and circus junk. If Daniel Burnham hadn't made his famous Chicago plan.

In 1909, Burnham wrote: "The lakefront by right belongs to the people. It affords their one great unobstructed view, stretching away to the horizon, where water and clouds seem to meet."

Beauty for the working class, he argued. A deterrent from vice and violence.

And so it happens that those of us who can't afford Michigan cottages and Wisconsin cabins meet for a few months every year along this lake that is by turns green or gray, blue or aqua, virtually every color but red.

It's not only cooler by the lake. In the summer, the lake makes us all a little more civilized. That's the best of the lake effects. It's hard to watch it wane.

The last item left on my desk in Tribune Tower was the final Sunday page of "Brenda Starr," which I wrote for many years.

When I decided to quit writing "Brenda Starr," the strip ended. My colleague Mary Elson framed the final page, drawn by the amazing June Brigman, for me.

In it, Brenda is leaving The Flash, the newsroom where she's worked forever. She's at a newsroom party, not so different from the newsroom toast we had in the Tower on our last day.

The final panel speaks to our leaving the Tower on Friday, June 8, 2018, as well as it does to Brenda leaving The Flash. It's worth noting that Brenda is walking into the sunrise, not the sunset, as she thinks: "Every ending is a beginning and every beginning carries the seed of its own end. As a wise man once said, so it goes . . ."

chapter 11

....

holidays

Grateful

Not long ago I took a long walk with a friend I've known since we were 17. I hadn't seen her in a while, so, knowing only the outlines of her latest accomplishments and troubles, I asked, "How has life in the 40s felt to you?"

She was quiet for a moment, then waved toward the sun and sky and said, "You know what I feel mostly? Grateful."

I nodded. "Me too."

On the surface, our lives are very different from each other's now. In the years since we overdosed on coffee and deep thoughts in the dorm at 1 a.m., we've had different joys, different griefs, different reasons to chafe occasionally against the boundaries of the lives we've built. But from our forked paths, we've arrived at the same conclusion: In the middle of life, the first word that comes to mind to describe our lives is "grateful."

Gratitude is one of those words that's so overused that you may hesitate to use it. It smacks of Hallmark cards and self-help books, of an industry that presumes we need to be taught gratitude, usually at full retail price plus tax and shipping.

But the truth is, just as dogs have to be trained to pipe down or roll over, we do need to be taught to pause and say thanks. Thanksgiving is our annual refresher course.

"Say thank you," adults are forever chiding children who have yet to compute that what they've been given wasn't rightfully theirs all along. That candy bar, the new doll, a compliment — most of us have to be taught that these are gifts, not entitlements.

So we learn to say thank you, though thanks may be less an honest expression of gratitude than a social ploy designed to keep the goodies coming.

As part of our instruction in gratitude, a lot of us are drilled to say grace before meals. "Bless us, oh Lord, for these thy gifts, which we are about to receive, etc." was the Catholic prayer my siblings and I had to recite before we were rewarded with supper. Desperate to get to the Spaghetti-O's, we raced through it with the same speed and reverence we brought to "Peter Piper picked a peck of pickled peppers."

I envied Protestants, whose snappy "God is great, God is good, let us thank him for our food" was an infinitely shorter route to the grub.

But somewhere along the way, after the rote recitations of gratitude we learn young, most of us learn to mean thank you. To feel thank you. To realize that almost nothing is entitlement, that everything's a gift and that most of it can be taken away. Our parents try to teach us this; then loss comes along to drive the lesson home.

Nothing teaches gratitude more efficiently than loss. The loss of people you love, through death or misunderstanding. The loss of youth. Of beauty. The loss of trust. Of money. The loss of a home or a job. By the time you're in midlife you've lost one or more of those. Having lost a few things, you more fully realize what those things were, and how lucky you were to have had them.

And once you've lost a few things you're attached to, you have two choices: grow bitter at what you've lost or start noticing how much you still have.

Have you ever noticed that after a catastrophe, many of the victims or the victims' relatives talk of gratitude? In the wake of the hurricane, the car wreck, the cancer, the terrorist attack, there are always people who respond by saying they're grateful to be alive. To have their health. To have their family. Grateful for a sunny day, or a rainy one, depending on the need.

They incarnate the simple truth that without loss, we're less likely to learn gratitude and more likely to take our good luck for granted.

It's a consequence of getting older, I'm sure, that recently I've found myself pausing regularly before I eat to look at my food and think, "Thanks." I'm glad in a new way for the food and a peaceful place to eat it. Glad to have had parents who taught me to say thanks before I understood the word. Glad for the life and the losses that helped me understand better. Glad for Thanksgivings that remind us all to say it.

WEDNESDAY, NOV. 26, 2008

The Troublesome Thanksgiving Guest

One of my brothers and I were making Thanksgiving plans, and the menu included trouble.

"What do you think we should do?" one of us said.

"I don't know," said the other. "What do you think?"

For the next few minutes, we circled around the problem like planes with nowhere to land.

Thanksgiving trouble can come in many forms. The turkey doesn't thaw. The flight is canceled. The corkscrew disappears.

But the toughest problem of all is the troublemaking dinner guest, and it's more troubling when that person is someone you love.

Sixty-four percent of families, according to a statistic I've deduced from friends' laments, have a troublemaking diner at Thanksgiving dinner. In some cases, it's the same person year after year who brings his or her life struggles to dinner and hurls them down next to the marshmallow yams.

All right, my brother and I plotted, we could make sure that the conversation centered on this person so that she didn't feel neglected. But, frankly, that was beyond exhausting and anyway we'd forget. What if we made sure not to make any jokes?

We went round and round on how to avoid the explosion, and then it hit me: If the explosion happens, again, so what? We'd survive. The point was to be together.

Thanksgiving isn't intended to be the most relaxing meal you ever had. You want mellow? Save it for some Saturday night.

Thanksgiving is a meal that formalizes through food your connections to the people you love, even if that connection sometimes sparks like a downed wire. It's a meal for savoring life as it is, not as it might be, and finding reasons to be grateful anyway.

It's easy to be grateful for life's good things. Good food, good health, easy friendship. Saying thanks for those is as simple as boxed stuffing.

But being grateful for the trouble? That's a different order of Thanksgiving.

I believe in the benefits of trouble. Through trouble, we inevitably arrive at some new place, a place where the light shines differently, and in that new light we see something we hadn't seen before.

Trouble might be a disease, the loss of a job or love, an accident. It might be some troubled person who makes our Thanksgiving dinners reliably difficult. But as my brother and I talked about that person in our family — who is guaranteed, I should note, not to read this — I thought of an e-mail another of my brothers sent his siblings recently after he was diagnosed with cancer:

"Every now and then I give Jasper and Ivan a lecture on the importance of family, the same one I remember Dad delivering to us over and over. And, like me then, the boys nod their understanding and ask if they can be excused now. Obviously, there's no lecture that can express the real value of having one's family there in difficult situations, and even the not-so-difficult ones. Maybe it requires being tired and middle-aged to fully recognize and appreciate the meaning of family, but I'm feeling the urge to sit the boys down and tell it to them one more time. Thanks to all of you for helping me feel less afraid and less alone, and more excited about being here."

Sometimes, we have to pass through trouble in one of its countless forms to know what we're most thankful for.

Turkey Trauma

Can we clear up one thing about Thanksgiving right now? A turkey is just a big chicken.

Please. Don't tell me clucking is not gobbling, etc. If we're ever going to restore some tranquility to Thanksgiving, we have to detraumatize the turkey-cooking operation, and to detraumatize we must demystify.

Yes, all you quaking turkey cooks, that roly-poly bundle is a bird, not an IQ test.

Something is very wrong with the fact that innocent turkeys are terrorizing Thanksgiving cooks from coast to coast. Listen to one typical woman, an otherwise confident professional and mother:

"I am to cook a 15-pound turkey and I feel intimidated," this friend recently e-mailed, unsolicited. "Can I fill that enormous cavity with stuffing which won't kill people with bacteria? Will the drumsticks dry out? Will I be okay even though the classy turkeys don't have buttons which tell you when they're done? I'm going to have to call that hot line they always talk about in newspaper articles."

Those newspaper articles. They're half the reason for our turkey terror. Every year the media gorge us with turkey troubles. Salmonella! Fickle ovens! Lousy stuffing! You'd think a PhD is required to get the turkey right.

To make the trauma worse, the articles assault us with so-called help, the most abusive and deceptive of which comes as recipes. Recipes and more recipes. Hundreds of new concoctions every year for making the perfect turkey.

Turkey a la mode. Turkey with poached bananas. Tutti-frutti turkey. There is no end to the manner in which the evil recipe inventors will make us doubt the ancient art of just sticking that baby in the oven, then kicking back with a margarita.

Why are we so susceptible to turkey torture? Partly because cooking a turkey is a rite of passage, like losing your virginity or getting your driver's license. Until you've done it — at least if you're a woman — you don't feel quite adult.

We're also susceptible to turkey torture because, as Americans, whether it's toothpaste or stock portfolios, we can't resist making ourselves miserable with our infinity of choices. We can't bear to be and do any less than the best; but how to choose the best when there are so many options?

So turkey cooking becomes a competition, a source of humiliation or self-esteem. We're only as good as the turkey we cook, and our turkey is good only if it's better than other people's turkeys. My turkey, myself.

"Yes, there's so much media coverage," said Chris Eilers, with comforting empathy, when I phoned the Butterball hot line in Downers Grove seeking counsel for turkey neurotics. She's one of 46 women in phone headsets who sit at long tables in front of computers talking turkey cooks through their troubles all the way through Thanksgiving Day.

"Gourmet recipes," she said. "Celebrities giving their recipes. Cookbooks with interesting new recipes. A lot of people call and say, 'This is the recipe I got from TV, but then this is what Martha Stewart says. What should I do?'"

To brine or not to brine, that is one of the big questions these days, said the Butterball Lady. (Only if the turkey's fresh, she said.)

Deep frying the turkey is another hot question. ("We don't think it's safe," the Butterball Lady said, noting that some fryers are prone to tipping over.)

What if your friends swear that roasting the turkey in a brown paper bag makes the moistest turkey ever? (Bad idea, said the Butterball Lady. The bag may contain chemicals or may burst into flames.)

So here's the Butterball Lady's best idea:

Put your sacrificial bird in an open pan. Brush oil on the skin. Cook uncovered at 325 degrees until it's two-thirds done, about 2 1/2 hours for a 10- to 18-pound turkey. Then place foil loosely on the breast. When a meat thermometer says the breast is at 170 degrees and the thigh is at 180, the turkey's done. Period.

"Not that different from cooking a chicken, right?" I said.

Except for placing the foil, said the Butterball Lady, not very.

So come on, turkey cooks: Shuck off the self-doubt. Pick your turkey path. Forget the roads not taken. And repeat after me: I am not my turkey. And my turkey, for which I am thankful, is just a big chicken.

Even the Terrible Things

My mother once said something that has played over and over in my mind in the few months since she died, and I hear it strongly as we get closer to Thanksgiving.

"Even the terrible things," she said, on a sunny day in what would be her last September, "seem beautiful to me now."

I rarely saw my mother cry, despite the many reasons she might have, but on that afternoon in her backyard, she cried a little, tears that I sensed were equally for the beauty and the sorrow in her life, and for the recognition that, when it's all done, beauty and sorrow are one and the same.

Even the terrible things seem beautiful to me now.

What she was saying that day, I think, was that it's all life. The things that hurt your heart, wound your pride, drain your hope, leave you lost, confuse you to the point of madness. That's life, life with its endless, shifting sensations and its appalling urgency and its relentless drive toward mystery.

What could be better than that? What could you be more thankful for than that?

At Thanksgiving there's a lot of talk about gratitude, a word that has been so merchandized — on calendars and coffee mugs and in self-help manuals — that when you hear it you may want to reach for the hand sanitizer to wipe away the goo.

In the commercial version of gratitude, life is filled with cozy meals, cozy weather, friends and relations who smother each other in hugs and greeting cards. To the extent that hard times figure in, it's only once they've been vanquished and can be toasted farewell with a glass of premium wine facing a perfect sunset.

It's easy to be grateful for such easy pleasures. Who can complain about cozy meals and friends who put up with your annoying behaviors?

But to see the beauty in the terrible things and to be grateful for those moments — that's an elusive art.

I think you have to be old to see how beautiful the terrible things are, my mother said that afternoon, and I suspect she's right.

Maybe we can't see the beauty in the terrible things until we're approaching the final beauty and terror. In other words, death: the ultimate proportion gauge.

Maybe only when you take your last step back from the canvas can you see how gorgeous all those wrong strokes and smudges look when viewed together.

All of the best times in my life have grown directly out of the worst times. What feels like manure often turns out to be fertilizer.

But what I took from my mother's remark wasn't just that good may grow out of bad. It's that the bad is its own beauty.

We all resist what's difficult and painful. We run from it. We curse it. It comes anyway, as inevitable as weather.

Most of us have gone through at least one time in our lives that we would call terrible. Everyone I know well certainly has.

A disease. A rape. A parent's suicide. The death of someone you love. The collapse of a dream.

These are things you would never wish on anyone, just as I would never have wished for my mother some of what befell her.

But as we approach Thanksgiving, I'm more grateful than ever to her for the ways she helped everyone around her understand that the hard times make you whole. They make you play the entire keyboard. They allow you to experience the full range of the most basic thing we give thanks for: being alive.

Say Thanks While There's Time

I always meant to thank Steve Wilson for browbeating me into buying the piano of my dreams.

Steve played bass for the Lyric Opera of Chicago, but to fill his time when the opera season ended, he tuned pianos. He was a short, talkative, earnest guy with a ready, staccato laugh, and for several years he bustled by my place every six months or so, toolbox in hand, then tried valiantly and vainly to nurse my old baby grand to grandeur.

My piano was respectable and fairly handsome, so, like someone in a comfortable if not thrilling relationship, I told myself I could live without having my heartstrings more passionately plucked. Until Steve Wilson started hounding me.

"When you're ready for a better piano, let me know," he'd say, head tucked under the piano lid, his nimble fingers fiddling with strings and dampers.

For a while I replied by grunting and mumbling. He escalated the coercion. "You feel you don't deserve a great piano, don't you?" he'd repeat, without irony. "You think you're not good enough." What? The piano tuner's a therapist now?

"When you realize you deserve a great piano," he'd say, "let me know."

Finally one day I let him know. He directed me to John Koelle, a local piano rebuilder. From Koelle I got a 1920s Steinway baby grand restored to its full glory. The first time I played it I wept.

I kept meaning to call Steve to say thanks for the inspiration and guidance. But no rush. I could say it when it was time to tune the new piano, and I knew he'd let me know when the time came. He sent out regular tuning alerts, which always seemed not just good business but a call to duty: Time to tend to the physical fitness of your piano, slob!

Not long ago, when a year had passed with no reminder, I called for an appointment. Steve had died in May. One night, at age 51, while his wife and three kids sat in the kitchen, he went upstairs to his home computer, logged in and had a heart attack.

I began obsessing over the fact that I'd never thanked Steve for shaming me into buying a piano whose beauty broke my heart. So a couple of days ago, thinking about Thanksgiving, our official day of thanks, I called his wife of 30 years, Georgene.

"You did, you called him," she said, "He played the message for me."

I did?

"He had the biggest smile on his face. You said how happy you were. He mentioned that you'd been wanting this piano for a long time."

I should have been horrified that I didn't remember making that call but I was too busy being relieved that I had. Bad memory aside, I know how many times I postpone saying thank you, waiting for the right moment, the right words, the perfect card.

Georgene Wilson, an attorney, talked for a while about her husband's work. She and three technicians he trained are keeping the business going.

"No matter what piano," she said, "the challenge for him was making it sound as good as it could. Each piano had individual idiosyncrasies. A piano is an instrument in addition to being a piece of machinery. It spends all this time under extreme pressure, affected by the temperature and humidity. His job was to make the piano sound as good as it could so the person playing it could achieve the maximum amount of joy from it. He took that responsibility seriously."

I recalled Steve berating me for keeping my piano next to a window, abused by sun and heat and cold. I mentioned how personally troubled — though I barely knew him — he had seemed that I was denying myself a first-rate piano.

"That would bother him," she said. "Because he was also a professional musician, he understood how making music individually can cause such extreme joy. And he wanted everybody to feel that joy."

I'm grateful that I did, after all, thank Steve Wilson for the joy he brought me. But there's still a lesson in this story: Is there somebody you've been meaning to thank for something? Do it while there's time. There may be less time than you think.

Forgettable Holiday Meals

"You won't mind, will you, if I write about your special holiday recipes?"

The look on my mother's face when I say this is briefly as blank as a winter sky.

In the background, the radio is on, another of those seasonal reports on the special family recipes that make the holidays a gustatory romp down memory lane.

"Holiday recipes?" says my mother, who is visiting, and in her look I see a mind roaming in search of the meaning of these curious words, like a cell phone seeking a signal.

Yes, I explain, you can hardly turn on the radio this time of year without someone cooing about Mama's legendary rolls, Grandma's heart-breakingly delicious dumplings, Great Aunt Minnie's soul-warming pearl onion casserole.

Heirloom recipes, I've heard them called. They're the coveted, often secret possessions of beloved women who pass down recipes the way men pass down stocks and bonds and carpentry tips.

My mother brightens.

"I always cooked a turkey," she says. Her shoulders shake with laughter. "Though I always forgot to thaw it until the last minute."

You're not likely to hear about it on the radio, but the Christmas season exposes a hidden truth about my mother and at least a few other women of her allegedly domestic generation: She couldn't cook. She didn't care about cooking. She passed on no secrets about cooking.

That's not to say she didn't cook. With the assistance of her daughters, in a household where responsibilities came with strict gender labels, my mother cooked for many, many years for eight children and a husband.

Her cooking, though, was the stuff of duty, not of folklore. She appreciated a good meal, prepared by others, but her creative mind ranged in different directions, toward words and music, dreams of travel.

"We must have eaten something besides turkey and stuffing," my mother muses. "We had a lot of things on the table. We probably had those tiny little green peas out of the can."

The memory — mushy little peas, a metallic aftertaste — flares in my mind like a freshly lighted Christmas tree.

"And I probably did something really clever, like make a fresh salad."

I arch an eyebrow.

"I didn't? Well, your father wouldn't have eaten that anyway. We based everything on what he would eat. And what he remembered about Christmas from his childhood."

He remembered sweet potato souffle, which I remember with a vague stomachache.

"And," my mother says, "after I served it for a couple of years and nobody ate any, including him, I said, 'Let's not have that anymore.' He said, 'We have to have that.' I said, 'Why?' He said, 'Because my mother always had it.'"

My mother was happy to indulge my father's Christmas memories as much as her culinary talent and curiosity allowed. And she wasn't a terrible cook, just a distracted one who had no romance about recipes.

"The scalloped potatoes," I say. "Those were always a Christmas hit. Nothing but butter and potatoes in a glass pie pan."

"I think there was a little milk thrown in," she says.

"And there was always creamed corn."

"Oh yes. There had to be creamed corn."

"Out of the can. And let's not forget the mashed potatoes. Flakes. Out of a box."

"Oh yeah yeah. Sure. And the turkey gravy came out of what?"

We laugh trying to remember what that container was.

These are not the kind of holiday food memories that merit radio reports. But it's funny. I feel as sentimental about the creamed corn, the canned peas, the potato flakes and the store-bought apple pie as anyone could feel for their five-star holiday cooking traditions.

Those childhood meals were as good as they needed to be, and they did what all the best holiday meals do.

Regardless of the menu, a good holiday dinner is one that makes you feel loved and safe, part of something that stretches back in time, and part of something you'll remember when you're old enough to laugh about it.

WEDNESDAY, DEC. 17, 2008

At Christmas, I Believe

I believe the holidays are as happy as you make them.

I believe in snow. It's fine to curse the snow in January, February, March and May, but in December, let it fall. No matter what your friends in Florida say, the holidays are not better with flamingos.

I do not believe in snow that turns to ice.

At the office holiday party, I believe, you should chat with your colleagues' spouses, even if you don't know them, because they may know nobody and are probably very tired of standing aimlessly in conversations about your office politics.

I believe in attending at least one holiday party that does not involve people in your office. You know all the reasons why.

I believe that you should not drive home drunk. From any party. Ever.

I believe in Rod Blagojevich. I mean that I believe that the governor of Illinois is a gift to every holiday partygoer stuck talking to a stranger. Simply say, "So how 'bout this Blagojevich thing?" and the conversation will open like a spring tulip.

I believe in holiday shopping within your means and helping out at least one stranger with lesser means.

I believe in live Christmas trees. I believe you still have a week to get one.

I believe that in the matter of Christmas trees and other holiday rituals "I'll do it tomorrow" too quickly turns into "Oh, well, next year."

I believe in Christmas cards, and that it's OK to mail them in January.

I believe we should not be offended by either the word "holidays" or

"Christmas." Arguing is contrary to the spirit of the (your adjective here) season.

I do not believe in Santa Claus, but I believe it's just fine to tell your children he exists. It is not fine to tell someone else's children he does not.

I believe in making those last-minute charitable contributions.

I believe in tipping the paper carrier. Many years, however, the little holiday tip envelope from Esperanza and Jose arrives in the plastic newspaper bag and sits in the mail pile until March, when I finally toss it out, defending my neglect with the thought that tips should not be requested and, besides, I've never met Esperanza and Jose. But these are tough times for everybody, and I bet they're especially tough for paper carriers.

I believe that if you're the one who travels every year to see your family, some year you should stay home.

I believe in singing holiday songs.

I believe that "O Holy Night" is the best of the schmaltzy Christmas songs and "Jingle Bells" is the best of the jolly songs and that "Frosty the Snowman" is a better song than "Rudolph the Red-Nosed Reindeer."

I believe that though the holidays start too soon, they never last quite long enough.

I believe that by next December you'll have forgotten most of the gifts you gave and most that you received, but you'll remember certain simple moments, like that walk you took to gawk at the neighbors' Christmas lights.

I believe in doing the relaxing thing you don't have time to do. I believe this even more during the holidays. No time for a workout? A walk? Yoga? Tea with a friend? That's why you should do it. The holidays are happier if you give yourself some time to breathe, which is one thing no one else can give you.

··

The Christmas Tree Therapist

The Christmas tree therapist is now in session.

Do you covet your neighbor's tree? Or perhaps you rage that that giant, pretentious thing next door is a blight on the environment?

Do your old ornaments make you sad? Or perhaps you fear you're losing your memory because you don't have a clue where you stored your ornaments last year?

Do you fret over fake vs. real?

Whatever your Christmas tree issue, you're safe with me because I've got issues too.

My issues are rooted where most Christmas issues are, in the rocky soil of childhood.

When I was very young, we always had a perfect tree, tall and bountiful, as bright and symmetrical as a diamond. At least that's how it looked to a 6-year-old.

The years passed, though, and times got hard in our family. When money's tight, it's hard to think ahead, so in the lean years, Christmas Eve would roll around and still we'd have no tree.

It became a family ritual that at some point on Christmas Eve, my father would dispatch my mother to find one.

He would hand her $10, dreaming of a tree that swooped from floor to ceiling. She would come home with whatever mournful cheap shrub was left on the lot.

You couldn't do better than that? he'd say. Not for $10, she'd say. He would suggest she hadn't looked very hard, and he may have been right. They played other issues out through the Christmas tree.

My brothers and sisters and I would decorate the imperfect tree, under my father's strict supervision: Tinsel goes on one strand at a time. No tossing it in clumps! String the lights evenly. Point that top star straight to heaven, no matter how cockeyed the tree.

When we were done, we'd snap off the room lights and admire the tree's glow. After a couple of drinks, my father always liked it too.

Unfortunately, after a couple more drinks, he saw all its flaws again.

In the Christmas tree, he seemed to find a mirror of his life. If he could get the tree right, his life, our life, would be fine. But the tree was never quite right, and his unhappiness with it made us all a little sad.

And that's my issue. When I look at a Christmas tree, anybody's Christmas tree, I never see just a tree.

I see the tree owner's back story. In a tree, I see expectation and history, hope and failure, a proxy for all sorts of relationships.

And for a long time, the only tree I wanted was the perfect one, which is why for a long time, I didn't have a tree. Life was simpler without one. Cheaper too.

But I came to miss the Christmas tree, the labor of it, its glow at night, the way it could warm a wintry room.

I learned, slowly, to expect less of a tree than my father had. It was OK if it was small. OK if it looked as if a bear took a big bite out of one side.

But the Christmas tree therapist is almost out of time. What are your issues?

You're anxious because you haven't gotten a tree yet? You don't have space for one? Money? Anyone to haul a tree for you?

Let me help. What about a tabletop tree? That's what I've got this year. Twenty-four bucks. Easy to decorate. Looks good in the window.

It is less than perfect, but even an imperfect Christmas tree is better than none.

SUNDAY, DEC. 24, 2006

Dad's La-Z-Boy

What kind of Christmas gift do you give someone who's dying?

The last Christmas of my father's life a couple of my siblings and I searched for an answer to that hard question.

We would not give Dad another shirt or tie.

No more Old Spice. Not another coffee table sports book he'd leaf through while he kept his true attention pinned on the TV football game.

He lived in a place too warm for sweaters. He didn't need another tool. He could have used a vacation, but he'd never taken a real one and wasn't about to start.

The things we would have most liked to give him — a longer life, peace in his anxious heart — weren't within our power.

We could give him our presence, of course, and hope that simply being there was proof of love, that proof of love was all he needed in whatever weeks remained.

That's what they say, isn't it? That in sickness or in health, love is the real gift we all hope to find in the mess of Christmas bows and boxes?

Even so, there's something to be said for a gift that can be seen and touched.

Choosing a gift for my father, even in good health, was tough. He had no hobbies, unless you count betting on the ballgames. In the middle of his life, in the midst of a crisis, he had turned his hobbies — carpentry and house painting — into his work, and he worked too much to cultivate new forms of recreation.

Free and easy time was as foreign to him as the body he had come to inhabit, whittled down by cancer to 120 pounds of bone. He still dressed every day in his painter's whites, but in the weeks leading to his last Christmas he spent more and more time in his chair.

Always the same chair. "Dad's chair." A wooden rocker with a seat so hard it may as well have been made of needles.

He mentioned occasionally that he just couldn't get comfortable in that rocker anymore, but given that he tended to equate ordinary comfort with luxury, luxury with waste and waste with sin, he wasn't about to buy himself a comfy chair.

So we did it for him.

The solution to our gift quandary appeared like a vision: a La-Z-Boy.

The La-Z-Boy store — the name was all wrong for a man who thought laziness was an E-Z pass to hell — was on a busy Phoenix boulevard about a mile from my parents' house. One of my sisters and I walked over. We picked a cream-colored recliner, an impractical fabric but it looked soft, hopeful.

The salesman said it would be delivered in a couple of days. Too long, we thought, for a man on a countdown.

So we carried the chair home, two young women lugging a La-Z-Boy through the streets, past the ranch houses, dodging cars, laughing all the way.

He liked his new chair. He got to sit in it for four months.

Occasionally all these years later when I visit my mother at Christmas, I stretch out in the La-Z-Boy, frayed now, and wonder why sometimes it's so hard to find gifts for people you love, why this last gift to my father was the only one I'd ever felt I really got right.

The best gifts any of us receive are the ones that make us feel that the giver has glimpsed in us some yearning, or some essence, that we may not even have known we'd revealed.

The best gifts we give are the ones that make the other person feel we've been paying full attention.

I like to think that's why the La-Z-Boy worked on both the giving and receiving ends, because my father wished for some ease, and though he couldn't say it we were able to see it.

Or maybe that was his last Christmas gift to us, the best present any gift recipient can offer: letting us believe that the thing we gave was perfect.

To Those Who Can't Be With Us

The father of my friend Laura died last Christmas Eve, and for all the grief it brought her family, there was a certain poetry in her father's timing. He was of Icelandic heritage and so Christmas Eve, in accordance with Icelandic custom, had always been the high point of the Christmas holidays for him and his wife and children.

Every year they gathered for a Christmas Eve dinner, then adjourned to the tree to open presents. Finally, stomachs full and gifts explored, they braved the cold night for the collective trip to church.

They spent Christmas Day at a more leisurely pace, unstuffing their stockings then lazing about until dinner time while Laura's father listened to Dylan Thomas' "A Child's Christmas in Wales," a ritual he conducted with headphones to spare his wife, who hated it.

He died in the afternoon of last Christmas Eve and so, to honor their father on his favorite night, Laura and her brothers that evening traded presents as they had year after year when they and their father were young. They weren't trying to pretend he was alive, simply to celebrate the fact that he had been.

Laura carries vivid memories of all those Christmases past into this year's Christmas, the first, as she puts it, in which her father is "truly absent." Last year, in the freshness of mourning, her family could simulate Christmas as it once was, but this year she and her mother planned on a quiet Christmas Eve, just the two of them, without the usual throng of relatives and the traditional meat pie.

"Somehow the usual ceremony seems to me to be too unbearably diminished to continue," Laura said. "It's as if our rituals have also died, or are at least in hibernation."

Few of us bring such an acute loss into this day whose official theme is joy, but for many of us, Christmas comes full of holes. A parent who died. A sibling who moved far away. A family member estranged from the family. Someone, it seems, is always missing, someone with whom we once shared Christmas and without whom Christmas seems a shade paler than before.

For years, it has been true in my family. No matter how big or festive the assembly, some ghost is always hovering near the turkey and the tree.

This year, three of my brothers and I, along with my mother, are assembling in Eugene, Ore., along with an assortment of relatives.

It's a cast that could fill a Cecil B. DeMille film, a film packed with subplots that make "The Young and the Restless" seem restful and still it feels not quite whole. The absences are as palpable as rain.

I have a brother in Moscow who can't afford to cross an ocean and two continents with his wife and baby. I have a brother in Colorado who is spending the holiday with his wife's family. I have a sister in Atlanta who for a variety of reasons can't make it and another in New York who for a variety of reasons doesn't want to. Our father died 11 Christmases ago.

But even as I lament that none of them will be with us, I know that all of them will. We'll do what families do, plugging the holes in Christmas present with memories of Christmases come and gone, telling stories to conjure up the ghosts.

We'll remember Melanie bustling around the kitchen with a surgeon's intensity and energy, elbowing intruders out of her path, and Chris hiding in his room reading Russian poetry. Bill's ghost will be there making sardonic jokes and Regina's will be there too, talking about her latest boyfriend.

And Dad, of course, will appear, standing in front of his handcrafted Nativity set, a drink in one hand, his other hand arranging and rearranging the three wise men, as if by achieving a perfect rendition of the first Christmas right there in our family room he could at last make his dream of the ideal Christmas come true.

The spirits of the absent guests always remind me that Christmas is never just one Christmas. It is the sum of all the Christmases you've known and all the people who have inhabited them.

Perhaps more than any other day, Christmas is the measure of passing time, the collective clock by which we count out our lives. It's a mutating event anchored in unchanging rituals. New characters join any family's cast — new spouses, babies, lovers — but the old cast is still clattering around in the wings.

In my family, we usually take a moment at a Christmas meal to raise a glass and say, "To those who can't be with us," and in that moment they are.

New Year's Purge

In the purgative spirit of New Year's Day, I stripped the past from my refrigerator doors.

Goodbye to the photos, quotes, poems and adorable children's drawings that over the years had finally combined to obscure every inch of stainless steel.

Farewell to ancient ticket stubs (Keith Jarrett, Cubs playoffs). Au revoir to friends' postcards (Parisian croissants, the Canal du Midi). Hasta luego to magnets (Costa Rica, Fiji, Pullman) that testify to my own wanderings.

This was no time for nostalgia. In the New Year's purge, nothing would be spared.

Not the photo of my brother waving goodbye through a train window to my mother and trying not to cry.

Not that postcard of the Chattahoochee River, despite the jolt I felt when I flipped it over and saw, in handwriting I will never see fresh again, the familiar words "Love, Mama."

Not the cartoon that shows a jocular boss patting an unhappy minion on the arm and saying, "You're better than ever at something we don't need done anymore."

Auld lang syne, my old fridge friends.

The typical American refrigerator door is a multipurpose object. It's a window to the owner's soul. It's a self-curated life story. It's a mirror. It's a canvas. It's a filing system. It's a nest.

On our refrigerator doors, we display the places we've been and the people we love, we reveal how we see ourselves and want to be seen. We post vital phone numbers. To dismantle this exhibition, built bit by bit, can feel self-annihilating, a trip into amnesia.

Too bad. This was 2012. Time moves forward, not back. It's basic digestive logic: Only by emptying out can you make room for the new.

And so on New Year's Day, I started snatching things off the double doors as if trying to beat a flood.

No, I would not get sidetracked by remembering that I'd once gone hang gliding in Rio de Janeiro and, equally fun, "butt-danced" in a suburban living room with a 5-year-old niece who is now grown, tattooed and pierced.

I would not linger over that photo of my father in his house-painter's whites standing next to his painter's van, nor would I gaze fondly at photos of friends' weddings and birthday parties.

This was like ripping off a Band-Aid. Liberation stings, but it hurts less if you act fast.

Occasionally, I paused to inspect one of the artifacts, my sticky hands proof that time creates grime.

I'd forgotten this quote, lost under a Geico 800-number magnet, from the writer Evelyn Waugh: "News is what a chap who doesn't care much about anything wants to read."

And this, ripped from a magazine short story by Alice Munro: "And it was possible, too, that age could become her ally, turning her into somebody she didn't know yet. She has seen that look of old people now and then — clear-sighted but content, on islands of their own making."

I smiled at a magnet given to me a long time ago by someone with whom I had a difficult relationship. "Resolve Conflicts Creatively," it said, then offered a series of numbered steps that began with "Calm Down."

Another magnet, also a gift, offered this counsel from John Steinbeck: "Unless the bastards have the courage to give you unqualified praise, I say ignore them."

I put that one back on the fridge.

But everything else went into a big bowl and then into a drawer, and my denuded refrigerator now gleams with the thing every new year encourages — relaxed space for the mysteries ahead.

This is one of Jason Wambsgans' beautiful photos of Tavon Tanner, a 10-year-old Chicago boy who was shot on his porch on a summer night in 2016.

The photos, which won a Pulitzer Prize, were published along with the story I wrote in December of that year.

When the story ran, a photo of Tavon holding up his shirt to reveal the long surgical scar on his abdomen dominated the Tribune's front page. It was a riveting portrait of beauty and violence and youth. Of Chicago. Of Tavon. Of strength.

This is a different look at Tavon's strength, and the photo I chose to keep on my desk.

chapter 12

the boy and the bullet

PART I

The Bullet

He wanted to see the bullet.

For weeks, he had felt it, a bump and an ache, lodged just below his left shoulder. Sometimes other kids asked if they could touch it, and he'd say yes, but not too hard.

If asked, he might pull up his shirt and show the long, fresh scar that snaked from his breastbone to below his navel.

"Thirty staples," he might say, shyly, wondrously, but even the staples in his tender skin didn't grip his mind the way the bullet did.

He had carried the bullet in his small body since the August night it pierced his back near the base of his spinal cord and ripped upward, ravaging his pancreas, his stomach, his spleen, a kidney, his left lung. He sometimes texted his mother in the middle of the night to tell her that it hurt.

Now, on a gray October day, a doctor is about to cut the bullet out, and he's hoping for the chance to inspect the little metal invader.

In a surgery prep room at Lurie Children's Hospital, he sits in a chair, leaning on his mother's arm, while doctors and nurses bustle around.

"How do you prefer to be called?" a doctor asks.

"Tavon," he said. Not Tay-von. Tuh-von.

He'll be under general anesthesia, the doctor explains, so he'll get an astronaut mask. Would he like it to be scented?

Before he can decide which scent — cherry, candy, bubble gum? — another woman enters, a specialist trained in the fears of children.

"My guess," she tells him, "is your imagination is working like crazy right now."

As she talks, he looks away, silent. Withdrawn behavior, the specialist knows, is common in children who have been shot.

When she tells him he'll be given laughing gas, though, he laughs, and for a moment a different boy flashes into view, the old Tavon, charming, lighthearted, graced with an incandescent smile, a 10-year-old boy known as joyful.

"What are you scared of?" one of the relatives gathered around him murmurs. "You don't know? Something. You tired of it? I know. You know what? It's almost over."

He isn't eager to get back into a hospital bed. He spent most of August and September in one, stretched out on his back for so long that he still has a bald spot where his head chafed against the pillow.

But he does what needs to be done, no complaints except the slump of his shoulders.

He slips out of his red Chicago Bulls T-shirt and black pants, into a blue hospital gown.

Climbs into the rolling, metal bed.

Allows strangers to bundle him in white sheets from his chin to his toes, leaving only his small face free.

Lies there wide-eyed and quiet as relatives pray over him, whisper in his ear, promise him hot wings when the surgery is over.

Then it's time.

PART II

Unintended Targets

From the first day of January through the middle of December this year, 24 children 12 or younger were shot in Chicago.

Shot stepping out of a car. Playing in the street. In front of a home. Outside a Golden Fish & Chicken.

They were shot in the jaw, the chest, the face, the arm, the groin, the back, the foot, the leg, the abdomen, the head.

A 1-year-old in the back seat of a car was struck in the neck.

Jamia, Jaylene, Khlo'e, Tacarra, Zariah, Corey, Devon. Their names varied — some publicly named only as John or Jane Doe — but all were considered "unintended targets," children who just happened to be in the way when the bullets flew.

Toward the end of this violent summer, I got in touch, or tried to, with parents of several children who had been shot, hoping to learn how the attacks had changed their families' lives.

At one girl's home, relatives said they didn't know where she and her mother had gone, maybe to a shelter. The official address of one boy turned out to be a vacant lot.

One friendly woman opened her door and said she knew who had shot her daughter — a family acquaintance currently hiding in Milwaukee.

She readily agreed to talk about it more, but when I tried later to reach her, she didn't answer her phone or her door.

I met the parents of another wounded girl one afternoon in the South Side neighborhood of Englewood. They were sitting on their porch while their daughter played with Barbie dolls. The woman invited me up, but it quickly became clear that the man wanted me to go.

"Why are you doing this story?" he asked.

A good question, fair.

I tried to explain that unless people understood how far and long the shooting of a child ripples, how it can alter the course of a life, a family, a neighborhood, how all of these shootings added together imperil the city, nothing in Chicago would change.

"People?" he scoffed. "What people?"

He looked away, down the block toward several young men clustered around an old car.

"It ain't gonna matter," he said. "This is Englewood, man."

Shock, grief, despair. Gang affiliations. Fear of retaliation. The desire to protect a child. The time-consuming business of just getting on with life.

There are many reasons the parents of a child who has been shot might prefer not to talk in public about what happened.

But Mellanie Washington was different.

Washington, who is 39, was hesitant at first, but she and Tavon came to believe that telling their story might matter. Let people see the damage. Let them know how the shooting of a child changes everything, and what it takes to recover.

"I want everybody to know what he's been through," she said.

She wants everybody to know one other thing as well.

"He's still here. He's still here."

PART III

West Polk Street

Even in the daily chronicle of this year's Chicago violence, Monday, Aug. 8, stood out: the city's deadliest day in 13 years. Nineteen people were shot, nine of them killed. Among the wounded was a 10-year-old boy who had been playing on his porch on West Polk Street in the Lawndale neighborhood.

Tavon Tanner.

As babies, Tavon and his sister Taniyah — the survivors of quadruplets — lived with their mother in the West Side home of Washington's favorite aunt. Their father, Andre Tanner, lived nearby.

"He grew up more ghetto," Washington says, adding that his "lifestyle" was different from hers.

Nevertheless, Tanner stayed involved with his kids until the night in 2007 when he died.

Sunday, July 1. Washington remembers the date because it was the day before her birthday.

Tanner was sitting on his grandmother's porch a few houses away from Washington's home, a party going on inside. At 1:50 a.m., his gun went off, and the bullet struck him in the abdomen. The official cause of death was deemed "undetermined"; the family believes it was an accident. Within an hour, he was declared dead. He was 28.

The twins, too young to remember, grew up knowing their father only through photographs and the stories their mother told them. One thing she told them is that guns are dangerous.

"So why did he have one?" Taniyah once asked.

Washington had no perfect answer.

By the time the twins were 9, Washington was eager to escape the old neighborhood. She loved her relations, but she was tired of the constant closeness and the neighborhood's "little madness."

"Let them miss us," she thought.

Financially, she was ready. She had a job as a dietary assistant at a suburban nursing home, where she prepared meal trays for the elderly. She also had a Section 8 housing voucher, her first, and with that help she went in search of a home on the North Side. Nowhere in Chicago was truly safe, she believed, but the North Side was safer.

One after another, the North Side landlords turned her down.

"That's how I wound up on West Polk," she says.

Lawndale, she knew, struggled with poverty and violence, and West Polk was an easy hop off the Eisenhower Expressway, a drug thoroughfare nicknamed the Heroin Highway.

Still, she was pleased with her new first-floor apartment in a graystone two-flat. It felt like luxury to have enough space for the twins, her older daughter and a young son. Tavon was happy.

"I liked the house," he recalls, "but it was a lot of shooting."

Washington resolved to keep her children safe.

"My kids stay up under me" is how she puts it.

She escorted her three youngest to school every weekday before setting out on the two-hour commute, via trains and buses, to her job. She forbade her kids to play on the basketball court at the end of the block where older kids gathered and trouble stewed.

The first and only time she let Tavon play there, someone stole one of his flip-flops. Never again, she vowed.

"They was the nicest neighbors I had in 40 years," says Betty Johnson, 79, who lives next door. "She was raising those kids right."

Awhile after Washington moved onto West Polk, another woman with kids moved into the apartment upstairs. Up on the second floor, people came and went constantly, and the place was loud.

But it was nothing more than ordinary trouble, or so it seemed until one night in August.

PART IV

August 8

He was staring at the moon.

That's what Tavon remembers about the moment before the bullet hit, how he was studying that bright light in the sky.

"We got that from our grandmother," his mother says. "Just something she put in us, to watch the moon."

It was a Monday. Summer. Warm.

From the front steps of Tavon's home, it was possible to glimpse the commotion at the end of the block, down by the basketball court, a swirl of police lights, yellow tape, officers and gawkers. Early that evening, someone had shot a man dead, in the head.

A couple of hours later, a new set of sirens launched into the night. Another block, another victim. From the back of his apartment, Tavon had heard gunfire and come to the front porch to ask his mother if she'd heard too.

She hadn't. There was so much noise on the street, on the sidewalks, from the stoops, people talking and laughing, cars whizzing by, that distant gunfire didn't penetrate.

The evening wore on. On the porch, Washington talked to her mother on the phone. Tavon's twin and one of Washington's sisters wandered in and out of the house. Tavon sat near his mother, gazing at the moon.

The bullets, when they came, seemed to come from nowhere, like the crack of thunder.

In Tavon's eyes, the world blurred.

Lord Jesus, God please protect my baby, just save my baby.

Washington still wonders how the 911 dispatcher understood her when she called, she was praying so loud and hard.

Lord Jesus, don't take my child.

"Ma'am?" she remembers the dispatcher saying. "Ma'am?"

Washington tells this story 2 1/2 months later, sitting in her aunt's house, the same cramped space the family occupied before they moved to West Polk. The living room is dim. The blinds are kept drawn. A TV flickers in an adjacent room, but nobody is watching.

"I've read stories about children who didn't survive," she says, "and it sits on my mind."

Tavon is on the couch, listening. When asked what he remembers of the night he was shot, he covers his face with his shirt.

"Holding it in's not good," his mother says, gently.

"I'm mad about it," he says, lowering his shirt. "It just make me sad."

He rubs his left leg, the one that now buckles when he jumps. It hurts.

Tavon doesn't remember much of what happened after the shooting, but his mother does.

The dusty smell when the bullets hit the house. The sight of her son bleeding. The keening of her 10-year-old daughter: "Twin, don't leave me! Twin, don't leave me!"

She can still see Tavon's bloated abdomen as he lay on a hospital gurney, feel herself pacing and pacing, smoking cigarette after cigarette, outside the emergency room, which was packed with relatives and friends.

She remembers Tavon's sister asking, "Is my twin going to live?"

Yes. She told her daughter and herself yes. No matter how many dead children she'd seen on TV, her child would not be one.

"I never once planned a funeral," she says. "I knew I wasn't going to sit in no front row at a funeral."

PART V

The Hospital

A small bullet travels through a small body with giant force. Tavon weighed 70 pounds.

"It would be like me being shot with a small cannonball," says Dr. Ryan Sullivan, a trauma surgeon on call the night Tavon was rushed into Mount Sinai Hospital.

Tavon lost his spleen that night, and with it his ability to fight infection. The abdominal surgery would leave him at permanent risk of internal obstructions. For the rest of his life, a long scar on his torso would look back at him from the mirror.

Leaving the bullet for the time being seemed like a wise choice, doctors thought, and so it stayed.

When Tavon returned to consciousness, after a couple of days on life support, he was panicked. He cried out:

Where am I?

Where's my twin?

Who did this to me?

I want my mama.

His friends sat by his bedside and cried with him. Tavon was especially bothered that one of them had seen the news on TV and thought he was dead.

Watching these little boys, Mellanie Washington cried too: What kind of childhood was this?

"Me, coming up, they didn't shoot into a crowd of kids," she says. "It was at night when the babies were inside. Now it's just gunfire everywhere. They just shooting to be shooting. Most gangbangers back in the day respected children and older people."

Mayor Rahm Emanuel came to visit, though Tavon was too sedated to remember. The Rev. Jesse Jackson stopped by, and a child star from the TV show "Empire." Day after day, teachers, friends and relatives kept vigil.

Once, at the hospital, Tavon thought he saw some boys involved in the shooting.

"The boys that shot me came up there with tattoos," he says.

His mother assures him he's mistaken. Whoever they were, their presence doesn't change how he answers when asked what he remembers most about his six weeks in the hospital:

"I feel safe."

PART VI

Home but Homeless

Mellanie Washington went back to the house on West Polk a couple of days after the incident.

"Incident" is her preferred term. The word "shooting" feels like an assault.

With the police at her side, she grabbed Social Security cards and birth certificates, a few clothes for her and her children. On the floor, bloody gauze from the night of the shooting lay next to the kids' uneaten chips.

So much for her dream of independence and escaping the little madness.

She moved back in with her aunt, in the old neighborhood, cramming the family's belongings into a rear bedroom. In the small house, two of her kids slept in the room with her aunt while she slept on the couch, or tried to.

Many nights she stayed up into the wee hours playing Candy Crush, hoping it could relieve her anger, wondering if she had somehow allowed this trouble.

"I felt like I had slipped a little bit," she says. She shakes her head. "No, I'm not going to fault myself. It's not like I was out partying. I was right next to my child."

On these sleepless nights, she also prayed that Tavon would be spared a life defined by anger.

"I don't want him growing up angry," she says, "so he wants to hurt others."

In late September, Tavon headed home from the hospital. But there was no home. The crowded house where his family was staying had nowhere for him to sleep comfortably, so he spent nights around the corner, with his grandmother and one of his aunts. It wasn't far, but at 2 a.m. or 3 a.m., plagued by nightmares and flashbacks, he wanted his mother.

In the darkness, they traded texts.

Mom are you woke?

Yes

I can't sleep

In her phone, he was listed as Baby Son, but the Baby Son she knew before the incident had changed.

The new Tavon was quicker to anger, slower to talk, easy to scare.

One day, after a Peoples Gas crew placed steel covers over holes in the street, he heard cars rolling across the metal.

"Grandmother," he cried, "they're shooting!"

No, his grandma remembers telling him, it's just the cars, and she took him outside to show him. Another day, he heard gunshots, real ones. He rushed to lock the door and make sure his twin sister and little brother were in the house.

It made him mad to think they were in danger, almost as mad as he was that his mother and his twin had been there to see him shot.

He was mad, too, that the tangible reminder of that scary night continued to live in him: the bullet.

PART VII

Life, Disrupted

Time changed.

"I used to mentally keep track of time," Washington says. "Before, everything was in order. Since Tavon was shot, I'm completely lost."

Since Tavon was shot. The preface to many sentences.

Since Tavon was shot, Washington no longer goes to work. Her employer at the nursing home offered her a year off from her job, with the promise that she could come back. She misses the salary but is grateful for the time.

Time to take Tavon to his frequent doctor's appointments, to look for a new place to live, simply to be home with her son.

But time, stripped of routine, is twisted now, unreliable.

She spends days indoors, with the blinds drawn, playing games with Tavon, reading online, thinking. Sleep is hard to find.

Since Tavon was shot, she wipes down everything with a mix of bleach, soap and water, knowing that without a spleen, he is highly susceptible to infections.

Since Tavon was shot, she has worried more about her other children.

Taniyah balked at entering fifth grade without her twin.

"It's an emergency," Washington told her daughter. "Show him how strong you are."

Talik, who is 7, seems lonely. He and Tavon used to play basketball and football together, ride bikes, chase each other around. Now, running and jumping are painful for Tavon, and so Talik plays alone.

But Tavon promised his little brother that they'd play again after the bullet was out. And on that October day, a week after his 11th birthday, he is rolled into an operating room at Lurie Children's Hospital.

Wearing his cherry-scented astronaut mask, he sees eyelashes fluttering above him, and then the room vanishes.

He drifts in a distant world while a doctor cuts into him with a scalpel, moves his skin and muscles aside, lifts the bullet from his soft body.

He is still sedated when the doctor, dressed in blue scrubs, walks into the waiting room where a dozen or so family members have congregated.

"The bullet is out," the doctor says.

"We got it!" someone cries.

Mellanie Washington rests a hand over her heart, her laugh a gust of relief. "The bullet is out."

But Tavon wouldn't get to see it after all. Police procedure. The doctor had passed it to a scrub nurse, who slipped it into an evidence envelope.

It isn't Tavon's only disappointment of the day. He'd hoped that the stent in his torso — a small tube that kept his insides working properly — would be removed. Instead, a new one was installed.

"They did it to protect you," his sister Tashyla, who is 20, consoles him. He had been rolled into a post-op room.

Wordlessly, he shakes his head, looking weary beyond his years, and gazes toward something far beyond the tigers painted on the walls.

PART VIII

Thanksgiving

One day in early November, Washington heard a knock on the door.

Two police officers stood out front.

"We found her," she recalls one of them saying.

"Her" meant Sirena Crosby, the woman who had lived above her family on West Polk.

Crosby had just been arrested and charged with the slaying of a 22-year-old man — the man who had been killed near the West Polk basketball court on Aug. 8, a couple of hours before Tavon was shot.

Mere coincidence?

Or was the person who shot onto Washington's porch that night retaliating for what Crosby, her upstairs neighbor, had allegedly done?

Tavon's case remains under investigation, and nothing in the public record draws the connection. Washington, however, is convinced Tavon paid for someone else's crime.

She feels sad for Crosby's kids — one was a friend of Tavon's — but the arrest gave her a sense of progress, and progress of any kind had been elusive since Tavon was shot.

Tavon would need counseling before he could return to school full time, they were told, but setting up the counseling had been complicated.

So was finding a new place to live.

After the shooting, Washington was granted a more valuable Section

8 "mobility" voucher, the kind intended to help her move into a neighborhood with less poverty.

Every day, she studied the for-rent ads, determined to get away from the dangers of the West and South sides. Every North Side landlord she encountered, she says, turned her down.

Meanwhile, her finances were a mess. Medicaid was covering Tavon's bills, but paperwork — police reports, doctors' reports, bills, applications, instructions — piled up. She stuffed the papers into bags and put them in the back room.

No proper home. Her job on hold. Her children struggling. Tavon in pain.

It was no year for Thanksgiving.

Then one afternoon a greeting card arrived in the mail. The cover showed a wreath of autumn leaves. It was from the Bailey family.

Thompson Bailey, a real estate investor in Denver, had heard about Tavon on the news.

"I have four kids of my own," he says. "I put myself in their shoes. I thought I should put some action behind my thoughts."

For weeks, he had been in contact with Washington, offering encouragement. He sent Tavon an iPad. Once, she mentioned that she didn't have the heart this year to do Thanksgiving.

Now here was a card. She opened it.

"Mellanie & Family —

I know this season or time in your lives has been traumatic & incredibly trying, and I know it has stolen some of the joy in your hearts. But it made me sad to hear that your family may not come together to celebrate Thanksgiving and what you do have. Please consider getting together & enjoying a great meal with one another."

It wasn't the $100 gift card that inspired her. It was the thought.

On Thanksgiving Day, she, her mother and her sister Harmonie cooked, and four dozen friends and relatives crowded into the little house to eat, drink and be grateful.

When the other kids danced, so did Tavon.

PART IX

Luck

Tavon is lucky.

Everybody around him says it.

Lucky to have good doctors, kind teachers, a strong family, the support of a good youth program, a relationship with police officers who care.

He's lucky to be young enough that his mind and body can heal.

Lucky to be alive.

Many children who get shot aren't so fortunate. They fall out of the reach of systems that can help them, stay trapped in families that can't or don't, get caught on long waiting lists for counseling.

But even with the best of luck, healing requires time.

After the surgery to excise the bullet, Tavon moved into his great-aunt's house with his mother. He lives there with his twin, his little brother and, lately, one of his aunts and four cousins. At night, he shares an air mattress in the living room.

And some days, while waiting to return to school full time, he goes to classes for a couple of hours.

On the Monday after Thanksgiving, under the drab skies of late November, Tavon gets ready.

In the shadowy house, his mother daubs cream onto his bald spot. He shrugs his backpack on. She goes with him to a charter school that opened in the neighborhood this year. He doesn't feel safe walking alone.

In math class, he sits in the last row by the window.

After an exercise involving the number 0.93 — he finds it difficult — the teacher announces a brain break.

Everybody stand up. Simon Says touch your head. Touch your nose. Run in place.

Tavon lifts one leg, the other, then grimaces and sinks into his desk.

"My ribs hurt when I get nervous," he says afterward. "Or when it rains."

At school, he has begun therapy.

"It's a lady, she try to get all that off my mind," he says.

"What she tell you?" his mother asks. They're sitting in the living room. "How lucky you are?"

He replies with a story about a teenager he met while he was at Mount Sinai. The older boy had been shot in the head.

"His speech is messed up," Tavon says.

"But see," his mother says, "you still talk normal. Different things happen to different people."

Tavon looks down at his phone, shrugs, smiles just a little.

PART X

Safety

The bullet that hit Tavon hurt everyone close to him.

His twin, who knelt beside him as he bled that night. His little brother, who misses his best playmate. His friends in the after-school program, who now wonder: If it could happen to Tavon, could it happen to me?

"With community violence, it's really hard," says Colleen Cicchetti, who runs the Center for Childhood Resilience at Lurie, where Tavon was recently matched with a counselor. "Unlike soldiers who went to some horrible place and then left, imagine if your traumatic reminders are your front porch. Every time you come in your house, you're reminded."

Everyone who loves Tavon is reminded, too, each time he grimaces in pain, snaps in anger, rubs his leg or his bald spot, peeks through the blinds to see who's out there.

But he doesn't complain much, and when he hears friends complain about this or that, he tells them to stop. He also tells them they should go to church.

While Washington was working, she seldom took her family to church. Sunday was her day of rest, and it could be hard to find a ride. It can still be hard to find a ride — she has never owned a car — but Tavon started pestering her to go.

Church, like the hospital, gives him something he craves: a sense of safety.

"When I go to church," he says, "like for the whole week, I can sleep."

On a snowy December Sunday, he and his mother and a couple of girl cousins file into one of the oak pews at the Greater Way Missionary Baptist Church on the West Side. It's a bright room, nothing fancy. No stained glass, just violence-resistant glass block windows.

Through much of the service, through the praying and singing and the preaching, Tavon nuzzles his mother's side. But toward the end, when the preacher names him, mentions that he was shot, he waves his arm.

"Amen!" the crowd calls. "Amen!"

"The reason why we clapping," the minister calls, "is you're still here."

"Amen!" the crowd cries.

When the preacher tells them that Tavon has another surgery coming soon, Mellanie Washington, from a pew toward the back, speaks up.

No, she says. The surgery was last Tuesday.

Surgery number eight. To remove the stent. The last surgery, if he's lucky.

The church fills again with shouts and applause for the boy who was shot.

Amen, amen, amen.

Awhile later, Tavon walks out into the falling snow. He skids around the parking lot as if it were a skating rink, laughing.

Still here.

"We live our lives, do whatever we do, and then we sleep—it's as simple and ordinary as that. A few jump out of windows or drown themselves or take pills; more die by accident; and most of us, the vast majority, are slowly devoured by some disease or, if we're very fortunate, by time itself. There's just this for consolation: an hour here or there when our lives seem, against all odds and expectations, to burst open and give us everything we've ever imagined, though everyone but children (and perhaps even they) knows these hours will inevitably be followed by others, far darker and more difficult. Still, we cherish the city, the morning; we hope, more than anything, for more."
—From Michael Cunningham's "The Hours"

"We live our lives, do whatever we do, and then we sleep . . ."

Through the years, readers have sent me beautiful poems and snippets of prose. I don't remember what occasioned this one, which is tacked to one of my cubicle walls. It's from Michael Cunningham's novel "The Hours."

I often think of the sentiment and rhythm of the lines above, especially the word "more," maybe because my mother told me that "more" was my first word. Or maybe it's because "more" would be a reasonable last word.

chapter 13

....

the journey of joan lefkow

PART I

Rain

Joan Lefkow thinks back now on a story her mother used to tell about their Kansas farm. She recounts it in the cadence of a Bible parable:

"There hadn't been rain. Then there was rain and everyone was happy. Then a hailstorm ruined the crops. My father looked out the door and said, 'The Lord giveth, and the Lord taketh away.'"

Out the door of the Chicago high-rise where Lefkow lives today, nine months after the murders that changed her life, federal marshals camp around the clock waiting, waiting, waiting for the next terror or, more probably, for the next time the judge is ready to step outside to Barnes & Noble or the hair salon.

"As a sojourner on this earth," she goes on, trying to explain how in these months she has kept her sanity and her faith, "I don't feel terribly entitled. I do believe the Lord giveth, and the Lord taketh away. It's your responsibility to accept the adversity as well as you accept the abundance."

"Adversity" is too small a measure of all that has been ripped from U.S.

District Judge Joan Humphrey Lefkow since the February evening when she came home from work, walked down to her basement and saw the blood on the floor.

Her husband. Her mother.

Her sense of safety. Her sense of self.

Her home.

All gone, along with her privacy, her autonomy, her vision of her future, certain dreams for her daughters, reliable sleep.

Now, U.S. marshals chauffeur Lefkow around in a van with dark windows, shepherd her into elevators and down hallways, lurk at a nearby table when she meets a friend for lunch.

Now, for reasons of safety, she goes to Office Depot to buy a paper shredder but then, for reasons of safety, won't have it delivered to her new address.

Now, the Marshall Field's clerk glances at the name on her credit card and offers condolences. Lefkow appreciates the kindness, but longs for the day she isn't recognized as the black-hatted widow at a funeral attended by the national media and a team of sharpshooters.

In the remains of this exploded life, Joan Lefkow reaches backward, back to the lessons about fate and fortitude she learned as a girl in a land where the summer sun was as pitiless as the winter wind and the snow along the empty roads could dwarf a man.

When people marvel that she's strong, as they so often do in admiration and bewilderment and relief, she shakes her head, says no, she's not strong. She's just from Kansas.

"It's something," she says, "about growing up in the Plains. Weather is harsh. The crops may fail. On the farm, you know your destiny is subject to the forces of nature in a way that people who grow up in cities don't learn."

The first time I met Joan Lefkow she said, "I feel dead inside."

This was on a sunny April day, six weeks after 2/28.

That's what she calls it, two twenty-eight, an icily precise term evocative of a terrorist attack.

On that day, Feb. 28, 2005, Lefkow's 64-year-old husband and 89-year-old mother were shot to death in her North Side home, because of her job, by a man who would have preferred to kill her. She found the bodies.

Even on days that impersonate the ordinary, that staggering array of facts never leaves her mind.

"It's like a ringing in the ears," she says.

In Chicago, around the country, "the Lefkow murders," as they were branded in the news, felt like both an alarm and an assault, as if what had happened to this judge had happened to us, to our rules of justice and to our faith that the law will keep us safe.

Then the alarm faded, drowned out in the public realm by other cataclysms, heartbreaks, horrors.

Joan Lefkow was left to salvage from the ruins.

At 61, Lefkow is slender and wide-eyed and with her thick brown hair she can look as girlish as a cheerleader, which she was back at Sabetha High School. On this April day, she'd extended her hand with a firm grip and a direct gaze. She smiled.

But the smile flickered like a candle whose wick is almost gone, and she seemed to float more than walk. Grief uproots and hollows.

She'd met me that day to decide whether she could bear from time to time over the coming months to talk about what happened to her on 2/28, about her life as it had been and would be.

How would she mend her family, remake a home? How would it feel to return to the job that had led to so much destruction? How would she view herself and the world from now on? How would she change, and not?

OK, she finally said.

OK, even though she cringes from publicity.

OK in part because among the things that had given her courage in the darkest days of her life, one was how much the people of Chicago had shared her sorrow. It made her feel as though she were living in a small town, where people are connected, where people care.

So, OK. She would let us share what happened next as she looked for what she would come to call her "little resurrections."

PART II

Home

She walks back into a still life of her lost life. Against a green wall in the dining room, her mother's gray crutches. On a bedside table in her blue bedroom, her husband's amber prescription bottles, a stack of his self-help books. "Compass of the Soul." "Wonderful Ways to Love a Teen." On a refrigerator magnet, a warning from Mark Twain: "In all matters of opinion, our adversaries are insane."

Except for plants as brittle as papyrus, everything in Joan Lefkow's house this April afternoon looks as it did when she walked in from work on that cold Monday evening in February, laid her purse on the dining room table, took off her jacket and wondered why her mother wasn't reading as usual in the red recliner in the front window, and why her husband hadn't returned her calls and why the house was so quiet.

She left her home that night in a blast of police and TV lights and went to live in hiding, estranged from her belongings, her routine and her past.

Now, after all these weeks away, she wanders the rooms and says, "It feels good to be home."

But where is home, really?

Is this home, this place where the familiar and mundane have turned into relics and omens? This house where cars slow and drivers gawk? This place without a husband?

Home is not the corporate apartment where she has been living, that blur of beige whose only charm is the gym where lately Darryl, one of the marshals, has persuaded her to go each day before breakfast even though she always resisted her husband's urgings to work out.

Home is not the apartment she's about to rent, the low-ceilinged high-rise place that yesterday when she'd pushed the door open for the first time made her feel her life had been shrink-wrapped.

Home is where her history is. Where her future was. Here. Home is still here.

And she can't stay. She can no longer risk living so exposed, even if she could live with the memory of the blood in the basement.

"There's the basement," she says, points, always quick to anticipate the needs of others. "You can go down."

From the basement of the house Joan Lefkow once considered home, you can hear the life above. Footsteps. Muffled voices. Notes plunked on the upright piano her parents gave her as a child.

The killer would have heard the lives upstairs as he waited with his gun down near the washer and dryer.

For 21 years, the house overhead vibrated with a family in motion. Four girls growing up. Michael Lefkow listening to Mozart, Aretha, bluegrass, opera. Joan cooking dinner, different meals for every girl, which she did most nights despite full days in court.

The Lefkows' colonial revival house, with the white vinyl siding they'd only recently stripped off and not yet replaced, was far from the grandest on their street in Chicago's Lakewood-Balmoral neighborhood. They spent their money on their daughters' educations, not on interminable home rehab. Or on pricey home security.

In many ways, they were an old-fashioned family. They didn't own a TV until their oldest daughter was 12. On Saturday afternoons, they held family meetings with bylaws and a minutes book to chronicle chores and vacations.

Then the girls grew up. One by one, the older three moved out, leaving behind their dollhouses, prom dresses, piano books and their youngest sister, Meg, who on this April day is looking for packing material.

"Mom," says Meg, rattling a New York Times stiff with age, "do you want the newspaper from February 27?"

Lefkow exhales half a laugh. She says, "Back when life was normal."

Back when life was normal, these rooms, closets and drawers could barely contain all the stuff that gave that life its weight and shape.

Look, says Lefkow now, all these earrings that have lost their mate. She polishes one on her jeans. And all these old credit cards. She goes in search of scissors. Here's a dusty flamenco doll Michael bought in Spain. She finds the vacuum cleaner and draws the cleaning brush over each tiny crease in the doll's skirt.

Dawdling in the clutter, she slows the dismantling of her life.

"I always had this desire for order," she says, pawing through her bedroom dresser. She plunges a dress into a plastic bag. She sighs. She slumps.

"But there is no order in life. It's all a fantasy."

Now every object is a memory, a decision. And every now and then, a laugh.

"Darryl!" calls a voice from the hall.

Darryl McPherson is the head marshal on Lefkow's protective detail. He's 31, trim and nimble, a former Alabama college baseball player who surveils the world around the judge with sharp eyes that used to watch for fastballs.

In these strange weeks McPherson has become brother, friend, handyman and coach to the Lefkow women. He scored them tickets to Oprah. The girls gave him one of their father's Brooks Brothers ties.

"Darryl, look!" says Helena Lefkow now, sauntering into the bedroom. Pretty in a fragile way, animated by a flinty mind, she makes it easy to imagine her mother at 25.

She dangles one of her mom's old party dresses, blue and black, short and strapless, in front of McPherson, who sits vigil in her father's rocking chair.

Judge, says the marshal, that dress would still look good.

The judge smiles. Extends a hand. Touches the old dress.

"Michael loved me in that kind of thing," she says.

Michael. Michael who, one of his sisters says, brought out the beauty in Joan, who helped the Kansas country girl believe in herself while she made him, the suburban boy, feel worldly.

Michael, whose own clothes — long-sleeve shirts, suit coats, pants jack-knifed over hangers — droop in the bedroom closet, where they'll linger for months before she can let them go.

Sometimes she'll stand alone and press the fabric to her face, searching for his scent, for proof of life.

She never finds it.

PART III
....

Michael

Michael Lefkow liked hats, which made him look taller, and he liked the snap of a starched white shirt. In his bedroom trunk, he kept a red cummerbund for flamenco dancing. When his daughters were young, his clothes sometimes made them groan. The Brooks Brothers suit he wore on a school field trip when the other parents wore jeans and khakis. The knee-high socks and little purple shorts he sported when he jogged.

He enjoyed clothes so much that before he was killed in February, he'd already bought a tux for his daughter Helena's September wedding.

Joan Humphrey met Michael Lefkow on Good Friday in 1965 in the Wheaton College library. She was a Wheaton senior, and he was a Northwestern Law School student who came to Wheaton to study. It was quiet there, unlike the nearby bungalow where, as the third of seven children, he'd lived with his family and a grandmother since his father died.

Wheaton students were supposed to be in chapel that afternoon. Anyone who stayed in the library was locked in. Joan Humphrey stayed, and introduced herself to one of the other inmates.

"He was intriguing looking," she recalls. "His grandfather was a Slavic Jew, a lawyer who knew seven languages."

That impressed the Baptist girl from the Kansas farm and the one-room schoolhouse.

When she arrived at Wheaton, a Christian college in Chicago's suburbs, Joan Humphrey was a shy, diligent, conservative 17-year-old who'd been so upset by Richard Nixon's 1960 presidential defeat that she helped make badges afterward that said, "We want a recount."

By edict of her church and family, she wasn't allowed to dance, so when she showed up for the occasional high school shindig, she sat on the sidelines. Movies were forbidden too, and though she sneaked off to "Elmer Gantry" at the drive-in and even lied to her mother so she could see "Summer Place" at the local theater, she wrote a paper in her first college semester denouncing movies as un-Christian.

The professor gave her a C.

"I was just spitting out dogma," she says now. "That was my first lesson in thinking for myself."

College was a constant test. Joan Humphrey had graduated second in her high school class of 47 students. At Wheaton, she struggled.

As a girl, she'd visited Denver, gone to the eye doctor in Kansas City and been as far as Arkansas to Bible camp. But college in the outskirts of Chicago was lonely in a way different from the loneliness of the small town and the farm.

She spent her first two years depressed — depression ran in the family — then, slowly, found herself liberated and liberalized.

"By the time I left college," she says, "I was divorced from the evangelicals."

Into her evolution walked Michael Lefkow. He was barely her height — 5-foot-6 — but he brimmed with personality, curiosity, generosity and ideas, big liberal ideas. He'd been to Spain.

"Want to go out for a beer?" he said one day when he cruised by her house in the cab he drove to pay for school.

She didn't drink. She said, "Maybe a Coke?"

That summer, on their first serious date, they went to see Federico Fellini's "Juliet of the Spirits." Michael laughed at the pretension of the allegedly great work of cinema. His contrariness irked some people, but Joan Humphrey grew to admire it.

"I'm always the one worried about how other people perceive me," she says. "He was always his own person."

Their courtship lasted for 10 years, complicated then and long afterward by the fact that Michael had fathered a child with another woman. Decades later, the fact that the other woman happened to be African-American would complicate their lives in a different way.

Finally, in 1975, Joan Humphrey and Michael Lefkow married, in a green wooden Episcopal church in the Colorado mountains. Michael wore a white Moroccan wedding shirt he'd brought back from Spain. Joan wore a white Moroccan caftan. They embarked on a life anchored by children, church and their shared zeal for the law.

Right after college, while she and Michael were still just dating, Joan had gone to work at an urban planning firm, ignoring the college career test that suggested law would suit her.

"There were no women in law," she says, "and I had no money."

But she was intrigued by Michael's job as a Legal Aid lawyer who helped the poor. One day, she said to him sheepishly, "Maybe I'll go to law school."

She was thinking Northwestern, but knew that if he balked, she wouldn't apply.

He said, "I think you'd make a very fine lawyer."

She said, "Really?"

If in the years that followed he ever minded that her career outshone his, he didn't let it show.

PART IV

Goodbyes

The last time Joan Lefkow saw her husband alive, on the morning of Feb. 28, he told her he wanted to use their 1998 Windstar mini-van that day instead of the 1992 Ford Tempo. He was staying home after surgery on an Achilles' tendon he injured playing tennis, and he wanted to drive to nearby Cafe Boost. She'd already loaded her work things into the mini-van. Wouldn't the Tempo suffice to get him to his morning coffee?

She was annoyed and he was annoyed, but they'd kissed goodbye as usual and he watched her from the doorway as she drove off in the van.

After that day, Lefkow would rarely cry in front of other people. Joan, her friends would say, was shouldering through as if grieving were just another job. Even at her husband's funeral she comforted weeping mourners more than she wept.

"I think she cries at night," one of her daughters said a few weeks later.

But on a day two months after Michael's death, Joan Lefkow goes to his office, looks around — at the swamp of papers, the poster of Spain, the family photos, the diplomas — and she weeps.

Michael Lefkow's little law office in the Monadnock Building in the Loop was nothing like his wife's suite in the federal courthouse catercorner across West Jackson Boulevard.

Hers: vistas of the lake and skyline, walls of polished bookshelves, Arts and Crafts lamps and chairs, a staff to take her calls, send her faxes, make the coffee.

His: a single room with an air conditioner in the window, a room barely big enough for his old walnut desk, bought used. His only staff was his daughter Helena, whom he'd hired as a temp and who affectionately despaired that her dad couldn't even make a computer file.

While his wife, with his proud encouragement, ascended the federal judges' ranks, Michael Lefkow had run for Cook County judge. He lost. But he didn't lose his vigor for his private practice. He was an old-style liberal who specialized in employment rights, and it energized his conscience that his clients were often broke.

In his office when he died:

Two 10-pound weights underneath the desk.

Fifteen years of appointment books squeezed into the cluttered shelves.

A 1960s valentine from his wife in a desk drawer near an e-mail from a daughter's boyfriend asking for her hand in marriage.

And everywhere lay records of the clients he loved, like the one who every two weeks mailed a check for $27.50.

On this May day, in the middle of his mess, in the void of his vanished life, his widow stands and cries.

"All this man's life activities," she says. "Phone message lists, calls to return. Now they're just papers in people's way."

A few days later, big men with big muscles and tattoos evacuate the house Joan and Michael Lefkow shared. Room by room, chair by chair, sofa, dining table, beds, a baggie that holds a baby's teeth.

She fusses over the movers. "Do you want water?"

She bends to straighten the plastic tarp on the stairway carpet. "I don't want anyone to stumble."

A neighbor stops by, they hug. She's losing the family of her neighborhood as well.

"You two were always the two who stopped and talked to everyone," the neighbor says. "How are the kids doing?"

Lefkow smiles the smile she wears like a uniform these days, tender, apologetic, as if she's sorry to intrude with this wreckage that is her life.

"Terrible," she says, but skimps on the details. She protects her girls like a bodyguard.

When the furniture is gone, she stands at a window in her bedroom, empty except for Michael's clothes, a box of his shoes, a jar of his pennies.

"My therapist told me to take a picture of what's out the window, like the tree," she says. "I haven't yet."

She gazes out at the red maple she'd watched from bed through so many changing seasons. So many things still to be done. Michael's headstone to buy. Two daughters' weddings to plan without the father of the brides. A job, the source of all this trouble, waiting for her return.

Suddenly, she recoils.

"They're filming me!"

Out front, a TV news crew aims a camera at the bedroom. She presses a hand to her heart, steps back. How do they know she's here?

Even at her own birthday party, attention makes her squirm. Now she's watched, always watched. By the media. The marshals. Who knows who else. In her solitude, she feels surrounded; in her loneliness, robbed of the right to be alone.

With a dark glance over his shoulder, McPherson sneaks her out the back door to a van idling in the alley.

PART V

Mother

Joan Lefkow grew up on 480 acres of farmland in the hills and creeks of northeast Kansas, where people were few and abundance came in the form of corn, oats, wheat, clover, sheep, hogs, cattle and sky. In the words of her brother John, "There wasn't too much to do, except what Dad told you. We didn't have a wide circle of friends."

It's a muggy June afternoon and John Humphrey, who is 70, sits in blue overalls in a white wicker chair on the porch of the empty Lefkow house. He's a big man with a broad, rumpled face and fluffs of white hair he's tamed with a green bandanna. He's come to Chicago from Colorado to help his kid sister, Joanie, fix up the house where their mother was shot to death.

His 43-year-old daughter, Anne, has come too, bearing sea salts to chase off evil spirits.

"A feng shui thing," she says, though she never scatters them as planned. Whatever demons had fouled the house, she determines, have already fled.

Now there are simply toilets to scrub. Baseboards to replace. The brute work of making the house appeal to a buyer undeterred by the killings in the basement.

"Hardly ever have I seen her be overwhelmed by circumstances," John says of his sister, "even this one." He then admits he doesn't really know how she is because she doesn't say.

Lefkow worries that her siblings — John, Judy and Tom — blame her for their mother's death.

"She shouldn't," John says. He raises his beer bottle, stares out toward the marshals milling on the sidewalk. "Anything like that just gets you right in the forehead. But it probably saved my mother 10, 15 really bad years."

Donna Humphrey wanted to die. At least that's what she'd told her children since October 2004 when a bout of sepsis, a blood infection, had sent her into the hospital and then into the home of her daughter Judy.

When Judy herself had to go into the hospital, around New Year's, Joan flew to Colorado and brought her mother to Chicago.

"Mother," Joan had warned, "you can stay with us as long as you tone it down with this 'I want to die.'"

Humphrey hated having to live with her children. She'd lived alone since 1977, when her husband, Jake, died; losing her independence deepened the depression that had dragged her down for most of her life.

"Here's the thing you have to know about Donna," eulogized a friend at her funeral. "She was almost never positive and upbeat. . . . Donna had been born to parents who didn't know how to show their love for her. . . . I think her early lack of love and acceptance made her unable to accept love from others later, and this included God. . . . But interestingly, it didn't keep her from feeling deep love for her own children."

The eulogist went on: "If you had told her on the morning of February 28 that this would be her last day, I believe she would have said, 'It's about time!'"

In rural Kansas of the 1920s, housework was more valued for girls than homework, and Humphrey had to quit school after 8th grade. She became her own teacher. Married, on the farm, she would sit under trees reading and eating apples, an inspiration to her studious daughter Joan, who nevertheless shrank from her mother's impatience and psychic pain.

"Her depression made me fearful she would leave, commit suicide," Lefkow says. "That theme of abandonment is a theme I've lived with."

In her mother's place and time, Lefkow says, the only anti-depressant was religion. Donna Humphrey gave her children a big dose of the Baptist fundamentalism that was her medicine.

Then a new pastor came up the grassy hill to little Woodlawn Baptist Church. He'd earned a master's at Wheaton College near Chicago. He encouraged Joan Humphrey to go.

And so, with a school loan and a little money her mother had inherited from her own father, she left the farm, her family, the burden of her mother's sadness and, eventually, the style of religion that sustained Donna Humphrey until her dying day.

By Feb. 28, 2005, Donna Humphrey had started to feel at home in her daughter's home. She talked more openly than ever before about her past, her regrets.

Joan Lefkow had come to find comfort in climbing the front porch stairs after work to see her mother illuminated in the winter window, reading novels or the Bible, keeping the home alive while she was gone.

On the evening of 2/28, Lefkow left the courthouse right at 5. All day she'd felt a pinch of anxiety. She'd called home several times. No answer. She'd phoned her daughter Meg, who'd slipped in after school to get her workout clothes and head to the gym.

"Have you seen Dad and Grandma?" Lefkow asked.

No, her daughter said. She figured they were sleeping.

The house was dark when Lefkow pulled up in the mini-van around 5:30. Puzzled, she scanned the living room, the dining room, the kitchen, checked the upstairs beds. Finally she descended the stairs into the basement, where Michael kept an office.

She flipped on a light.

Saw blood pooled on the floor.

She opened Michael's office door.

Saw his body. Then her mother's.

Her mother, she noticed, was wearing the bright blue caftan they'd just ordered from the Smithsonian.

She pulled the door shut. And listened to the silence.

PART VI

Mysteries

What do you do with the memory of a murder? Of two? How can you witness annihilation without it annihilating part of you? Write it down, Lefkow's therapist tells her. So on a laptop in her corporate apartment, with the marshals on guard outside, she starts writing one day in late April. Stops. Resumes the day before the movers come to the house in May. She writes in the naked style of a legal brief.

The bodies. 911. The phone call to a daughter's fiancé.

She writes of how she called one of her girls that night and shouted, "Come home! Run!" How she reached another in California, told her to get on a plane, now, heard her daughter say, "No. No. No. Mom, you're joking."

She keeps typing.

The ride to the police station. The friends who gathered there to cry. The interrogation, then the ride to the hotel where her family hid for the next two days.

More than once she types, "I don't remember."

Other people who were there that night and the days right afterward would remember things she didn't remember, or didn't feel inclined to write:

The rumpled hotel beds and curtains drawn against the daylight. The girls drifting in and out of rooms, holding each other, weeping.

One daughter sobbing, "I want my daddy, I want my daddy, I want my daddy."

Joan rocking her daughters in her arms.

Joan shrunken to the bone.

Joan, composed, signing funeral papers.

The sleeping pills.

The rifles.

The marshals hoped the family didn't know about the weapons propped against a wall in a room down the hotel hall, on alert for the next attack by an unknown killer who had left no explanation beyond a cigarette butt in the kitchen sink.

In her typed account, which she titled "Our Tragedy," Lefkow also mentions Matt Hale.

"You know who I am," she'd said to the officers who swarmed into the house that night. "I'm the federal judge that was threatened by Matt Hale's group."

By February 2005, Lefkow and her family had grown accustomed to the notion that someone wanted her dead.

That someone was Matthew Hale, the so-called Pontifex Maximus of a racist so-called church he ran from a bedroom in his father's house in East Peoria. He was engaged in a trademark dispute with a New Age group in Oregon. Lefkow initially ruled in Hale's favor but when an appeals court overturned her, she ordered his church to give up its name.

Out on the Internet, Hale and his followers took to vilifying her as a Jew judge, though she's Episcopalian, and as the grandmother of biracial children, children she loved but was related to only through marriage to Michael. The haters posted her address.

"During the Spring," reported the 2004 Lefkow Christmas letter, in Michael's cheerful voice, on stationery rimmed with holly, "Joan was called as a witness at the trial of Matthew Hale, the white supremacist charged with soliciting her murder. A supporting family cast on the benches saw her acquit herself well in the witness chair, a seat she is unused to filling. The jury, by the way, convicted Mr. Hale of the crime and he awaits sentencing."

Had Hale manipulated the February killings from his jail cell, where he reportedly sat singing opera, taking Prozac and complaining of his persecution? If not him, who?

For nine days, Lefkow lived not knowing where the next shot might hit, or why, sure of one thing only: This happened because of her. Her work.

She was sitting in her sister's house in Denver on March 9, preparing for her mother's funeral, when a marshal walked in.

Some guy, an out-of-work electrician, Polish, had just shot himself to death in a van near Milwaukee. He left a confession. Had she heard of him?

"I did remember him," she says now. "And it made sense to me that he had done it. I felt empty. The absurdity of it all."

Him. She won't say the name. Won't write it.

To her, Bart Ross is simply "the perpetrator," the man who broke into her basement through a window, then shot her husband and mother for no reason other than that they stumbled on him as he lay in wait for her.

"They were innocent," she says, "and I was the sinner."

Lefkow can still see the perpetrator's cancerous jaw, how the day he brought his malpractice suit into her courtroom his mouth opened so slightly that each word seemed to leave a new wound.

She felt sorry that no one was there to calm his rant about the doctors, lawyers and judges who had ruined his life, sorry that she had to command him to sit down.

"He was pathetic," she says. "My heart went out to him."

She dismissed his case, but for a while afterward kept a clipping from a friend about jaw reconstruction, wondering if she could help.

"Last night I was thinking, if only we'd had security cameras," she says one spring day in a bookstore cafe, her fingernails painted bright red by one of her daughters. "If only we'd had a dog."

If only, if only. Regret's incantation.

Maybe, she says, she should have spied the warnings in the perpetrator's lawsuit, detected that denying him would detonate his rage. Maybe she should have been more imperious, less inclined to look him, like everyone who comes before her, respectfully in the eye.

"I am such a sap," she says and sighs.

But what was done is over. Lives extinguished, killer found, mystery solved.

Now the new mystery: How would Joan Lefkow reconstruct her mutilated life?

PART VII
. . . .

Who Am I?

"It sounds silly for a 61-year-old woman to be saying this," Lefkow says one morning in June, "but who am I?" She sits barefoot on her old sofa in her new rented apartment. Out the big corner windows gray clouds press on the brick-and-steel city. This is a modern high-rise, guarded by a doorman and her federal marshals, nothing like the big old house she has abandoned.

She is so determined to keep the address secret that she has rerouted her mail to her office.

"Should I retreat to a mountain to read and write?" she says. "Live on the ocean? Or live in Europe? These things are all possible now."

Possible, but not likely. Money's tight. Her husband died with little life insurance. She needs to go back to work, wants to. But not yet.

There's still Michael's headstone to choose. The house not ready for sale. Michael's clothes still in their bedroom closet. So many burdens that double as distractions, goals.

And she's still not ready for a routine life without the twin anchors of the old one — conversation with her husband when she wakes up and goes to sleep.

Once, she called his voice mail just to hear him talk.

These days she devotes herself to the business, the busyness, of grief. She packs. Unpacks. Untangles the family finances.

One day the marshals drive her an hour north to buy a baby grand piano. It's a squeeze in this apartment, but her mother bequeathed her a little money with instructions to replace her battered childhood spinet.

Some days she lunches with friends, by unspoken agreement avoiding discussion of "that night," "the tragedy," "2/28." The marshals chide her if she sits exposed on a restaurant patio. The pleasures of natural light and fresh air have been reclassified as dangers.

On Sundays there's church and once a week there's therapy.

Religion, she says, "is the floor I stand on." Therapy coaxes her below ground.

"I have a hard time digging into what I'm feeling," she says.

She'll concede to sadness. It shows in the sag of her voice, in the weariness that sometimes descends like a swift fog from out of nowhere. She can admit, quietly, that she feels betrayed by life.

But anger? The full scream? Not yet anyway.

"This whole anger thing is pretty deeply buried in my soul," she says. "I learned early on that anger is not an emotion you could appropriately express."

Every now and then, as the anesthesia of disbelief wears off, she feels the anger scorch. Not for herself, not that she can recognize, so much as for her daughters.

There's Maria, dark-haired and outgoing, reminiscent of her dad. Helena, more demure and watchful, more like her mom. Laura, taller than them all, a college junior with a lawyer's love of argument. Meg, a high school junior, who wears a lip ring and dyes her hair and who lately has grown up fast.

What can she say when one of the girls phones at midnight sobbing? When another wonders how she'll tell her own children that her father was murdered?

What can she say when a daughter climbs in her bed, weeping that she can no longer envision her father's face? When another cries to think of a wedding day without her dad?

What can she say when one of them tells her she's become too needy?

What can she say when they cry for the injustice of what's been stolen from them, except to say this is not an issue of justice?

She can't tell them Dad and Grandma have gone to a better place. Or that they died because God decided it was time. Despite her deep faith, she's not convinced of either.

"Mostly," she says, "I just hug them and let them cry."

Into this interminable darkness shines the light of one clear thing: She must take care of her girls. Duty is comfort.

The girls take care of her too.

On Easter, they made her laugh by teaching her dirty words, a few of which she painted on an Easter egg.

On her 30th wedding anniversary — "Take me to Hawaii, I've never been to Hawaii," she'd said to Michael — they took her to dinner.

Mother's Day. Father's Day. Each official festive occasion passes like another hurdle jumped in the psychological escape from 2/28.

The unnamed, uncelebrated moments are hard in a different way. It's on solitary mornings like this one, when the two girls who are home for the summer have gone off to work, that Joan Lefkow sits alone in the stillness, baffled.

"I have to keep reminding myself that this really did happen," she says. "There's something about death that's so stark and shocking. A person who was with you for 40 years is gone! Just gone!"

She tosses her arms into the air. Lets them drop. Tears fill her eyes, but don't fall.

Memory is gravity. It tugs her down and back. She fights to look up, move on.

She changes the picture on her cell phone from one of her husband's grave to one of her daughter Maria trying on a bridal gown.

Now, the phone rings.

"Just the marshals," she says. "Checking on my schedule."

They're a rotating squad, mostly strong men half her age, from places like Arkansas, Missouri, Kentucky. Mostly they disagree with her on politics, but they admire her grace and strength while they hover around the bridal shop, the theater or the grocery store with their sunglasses and their cell phones.

She has learned to stop mothering them as much as she did at first. They'll figure out when they're hungry or need a bathroom break.

Still, she and they trade kindnesses. They carry her groceries, fix a light. After one of her mother's memorial services, a marshal taught her a few pool moves in a small-town Kansas bar. She once made the guys pancakes.

The polite tenderness they exchange sometimes looks a lot like love.

The marshals are there to make her less afraid, but their presence tells her to be wary. Wary of her reflex even now to trust.

Out on the Internet, the ignorant and hateful still spit on her name. In May, she was dining in a Thai restaurant when someone posted a nasty note, seemingly aimed at her, on the window.

Every time she phones the CP, the marshals' command post, to say she's ready to go outside, she's reminded that she's not just a victim of violence, not just a widow navigating the ordinary obstacle course of grief.

She remains a judge, made vulnerable by her power.

PART VIII
. . . .

Judge and Witnesses

After the murders, she turned down plea after plea to speak in public. No to Larry King. No to Diane Sawyer. Yes, she says, when U.S. Sen. Arlen Specter asks her to fly to Washington to testify about judicial security in front of the Senate Judiciary Committee. Temporary pain relief: Be useful.

What had happened to Lefkow hadn't happened just to her. The assault on her family felt like an attack on all judges, on the family she joined the day she first put on her black judicial robe. She gives the date as reflexively as if it were her birthday: Nov. 9, 1982.

Lefkow figured early in her career that she was too shy to be a strutting courtroom attorney. But a judge? She liked to read and write. She liked to listen. She even liked lawyers.

More than that, she believed in justice and the justice system as deeply as she believed in God, the right to vote and the separation of church and state.

She also believed that every criminal was somehow crippled.

Female judges were scarce when Lefkow was appointed a magistrate, but the field was good for women. Pay equal to a man's. Negotiable hours that made it possible to bring up children. Respect.

When she had her fourth child, at 44, she helped start a child-care center in the Dirksen U.S. Courthouse. It's still there.

By 1994, President Bill Clinton was scouting for women to name as federal judges. Lefkow applied. She wasn't chosen.

For the next six years, even as she became a U.S. Bankruptcy Court judge, she applied over and over. Over and over, other women, her friends, got the job.

Finally, on Sept. 7, 2000, in proof of what one speaker that day called her "absolute, enduring persistence," Lefkow stood in a crowded courtroom to take the oath of office. She felt like Dorothy in Oz.

She talked about the family farm, the Kansas plains, her small town and the unknown world into which her mother had dispatched her for an education.

She placed a hand on a Bible held by her daughter Laura and, with her children, husband, siblings and mother as witnesses, solemnly swore to administer justice equally to rich and poor.

So help her God.

On a bright May day almost five years later, she walks into a dim, paneled Senate hearing room. She has become what she ruefully calls "the poster child" for the hazards of the judge's job.

She flinches at the pack of photographers crouched on the floor, clicking, clicking, clicking at the widowed judge in her cream-colored skirt suit and fresh haircut.

Her voice is strong, though, as she speaks, sitting at a massive table, sometimes looking down at the text she'd labored on for days, sometimes glancing up at the three senators who'd shown up to listen.

Dick Durbin and Barack Obama of Illinois are there and from Pennsylvania, Arlen Specter, the lone Republican.

Occasionally she adjusts her reading glasses as she talks of the need to make judicial safety a priority. To better fund the U.S. Marshals Service, which protects judges and their courtrooms. To finance home security systems for judges. To limit the Internet posting of judges' addresses and personal information.

She quotes from Bill Clinton's condolence letter: "the madness in the shadows of modern life."

Her daughters sit behind her, but she has deleted their names from her speech, an attempt to protect their privacy and safety.

The next day, Lefkow's picture is on the front page of the Chicago Tribune and the New York Times. AOL features her on its main screen, with a poll. Do you agree with this judge? Should Congress condemn anti-judge rhetoric? Could recent harsh comments about judges encourage violence?

Her own answer is such a stern yes that a few weeks earlier, after Republican Sen. John Cornyn of Texas linked violence against judges to their "political" decisions, she shot him a letter.

"Sir," she wrote, "I challenge you to explain to my fatherless children how any judicial decision that I ever made justified the violence that claimed the lives of my husband and mother. As I will not reveal my daughters' names or addresses, I will be glad to convey to them any statement you wish to make that might ameliorate the further pain that you have caused my family."

She never heard back.

Then the trip to Washington is over. So is the brief, sharp purpose it brought to her shapeless new life. She flies home to Chicago, to gray skies and a cold. She knows she should go back to work. But more than ever now, she feels tired, exhausted by the realization that there is no quick way out of grief, just a slow trek through the days.

PART IX
. . . .

Work

By 9:15 a.m. on July 12, Lefkow has had four cups of coffee, received calls from three of her daughters and shown a couple of relations from Topeka around her courtroom. "This," she tells her relatives, sweeping a hand around the room with a homeowner's pride, a mother's tenderness and a pilgrim's awe, "is Mies van der Rohe at his best." This, courtroom No. 1925 in the Dirksen U.S. Courthouse, is also where Lefkow met at least two men who hoped to kill her, Bart Ross and Matt Hale.

Day after day, the angry and afflicted ride the elevators up the glass-and-steel skyscraper into these windowless, towering, walnut-walled rooms where law is intended to civilize emotion. Emotion, it turns out, sometimes rules.

On this Tuesday, her first day back on the bench, Lefkow's staff is afraid of emotion in the court. They persuade their boss to post a sign on the courtroom door. It thanks everyone who has expressed condolences and ends in bold type:

"In court proceedings, Judge Lefkow respectfully requests that no reference be made to the matter."

In her chambers, Lefkow is elated, nervous. Can she even remember how to navigate through a database to find a court case?

"Hey, it came up!" she says, sitting at her computer. "Isn't that so cool?"

She squeezes her lips, leans into the screen and studies a case about alleged police misconduct in suburban Markham.

"Judge," says her courtroom deputy, Mike Dooley, poking his head in the doorway, "your guests are here."

For the first time since Feb. 28, she shrugs on her black robe, a cheap old polyester and cotton gown she's too thrifty to replace though she hates the way it hangs.

She zips.

In the hallway, she stands flanked by marshals, like an actor poised for curtain call. She curls her knuckles under her chin, the way she often does when she's thinking or self-conscious or fighting tears.

Then she's back, back up there in her old seat on the bench, smiling at the attorneys, listening to the facts, asking questions, riffling through papers, making decisions.

No mention is made of "the matter."

The procedure is as familiar as breath, the place as familiar as home. The only visible change is the big old walnut desk on her left. Michael's. He's no longer around to pop by and wave from the courtroom's back row, but she has brought over his office desk to keep her company.

"So," she says, back in her chambers, her grin mixed with a wince, "how'd I do?"

"We got one under our belts, Judge," says her assistant, Krys Juleen, and hugs her boss, hard.

"You want some coffee?" asks a clerk.

"Do you have coffee?" Lefkow says.

"It's all made."

Over her fifth cup of the day, Lefkow leans back in her desk chair. Chicago flexes outside the plate glass windows, a sweep of mighty towers and a great turquoise lake, her city, always changing and enduring.

She tilts her head. "I'm very much intrigued," she says, "by how much we live in the present."

That night, she brings flowers to a friend's home for dinner with three judges, women who often lunch together in the courthouse.

"I went back to work today," she says softly.

How'd it go? her friends cry.

"It felt good."

Over pasta and wine, they chat like any gang of friends, about jobs, politics, the Supreme Court, kids, nutritionists.

"You're eating much more now, Joan," says one.

"I put back all the weight I took off," Lefkow says. She laughs and shrugs.

"I didn't mean that."

Soon the coffeemaker is popping and Lefkow empties two big grocery sacks on the table.

"So there's the mail."

Condolence letters. She has received more than a thousand. Her friends hold note-writing parties to address envelopes while she signs cards.

"My heart goes out . . ." "The world has been cruelly robbed . . ." "We feel so helpless . . ."

A thousand different ways to say what can't be said.

The cards are from strangers mostly, including more than 200 judges and a story development team at ABC-TV.

The sympathy keeps her grief more vivid than she wants, but with the same gratitude that moved her to go to the police station and shake hands with the officers who helped her on the night of the murders, she has vowed to answer every one.

"Very Lefkow of you," one of the women says.

For the next couple of hours, they work, sometimes without a word. They're not judges right now, just friends finding comfort in the ability to help and be helped, in the scratch of pen on paper.

PART X

Alone

Sunlight and dust motes. That's all that's left in Joan Lefkow's old bedroom on a morning in late July when the men from St. Leonard's House walk into the closet, sweep her husband's hangers off the rods, then cart them down the stairs and out to a truck on the shady street.

"You help men getting out of prison?" Lefkow says to the manager of St. Leonard's, a West Side shelter.

She stands near the front door, arms crossed, as her husband's life whisks past. For weeks after clearing out the house, she has hung on to his clothes as if holding on to hope.

The man from the shelter nods. "Yes, it's all about saving lives."

She nods. Good. Let some ex-con wear Michael's camel jacket, the suit still in its dry cleaning bag, the cowboy boots he bought in Colorado when they were married 30 years ago. Let his death help to restore a life.

Then the truck pulls off, and just like that, the clothes are gone.

Her teenage daughter starts to cry. Lefkow hugs her and they lean murmuring against a door jamb, the mother stroking the daughter's face and hair, the girl stroking the mother's, until they both stand up tall and move apart.

Another little death, this end of Michael's clothes. A death that makes more room to breathe.

"I've had enough for today," Lefkow says abruptly.

She walks outside to the marshals' van. The sky is blue, a lawnmower whirrs, a bus belches past. The world hums on, regardless.

"The thing that's beginning to hit me now," she says a few days later, "is that this isn't a phase of life that you get through and it's over."

She sits in the red recliner her mother liked, next to her newest book. Lately she reads more than she's read in years, often at 3 a.m., reading to staunch the memories. This book is "The Way We Never Were," a feminist history of the American family.

"Your view of the future is different," she says. "All these assumptions, good or bad, about the future have changed. There are so many older women alone. It's a new version of myself."

Her daughter Laura glances up from the family photos she's sorting on the couch. Her dad in an Afro. Her mom in a miniskirt.

"You're not alone," Laura says in a tender voice. "You have us."

"There's this whole social conditioning," Lefkow goes on. "You have a husband. People treat you in a certain way because you have a husband, no matter how unhappy the marriage is. To say the least it's uncharted territory."

She circles her teacup in the saucer. The china clinks in the quiet room.

She stands up, brightens. "Did I show you my dress for the wedding?"

PART XI
....

A Wedding

On a Saturday in September, Helena Lefkow, daughter of Joan and Michael Lefkow, marries Jake Edie. The groom wears the tux Michael Lefkow had planned to wear to his daughter's wedding.

The fatherless bride wears an ivory gown and, on her right forefinger, her father's wedding ring.

The flower girls — twin daughters of the daughter Michael fathered with another woman — wear mango-colored sashes made by Joan.

The marshals wear their Sunday suits.

Relatives, judges and lawyers have come, friends from the old church and the old neighborhood, a full assembly of the Lefkow family's shattered community.

At a pre-wedding party with an Elvis Presley theme, Joan Lefkow had dressed like a backup singer, in a cat suit and a big teased wig.

On the wedding day, she wears a strapless periwinkle Nicole Miller gown as she stands to address the gathering:

"The poet Diana Der-Hovanessian wrote, 'When your father dies, the sun shifts forever, and you walk in his light.' I shall not attempt to put a good light on what happened to deprive Helena's father of his great joy of being here tonight to celebrate and amuse you all with a cleverly eccentric blessing of his daughter Helena's marriage.

"But I do know that the light cast by his life on his daughters and the family and community in which he lived and worked will sustain you, Helena, and all of us as we go forward without him.

"And let us also acknowledge another person we miss, Helena's grandmother Donna, who always said goodbye with 'this is my last trip to Chicago' but always pulled herself together to be there for every christening and graduation, and many birthdays and Christmases. We miss her warm presence with us."

PART XII

Faith

Often in the seven months I spent talking with Joan Lefkow, I would look at her, this strong and tender woman, and repeat to myself the soul-rattling thing that when you're with her you can never quite forget and never quite believe: Her mother and her husband were murdered. In her home. Because of her job. By someone who wanted to kill her. She found the bodies.

How had it happened that the ordinary things this humble woman loved and wished for most — family, home, meaningful work — converged and exploded on one awful winter day in the middle of her life?

You could chalk it up to fate, to the inexorable drive of the actions of her life toward a single point. You could subscribe to the dark theory, "Your luck is your doom."

If you're Joan Lefkow, when you think about fate, you also think about faith. You think about the universality of suffering and the promise of rebirth. And you still oppose the death penalty.

"The wedding was a resurrection of sorts," she says in a dark wine bar on a rainy night with autumn rolling in. "A new family being created."

She's shucked off her shoes, tucked her feet underneath her on a couch, ordered a glass of Chianti. In her pink shirt and black suit, she no longer looks like the ghost who when I first met her in April had said, "I feel dead inside."

Resurrection. It's one of her favorite words. Little resurrections are the signposts she seeks out in the foreign land of this new life.

The plant that didn't die in the old home and lives on in the new one. Her piano lessons resumed. Work.

She's still waiting for the resurrection in her refurbished house, the young couple she hopes will buy it and make a new family.

Tonight, a buxom blond singer in a black dress is perched on the ebony piano, waggling a stiletto heel in time with "You'd Be So Nice to Come Home To."

"I like this song," says Lefkow. Maybe, she says with a laugh, she'll become a lounge singer. She hums a couple of bars.

Her loneliness grows starker as the shock wears off. From day to day, she ricochets from disbelief to acceptance and back again, from energetic determination to fatigue no sleep could cure.

And yet, she says, cupping her chin in her hand, leaning an elbow into the couch, she feels her voice growing stronger.

She gets invitations to speak now. She grows more inclined to accept. She feels an obligation to the issues of justice that roused Michael.

"I've found my voice in a way I didn't have yet," she says. "I don't have forever to be an influence on other people. Michael's not there to speak, so I must speak louder. I'm less afraid."

She's musing on courage when the singer croons into the microphone, "Good to see you, Judge."

The woman, a stranger, hops off the piano, walks over to Joan Lefkow and hugs her. For a flicker, Lefkow shrinks away, then she hugs back, because this is who she is now, a shy woman from the Plains connected to the world by everything she has lost.

Michael Lefkow once asked his wife, "Even if there is no God and even if evil prevails, would you live your life differently?"

She told him no. She still thinks no.

"I have some core value that searching for the good and the honorable is the way to live," she says. "God is the spirit of good in the world. God is the spirit of love in the world. That belief is so engrained in me that even if someone proved point by point that it wasn't true, I'd still believe it."

FROM
THE
DESK
OF

Mary Schmich

It's all boxed up or gone now.

- The notes on stories I've cared about.
- The old Rolodex.
- The T-shirt of the Tribune's front page on Jan. 1, 2000. In the fine print on the side is a refer (pronounced reefer) to a story I wrote from Pitt Island, New Zealand, where I witnessed the first sunrise of the millennium.
- The faded autograph from B. B. King, from a riverboat cruise on the Delta Queen down the Mississippi River.
- And a Wendell Berry poem that makes me feel a little saner every time I read it. It's called "The Peace of Wild Things."

chapter 14

························

2012 pulitzer prize winners

Gina

My sister Gina received her first cellphone as a birthday gift a few days ago.

Until recently, Gina had insisted that a cellphone was too complicated for her, a plausible statement given how many things she finds hard.

For years, she found bathing complicated, so she rarely stepped into a tub or shower. Brushing her teeth felt complicated, so her teeth went bad. Cleaning her room felt like climbing a mountain, so her room devolved into a jungle of junk with a skinny path to the unmade bed. In the final weeks of her old cat's life, she found it too complicated to pick up the cat feces on the carpet, so she neatly laid a paper towel over each set of droppings.

When Gina was little, doctors said she had an IQ of 34, and though they were far wrong, the right diagnosis has never been clear. Mild autism. Borderline personality disorder. The verdict seems to have changed almost as often as her medications.

What is clear is that Gina is different, so she always lived with our mother and our mother lived with the question: What will happen to Gina when I die?

Gina worried too. As Mama grew frail, Gina often climbed in her bed in the middle of the night to weep.

"Honey," my mother would soothe her, "you'll be OK," and my siblings and I, unconvinced, told our mother we'd make sure she was.

In the months leading up to my mother's death, Gina began to change. She calmed down, some. She took pride in making Mother's morning coffee. When one of my brothers or I bathed our mother, Gina held the towels. When we'd lift Mother off the portable commode next to the sofa where she slept, Gina was quick to say, "I'll empty it."

But after Mama died, we braced for Gina's familiar rages. We talked about how to handle her when she burst into shrieks at the memorial.

On the morning of the service, she found me while I washed my face.

"Do you think," she began. "Do you think it would be OK if I don't go? I just. I just think the best way for me to honor Mom today is to take a shower and brush my teeth and go out on the bus."

And that's what she did.

With clean hair, in new brown capris and shin-high socks from Target, she rode the bus from store to store that day, along a route she rides for hours almost every day just for fun. She visited with clerks and pharmacists she considers her best friends, telling them her mom was gone.

"Mom would be proud of me for being independent," she said when she got back.

In the year since, Gina has lived alone, next to one of our brothers. She has given up soft drinks, after years of a dozen a day. She has gone to the dentist, and her teeth, minus several that had to be pulled, are white again.

She showers.

And now, thanks to two brothers, she is a modern woman with a cellphone. I called her on it last week.

"I'm doing a lot of things I never thought I'd be doing," she said with a big laugh. "Living alone! And a cellphone!"

I try to understand my sister's transformation, to trust that it will last. It's one of the most mysterious and beautiful things I've ever witnessed, though maybe it's no more complex than this:

When your greatest fear comes to pass and you survive, you discover who you really are.

A Memorial Mission

The woman walks toward the wall.

She presses a fingertip into the shiny, dark stone, traces it down the wall, left to right, left to right, name after carved name, a roster of the dead palpable against her skin.

Jim Zwit is about to leave when he catches sight of the woman. He has been on the Washington, D.C., mall with two old Army buddies for several hours on this sunny April day, the 40th anniversary of the 1971 firefight that killed eight of his fellow soldiers. He has cried a little, reminisced and prayed, talked to the kids who arrive by the busload to see the memorial and learn what the Vietnam War was really like. He's ready to go home.

The woman bends, her eyes scan lower.

Zwit, noting that she is middle-age and black, thinks: It can't be. Can it?

Zwit knows this stretch of wall as well as he knows his scars, the pink welts that run from below his navel to his right nipple, the sinkhole of puckered skin where he once had ribs.

This is Panel 4W. The names of the eight men who died the night he earned his scars begin close to the bottom, at Line 123.

Robert. Jerry. Charles. Terry. Ronald. Rex. Paul. William.

Over the past four decades, Zwit has dedicated himself to finding their families so he could tell their mothers or fathers, their brothers or sisters or cousins, how they fought, how they died, and that they weren't alone.

He has tracked down relatives of all the men. All except one. William. William Ward. No matter how he searched, every clue went cold.

The woman drops onto a knee. Zwit walks over, kneels down next to her, rests a hand on her shoulder. He feels the rustle of a dormant hope.

"Can I help you find something?" he says.

In April 1971, Jim Zwit, the second in a family of nine children from Chicago's South Side, trekked with his infantry company down into the A Shau Valley and up onto an enemy ridge to retrieve the body of a soldier killed two days before.

Like the other 77 men known as the Delta Raiders, he carried 80 pounds in his rucksack. His M60 machine gun weighed 28 pounds more. He had just turned 20 years old.

At dusk on the second day, the men trudged up a trail littered with trees toppled by American bombs, swatting machetes at the suffocating jungle. They could sense, but couldn't see, the underground tunnels and bunkers of the North Vietnamese soldiers who had lured them deeper into danger by moving the body they came to get.

Shortly before 7 p.m., in the dying light, the quiet jungle erupted.

Explosions, the pop of machine guns, shouts and screams, bullets, blood, shrapnel, the stench of sweat and burnt gunpowder.

Then silence.

From up the trail, in the kill zone, a voice floated back toward the men hunkered behind a felled tree.

I'm hurt. I need a medic.

Zwit recognized the voice. It belonged to Paul McKenzie, the only black lieutenant in the company, a guy who never put you in danger without standing next to you.

Zwit was big and blond in those days, a wrestler and a hockey player whose Chicago friends called him a Pollock even though his parents were of Slovakian and German stock. He'd also been called hyperactive. Outgoing. Life of the party.

Now he jumped over the protective log and darted up the trail.

From the brush, he heard Vietnamese chatter. Spying the entry to a camouflaged bunker, he walked over, aimed his gun into the hole and fired.

Forty years later, in his La Grange Park kitchen, he will close his eyes and squeeze his crossed arms tight across his scarred chest when he recounts how the bunker suddenly went quiet. He had never killed before.

Zwit lugged McKenzie over his right shoulder and was halfway down the trail when the second mad minute — that's what the soldiers called the bursts of violence — struck.

McKenzie died almost instantly, hurled to the ground, riddled with metal fragments and looking Jim Zwit in the eye.

Without the shield of McKenzie's body, Zwit may have been killed too. As it was, he was just bloodied and broken. When the rescue helicopter finally arrived, it couldn't land, so Zwit was reeled up, slamming from tree to tree as the chopper lurched to avoid gunfire from the ground.

This is how Zwit remembers it. Others who were there that night tell a similar story. There are a few hard documents that testify to what happened, like the handwritten military report for April 15, 1971, that noted Zwit's condition when he arrived at the hospital:

"Multiple frag wounds to chest . . . Doctors do not believe he will live."

He lived.

He lost his right kidney, a piece of his liver and four ribs. He would spend the rest of his life with shrapnel in his abdomen. But he did what eight men he fought beside that night weren't allowed to do. He lived.

After a couple of years of surgeries, he got a job as a Chicago cop. He married, had two kids, divorced, remarried in 1987, would soon have two more kids. He left the police force to go into business as a process server who also did investigations for law firms.

And through it all, he kept thinking about the promise he'd made to Bob Hein.

Hein was one of the men who'd carried him over the log to safety the night of the firefight. In the hours before the rescue helicopter came, Hein dashed back repeatedly from the combat to bring Zwit water, until, at some point, he didn't come back.

Months earlier, the two had made a pact: If only one of us gets out, the survivor has to find the family of the other guy and tell them how it happened.

Somewhere between Vietnam and home, Zwit lost Hein's address, and in those days, it was hard to find people. There was no Internet, no Facebook, no email. War documents were classified. Nothing was digitized.

Zwit remembered Hein was from Sacramento, though, and once a friend visiting California ripped the "Hein" pages from the Sacramento phone book. Zwit called every one. No luck.

When he heard about a Sacramento TV anchor involved in a California memorial for Vietnam vets, he wrote and asked for help. The anchor sent his letter to the commission handling the memorial. One of the men on the commission was a vet and a property appraiser; he scoured property tax records. No luck.

Finally, in 1988, a chain of coincidence led Zwit to Hein's mother. She still lived in Sacramento, but she'd remarried and changed her last name.

The day he called her, she told him that Bob had received a posthumous medal for carrying one of his comrades to safety.

"Mrs. Hein," Zwit remembers saying, "I'm the guy he carried back."

After that, Zwit went, in his words, a little bonkers. He vowed to find the families of the other seven dead soldiers.

He made call after call to the National Archives in pursuit of leads. He phoned newspapers in tiny towns, searching for obituaries. He narrowed one search with the help of a private investigator buddy who had access to a credit-check company.

One by one, he found the dead men's relatives. In West Virginia. Oklahoma. New York.

One by one, they thanked him, for giving them more details than what came in the curt government notification, for bringing what was lost briefly alive again.

"We got no personal belongings of Terry's back," one mother wrote him in a shaky hand, from Nashville, N.C. "Not even his glasses. He had worn them since 2nd grade and wore them all the time except when sleeping or bathing. I'm sure he died with them on his face . . . I am sending a picture of Terry that I have cherished for years."

Only once did Zwit feel that his overture was unwelcome, and he understood.

And only one family's whereabouts eluded him. William Ward's.

"Can I help you find something?" the man asks.

But Lois Daniels has just seen the one name, the one out of the more than 58,000 names on the black wall, that she's looking for.

"William Ward," she murmurs.

She points her camera. The gleaming stone reflects the image of the big guy in blue jeans, with wispy faded blond hair, who has appeared beside her.

"Did I hear you right?" the man says. "Did you say, 'William Ward?'"

Does he say it before she stands up? After? When they tell it later, they won't remember it exactly the same.

But he has heard her right.

She says she grew up in the North Carolina countryside near Ward's family, is married to his cousin. She says Ward's mom and six younger siblings are still alive, though no longer on the North Carolina farm.

Two men who have come to the wall with Zwit today join them. One is the helicopter pilot who pulled Zwit out after the firefight. The other is Bob Gervasi, a platoon buddy who carried Ward's body away.

Soon, they're all hugging and, as Gervasi will say later, a little wet behind the eyeballs.

"It's great you came for the anniversary," Zwit tells Daniels.

She says, "What anniversary?"

She doesn't realize that April 15, 2011, is the 40th anniversary of Ward's death. She's here only because it's grandparents day at her grandkids' school. Her daughter in nearby Maryland has invited her to join them on a drive to D.C. It is her first visit to the wall.

"It was," she'll say afterward, "a divine appointment."

A month later, in May 2011, the Ward family held a reunion.

Among other events, they gathered to watch a video Jim Zwit sent of the slim, young guy they called Spooky.

For years, Ward's family didn't talk about his death, though year after year, on the anniversary, his mother placed a photo of him, in uniform, in the local paper.

They knew little about how Ward died, nothing about his comrades. They are grateful for what Zwit has told them, especially for the reassurance that, unlike so many other men, he went fast and didn't suffer.

"It feels good to know the full story," said his sister, Ethel Carter. "Maybe that's why I couldn't talk about it. I didn't know what I was talking about. Now I know."

When they played the video at the reunion, several people whooped in delight.

Look. Spooky, in Vietnam, down by some water, in his green uniform. Smiling, just like he did the day he left for the airport and said, "I'll see you all."

But then someone noticed Ward's mom. The video had upset her.

They cut it off.

Later, several of William Ward's siblings made plans to go to the wall this Memorial Day, for the first time in many years, for which they thank Jim Zwit.

Remembering is a mixed blessing.

Some people like to remember what's difficult as a way to preserve life or to understand it. Others try to forget.

Jim Zwit has wanted the knowledge he has shared with the families of eight dead soldiers to give them a choice about what and how they remember.

And he has, no doubt, wanted something for himself, too, something to do with his own memories, even if he's not sure what.

SUNDAY, JUNE 12, 2011

Save a Little Outrage

The woman answered my knock by opening the door a crack. She was neatly dressed in blue jeans and a blue shirt.

Was this Dvonte Sykes' home? Was there someone I could talk to about what happened Saturday night?

"I'm his mother," she said, warily.

It was Friday, midday, not quite a week since Tonia Rush's son was arrested. He and four other teenage boys were charged with mugging five people in an affluent, touristed part of downtown Chicago. She didn't want to talk, but said she would, outside, on the stoop of her two-story graystone duplex.

Had Dvonte been in trouble before?

"No. Never. He's a pretty good kid."

She reached absent-mindedly into her mailbox, pulled out several envelopes.

She said Dvonte had planned on going to summer school to earn credits to complete his junior year of high school.

Instead, at 17, he has been charged as an adult with robbing a Thai tourist and participating in a "mob action" in which a group of teenagers tried to steal another man's scooter.

"Now we're going to throw the book at him," she said, "going to use him as an example."

What he's accused of doing is really bad, right? When I asked, she didn't hesitate.

"Yes. It is. Absolutely. If he did it, he needs to be punished. But how it's blown up is not making it any better."

Nearby, the Englewood neighborhood was humming with young men. They clustered at the bus stop, next to cars, outside Stewart's Cut Rate

Liquors. A couple of guys played a game of quarters, tossing coins on the sidewalk, aiming at the cracks.

But Rush's block, which has houses on only one side, facing elevated Metra tracks, was quiet except when a train roared by.

She said that since she moved here from Hyde Park because it was all she could afford, the neighborhood has gotten worse.

"I can walk to the bus stop and hear gunshots. People getting murdered, drive-bys every day."

After her son's bond hearing, she told a reporter that his $250,000 bail wouldn't have been so high if he'd committed crimes on the South or West sides. Her remark ignited outrage. She holds to her opinion.

"Politics, money, race," she said when I asked why she thought this case was so big. "Pick any one of them. New police chief. New mayor. They're going to make sure they're setting an example for everybody."

Rush was polite, but short on details. She said she works part time. She said she'd never heard of the two other teenagers charged as adults with her son. She said his father had seen him since the arrest.

What would she like to say to Dvonte in jail?

"That I got his back 100 percent. I'm here for my son. I'm not here for the media, nor anybody else."

Then from her handful of mail, she picked up a postcard. She flipped it over, flipped it back.

"How did they get this address?" she said.

She passed it to me. The card, handwritten to her son, used a racial slur: "You and the other (expletive) don't seem to be able to quit acting like (expletive). Hopefully, they will now put all you (expletive) away."

"I have no comment on this," she said.

Her voice stayed level. She walked back inside and closed the door.

The marauders who beat five people in downtown Chicago last Saturday did something very bad. They hurt those individuals, and they hurt the city. But let's save some righteous anger for the unseen assaults that happen in Chicago every day.

Forget High School

We can all agree that certain kinds of people are unfit to be mayor of Chicago.

Crooks. Wimps. Anyone who can't at least pretend to love baseball.

And how about people who went to high school on the North Shore?

When the rivals to replace Mayor Richard Daley met for a debate Thursday, Gery Chico suggested that Rahm Emanuel doesn't pass mayoral muster because of where he's from.

"He comes from the wealthy North Shore, I come from the Back of the Yards," Chico said, talking with the media after the debate. "If you come from the South Side, you think of Chicago like a South Sider. He's North Shore wealth, entitlement and privilege."

Chico pointed out that Emanuel attended "the wealthiest high school in the state of Illinois." That's New Trier in Winnetka.

"If you come from Wilmette, Winnetka, Lake Forest, that's what you think like," Chico said. "I didn't go to some elite high school. I went to Kelly High School."

Chico is partly right. The North Shore is different from Chicago.

The city is fast, vast, rich, poor, bleak, gorgeous, multicolored. The lakeshore towns to the north are small, clean, green, serene; if you lived there and never ventured out, you might have trouble fathoming Chicago.

Emanuel, of course, has ventured beyond the North Shore. He was born in Chicago, moved back as an adult, and from 2003 until 2009, when he went to Washington as President Barack Obama's chief of staff, represented a varied swath of the city in the U.S. Congress.

But Chico is right about another thing: He and Emanuel are different kinds of Chicagoans. Chico was bred in the city, in a time when neighborhood identities were even stronger than they are today.

When he questions Emanuel's city cred, he's appealing to a certain Chicago tribalism, the belief, held especially by some longtime natives, that only those who rise from Chicago's grit can understand or claim the city. He's also tapping into the fear that anyone who grew up rich can't care about the rest of us.

But I'm guessing that Chico is doing more than just playing the politics of class and place. Though he's a wealthy lawyer now, he's still a guy from the Back of the Yards. When he talks about Emanuel, he's talking about something personal.

I grew up as the daughter of a struggling house painter. If you grow up without monied privilege, you'll always see life through the lens of that upbringing, even if your circumstances change. You'll always sense that people who grew up with money have a different lens.

So, yes, Gery Chico undoubtedly understands some things about Chicago that Rahm Emanuel doesn't.

But that doesn't indicate who can best manage this city. Governing a city requires seeing it on many levels, and sometimes an outsider's eye is the clearest one.

Emanuel, insider and outsider, is the front-runner in the mayor's race. Chico is his closest rival. They'd both, probably, make decent mayors.

And Chico's right about another thing. Social class does matter in Chicago, just not in the way he suggests.

The city remains deeply segregated, racially and economically. Its mansions and skyscrapers are surrounded by neighborhoods where jobs are scarce, guns are abundant, schools are chaotic and it's hard to buy a fresh vegetable.

The candidate who sees those divisions clearly, and has the best plan for repairs, is the one to vote for, regardless of where he or she went to high school.

SUNDAY, OCT. 2, 2011

The Harris Family

The Harris family's life began to unravel around dawn on the last day of August.

R.J. Harris, who is 77, was in bed when a noise jolted him awake.

Bam. What was that?

Bam. It sounded like an explosion.

Bam. The front door swung open and officers in masks swarmed inside, pointing rifles.

Police! Hands up! Police!

Harris' wife, an aunt, a son, a grandson, a granddaughter, a great-grandson and a cousin all bolted awake. From the floor above, where one of the Harris daughters lives with her family, came the blast and stench of smoke bombs.

Mr. Harris, standing in the middle of the house that he bought 41 years ago, that has lodged his large family through the neighborhood's gentrification, kept thinking: All you had to do was knock.

Outside on Sheffield Avenue, more officers gathered, shooing away neighbors. One neighbor described the scene on her blog.

"I felt like I was on 'The Wire!' Fantastic," she wrote. ". . . The neighbors hung out near our fence, trying to appear as nonchalant as possible, you know, as if this sort of thing happens every day in Lincoln Park. I watch 'Breaking Bad,' yo, I know about meth. I bet they were totally cooking in there."

No meth was found inside the Harris home.

The police did arrest two family members on animal-related misdemeanors, and took away four dogs. But they found no evidence of the crimes some neighbors had suspected, the kind that typically call for 40 officers.

No drugs. No guns. No dogfighting.

The 40 officers on the scene — from the Chicago Police Department Animal Crimes Unit, two SWAT teams and the Cook County Sheriff's Department — left.

The raid was over.

For the Harris family, however, the shocks had just begun.

As the smoke cleared, a building inspector arrived. The Harrises knew that their house was rundown. In a neighborhood of new mansions, it stood out, with its bedraggled American flag, the window fan, the brown wooden steps that sloped straight to the sidewalk.

But they had never been issued a building code violation.

Now the inspector wrote down dozens of infractions and made another list for an adjacent home where two of the Harris daughters live. Bad wiring, clogged gutters, torn siding, broken plaster, rotting window sashes, unsanitary living conditions.

An emergency order to vacate was issued.

And just like that, out of the blue of a summer morning, the Harrises lost their home.

"I never seen so much hate build up in one minute," Mr. Harris says. "For what?"

Now as they pack to leave this week, not sure where to go, that's the question that burns in them and some of their neighbors: For what?

What did they do that merited this kind of force and such harsh, swift punishment?

When R.J. Harris bought two houses on Chicago's North Side in 1970 — $65,000 for the pair — the neighborhood was not yet one of Chicago's most coveted.

The shopping empire that would eventually rise on nearby Clybourn Avenue — Whole Foods, Patagonia, Bed Bath & Beyond — was years away. The residents were Puerto Ricans, Italians and Germans, but most, like the Harrises, were black.

The neighborhood had its troubles, but it was better than the Wentworth Gardens public housing project, where Mr. and Mrs. Harris started out raising their seven children.

"We had a dear friend said, 'You don't need to be in the projects with these children,'" Mrs. Harris says. "'I have a house I'm going to sell you.'"

R.J. and Josephine, who married in 1954, met in St. Louis after Mr. Harris, who grew up picking cotton on an Alabama farm, had come north at 14 to look for work that paid.

Through the years, he found it: dumping rocks, loading ice, piling huge water jugs on skids. For 25 years he worked as a custodian for the Chicago Housing Authority and left on disability only after he blew a disk in his back carrying a 55-gallon garbage container. Mrs. Harris worked as a file clerk.

From the beginning, friends and relations were in and out of the Harris house on Sheffield. Mr. Harris masterminded the community garden. Friends sat out front talking, drinking and playing checkers, customs the family maintained through the decades, sometimes to the consternation of new neighbors who conducted their social lives in the privacy of back patios and decks.

As new, mostly white people moved in, and almost all the other black families moved out, the Harrises sometimes felt marginalized. Still, when developers knocked, they said: Not for sale.

Houses weren't just real estate. They were homes.

Besides, it was safe here, and the men of the family could find odd jobs with the new neighbors, shoveling snow, mowing lawns, fixing cars.

Some of the Harrises' offspring got in trouble, from the minor to the major. More than once, Mr. Harris ejected his son Michael — who has been in and out of prison for such crimes as burglary and shoplifting — but he always let him come back because that's what families do.

He fretted over his kids who didn't work, but felt good that most did and that as his grandkids grew up, most made it to college. He and his wife were proud that in a time of fractured families and hard finances, they kept their family together.

And then came that August dawn.

Here's how the police see it.

In July, Ald. Scott Waguespack's aides contacted the Chicago Alternative Policing Strategy office for the 18th District The alderman's email noted that some neighbors had complained about unleashed dogs and drugs in tiny Privet Playlot Park. The playground is separated from the Harris home only by a vacant lot.

While the alderman himself says that he had not focused on the Harrises as a major problem — he was more concerned about nearby empty lots and vacant houses — his office also forwarded to CAPS a complaint letter that had arrived with a photo. In the photo, a little girl stands in the playground staring down at drug paraphernalia.

The CAPS office told the beat officers to be on alert.

Soon afterward, at a beat community meeting, some neighbors expressed similar concerns.

A few days later, an anonymous caller to 911 reported an ailing dog on the sidewalk. The man with the dog was the elder Harrises' son Michael.

According to the police, Michael took the dog to the vet that day, but it was malnourished and had suffered heatstroke and it died; the vet gave his report to a police officer.

From there, the case went to the Animal Crimes Unit, which, after surveillance, felt there was sufficient cause to enter the Harris home and to do it with enough force to protect its officers.

After the raid, a news release about it appeared on the 18th District CAPS website.

The release, noting that citizens had complained of animal cruelty and "gang/drug sales," concluded with the statement: "This is an excellent example of the police and citizens working together."

What the release did not note, however, was that no one was charged with "gang/drug" sales.

It did not note that Michael Harris was arrested only for the largely unknown misdemeanor of being a felon in possession of non-neutered dogs. After he got out of jail, he collected money from neighbors to have one of the dogs, Kiki, spayed and returned to the family.

Meanwhile, the case against one of the Harrises' grandsons, Andrew, 21, remains in court. According to the misdemeanor charges, his two pit bulls were malnourished and mistreated. According to the family, they were fed and watered daily and never used to fight.

As for the dog that died in Michael's care, the family insists there was a misunderstanding. Kiki was treated in July for heatstroke and survived. Around the same time, the family's old dog, Snow, died. They buried her in the side yard.

In the days after the raid, unsubstantiated rumors bubbled through the neighborhood.

Tales of Harris pit bulls attacking neighbors' dogs, of dogfighting, Gangster Disciples filling the house, children who didn't go to school.

Strangers, family members say, drove by and shouted curses, perhaps fueled by a radio news report that had mentioned dogfighting and neglected to report the raid's outcome.

Neighbors who have known the Harrises for a long time were aghast.

"I've petted a couple of those pit bulls," says Wendi Taylor Nations, who is active in animal-rescue causes and whose front window looks out on the tot lot and the Harris homes. "I've never seen abuse. Had there been, I would have been ahead of the police. We're just heartbroken for them."

"They're good people," says neighbor Chris Swindells. "I'm just so sad."

Some neighbors feel the Harrises are the target of a small, unhappy group, but even the family's supporters understand why others might be perturbed. The family's young men hang out in the gangway. Their friends visit. They can be loud. And not every neighbor sees the same things.

"It's not an easy time in this city," says Dorothy Collin, a Harris neighbor and former Tribune reporter distressed by their treatment. "Every time you turn on television you see things about shootings and crime. I also understand people are worried about their property values. What you've got is a different way of life, an old Southern way, or the old South Side of Chicago way. Now it's surrounded by the new way of life. It's a real collision of cultures."

Shortly after the raid, one of the Harrises' daughters, Yvonne, stood up at a CAPS meeting.

"I said: 'If you all had a problem with us, all you had to do was knock on the door. Let me know. I will address it.'"

She recalled the meeting as she sat in her parents' living room last week, surrounded by packing boxes.

"We're not the cream of the crops here," she said. "We didn't have the money to fix up the property like other people fixed up theirs. We living. We try to maintain here as a family, keep our parents comfortable."

At the CAPS meeting that night, several people who had complained about the family were in the audience. None of them said a thing.

"Sometimes," said Mr. Harris, with a weak smile, "you just have to move on."

"I'd move on," said his wife. "But I just don't know why. Why? And we got nowhere to go."

It was a gray morning. In the mess of clothes and boxes, Mrs. Harris, who is 80, slowly folded a pair of pants.

They could come back to the house if they fixed it up in the next nine months. They have no cash to do it. They're sitting on a fortune in land, but the million or more they might eventually make by selling doesn't pay a rental deposit this week.

Maybe a new place wouldn't be so bad, somewhere fresh with a garage, a garden. But they can't buy before they sell.

And no amount of money will erase the humiliation.

"Do you know how bad you feel when you come out and everybody's laughing at you?" Mr. Harris said.

The family doesn't blame the police. They have nothing bad to say about their neighbors.

Mostly, they're hurt and mystified and convinced, as some of their supporters are, that they are up against forces of development too big to fight.

Mrs. Harris propped her head on one of the boxes. She gazed out the window, silent, toward the playground, where on Sunday several neighbors will throw them a farewell party.

"It's not the dogs," she finally said. "It's not us. They just want this property."

The facts in this case can be argued. So can what they mean.

But what happened to the Harrises should not have happened, not this way, so abruptly, without mercy and without help and with no proof of great crime. It is simply wrong. It divides a divided city even more. Chicago is better than that.

Lost, Word by Word

The day David Foote had to admit that words were leaving him, he was standing at a blackboard at Lake Forest High School, lecturing on "Romeo and Juliet."

Mercutio. Montague. Lady Capulet.

He knew the characters as well as he knew his bow ties, but now, poised to explain the play to a room full of teenagers, every one of those Shakespearean names escaped him.

His wife had already noticed changes in his speech. He'd started scrambling pronouns. "I" exited his mouth as "they." Nouns vanished.

His wife knew it was odd that he had anything less than perfect control of his basic tools. An English teacher who confuses words is like a carpenter who mixes up nails and screws.

"I'm fine," he'd say when she'd bring it up. "I'm fine."

That day at the blackboard he had to admit he wasn't.

Foote was only 58 when he discovered he had a little-known form of dementia known as primary progressive aphasia. PPA, for short.

Alzheimer's, the dementia we all know, steals memory. PPA begins by destroying nerve cells in a part of the brain that controls language. In other words, it steals words.

"I can find the real world," Foote said Friday. He paused, revised. "Word. I can find words, but sometimes through circuitous routes."

He was sitting in his Wilmette living room with his wife, Cathy Donnelly. They agreed to be interviewed because a big conference on PPA is coming to Chicago this week, and though they haven't discussed his condition even with some of their friends, they believe it's important to help others understand the disease.

"It's my coming out, I guess," Foote said.

Now 66, Foote still looks like a parent's reassuring dream of an English teacher. His full gray hair is as neat as his sweater vest. His smile and gentlemanly humor are intact.

But listen.

He says "toy" when he means "treat." "Prominent" when he means "permanent." Sometimes he's as articulate as you'd expect of a man who taught English for 22 years at Evanston Township High School and another 15 at Lake Forest. Other times, he's lost in a verbal maze.

"My life has been talking," he said. "And teaching. And helping kids learn to write. And telling stories. I felt there was. I knew. I felt. I guess."

You could almost hear his mind. Scanning. Searching. Shuffling. Waiting. Finally, the words: "I felt parts of me were falling off."

Reading is one part that has fallen off. If he reads now, he has to do it out loud.

And spelling. "Come on, I can do this," he told himself when letters started going haywire. But he couldn't.

And numbers.

"Here's my watch." He held up a wrist and on it, a watch made for the blind. He punched a button on the side. The watch announced: "The time is 11:32 a.m."

A few minutes later, his wife asked if he could read the hour. He gazed at the round dial.

"It's 10. No. It's 11." He looked up. "I don't know."

Because PPA creeps into a mind earlier than most dementias, it often goes unrecognized. Foote was lucky enough to find his way to Northwestern's Cognitive Neurology and Alzheimer's Disease Center, the sponsor of the upcoming conference, where he was diagnosed.

At Northwestern, he learned the bad news: There is no cure. Unlike stroke victims, people with PPA can't recover speech through therapy. Eventually, memory goes too.

At the same time, he learned that people with PPA often develop skills that don't demand much talk. Some garden. Or build things. He has taken up watercolors. He also hangs on to his job as a docent at the Loyola University Museum of Art.

Some days he goes to a support group at Northwestern. It's a place where people who have trouble talking feel safe talking to each other.

"I used to be able to," he said. "To. Be able. Help."

"Help other people," Cathy said.

She finishes a lot of his sentences. She pays the bills now too. The numbers were too much for him. But he cleans and cooks, and if his trouble with measurements results in some strange dishes, she doesn't mind.

"For a while there," he said, "I was, I was driving in the evening and there was a little . . ."

He waved his hands, smiled, let the unspoken words drift off.

To prepare for our interview, Foote scribbled two lines of a Dylan Thomas poem on a small yellow sheet of paper. He picked it up to read.

"Do not go dentle," he said. Paused. "Do not go gentle." Pause. "Into there."

The lines as he had written them were this:

Do not go gentle into that good night,
Rage, rage against the dying of the light.

"Fight it," he said. "Fight it. I'm not fighting it to be angry. I keep raging to make sure I can keep doing things."

Cathy reached out, clasped his wrist, blinked back tears.

"He's the most upbeat, enthusiastic, joyful man," she said. "But there's going to come a time."

Her words, too, drifted into silence.

SUNDAY, MAY 15, 2011

Ode to Mayor Daley

And now it's goodbye
To the Rich Daley reign
The fun and the glory
The pleasure, the pain.
For more than two decades
He ruled like a king
And answered his critics:
"Put dis up your thing!"
They called him "Boss Junior"
A nod to his dad
Who also was mayor
For good and for bad.

But Richard M. Daley
Was not Richard J.
He made his own city
He had his own way.
He said, "I will make
Dis old town like Paree!
Tres chic and tres global!"
His minions cried, "Oui!"
The sky filled with towers
The parks with cute chairs:
A glitzy new look
For da city of Bears.
The streets sprouted tulips
And wrought-iron rails
(And meanwhile his cronies
Were hauled off to jails.)
He knew every alley
Each corner and wall
(But nary a thing
About rot in the Hall . . .)
He moved out of Bridgeport
His old Irish spot
As downtown went upscale
And condos got hot.
He biked and he peddled
His countless grand schemes:
"Let's plant on the rooftops!
Let's dream the big dreams!
Let's get the Olympics!
Let's court the Chinese!
Let's name streets for Oprah!
I'll do what I please!"
He took over schools,
And in cover of dark
He bulldozed Meigs Field
To make way for a park.
He tore down the projects
His father had built

But poor is still poor
In Chicago's new gilt.
No, all was not gold
In the Kingdom of Rich
The people got angry
They often did (express their grievances impolitely).
He chewed up the language
He barked at the press
And, yes, he sure bungled
That parking-box mess.
The budget's a wreck
And recycling still stinks
(At least we can still
Eat foie gras with our drinks.)
And yet in the end
Richard Daley was great
A leader, a thinker
Who guided our fate.
In Uptown and Pilsen
Along Lake Shore Drive
Chicago was changed
By that big Man on Five.
For all he did wrong,
He did good with his clout
He made this town better
And loved it full out.
So now he retires
To be with his wife
Chicago's next chapter
Will start his new life.
Yes, time marches forward
And Rahm marches in
A new gang's in power
The new games begin.
But in this last moment
Let's make a brief stop
To say we were lucky
With Daley on top.

Dear Rod

Dear Rod,

You just got handed an opportunity.

It can't have felt like opportunity to you Monday, sitting in the court-room in the avalanche of that verdict.

Guilty, guilty, guilty, guilty, guilty, guilty, guilty, guilty, guilty, guilty, guilty, guilty, guilty, guilty, guilty, guilty, guilty.

Seventeen counts of guilty, and each time the jury foreman uttered the word, it was like another boulder rumbling toward the defendant's table. The defeat was crushing.

No wonder your wife cried. No wonder she said she just wanted to go home.

But you came down to the courthouse lobby anyway and waded into the media mob.

"I, frankly, am stunned," you said.

Even people who think you're a liar can believe that. Of course you were stunned. Defeat, for the hopeful, is a kind of death, and like death, it takes awhile to process.

And after all these years of pleading innocence, of making your case on talk shows and sidewalks, of turning yourself into a well-dressed clown on a crusade to persuade, you may have come to believe you'd done nothing wrong.

Lies are mutants. The lies we tell others have a way of morphing into truth in our minds. Self-delusion begins as a kind of survival instinct, then turns out to be a self-ingested poison.

So the opportunity the jury gave you Monday is this: to tell yourself the truth.

Short of a miracle — i.e., a mistrial — your fight is over. Now you have the chance to look hard at what you did. Look at it from the angle of the law. Look at it from the angle of the people who elected you.

Maybe you really did think that your wheeling and dealing was just how the game was played. You once said that everything's a deal. You're right.

And you're right to think that you were hardly the only political wheeler-dealer in Illinois, others of whom are still illicitly glad-handing and strong-arming their way through power. You'd even be right to think that your downfall came with a whiff of mob mentality.

But those truths aren't the point now. A jury — one that weighed the charges long and hard — just found you stepped out of the legal bounds 17 times.

You've been handed opportunities all your life. Parents who helped you. Allies and in-laws who boosted you. You were endowed with a certain charm.

With these gifts, you had an extraordinary shot at power and at using it well. You blew it.

There are people who revel in your disgrace. I heard some yell "boo" as you left the courthouse. One yelled "crook." When the verdict was read, I saw a few smirk.

But there are others who take no pleasure in your fall. A lot are sad to see your family suffer.

Now you have the chance to think how you blew it and how you might make amends, especially to the people who matter most to you. Your wife, your kids, your brother. Honesty is the only place to start.

You're a Winston Churchill fan, so maybe you've heard this quote: "Once in a while you will stumble upon the truth but most of us manage to pick ourselves up and hurry along as if nothing had happened."

You're not likely to hurry far from a prison cell for a while, but you'll have the opportunity to linger over the truth of what happened, to understand your part in it. If you can do that, you'll come closer to being the man you wanted to be and might have been.

FRIDAY, JULY 15, 2011

Marilyn, Big and Bad

It should be good news that a giant statue of a woman rose over one of Chicago's most conspicuous public spaces this week.

Chicago, a city that has almost as many statues as it has potholes, is notoriously short on statues of women. Mile after magnificent mile, our city teems with large reproductions of presidents, philosophers, sports stars, warriors and saints, almost every one a man.

Finally, we get a highly visible statue of a woman. Twenty-six-feet tall. Looming next to North Michigan Avenue at the Chicago River. As obvious as a skyscraper.

And as tawdry as a peep show.

"Relax," an inner voice chided the other day when I wandered out of Tribune Tower and immediately ran into workers installing what appeared to be a humongous Marilyn Monroe.

Her famous white skirt swooped toward the heavens. Her underwear was in full view. Her head remained a mystery, wrapped in plastic with a cord at the throat, unpleasantly, if unintentionally, adding to the pornographic feel.

"It's just a tourist attraction," the inner voice clucked when I cringed. "Walk on."

So what that men were standing dwarfed between the giant legs of the fake Marilyn, shooting photos of her crotch while one stuck out his tongue to mime a lick? So what if there were guys leering at her underpants and her exposed backside? Hey. Whatever makes people happy. Women were there laughing too.

"Chill, Hon," said my inner voice. "If you don't think this is fun, you must be getting old."

So it was with relief that a while later I stumbled on an item by ChicagoNow blogger Abraham Ritchie, who had the guts to sum up the sculpture in four perfect words: "Downright creepy and sexist."

The statue, whose head will be unveiled Friday, could prove to be someone besides Marilyn Monroe. Maybe the head will look like Barack Obama's. Or John Boehner's.

No matter whose head it is, though, the rest is Monroe, clearly derived from a scene in the 1955 movie "The Seven Year Itch," in which a gust from a sidewalk subway grate blows her full skirt skyward.

Photos of the scene, shot in Manhattan, have been wildly popular for decades. In the best-known of those photos, Monroe hugs her knees together as she presses her skirt down. The billowing cloth offers just a glimpse of underwear.

The original image is coy. Marilyn on the Mag Mile is crude.

"This work is totally objectifying," said Ritchie when I called him Thursday, curious about his perspective as a young male art critic. "It's not even the subtle eroticism of a pinup of the 1950s or of the original photo. It's a stiff representation of sexual voyeurism."

The Monroe statue is the work of J. Seward Johnson, an artist who isn't from Chicago or based here but who is a favorite of Chicago's Zeller Realty Group, which has put other of his giant sculptures in Pioneer Court. The one before this was a huge reproduction of the farm couple from the painting "American Gothic." Art critics often refer to his work as kitsch.

Kitsch is in the eye of the beholder, and there's a place for kitsch in this world. There's also a place for art that makes you think about sex and the human body. There's a place for all of that in public.

But this sculpture doesn't merit its primo place in Chicago. Its only distinguishing feature is its size, which brings to mind some 1950s B movie about giant women.

What's most disturbing about the sculpture, though, is not that it's mediocre. It's the fact that Marilyn Monroe was real. She wasn't a sci-fi amazon. She was more than an image. She was a real woman who died at the age of 36 of a drug overdose, perhaps by suicide. Inviting people to leer at her giant underpants is just icky.

The next time someone wants to fill a public space with art, why not find a Chicago artist? Or a Chicago theme? Or a great piece of art from somewhere else that makes the point that Chicago is a city where great artists show their work?

How about a statue of a woman that focuses on something besides her underwear?

SUNDAY, NOV. 20, 2011

The Ice Cream Man

I was thinking about Thanksgiving recently when a memory snapped into view as unexpectedly as a computer pop-up window.

In the memory, it was summer, not November. I was 10 years old, wearing shorts, flip-flops and a sleeveless button-up blouse. The day was sticky hot, and from somewhere outside came the bell of the ice cream man.

My 10-year-old self hurried to the porch to watch as kids from up and down the street flew out of their front doors toward the truck, hungry for Eskimo Pies and Nutty Buddies.

A couple of my brothers were in the jostling crowd, which puzzled me since I knew we had no money for the ice cream man. All I could figure was that they were selling handmade Bugler cigarettes, the cheap kind we rolled for our parents, to the neighbor boys.

Suddenly, from my porch vista, I wanted a Nutty Buddy like I'd never wanted a Nutty Buddy before, like I'd never wanted anything. I deserved a Nutty Buddy. I would demand a Nutty Buddy.

My father was sitting in a rocking chair downstairs. He looked odd, at home in the middle of the day, no cuff links or tie, watching TV. He was out of work and had nowhere to go. I gathered my courage the way you might hug a thin coat to your chest in an icy wind.

"Can I have some money for the ice cream man?"

In my memory, just before he says no, my father looks as sad as I ever saw him. I knew we were broke, whatever that meant, though I didn't know then that his business had gone bankrupt. The desire for that Nutty Buddy swelled within me anyway, and words that I had never consciously formed burst into the room with the ferocity of bulls.

"I hate being poor!"

There were things you weren't allowed to do in my father's house. Curse. Lie. Leave lights on in empty rooms or dirty dishes in the sink. Of all the sins, the greatest was talking back, so I spun on my flip-flopped heel to get out of there, and fast.

"Mary Theresa."

He used his children's middle names only when trouble loomed. I turned back toward him, the metal boot of dread stomping on my heart.

"You never ask for anything," he said.

He was standing up, fishing in his pants pocket. He pulled out some change, counted it in his palm, pressed it into one of mine. "Buy something for your brothers too."

I was scurrying away, elated and mystified, afraid the ice cream man would escape before this miracle came to fruition, when he spoke again.

"Mary Theresa."

Again, I turned around.

"Yes, sir?"

"We don't have money. But we are not poor. Poverty is a state of mind."

Off and on for years since then, the vision of my father giving me money that was hard to spare has come back to me. I think that's why the memory surfaced when I was thinking about Thanksgiving.

This week begins the official giving season, a season that also comes with wishing, expecting, demanding. There's a temptation to feel that what we get, or what we give, is never quite enough.

I don't agree that poverty is entirely a state of mind, but I know what my father meant. And part of what he meant is that no matter how little you think you have, there's always enough to give some away, and no matter how little you think you've gotten, you may understand later that it was huge.